BLACK JACK PERSHING

RICHARD O'CONNOR

BLACK JACK
PERSHING

RICHARD O'CONNOR

ILLUSTRATED WITH PHOTOGRAPHS

DOUBLEDAY & COMPANY, INC., GARDEN CITY, NEW YORK 1961

CONTENTS

Part Three: SOLDIER IN RETIREMENT

FOREWORD

This is not an "authorized" biography of General Pershing in the sense that it was written with his family's blessing or encouragement. His son Warren, however, did make available his personal recollections in his usual gracious manner and gave permission for examination of the Pershing Papers in the Library of Congress's Manuscript Division, which were admirably collected, indexed, and boxed only in the past several years. No previous work on Pershing's career included these voluminous papers, diaries, letters, and journals.

My acquaintance with the general was limited to a few minutes' interview in his office when I was a reporter in Washington, and the city editor, who had a grisly sense of humor, insisted that I try to enlist his opinion of General Douglas MacArthur's dispersal of the Bonus Marchers, most of them men who had served under Pershing.

The general, of course, wouldn't talk. He was grimly courteous, impassive, and understandably eager to be rid of me. The nauseating phrase, "No comment," had not yet come into common usage, but that was what his few curt remarks added up to. He was an expert at ridding himself of newspapermen, most of whom he disliked on principle, and a few minutes later I found myself out on the street, dismissed with a grunt and a nod. I didn't much like the old General of the Armies. I had known Chicago gangsters who were friendlier.

Now, a quarter of a century later, I find him more understandable. The aim of this biography is to do the same for the reader.

PART ONE

SOLDIER
ON THE FRONTIERS

1. Plowboy, Officer, and Gentleman

The two leading American military crusaders in Europe during the first and second world wars were men of strikingly similar background. Both sprang from mid-continent America, from similar racial stock and much the same kind of hard-working, unpretentious people who had come west with the wagon trains and settled along the Middle Border. But the times in which they lived, their differing experiences, and their own remarkably opposed personalities shaped them in diverse fashion. Rarely has a general acquired the popularity of Dwight D. Eisenhower; his was the smiling brotherly image, agreeable, democratic, rarely stern or authoritarian. He delegated responsibility whenever possible, and his plans and decisions were formulated in the homogenized atmosphere of staff conferences and group thinking. Supreme Headquarters functioned along corporate lines; its natural habitat was the monolithic office building, and Eisenhower was its urbane and tactful chairman of the board.

John J. Pershing, commander in chief of the American Expeditionary Force, evoked no such enthusiasm at home or abroad. Among World War I generals, a well-publicized paternalism was regarded as necessary equipment for high command—"Papa" Joffre pulling the ears of his *poilus* and calling them "my children," Hindenburg gruffly representing himself as the massive father image of the German armies. But, as a perceptive American war correspondent named Heywood Broun observed, "they don't call him Papa Pershing." There was nothing paternal about Pershing, who had little talent and less respect for posturing of any kind. To the doughboy he was simply a hard-boiled, super-drill sergeant. He didn't expect to be venerated by the men he sent into combat and death any more than their top kick did when he blew his whistle and shoved them into no man's land; nor would he allow the arts of publicity to be applied on his behalf and picture him as anything but what he was—a practical, unsentimental soldier doing his job.

Instead of delegating authority, he kept his hand on every lever of the A.E.F.'s operations and yielded responsibility grudgingly, if at all. He organized the American forces in Europe with himself as their model, causing one writer to observe, "When you stumbled upon a lost American doughboy in a God-forsaken hamlet, his bearing, the set of his tunic, his salute, all authentically recalled the general who sat in Chaumont." He was a hard disciplinarian, unashamedly ambitious, jealous of his authority, ruthless with major generals who had served with him in Mexico or the Philippines, harsh with homesick boys who faltered in their duty. Even his oldest friends were given just one chance to prove themselves. He accomplished what he set out to do—build a modern, war-worthy American Army, keep it separate from the Allies, and help beat the Germans—but few loved him for it.

The presidency was Eisenhower's for the taking. With Pershing, even had he admitted to wanting it, it was a different matter. Politicians who tested sentiment among his former soldiers and civilians at home to determine whether Pershing could not be propelled into the White House, much as Ulysses S. Grant had been nominated through the political backing of the Grand Army of the Republic, found that both classes were as opposed to the idea of "Pershing for President" as the general himself professed to be.

Everything about Pershing seemed to be sternly and exclusively military. He never softened an order with a smile, rarely with an explanation. He did not expect popularity but demanded obedience. Soldiering was the harsh profession he had learned while galloping pack trains through Apache country, storming Moro forts in the Philippines, chasing Pancho Villa through the badlands of northern Mexico. He resisted change, and, even as late as the summer of 1918, was demanding two cavalry divisions for service among the barbed wire, the machine-gun nests, and trench systems of the western front. In his lifetime of eighty-eight years, weaponry developed from the cavalry saber to the atomic bomb, with rapid-fire armament, tanks, aircraft, and poison gas in-between, but he always regarded warfare as a matter of men with guns in their hands. Self-confidence was the keystone of his career, and firmness, if not granitic stubbornness, was the main element of his character. On being jumped from command of a border division to commander in chief of the A.E.F., he remarked, "There never was, then or at any other time, any doubt of my ability to do the job, provided the government would furnish me with the men, the equipment, and the supplies." He had the kind of vast self-assurance that enabled him to "believe in himself without thinking of himself." Newcomer to modern total war and large-scale operations though he was, he refused to be overawed by the towering reputations of the French and British military leaders or persuaded against his will by the eloquence of their civilian chiefs. If they wouldn't take a simple "No," he did not hesitate to raise his voice and bang his fist on the conference table to make it more emphatic.

During a crucial meeting of the Supreme War Council in May of 1918, when the Germans had broken the Allied front, he refused to be coerced on an important issue, and Lord Milner whispered to Prime Minister Lloyd George, "It's no use. You can't budge him an inch." When he was finally budged, it was because he judged that the time and circumstances were proper for co-operation. He had been unbudgeable all his life and didn't propose to change in the rarefied atmosphere of European war councils.

His nickname was significant. They called him Black Jack Pershing. . . .

For a man whose lifelong concern was organized violence, he was born in the proper time and place, less than a year before the Civil War started and in a section of Missouri which was overrun by guerrillas, border fighters, and bushwhackers of all persuasions. He was literally under fire before he was four years old. He drew his "daily ration" from a friendly Union Army sergeant. He watched the gaunt men from both armies return to their homes, many of them maimed or diseased, most of them disillusioned, all of them hating war more than they hated each other, after the surrender at Appomattox. War deeply scored the earliest conscious moments of his life.

John Joseph Pershing was born in a section house of the old Hannibal & St. Joseph Railroad on the outskirts of Laclede, a village in northeastern Missouri, on September 13, 1860. His father, John F. Pershing, was a section foreman on the railroad at the time of his first child's birth, but his ambition and energy were to make him one of Laclede's leading citizens within a few years; his mother, the former Ann Thompson, was descended from old Virginia stock. There was small chance that "Jackie," as his family called him even after he became an imposing national figure, would be spoiled. He was the first of nine children. Three of the children died in infancy—not a bad proportion in those days—but two brothers and three sisters survived.

The Pershing ancestry was a purposeful mixture of Anglo-Saxon on his mother's side of the house, Alsatian and German on his father's. His great-grandfather, Frederick Pfoerschin (the name underwent a sea change to Pfershing, then was further Anglicized by dropping the *f*), migrated to the United States from the French province of Alsace, landing in Philadelphia on October 2, 1749. Frederick Pershing, a Lutheran who spoke both French and German, came over as a "redemptioner" on the sailing ship *Jacob,* indentured to the ship's captain until he had worked out his passage over. "Service in redemption," as his great-grandson wrote after research into the family history, "was based upon a contract or indenture entered into between the captain of the ship and the passenger by which the latter agreed for a certain period after his arrival in America to render whatever lawful service or employment the captain or his assigns might exact." Once that obligation was settled, Frederick Pershing moved to Westmoreland County, Pennsylvania, married Maria Elizabeth Weygandt, and worked a farm to the end of his days.

In succeeding generations, part of the Pershing family stayed behind in Pennsylvania and part joined the movement westward. "Each generation," John J. Pershing wrote with pride, "furnished pioneers as the frontier moved westward. They were found in the columns that settled the Western Reserve; in the trains that carried civilization to Indiana, Illinois, Missouri and the Middle West, and were represented among the early settlers of Oregon and California. Their log cabins have dotted every state from Pennsylvania to the Pacific."

One of Frederick Pershing's sons, the Reverend Conrad Pershing, accompanied Captain Campbell's punitive expedition against the Indians near Fort Ligonnier in 1792. Scouts located the Indians' camp and an immediate assault was ordered by Captain Campbell. This was delayed when Conrad, as unofficial chaplain of the expedition, insisted that they all get down on their knees and pray. Conrad prayed so loudly and fervently—possibly on purpose—that he had to be silenced by his more military comrades. An hour later the company descended on the hostile camp to find it deserted. "Whether a spy from the Indian camp, or his loud praying, caused the Indians to flee is not known," a Pershing family historian wrote, but the Reverend Conrad was requested to stay at home when any other forces took the field.

General Pershing, who came across this account in his later years, scrawled on its margin a disapproving comment on his great-uncle's pious lapse: "Hardly a military proceeding."

John F. Pershing, the general's father, migrated to Missouri by working his way down the Ohio on flatboats and was hired as boss of a track-laying gang pushing the railroad across northwestern Missouri. He met Ann Elizabeth Thompson, who had been born twenty-four years before in Blount County, Kentucky, while she was living on her family's farm outside the town of Warrenton, Missouri. They were married in 1859 and settled down in the section house outside Laclede, where neighbor women assisted in the birth of their first son.

The family soon moved out of the section house to a more substantial two-story frame house in town, with a porch, bay windows, and outbuildings. John F. Pershing had already started rising in the small world of Laclede, had opened a store, had been appointed United States postmaster and elected captain of the Home Guard. Remote and sylvan though that corner of the state was, Linn County knew sectional strife long before most of the country. Many of the Pershings' neighbors were pro-slavery—there were $30,000,000 worth of slaves in Missouri's border counties, and Laclede itself numbered more Negroes than whites among its population—and one of their nocturnal pursuits was raiding across the line into Kansas and attempting to drive out the equally fanatic Free-Soil colonists. The elder Pershing had, of course, declared for the North and the Union. His mother's family, General Pershing said, was "distinctly southern in manners and habits of thought," but opposed to slavery. So there was no argument over national issues in the Pershing house.

When war came, John F. Pershing, whose interests were more mercantile than military, marched off with the 20th Missouri Infantry as its sutler. His connection with the war, even in this peripheral role, was limited to a few brief campaigns. Perhaps the most venturesome of his wartime experiences was going to Vicksburg and bringing back his wife's brother, who had been wounded in the siege and was incapacitated for further service.

Young John Pershing may not have been able to recall in later years the talk of Shiloh, Gettysburg, and Chickamauga that echoed through his earliest childhood, but what he called a "vulgar and vicious" kind of war came to his doorstep when he was not quite four years old. On June 18, 1864, a mob of Confederate bushwhackers led by a Captain Holtzclaw, the terror of the neighborhood, rode into Laclede. The earliest recollection of his life, as Pershing wrote in a draft of the unpublished memoir of his pre-1917 years, was of the raiders galloping into the town, riding around the square and through the streets, firing their guns into the homes of known Unionists. Several men who tried to resist them were shot.

The Pershings were among the most prominent Unionists in Laclede, and their house, with the United States flag flying outside, attracted the bushwhackers' attention immediately. Pershing's father took his double-barreled shotgun and headed for the door, but his mother threw her arm around him and "begged him not to be so foolish." The Pershings barricaded their doors and took shelter behind the furniture as the raiders emptied their guns into the house. Fortunately their aim did not match their enthusiasm, and the family survived the brief siege without harm. For more than an hour the raiders terrorized the town; then the triumphant blast of a whistle sounded from the Hannibal & St. Joseph tracks. A trainload of Union soldiers, summoned by telegraph from the nearest garrison, arrived to send the bushwhackers ingloriously flying. The boy's next martial memory was less violent: the weary files of Union and Confederate soldiers straggling back to their homes, neighbors once again, after Appomattox.

With his father prospering and the family increasing at the rate of a child a year, Pershing's boyhood was the kind of rough and carefree idyll such as another Missourian would be describing in the adventures of Tom Sawyer and Huckleberry Finn. The country around Laclede was sparsely settled, making it ideal for boyhood's purposes. Young John knew the best places for hunting the quail, squirrel, coon, and wild turkey which abounded in the thickets, the most promising fishing holes in Turkey, Locust, and Muddy creeks. In the spring he and his friends would make catches by the wagonload when the streams flooded, then receded, and left hundreds of fish trapped in the isolated pools. They spent hours frolicking in the swimming holes at Pratt's pond and the Woodland Mills dam, where the mill itself hung over the water on stilts. On long summer days, wearied of other sports, he and his friends would lie under the giant cottonwoods along the creek bottoms and discuss the latest exploits of the James boys, the Younger brothers, and other offshoots of the Quantrell raiders for whom the war would never end. In the library at home, Pershing recalled in mature years, there was an assortment of good reading: the Bible, *Pilgrim's Progress, Aesop's Fables, Robinson Crusoe,* the works of Shakespeare, Scott, Poe, and Byron, but he surreptitiously devoted himself to the paperback volumes of Beadle's Dime Library and once in school was caught poring over one of them behind his geography, because "I became so absorbed in the hairbreadth escapes of the heroes of those blood-curdling tales."

The most humiliating of his boyhood experiences, one which contributed to his lifelong shyness and made him ill at ease when he was called upon to speak on any formal occasion, occurred when he was only five or six years old. He was supposed to recite *Mary Had a Little Lamb* at a school exercise to which the parents were invited. Every gruesome detail of that recitation stuck in his mind ever afterward. "Mother had dressed me up in my best clothes, to which a blue bow tie gave a fancy touch." He was the first pupil called upon to recite. "I was stagestruck. The words entirely left me. After a dreadful pause, Mother, who sat well up front, came to the rescue, whispering the first line loud enough for me to hear." The boy had to be prompted through every line of the nursery rhyme. "My embarrassment was so painful that the memory left with me was lasting . . . and often to this day when I get up to speak the latent memory of that first experience comes over me with distinctly unpleasant effects."

His brother Jim, born a year later (and followed by Bess, May, Grace, and Ward among the surviving children), was regarded by the townspeople as being brighter, livelier, and more popular. If any of the Pershing boys made good, they believed, it would be Jim, who seemed to have more "push." Perry Floyd, the town blacksmith, remembered John as having "devilment in him—nothing mean—just a little quiet sly devilment." It had to be quiet; the elder Pershing was prominent in the Methodist Church and had no intention of letting any of his boys get mixed up with the "bad element," and his mother kept warning him against his less respectable friends, the local Huck Finns, with the fine old rural proverb, "If you lie down with dogs, you will get up with fleas."

One instance of "devilment" occurred when John and two other boys locked their teacher, Old Man Angell, out of the schoolhouse in retaliation for his practice of lashing the legs of tardy pupils with a switch from a bundle kept fresh and limber in a corner of the schoolroom. John, whose lifelong failing was an habitual tardiness, was a regular target of the schoolmaster. The lockout caused almost as much of a stir in town as Holtzclaw's raid. It took the local pastor and the whole school board to persuade the boys to remove the ladder barricading the door. It was also John's last known defiance of authority in any form.

He learned to chew tobacco and smoke a corncob behind the tobacco barn owned by Clay Biggers's father. Clay, the future mayor of Laclede, shared a seat with him in school and squared off with him in schoolyard fights. "I've had many a fight with him and I could always whip him because I was bigger," he said, "but he was always ready to keep right on fighting. Whip him one day and he would be right back to tackle you the next. He was the gamest boy I ever knew." As General Pershing remembered his schoolboy fights, "I was *always* able to hold my own." He scratched out the *"always,"* however, and substituted "usually."

He looked on his elders with the skepticism of one of Mark Twain's observant young characters. The people of Laclede, he noted, made a great show of being religious, but "they did not always live up to the tenets of their church . . . and were known as backsliders. But they usually came back into the fold during the revivals held each winter, when they would express deep regret at their conduct, only to fall from grace later on. This hypocrisy did not escape the observation of even the growing children."

Not unexpectedly, perhaps, the heroes of his boyhood were the soldiers who guarded the army storehouse in Laclede. He made friends with the sergeant of the guard, who gave him a piece of hardtack every day which he solemnly brought home and presented to his mother as "my day's ration." Despite his occasional waywardness, he was closer to his mother than any other adult. He resembled her in looks and temperament, having inherited her square jaw, wide brow, well-spaced eyes, and firm mouth, her common sense and competence in everything she undertook. He recalled in later years that she was perhaps the most accomplished horsewoman in that section. His brother Jim, on the other hand, inherited their father's hearty outgoing per-

sonality and ability to make himself popular. Of these paternal qualities, the older boy received scant measure.

There was little in his early years to suggest that John would be
much different from the boys he played and made mischief with, who
grew up to be farmers, clerks, day laborers, and drifters.

As the boy grew older, however, his parents made him aware of the
fact that more was expected of him than running wild in the woods
and creek bottoms. John and Ann Pershing wanted something better
for their family than ordinary, obscure, and aimless lives. The elder
Pershing had become a leading merchant and landowner, president of
the local school board, and superintendent of the Sunday school at the
Methodist Church. He planned a college education for John and the
other children, so they were expected to work hard at their studies.
John, as the oldest boy, was also introduced early, before his twelfth
year, to the virtues of manual labor. On farmlands acquired by his
father at the edge of Laclede, John learned to plow the soil, plant
and cultivate long rows of corn, feed and otherwise care for the hogs
and cattle, all the farm chores which began before sunup and ended
just after sundown. It was noted that the young plowboy hated a
crooked furrow; he'd sweat and strain for an hour to remove a rock
from the path of his plow and keep his rows straight . . . an early
instance of his notable, career-long insistence on heading straight for
an objective, sweeping everything aside.

John's apprenticeship was doubly valuable when in the panic of
1873, his father's holdings were almost wiped out. The elder Pershing
had bought up a number of farms with the help of bank loans, and
with the postwar depression came the inevitable foreclosures. The
Pershings lost all but one farm, which John was to work singlehanded
at the age of fourteen while his father went out on the road as a
traveling salesman for several years for a Saint Joseph clothing manufacturer and later for a Chicago firm. It was left to John, through the
remainder of his teens, to act as head of the family while his father
was on the road, keep up his schooling, and make the farm on the outskirts of Laclede pay its way. A sense of responsibility was thus in-
grained into him permanently. It was just as well that he had those few
carefree boyhood years before he was introduced to the sterner realities,
because he never was released from them until he was a very old man,
so old and ill that he was the captive of his doctors and nurses.

For the rest of his youth, unwittingly enough, he might have served as a model for one of Horatio Alger's all but incredible heroes. There was an almost dreary sense of rectitude, striving, and achievement about the years of his youth; yet it was not at all uncommon in those times, when so much more was demanded of young men. From all accounts, he accepted his lot cheerfully and without giving himself any airs or assuming that he was a martyr to family responsibility. At the age of seventeen, when he might have been entering college if his father had been less optimistic about the value of Linn County farmland, he qualified as a teacher at the elementary school at Prairie Mound, where he was paid thirty-five dollars a month, cash money, for drilling the fundamentals into those pupils who came to learn and thumping discipline into those who slouched at their desks and tried to interfere with that process. John had a way with rebellious and disorderly louts as well as the more receptive pupils, and he was asked to come back a second year.

One significant episode of his two-year tenure as teacher at Prairie Mound's one-room school survives. W. H. Blakely, who had been one of Pershing's pupils, told a Kansas City *Star* reporter during World War I how a burly redheaded farmer rode up to the schoolhouse one morning, brandishing a revolver and roaring out demands that the teacher show himself. Pershing had whipped his oldest boy for having kicked a dog which had strayed into the schoolroom.

Blakely remembered how the farmer "rode up cursing before all the children in the schoolyard and how another boy and I ran down a gully because we were afraid. We peeked over the edge, though, and heard Pershing tell the farmer to put up his gun, get down off his horse, and fight like a man. The farmer got down and John stripped off his coat. He was only a boy of eighteen . . . but he thrashed the old farmer soundly." When he had dusted himself off, the farmer generously conceded that John was "a better man than I thought you were," and added, "If that boy of mine does any more cutting up, I want you to lick him good." From then on, the older boys, some of whom were almost John's age, kept the peace while in his schoolroom. In later years, too, Pershing did not hesitate to use his fists, if necessary, to make a point.

He saved the money earned from teaching to attend the 1879 and 1880 spring terms at the State Normal School at Kirksville (now the Northeast Missouri State Teachers College) and on June 17, 1880, was awarded the degree of Bachelor of Scientific Didactics, an educational whimsey of the time. In Kirksville he lived with an uncle, William Griffith, and nights, after putting aside his textbooks, he began reading his way through Blackstone. His ambition then was to become a lawyer; the career of a professional soldier had never occurred to him at an age when most boys intent on a military career were entering or applying to enter West Point. Meanwhile, he continued to teach school and work the family farm. As he turned twenty-one, his sister May recalled of him, John was very particular about his appearance, used to keep his Sunday trousers pressed between the mattresses on his bed, and was exceedingly proud of the gray kid gloves his father had given him as a birthday present.

The whole course of his life, which might have proceeded along the quiet channels of a small-town legal career, was changed by a few inches of type appearing in newspapers published throughout the Second Congressional District under the signature of Congressman J. H. Burroughs. It read, "On July 15th there will be a competitive examination for the appointment of a cadet at the United States Military Academy at West Point. All honest, strong, God-fearing boys of this district may take part."

John decided to take the examination after much soul-searching and over the objections of his mother who, to the end of her days, would have preferred the title of attorney at law to the one which he finally attained—and shared only with George Washington—General of the Armies. The military profession was generally held in low repute and regarded as a refuge for misfits, drunkards, and ruffians. A familar jeer at the sight of a uniform was, "Soldier, will you work?" As John rationalized it, however, West Point would provide a first-rate education at government expense, and he was privileged to resign from the military life after graduation. Some of America's best soldiers have been hooked with this bright lure, the chance of a "free" education.

Eighteen candidates took the examination that summer at Trenton, with the result that Pershing received the highest grades and the appointment to the military academy was his, provided he could pass its more stringent academic board's requirements. On December 28, 1881, the Laclede *News* announced: "John J. Pershing will take leave of home and friends this week for West Point, where he will enter the United States Military Academy. John will make a first-rate, good-looking cadet with Uncle Sam's blue, and we trust he will ever wear it with honor to himself and the old flag which floats above him. John, here's our hand! May success crown your efforts and a long life be yours!"

Actually, unsure whether his degree of Bachelor of Scientific Didactics had completely equipped him for West Point, John was heading for Highland Falls, New York, where the white-bearded old Caleb Huse (West Point '51) had established a preparatory school for Academy hopefuls. The shaking-down process which stood between him and graduation was formidable. Of 183 appointees in his class, only 129 passed the examinations, and of those 129 only seventy-seven received their diplomas in 1886. John applied himself, as usual, and passed the West Point examination, entering the Academy as a plebe in July, 1882, just short of his twenty-second birthday (the legal limit for admittance) and six years older than the youngest member of his class.

Demonstrating, at least, the diversity of American character, some odd types managed to survive the Academy's screening process. Avery D. Andrews, Pershing's classmate and a somewhat more sophisticated easterner, recalled that among them were some amusing specimens whose eccentricities would require all the grooming and standardizing that West Point could apply. "One tall and lanky candidate from Texas appeared in a long black coat, then commonly known as a Prince Albert, and a vest which no doubt was white when he left Texas. . . . Another boy from Oregon walked over one hundred miles to a railroad station and then traveled by train for the first time in his life." But the giddiest character of all, perhaps, was a comical fellow named Wiley Bean who showed up in a seersucker suit and soon after meeting Pershing went around telling everyone that "Pershing will be President one day."

Almost thirty years later Pershing provided his own first impressions of West Point:

"Marching into camp, piling bedding, policing company streets for logs or wood carelessly dropped by upper classmen, pillow fights at tattoo with Marcus Miller, sabre drawn marching up and down superintending the plebe class, policing up feathers from the general parade; light artillery drills, double timing around old Fort Clinton at morning squad drill, Wiley Bean and the sad fate of his seersucker coat; midnight dragging, and the whole summer full of events can only be mentioned in passing. No one can ever forget his first guard tour with all its preparation and perspiration. I got along all right during the day, but at night on the color line my troubles began. Of course, I was scared beyond the point of properly applying any of my orders. A few minutes after taps, ghosts of all sorts began to appear from all directions. I selected a particularly bold one and challenged according to orders, 'Halt, who goes there?' At that the ghost stood still in its tracks. I then said, 'Halt, who stands there?' Whereupon the ghost, who was carrying a chair, sat down. Then I promptly said, 'Halt, who sits there?'

"After plebe camp came plebe math and French. I never stood high in French and was prone to burn the midnight oil. One night Walcott and Bentley Mott came in to see me. My roommate, 'Lucy' Hunt, was in bed asleep. Suddenly we heard Flaxy, who was officer in charge, coming up the stairs several steps at a time. I snatched the blanket from the window, turned out the light and leaped into bed, clothing and all, while Walcott seeing escape impossible, gently woke Hunt, and in a whisper said, 'Lucy, may I crawl under your bed?' I paid the penalty by walking six tours of extra duty."

Civil War glamour still provided a thick overlay on the Academy's tradition, and, as Pershing noted, "The West Point under Merritt, Michie and Hasbrouck was still the West Point of Grant, Sherman, Sheridan, Schofield and Howard. The deep impression these great men made during their visits to West Point in our day went far to inspire us with the soldier's spirit of self-sacrifice, duty and honor." During Pershing's term at the Academy, the one-armed General O. O. Howard was superintendent, soon to be succeeded by the dashing General Wesley Merritt, who had commanded a cavalry division under Sheridan at the age of twenty-seven.

The clearest picture of Pershing as a cadet was provided by Robert Lee Bullard, who was in the class ahead of him and who subsequently commanded the Second Army in France under him. Bullard, a southerner, was cadet lieutenant while Pershing was first sergeant of A Company of the Cadet Corps and apparently observed him closely. Bullard noted that Pershing had it easier than most of his classmen— who were an average three years younger—because he was "more mature than most cadets" and quickly developed the "right idea of command and authority."

Pershing had "regular but not handsome features and . . . a robust strong body, broad shouldered and well developed; almost or quite six feet tall; plainly of the estate of man while most about him were still boys; with keen searching eyes and intent look . . . Pershing inspired confidence but not affection. Personal magnetism seemed lacking. He won followers and admirers, but not personal worshippers. Plain in word, sane and direct in action, he applied himself to all duty and all work with a manifest purpose, not only of succeeding in what he attempted, but of surpassing, guiding and directing his fellows in what was before them. His exercise of authority was then, and always has been since, of a nature peculiarly impersonal, dispassionate, hard and firm. This quality did not, as in many, give offense; the man was too impersonal, too given over to pure business and duty." Pershing's manner even as a cadet, when most of his fellows were a trifle shaky-voiced and shamefaced about snapping orders and were far from having acquired the "habit of command," indicated clearly that he believed he had an "unquestioned right to obedience," Bullard noted.

This instinctive grasp of the "right to obedience" led Pershing steadily upward through the West Point ranks, until he was first captain of the Cadet Corps, "the most coveted place a cadet can hold."

With the girls who came up to West Point for the hops, Pershing was more popular—and a lot more relaxed—than with his fellow cadets. Then and for the rest of his life he loved dancing, and he became another man in the company of women; the icily commanding manner was defrosted and the hard look in the eyes melted amazingly. Pershing was attractive as well as attracted to the opposite sex, with his tall erect figure, dark blond hair, and gray-blue eyes. "He was a hop-goer," Bullard noted with disapproval, "what cadets called a 'spoony' man. He loved the society of women. That, too, like other early characteristics, seems to have held with him. . . ."

Pershing was neither the best disciplined nor the most scholarly of his class, but his fellows and his instructors agreed that he was the most "soldierly." On graduation he stood No. 17 in discipline, most of his demerits being for tardiness in appearing for formations, a tendency which would hardly have surprised his old schoolmaster. This peculiar flaw in a man otherwise so sternly self-disciplined and so impatient with his own and others' human frailties, this almost comic lack of time sense, was to become exaggerated, if anything, with the passage of the years and cause amusement and consternation, not to say vexation, from Paris to Tokyo; it was to confound important personages who had never been kept waiting in all their lives; but it was never to be cured.

In scholastic standing he ranked No. 30 in a class of seventy-seven survivors. The French class was the scene of his bitterest torments, which would have been no surprise to those who watched and listened to his struggles with the language many years later in France. His classmate Walcott told of coming upon Pershing "immersed in his French books" with "an expression of hopelessness and discouragement that indicated he felt he would sink." The Missouri twang was an insubstantial foundation for attempting the intricacies of French pronunciation.

Sometimes he foundered in English, too, according to Walcott, and occasionally his recitations in that class were "painful." Walcott recalled that once Pershing was called upon to discuss "pseudo-metaphors" and "made a great struggle to clarify the subject . . . great beads of perspiration standing out on his forehead." Pershing collapsed ignominiously when the instructor finally rapped out in exasperation, "Mr. Pershing, what *is* a pseudo-metaphor?" He could only run up the white flag and sit down.

Perhaps the solemnest moment of his cadet career came in his fourth year at the Point. General Grant's funeral train rolled down from Albany, where he had lain in state, and passed through the West Point station of Garrison, across the Hudson from the Academy. As the black-draped train slowly passed on its way to New York City, the whole undergraduate battalion with Cadet Captain Pershing at its head stood at present arms. It could hardly have occurred to him that in character and military aptitude, even to some extent in personality, he would more closely resemble Grant than any other eminent American commander . . . but his fate on the whole was kinder. He managed to escape the presidency.

Thus in the spring of 1886, commissioned a second lieutenant in the cavalry by President Grover Cleveland, his ill-defined hopes for a legal career deferred at least temporarily, he entered the Regular Army, then an establishment of less than 25,000 officers and men, with the Indians all but pacified and war not even a smudge on the horizon. It was a career that most young men would have regarded as the starkest of dead ends. But Pershing entered on the professional military life with hope and enthusiasm; he and his classmates celebrated their graduation in high glee with a dinner at Delmonico's the night of June 12, with Pershing at the head of the table as class president.

Their high spirits evidently were still undampened when he and several of his fellows entrained for Fort Bayard in New Mexico, the headquarters of the 6th Cavalry, to which they were posted. On the train from brawling Dodge City, over the Atchison, Topeka & Santa Fe, "we told stories, sang class songs, cleaned out eating houses, fired at prairie dogs, hazed the peanut boy, and practically ran the train," Pershing related. "Our stories came to be such chestnuts [that is, stale jokes] that Bean bought an old-fashioned doorbell which was used as a chestnut bell with which we had great fun. . . ." Apparently the antics of the young officers bound for their first post palled on at least one of their fellow passengers because "the bell was retired" after a train-riding cowboy grimly objected to its clamor. None of the high-spirited young men cared to shoot it out with this dour specimen, nor to risk having a brawl with a civilian the first entry on their records.

Pershing's first assignment landed him in the heart of the Apache country during the last campaign against the dissident Apache chiefs, the most notable and possibly the most ferocious of whom was Geronimo. Months before, Geronimo, roaring drunk on mescal, had fled the reservation with his braves and struck terror into settlements in New Mexico, Arizona, and Old Mexico with his cunning and merciless raids, killing, burning, and torturing. The Army eventually gathered up a total of 5000 troops to run down less than a tenth of their number—but they were Apaches and Geronimo was their leader. They kept ducking back and forth across the international boundary until both American and Mexican governments agreed that the U.S. forces would be allowed to follow the Apaches into Mexico when and if necessary.

In April of 1886 General George Crook, whom Commanding General Philip H. Sheridan did not believe was ruthless enough in his operations, requested that he be relieved of command. He was replaced by Nelson A. Miles, one of the more successful Indian-fighting generals on the frontier, who had been the youngest corps commander in the Union Army. General Miles said later that he "adopted the same methods used to capture bands of wild horses years ago on the plains of Texas—by constantly pursuing, putting in fresh relays and finally wearing them down."

His first need was a device for speeding and maintaining communications, since the Apaches shrewdly persisted in chopping down telegraph poles. The heliostat, later known as the heliograph, was the instrument of his choice; it was a mirror mounted on a tripod which, by reflecting sunlight, could flash messages in Morse code for fifty or more miles. Years before, an English officer in the Indian Army had

invented the heliostat, and it had worked out well there. Miles also
had tested it during campaigns in the Northwest. Placing heliostat stations on twenty-seven mountain peaks in Arizona and New Mexico,
with signalers and infantry guards at each station, Miles was enabled
to keep watch over a 600 square mile area, transmitting and relaying
more than 2000 messages during the Geronimo campaign and pushing
his troops in for the kill on orders blinked in Morse code over the
mountains.

Lieutenant Pershing's first job was taking command of a detachment charged with locating a line of heliostat stations between Forts
Bayard and Stanton. It was dangerous work, since the Apache bands
still hadn't been brought under control and were striking like forked
lightning over the desert floor, attacking settlements, stage stops, water
holes, and cavalry patrols. Later, when the chain of heliostat stations
was in working order, he was placed in command of a pack train which
took supplies to isolated posts throughout the Apache country. It was
brutal work. At any moment his mule train and escort of a dozen or
so troopers might be ambushed. Every arroyo, mesa, and clump of
brush might conceal a war party. All along his route smoke signals—
the Apache equivalent of the heliostat and almost as effective—rose
from high ground, tracing his progress. Pershing and his troopers
would spend sixteen hours a day in the saddle, hurrying through the
hostile country, and at night when the supply-laden aparejo would be
slipped off their mules' backs the animals would collapse in puddles
of their own sweat. Eventually Lieutenant Pershing was commended
for "having accomplished a particularly fine piece of work" in maintaining the supply lines.

His only brush with the Apache raiders occurred one day while
he was waiting at Fort Wingate to take out another pack train. A
wounded cowhand rode into the fort with news of a night raid on the
ranch where he was employed. Scores of hostiles were circling the
place, to which the cowhand and a number of his friends had repaired after pursuing and catching several cattle thieves. Now thieves
and honest cowhands alike were holed up and facing a common fate.
A troop was placed under Pershing's command to ride to the ranch
and rescue the besieged. When they approached the place, Pershing
ordered his patrol to attack in extended order so the Apaches would
be given the impression they were confronted with a superior force,
especially since Pershing and his command swept down on them from

a hillside at their rear. The Apaches were taken by surprise and chased away; the ranch party was rescued, with several dead among them. And there was an unsentimental footnote to the affair; the cattle thieves, though they had helped drive off the raiders, were duly hanged.

Pershing was learning the cavalryman's trade under the pressure of active campaigning. A photograph taken of him with the officers of the 6th Cavalry, their wives, and children indicated a hardening in the smiling cadet of only a few months before. He was lounging on the porch of the officers' quarters with his arms around a little girl, his face leaner, older, and tougher. He had grown a blondish beard and mustache and looked every inch the veteran cavalryman. (One of the features of his inveterate professionalism was his striking ability to look the part, whether he was suddenly called upon to perform as a military attaché abroad, lead a cavalry column into some wild interior, or command a group of armies.) With his cape thrown back over his shoulders and his cap with the crossed sabers tilted over one eye, he looked as though he had spent at least ten years chasing Apache war parties.

The hard-nosed quality in Pershing was conveyed to the men under his command very early in his career. It was an Old Army legend that shortly after his arrival at Fort Bayard one of his troopers took exception to his insistence on Academy standards of discipline and obedience, which were somewhat more rigid than those of a frontier regiment. Pershing's only recourse, as with the redheaded farmer in the schoolyard at Prairie Mound, was to show him who was the better man with his fists, although a fight between an officer and an enlisted man was theoretically taboo. Pershing won, of course; he always won in any contest over his right to command, whether it was over the polished wood of a conference table or the trampled straw behind the stables. Robert Lee Bullard, who was stationed nearby, heard of the bare-knuckle encounter and years later recollected that Pershing had been challenged by his subordinates only twice in his career—"once by one who, as I heard, was convinced by Second Lieutenant Pershing in his shirt-sleeves, and once, I knew, by one who within forty-eight hours had paid with his life for his disobedience to Captain Pershing —dying of cholera. I buried him."

It didn't take long for Pershing to acquire the reputation throughout the small Regular Army of being a hard but fair young officer.

Some years later he would be called Black Jack Pershing, which seemed a perfect description of his forceful character. Men learning that they were to fall under his command knew what to expect, what was expected of them, and conducted themselves accordingly. The other side of the coin was the fact that Pershing looked after his men more diligently than most officers, keeping a close watch over their food, equipment, living quarters, and sanitation—the mark of the best kind of company officer.

As soon as he had the troops firmly in hand, he turned his attention to more scholarly matters in his spare time. He absented himself from the poker games at the post trader's store, after becoming so fascinated with the game that "I began seeing poker hands in my sleep." Boozing had never appealed to him, popular as it was in the frontier posts. In place of those amusements he read his way through the post library and devoted himself to learning the Indian dialects from tame Apaches and civilian scouts hanging around the fort. Soon he was able to speak in the Apache tongue and had mastered the sign language which was the *lingua franca* of the Plains. Only a handful of officers took their profession that seriously.

After sixteen months of rugged campaigning, of ambushes and fire fights in the mountains, of forced marches so grueling that even the mules couldn't stand the pace, General Miles's flying column commanded by Captain Henry W. Lawton of the 4th Cavalry drove Geronimo and less than a hundred of his followers to the end of their resources high in the Sierra Madre. Geronimo agreed to surrender and was sent into exile in Florida, then a sort of American Devil's Island, along with his die-hard followers and their families.

General Miles was not entirely satisfied with the Army's performance in that campaign or the fact that it took one year and four months for 5000 troops to round up a handful of unruly Indians. He called for large-scale maneuvers during the autumn of 1887, only a few months after active campaigning ceased. The handsome, white-maned, and egocentric Miles did not distribute compliments lavishly among his subordinates, but he found occasion to praise Lieutenant Pershing for "marching his troops with a pack train of 140 mules in forty-six hours and bringing in every animal in good condition." Pershing's long and intimate knowledge of the Missouri mule, first acquired from behind a plow, enabled him to take his first step up the ladder of recognition.

He was soon transferred to command of a troop at Fort Stanton, and again distinguished himself in the "raiding games" ordained for the instruction of young company officers by the department commander. One lieutenant and his troop would be assigned to enact the roles of Apache raiders, and another would be detailed to their pursuit. Colonel Eugene A. Carr, commander of the 6th Cavalry, singled out Pershing as one of the more vigorous troop commanders.

At Stanton, Pershing became acquainted with a number of ranchers and their families who had their spreads along Eagle Creek, to the south and west of the fort. Among them were Pat Garrett, the ex-sheriff of Lincoln County, and John Poe, a former cattle detective. Half a dozen years earlier, with one of Garrett's deputies, the two men had stealthily approached the main building on Pete Maxwell's ranch at old Fort Sumner in search of an elusive young man named William H. Bonney, better known as Billy the Kid, and Garrett had shot and killed the Kid in Maxwell's bedroom. Pershing met Garrett and Poe when they came to Fort Stanton to pick up their mail and frequently visited them and their families at their ranches on Eagle Creek.

Poe's wife, Sophie, remembered Pershing as a friendly and unaffected young man. He and two other young lieutenants were known to the people in the neighborhood as "The Three Green Peas," who went riding around the countryside in their off-duty hours, exploring the desert and foothills under the white peaks of the Sierra Blanca. One of the places they often visited was a roadside inn kept by Mr. and Mrs. Frank Lisnet. Once they went boar hunting and shot one of Mrs. Lisnet's pigs under the misapprehension that it was a wild and ferocious tusker. Mrs. Lisnet gave them a dressing down that fairly crisped the air around them; however, they soon managed to re-establish themselves in the Irish lady's good graces.

Almost thirty years later, a brigadier general with a distinguished record, Pershing stopped off at Roswell to inspect the New Mexico Military Institute. He heard that the Lisnets were living in Roswell and went to look them up.

Mrs. Poe said that Pershing approached Mrs. Lisnet with a smile, saying, "How do you do, Mrs. Lisnet! Remember me?"

"Sure and that I do," replied the old lady. "You're the lieutenant that was always killing me pigs!"

During his stay at Fort Stanton, Pershing was visited by his sisters May and Grace. Trotting unmarried female relatives around the post was then one of the duties of a young officer. Lieutenant Paddock, one of the "Three Green Peas," was taken with Grace and they were soon married. A little more than ten years later Grace was widowed when Paddock was killed in China during the Boxer Rebellion.

On May 9, 1889, Pershing was given a mission both delicate and dangerous by Colonel Carr. Three white men had raided the Zuñi reservation for horses and killed three Indians while trying to make their escape. The three horse thieves were tracked down and surrounded by 150 Zuñis in a building on the S Ranch. Pershing was sent from Fort Wingate with ten troopers as an escort to stop the battle. He persuaded the enraged Indians to call off their attacks, then crept up to the cabin where the white men were holed up. Kicking in the door, he confronted the three renegades with a revolver in his hand. He promised them safe conduct past the encircling Indians, and their situation being hopeless under siege they agreed to accompany him. The Indians accepted Pershing's word that the renegades would be punished. Pershing brought the thieves safely to the Fort Wingate guardhouse, where they were held for trial.

He spent a little more than four years commanding a troop in the 6th Cavalry at Forts Stanton, Bayard, and Wingate. Then, late in 1890, the nation had its last big Indian scare. Again the Sioux threatened to rebel against the relentless encroachments of the white man. Setting off the uprising was a religious craze called the Ghost Dance, which spread through most of the Indian tribes in the West, but affected the Sioux most strongly. The Indians believed that the second coming of Christ was at hand, but this time the Messiah would be an Indian, who would disperse the whites, bring back the buffalo, and restore the ancient freedom of the Plains. Sitting Bull, the symbol of Sioux resistance, went along with the Ghost Dance propaganda. Two years before, the old Sioux who had been one of the leaders at the Little Big Horn when the 7th Cavalry was shattered had blocked the sale of 11,000,000 acres of Sioux land at fifty cents an acre. Now the whites would have their revenge. Washington decided that Sitting Bull and his few hundred followers at Grand River must be disarmed.

What followed was simply a merciless police action in the winter-locked badlands on the Dakota-Nebraska border. "If the so-called Messiah was to appear in that country, Sitting Bull had better be out of it," as Miles, the commanding general, cynically put it. In justifiable anticipation of trouble over the old chief's arrest, Miles ordered troops

from Chicago to San Francisco concentrated at and near the Pine
Ridge Agency in South Dakota, a mobilization aided by the fact that
the Burlington Road's lines penetrated deep into the Sioux country.

Early in December 1890 the 6th Cavalry received its marching orders, concentrating at Albuquerque for the long train ride north to the
railhead at Fort Niobrara, Nebraska, just south of the Dakota line
and the Rosebud Agency. Pershing and his regiment formed part of
the picket fence around the Sioux country, a cordon which was to seal
off the hostiles until they decided to surrender.

On the night of December 14, Sitting Bull was shot to death by an
Indian Police sergeant as he was being hauled out of his cabin at
Grand River. A battle broke out between the arresting force and his
followers, and the thirty-two day "war" against the Sioux was on. Its
sorry culmination was the so-called Battle of Wounded Knee, December 29, when upwards of 150 men, women, and children of Big Foot's
band were slaughtered. All over the vast, snow-covered reservation
for the next several days there were skirmishes and running battles
as bands of Sioux warriors tried to break through the Army's cordon.
Pershing and his comrades on the outer perimeter took part in two
brief skirmishes with the hostiles as they patrolled the ice-slicked line
of the railroad south of the reservation.

Now commanding a company of Sioux scouts, Pershing was patrolling Little Grass Creek a few miles from Daly's ranch when they
were attacked on January 1, 1891, by Kicking Bear and his band,
who were close to starvation and hoping to raid one of the nearby
ranches for food. Pershing and his command drove them off, killing
four of the hostiles. The brief skirmish provided the first combat cita-
tion on Pershing's record—"Action near mouth of Little Grass Creek,
South Dakota, January 1, 1891." Pershing later wrote that he "found
much that was fine in Indian character" while commanding the company of Sioux scouts.

Two weeks later, sick and starving, the Sioux decided that the Messiah would not be coming to their rescue, and there was a mass surrender at the Pine Ridge Agency. The last of the Indian wars was over.
To impress the Sioux further with the white man's military power, a
review of all the troops participating in the campaign was held at Pine
Ridge. Then Pershing, with Troop A, and four other troops of the
6th Cavalry were sent back to Fort Niobrara. On the march they were
overtaken by a blizzard which smothered the Dakota country and

took many lives. Fortunately Pershing saw to it that his men were equipped with canvas overcoats, felt oversocks, and overshoes before they set out from the agency. Troop A long remembered how Lieutenant Pershing made certain that his troopers muffled their faces with towels, pegged down their tents securely, and were supplied with cooked rations on that march through the blizzard. Not a man was lost. Years later Sergeant Tom Stevenson, a Civil War veteran, told an interviewer, "That's the sort of officer Pershing was, always thinking about his men, and that's why the men would do anything for him."

When Pershing took up his next assignment, Colonel Carr briefly summed up his years with the 6th Cavalry in a fitness report which read: "Professional ability, most excellent; capacity for command, excellent."

2. A Silver Star for San Juan Hill

Early in the nineties one of the most admired figures on the campus of the University of Nebraska, a land-grant school in Lincoln, was a keen-eyed young man whose back was straight as a slide rule and who marched from building to building as though their ivyless walls enclosed a parade ground. Against all odds, the young man had won the respect of the faculty and was idolized by the student body. One of his admirers was a young lady named Dorothy Canfield, the daughter of Dr. James Hulme Canfield, the president of the university. As Dorothy Canfield Fisher, she was to become a celebrated novelist and essayist. One of the more impressive memories of her student years was how Second Lieutenant John J. Pershing assumed the rather despised post of Professor of Military Science and Tactics, as well as Commandant of Cadets, and made something of it. The school, under terms of its government grant, was required to place an army officer on its faculty, but until then none of Pershing's predecessors had succeeded in making anyone like the idea. Until Pershing's appearance, President Canfield noted that "interest in the battalion was weak, the discipline next to nothing, and the instincts of the faculty and the President of the University against the Corps."

Pershing had heard of the vacancy through his brother Jim, a clothing salesman, like his father, with headquarters in Lincoln, and applied for it through channels. In September of 1891 he was assigned to the post. The assignment was regarded among his fellow officers as a sinecure, and Pershing was congratulated on being given a long vacation with pay. Nominally his duties would include a few hours on the drill field and a few more in the classroom. Otherwise his time would be his own. He could expect to be greeted with even more contempt and indifference than was the military man's usual lot among civilians, but doubtless he could find ways to amuse himself off-campus.

Pershing, however, had decided that if he could learn to get along with the sullen conquered Apaches of the Southwest he ought to be able to win the confidence of paleface college boys in Nebraska. Obviously it wasn't going to be easy; only a few men were still willing to come out for drill, and his classes in military science and tactics were composed of a few yawning, sleepy-eyed students. Amid the general apathy, Pershing decided to show the student body and the faculty that a professional soldier wasn't necessarily a red-faced dolt dreaming of old battles. He immediately informed President Canfield that he was there both to teach and to learn. The school was short of mathematics instructors, so he volunteered to take classes in that subject in addition to his prescribed duties. (Among his students were Dorothy Canfield and Willa Cather, but as he commented later, "I doubt that the study of mathematics gave either one of them a taste for literature.") Furthermore, he entered the law school, still determined to fulfill his ambition to be admitted to the bar.

He was still fond of dancing and attended most of the students' social affairs. At thirty-one, he was a good ten years older than most of the students, but he cut a fine figure on the dance floor, partnering with all the coeds impartially and rarely dancing with any girl more than once in an evening. He was both too discreet and too ambitious to become involved emotionally, though "crushes" on a young instructor were an unofficial part of the curriculum.

More and more of the men began volunteering for the cadet battalion. Inobtrusively, and partly through the visible admiration of the coeds for Lieutenant Pershing, he managed to invest the military with a certain amount of glamour, and his recruits were no longer regarded as servile clods marching to the orders of a stiff-necked West Pointer.

Not that he relaxed discipline in the battalion to make it more attractive; on the contrary, he made it stricter. Athletic Director Best (in an interview with a New York *Times* correspondent during World War I) recalled that Pershing took his cadets in hand the first day they reported for drill:

"It had been their habit before this time to come to drill with shoes blackened or not, just as they pleased. When Pershing took hold the first thing he looked at was to see that all shoes were well blackened and that the heels looked as good as the toes. He was just that thorough-going in everything all the time."

Best said that Pershing was "mighty dignified in his work, but he had a way of getting next to the new men." And he added:

"I just worshipped that man and everybody around the University felt the same about him."

One of Pershing's cadets, William Hayward, who became a colonel and commanding officer of the 15th New York Infantry during World War I, recalled that "Pershing was as severe a disciplinarian as a kindly man can be. He was always just. He had no pets. Punishments for derelictions of duty came no swifter than his rewards for faithful performance. . . . Lieutenant Pershing had a very keen though grim sense of humor. How he laughed when we appeared for the first time in white duck trousers as part of our uniform. They were made under contract from measure by a concern which made tents and awnings, and the goods must have been cut out with a circular saw."

In his mathematics class as well as the drill field Pershing was a sympathetic and intuitively helpful instructor. One of the shyest boys in school, as his sister afterward told an interviewer, was asked to stay after the class was dismissed one day. The boy, tongued-tied as usual in recitation, had failed to finish his demonstration of a problem at the blackboard. But Pershing told him, "All that kept you from working out that problem was your nervousness. I have marked you as though you had succeeded." In subsequent after-class sessions, his sister said, Pershing "braced him up and put him on the road to self-confidence."

Off-campus, Pershing also made friends. Grimly and typically military though he seemed in later life, he had a broader range of interests than most of his fellow officers, and a much greater talent for friendship with civilians, which most of his comrades avoided in preference to the closed-in and somewhat stifling society of Officers' Row, the regimental mess, and the post trader's saloon. Pershing not only had very little anti-civilian prejudice but was still thinking seriously of returning to civil life; instead of regarding the civilian with suspicion and a touch of contempt, he was curious about other people, the way they lived and thought.

Pershing also had the valuable knack of forming associations with men on the rise, like himself, or perhaps it was the mutual attraction of men of aspiration and ambition. Such men, caught in the backwater of the Nebraska capital, would naturally be drawn together.

After classes and drill were over for the day, he often dropped in at the law office of Charles E. Magoon, the future governor general of Cuba. Another firm and long-lasting friendship was formed in Lincoln with Charles G. Dawes, also a young lawyer, who in a remarkably short time was to leave his inconsequential practice in the frontier capital, make his way upward in Chicago financial circles, and eventually land in the vice-presidency under Calvin Coolidge.

Pershing and Dawes fell into the habit of dining together at Don Cameron's ten-cent lunch counter, where they discussed the law and the possibility of Pershing's hanging out his shingle once he received his degree at the university. The affection and respect engendered in those bull sessions over Cameron's bean suppers resulted more than twenty years later in Pershing's reaching down into an engineers regiment and selecting Dawes to supervise all the American Expeditionary Force's purchases in Europe.

Dawes was tall and loose-limbed, easygoing and gregarious; had a big nose and a wide humorous mouth, red hair and a rather absurd but currently fashionable handle-bar mustache; and was amiably inclined toward the dandyism of that decade. He was a great talker and Pershing a great listener, a perfect combination in a time and place where men had to depend on their own resources for entertainment. A native of Marietta, Ohio, he was the son of General Rufus Dawes, who had served in Congress with William McKinley, a family friend who in 1898 would appoint the younger Dawes as his Comptroller of Currency. Most people thought Dawes something of a lightweight, with few of the steelier qualities required for success, and even the usually perceptive Mark Hanna remarked after his first meeting with him, "He doesn't *look* much, does he?" Pershing saw that there was much more to the young Ohioan than a talent for conversation and a fondness for expletives which were to become one of the more colorful adornments of the Coolidge administration.

At the end of his second year as drillmaster of the university cadets, Pershing was so confident of his battalion that he entered it in the interstate competitive drill, placing it on display against the crack companies of many other schools. To everyone's surprise, Nebraska won the silver cup and $1500 in prize money for its efforts, allowing President Canfield to boast, "We have the second best corps of cadets in the United States according to the reports of the United States inspectors, the first being the corps at West Point. Lieutenant Pershing made the corps what it is today." That same year Pershing was given his first promotion, to first lieutenant, after a half dozen years' service in the lowest commissioned rank.

In the last year of his assignment at the University of Nebraska, President Canfield wrote the War Department a letter of praise for Pershing that was rarely surpassed in his later career. "I know something about the duties of his position, and I know something about officers of the army. I speak with both experience and observation, therefore, when I say without the slightest reserve that he is the most energetic, active and industrious, competent and successful I have ever known in a position of this kind. . . .

"While he has been here he has taught three hours a day in mathematics, with just as much success as he has conducted his work as Commandant. He is thorough in everything he undertakes, a gentleman by instinct and breeding, clean, straightforward, with an unusually bright mind; and peculiarly just and true in all his dealings. In addition to his work as instructor and his official duties, he has carried the course in our law school, and graduated last week with high standing. He is a man of broad outlook who sees things in their true relations, and who desires to know and be more than he is."

University life apparently encouraged second thoughts about his future career. He had been admitted to the bar of Nebraska and was seriously considering the possibility of resigning his commission and taking up a law career.

There were several factors influencing him, in addition to the newfound attractiveness of civilian life. Inwardly he had never been fully committed to a lifetime of soldiering. He had entered West Point because it offered a more complete education, had stayed in the Army because he felt that he owed it to the government. But there were facets of a military career that he found repellent—its narrowness, its caste consciousness, its smug self-sufficiency. The romantic aspects of soldiering on the frontier escaped him completely—though as an old man he recalled those days with a nostalgic affection—and the prospect of spending endless years policing the Indian reservations was anything but inviting. Furthermore, his mother still hoped that he would leave the Army; soldiering to her was the memory of her brother being brought back maimed and helpless from the siege of Vicksburg.

There were also more practical reasons for leaving the service. He was still a lieutenant at thirty-five—an age at which a man is supposed to make sure of his course before it's too late to change—and he had grave cause to wonder whether he had any real future in the Army. Promotion was so slow that many captains were white-haired. A number of his classmates who had resigned their commissions, on the other hand, were successful in civil life.

Yet the odds were all against resignation from the Army. West Pointers, it is evident from Academy records, either leave shortly after graduation or serve until retirement. Pershing had sunk too deeply into the familiar rut, though his university experience had temporarily persuaded him otherwise. Hanging out his shingle at his age wouldn't be easy either, and besides he apparently realized that his reserved temperament was ill-suited to the rough and tumble of provincial courtrooms. It was a hard decision, but Pershing finally came to the conclusion that the Army was his fate. He had hated crooked furrows as a young plowboy, and that prejudice remained with him. Never again was he tempted to change professions.

In the spring of 1895, just before leaving the University of Nebraska, he learned that there was a vacant captaincy in the Quartermaster Corps. He wanted that post because he might have to wait for years for another promotion in the cavalry; besides, in the event of a still unforeseen war, he could always transfer back to a line regiment. Generals Miles and Merritt supported his application, but Adjutant General Henry C. Corbin and his fellow bureaucrats still ruled the Army and to their clerkly minds a cavalryman ought to stick to his trade. Application denied.

Instead he spent a year at Fort Assinboine, Montana Territory, commanding a troop in the 10th (Negro) Cavalry, much of it in rounding up 600 renegade Crees and escorting them over the Canadian border. Then Miles, now general in chief, summoned him to Washington as his aide-de-camp. General Miles's sponsorship was valuable in at least one respect: he saw to it that Pershing was posted to West Point as an assistant instructor, an assignment which suggested that an officer was capable of thinking as well as fighting.

Before he began his year at West Point, another of those fortuitous meetings with an upcoming man occurred. Perhaps no other encounter of his career was so important to its advancement. General Miles sent him to observe a military tournament at Madison Square Garden in

New York during January 1897. His classmate, Avery D. Andrews, who had resigned his commission and was serving on the Board of Police Commissioners with Theodore Roosevelt, had taken a box for the tournament and invited Pershing to be his guest.

Roosevelt, busily cleaning up the graft-ridden New York Police Department then but soon to be appointed Assistant Secretary of the Navy, was another guest in the Andrews box. He and Pershing hit it off immediately, as was entirely predictable. Roosevelt was the premier western buff of all time, and not the least of Pershing's fascination for him was his facility with the Indian dialects. They spent more time swapping stories and comparing linguistic notes than watching the maneuvers on the tanbark that evening. "Both were enthusiastic and expert horsemen and both had seen much of the West," as Andrews recalled. "Both knew the Indians and the Indian Country, and both spoke the language of the plains and mountains. They spent the evening in a lively exchange of views and stories of the West and formed a friendship which lasted through life."

From then on, in and out of the White House, Roosevelt followed Pershing's career with great interest and sympathy, and his conviction that Pershing was destined to become one of the country's ablest military leaders resulted in the key promotion of the latter's career. Without that meeting at Madison Square Garden, Pershing's life would have been vastly different.

As a tactical officer at West Point, Pershing was considerably less popular than he had been at the University of Nebraska. He was charged with the immediate supervision and discipline of the cadets and believed that the Academy's standards of order and obedience should be kept at the same level as when he was a cadet.

Company A of the Cadet Corps, which was his immediate responsibility, chafed under Pershing's relentless demands and frequently abrasive personality. Being healthy young Americans, they plotted mischief against their taskmaster. Some of the cadets of Company A balanced a bucket of water on a door, placing it so that Pershing would be doused. That particular trick had whiskers on it when Pershing was a cadet himself, and he spotted the trap before it could be sprung. He ordered a janitor to remove it and said nothing. The matter would have ended there, presumably, except that the janitor did not understand that he was walking into a trap and inadvertently became the victim of the cadets' prank. Soaking wet and thoroughly enraged, the janitor complained to the authorities. Each member of Company A was summoned before the superintendent and questioned, but none would say who was responsible. The whole company was sentenced to thirty days' confinement.

First his own company and then the whole corps took to calling Pershing "Nigger Jack" well out of hearing. This, of course, referred to his service with the colored troops of the 10th Cavalry. Later the sobriquet was tidied up and became "Black Jack." The whole army adopted it, possibly because many thought it compared him to the small blunt instrument known as the "blackjack." In any case, it followed him through the dignities of high command to his grave.

Pershing had spent less than a year as a West Point instructor when the war with Spain broke out. The mysterious sinking of the battleship *Maine* in Havana harbor, the sympathy for Cubans rebelling against the harsh Spanish colonial rule, and the national enthusiasm for joining the other great powers in acquiring colonies—with Cuba, Puerto Rico, and the Philippines rich prizes to be loosened from the palsied grip of the Spanish Empire—all contributed to the declaration of war on April 25, 1898. The ethics of that declaration did not concern Pershing any more than it did the majority of his fellow citizens; his main consideration was getting away from the classroom and into the fighting. The thought of sitting out the war on the palisades of the Hudson while his fellow officers were winning glory and promotion in the Caribbean and the Pacific was maddening.

Yet regulations, it seemed, would keep him at West Point even while the Army in the field needed every experienced officer to train and lead its combat forces, and while the Regular Army was doubled in size and the President was calling for an additional 125,000 volunteers. Theodore Roosevelt, raising the regiment of Rough Riders with Leonard Wood as its colonel and himself as its more prominent second in command, bitterly remarked on "fat old colonels who fall off their horses or cannot stand a five-mile march." Yet a young and vigorous, highly trained and widely experienced officer like Pershing was to be kept out of action. The War Department bureaucracy had ruled that no officer was to be detached from the Academy's faculty to serve in the field.

Pershing considered resigning his commission and joining either Roosevelt's Rough Riders—few people thought of the regiment as

Wood's although he was its nominal commander—or joining his class-mate Andrews in the New York National Guard.

Instead he obtained permission from West Point's sympathetic superintendent, Major Oswald H. Ernst, to go to Washington and plead his case. He went over Adjutant General Corbin's head, probably with an assist from General in chief Miles, and pleaded for return to regimental duty before Secretary of War Russell A. Alger, himself a cavalry veteran of the Civil War. His appeal was persuasive enough for Alger to override his bureau chiefs and send Pershing back to the 10th Cavalry. Since there was no troop command vacant, he was attached to Colonel Baldwin's staff as quartermaster.

Watching and participating in the weirdly incompetent embarkation of the expeditionary force for Cuba early in the summer of 1898 must have been an invaluable experience for Pershing, a lesson to be recalled when he launched his own expeditionary forces in the Philippines, Mexico, and France. He arrived in Tampa, Florida, just in time to accompany his Negro cavalry regiment in the landing on Cuban shores.

The sorry history of that movement does not require much recapitulation except in relation to Pershing's education in how *not* to conduct an operation overseas. Practically everything went wrong. By mid-June Major General William R. Shafter, as commander of V Corps, which was to undertake the invasion, had managed to scrape together only 16,000 men, and barely enough transports, civilian and naval, to carry that many to the unmapped and unreconnoitered Cuban shore. Most of the troops wore the Old Army's blue flannel for summer campaigning in the tropics; only the Rough Riders were suitably clad in lightweight khaki. The canned beef was bluish; other rations were wormy or moldy. Virtually no preparations were made to handle the sick and wounded. Black powder was used to fire the American artillery's guns and the infantry's rifles (while the supposedly antiquated Spanish Army was equipped with smokeless powder and modern Mauser rifles). When the first regiments were finally landed near the villages of Siboney and Daiquiri, the invading force was a tangled, seasick, and homesick mass, separated from their supplies, confused by a lack of leadership. General Shafter was a fat gouty old man who had to be boosted into the saddle from a platform; General Joe Wheeler was a frail and white-bearded, but high-spirited veteran of the Confederate cavalry, who led the cavalry division when he was able, and many of their juniors were equally unfit for service in a jungle campaign. Pershing, however, loyally excused the miseries of the invasion as being due to the "inexperience of officers in transporting troops by water" and the "uncertainty as to whether or not the Spanish fleet was really confined in the harbor of Santiago."

One of the first reactions of the liberators was that the Cuban rebel army, whom they had come to sustain, succor, and ally themselves with, was a contemptible rabble. The same attitude toward native allies, carried intact across the generations, was visible in the early stages of the Korean War. At first sight and in the first brief actions against the Spanish forces, the Americans decided that the Cubans were all too ready to leave the fighting to the newcomers. Pershing was more liberal-minded. "Ragged, some half naked, wearied from hunger, laden with huge earthen water pots, heavy packs and cooking utensils slung over their backs, armed with every conceivable pattern of gun, it is no wonder that they dared not face the deadly Mauser rifle; we ourselves had much less contempt for Spanish arms after we had met them face to face on the battle field."

The idea behind the overland campaign—one could hardly call it strategy since General Shafter himself said "there was no strategy about it" and his only concern was to "do it quick"—was to march through the jungle, overwhelm the fortified ridges known collectively as San Juan Hill, and demand the surrender of the port city of Santiago. General Shafter, lying in a hammock with a malarial fever, was confident that all opposition would be swept aside; he even rebuffed the offers of naval gun support from U.S. battleships at the mouth of Santiago harbor. The job, he felt, could be quickly and smartly handled by Lawton's infantry division, based on Daiquiri, and Wheeler's cavalry division, headquartered at Siboney. The infantry was to take out El Caney, a fortified spur which jabbed into the flank of the proposed American advance, while the cavalry stormed San Juan Hill and its line of stone blockhouses.

Dismounted, the cavalry slashed its way through the tropical forest, matted with vines and spiked with Spanish bayonet, and arrived in position several hours before the general advance scheduled for the morning of July 1.

Before El Caney, to the north, U.S. batteries opened fire at daylight and the attack on the landward defenses of Santiago was under way. The 10th Cavalry and its Negro troopers waited to go into action with S. B. M. Young's brigade, which was to advance in two columns, the 1st and 10th Cavalry on the left, the Rough Riders on the right. The scene (as Pershing described it five months later in a well-wrought address before a Chicago church group) was "ideally beautiful; the sky was cloudless and the air soft and balmy; peace seemed to reign supreme, great palms towered here and there above the low jungle. It was a picture of a peaceful valley. There was a feeling that we had secretly invaded the Holy Land. The hush seemed to pervade all nature as though she held her bated breath in anticipation of the carnage."

An artillery duel opened proceedings on the 10th Cavalry's front. "A slug of iron now and then fell among the surrounding bushes or buried itself deep in the ground near us. Finally a projectile from an unseen Spanish gun discharged a Hotchkiss piece, wounded two cavalrymen and smashed into the old sugar mill in our rear, whereupon the terrorized insurgents fled and were not seen again near the firing line until the battle was over."

Pershing was standing at the roadside, watching a battery of field artillery crossing a stream and moving up to counter the Spanish batteries' fire, when he heard a young officer express his bitterness against the confusion and lack of direction attending the advance by denouncing General Shafter as a "fat old slob." Pershing was outraged; publicly criticizing a superior in the midst of a battle, no matter how great the provocation, was unthinkable to him.

He rounded on the younger officer, demanding of him, "Why did you come into this war if you can't stand the gaff? War has always been this way. Did you expect to see the Old Man standing out here with a book in his hand, telling these mule-skinners how to handle their outfits? The fat Old Man you talk about is going to win this campaign. When he does, these things will be forgotten. It's the objective which counts, not the incidents." Pershing was less than prophetic about the high-level incompetence of the Santiago campaign being "forgotten." The ubiquitous war correspondents—there seemed to be one behind every tree, mostly wearing the Hearst colors—kept the public at home informed of the rudderless careening in Cuba and it was all that Shafter's chief supporter, Secretary of War Alger, could do to fend off demands that he be superseded.

Out of touch with V Corps headquarters, since Shafter had a direct cable and telegraph connection with Washington but none with his divisions at the front, the battle for Santiago proceeded on the initiative of the junior officers, the noncoms, and the troops themselves. Lawton's infantry got stuck in front of El Caney, but the two cavalry columns pushed on toward San Juan Hill.

Without mentioning his own role in the assault on the fortified ridges, Pershing continued in his account: "Then the balloon [an observation balloon sent aloft to report on any Spanish troop movements] had become lodged in the treetops above and the enemy had just begun to make a target of it. A converging fire from all the works within range opened up on us that was terrible in its effect. Our mounted officers dismounted and the men stripped off at the roadside everything possible and prepared for business."

Meanwhile, the 71st New York Volunteers, badly officered, were moving up on the left to lend flank support to the dismounted cavalry's attack on the ridges. Under heavy fire as they advanced through the jungle, they panicked and fled rearward for safety. Not even the threats and entreaties of the divisional commander and his staff could persuade them to move forward again.

Pershing and the 10th Cavalry's Second Squadron, which he was accompanying as a possible replacement for any officer who fell in action, took shelter under the bank of the San Juan River and "stood in the water to our waists waiting orders to deploy. Remaining there under this galling fire of exploding shrapnel and deadly Mauser bullets the minutes seemed like hours.

"General Wheeler and a part of his staff stood mounted a few minutes in the middle of the stream. Just as I raised my hand to salute in passing up the stream to reach the squadron of my regiment, a piece of bursting shell struck between us and covered us both with water.

"Pursuant to orders from its commander, with myself as guide, the Second Squadron of the 10th forced its way through wire fence and almost impenetrable thicket to its position. The regiment was soon deployed as skirmishers in an opening across the river to the right of the road and our line of skirmishers being partly visible from the enemy's position, their fire was turned upon us and we had to lie down in the grass a few minutes for safety. Two officers of the regiment were wounded; here and there were frequent calls for the surgeon."

Now the time had come for the direct assault on San Juan Hill, through barbed-wire entanglements (the first ever encountered by

American troops, and a bitter surprise to them) and under heavy fire from the Spanish artillery and the riflemen crouching behind the slits of their blockhouses and in trenches snaking their way across the ridges. Three cavalry regiments made the charge—the regulars of the 1st and 10th, the volunteers of the Rough Riders. Theodore Roosevelt, waving his campaign hat à la Phil Sheridan, led the westerners in person, Leonard Wood being occupied with higher command duties, and charged right over the hill and into the White House. His Rough Riders, of course, received most of the glory, but the regular cavalry deserved at least an equal share of the credit.

As Pershing recalled, "Through streams, tall grass, tropical undergrowth, under barbed wire fences and over wire entanglements, regardless of casualties up the hill to the right, this gallant advance was made. As we appeared on the brow of the hill we found the Spaniards retreating only to take up a new position farther on, spitefully firing as they retreated and only yielding their ground inch by inch.

"Our troopers halted and laid down but momentarily to get a breath and in the face of continued volleys soon formed for attack on the block houses and intrenchments on the second hill. This attack was supported by troops including some of the 10th who had originally moved to the left toward this second hill and had worked their way in groups slipping through the tall grass and bushes, crawling when casualties came too often, courageously facing a sleet of bullets, and now hung against the steep southern declivity ready to spring the few remaining yards into the teeth of the enemy.

"The fire from the Spanish positions had doubled in intensity. There was a moment's lull and our line moved forward to the charge across the valley separating the two hills. Once begun it continued dauntless in its steady, dogged, persistent advance until like a mighty resistless challenge it dashed triumphant over the crest of the hill and firing a parting volley at the vanishing foe planted the silken standard on the enemy's breastworks and the Stars and Stripes over the block house on San Juan Hill to stay.

"This was a time for rejoicing. It was glorious."

Pershing also told of watching "a colored trooper stop at a trench filled with Spanish dead and wounded and gently raised the head of a wounded Spanish lieutenant and give him the last drop of water from his own canteen." The 10th Cavalry had lost half its officers and one fifth of its enlisted men in the charge uphill. The troopers had behaved so gallantly that, Pershing said, their officers "could have taken our black heroes in our arms." In the Santiago campaign Pershing acquired a lifelong respect and affection for the Negro soldier.

Next day the U.S. troops on San Juan and Kettle hills strengthened their positions. On the following day the fate of the Spanish forces in Santiago was sealed when the enemy fleet was destroyed in attempting to escape from the harbor. A truce halted the fighting around the land defenses of the city, but "the rainy season had set in in earnest and the trenches at times were knee-deep with mud and water. The constant exposures to the heat and rain together with the strain of battle began to have its effect upon even the strongest of us. Our sick list gradually grew and the dreaded yellow fever appeared in our ranks; the field hospitals already overcrowded with wounded were compelled to accommodate the increasing number of fever patients; medical supplies and food for the sick were lacking. . . ." Meanwhile, with the American Army succumbing to fever in its trenches and camps all the way back to Siboney and Daiquiri, negotiations were opened between General Shafter and the Spanish Army for surrender of the city. Santiago was bombarded for two days by the U.S. artillery to help the Spanish commander make up his mind, with the American fleet's guns joining in offshore. The Spanish finally capitulated on July 16.

In his account of the campaign, Pershing neglected to mention his own role in the fighting. It was not, however, ignored by his comrades. Lieutenant John Bigelow, Jr., Troop D, reported he was "disabled by three bullet wounds received simultaneously" on the approaches to San Juan Hill and Lieutenant Pershing took over his command. Major T. J. Wint, commanding the Second Squadron, informed the Adjutant General's office in his report dated November 28, 1898, that Pershing "was with the Second Squadron when passed on Sugar House Hill and during its advance on San Juan Hill he conducted himself in a most gallant and efficient manner." Colonel Baldwin, the regimental commander, cited Pershing for "untiring energy, faithfulness and gallantry during this engagement." Even more enthusiastic was the brigade commander's praise. General S. B. M. Young, a Civil War veteran, declared that Pershing was "the coolest man under fire that I ever saw."

The upshot was that Pershing was awarded the Silver Star, the second highest combat decoration, for "gallantry in action against the Spanish forces, Santiago, Cuba, July 1, 1898."

He was also brevetted a major in the volunteers and, more importantly, promoted to captain in the Regular Army.

Within a month Pershing was ordered back to Washington to duty in the War Department. His first post, assumed on August 18, was chief ordnance officer, which he held until December 20. Then he was assigned to organize the Bureau of Insular Affairs, which was to oversee the military administration of the islands wrested from the Spanish.

As head of this military government bureau, he fell under the close and favorable attention of Elihu Root, the prosperous New York lawyer who was appointed Secretary of War to succeed Russell A. Alger, the moribund condition of the War Department having been harshly revealed to President McKinley in the supply, organization, and direction of the Cuban campaign. Root was a deceptive man, mild and modest in appearance, with his hair worn in thick bangs over an intellectual forehead. But underneath the detached and professorial manner was an incisive and ruthlessly efficient mind; only occasionally his face relaxed in what one associate called a "frank and murderous smile." There were protests against the appointment of a corporation lawyer without military experience to direct the War Department, but the President insisted that he had to "have a lawyer to direct the government of these Spanish islands."

Root was naturally impatient with the pettifoggery, the paper shuffling, the military vanities and foibles he found among his new associates. Captain Pershing intrigued him immediately, not only because a soldier with a law degree was such a rarity but for his plain speaking and his contempt for bureaucratic quibbles. Root found that Pershing was the rare officer who could carry out a directive without delay or confusion, who was willing to make decisions and assume responsibility without buck passing. Together they confronted the problem of the corruption and scandal in the military government of Havana and worked on plans for the pacification of the Philippines, where native guerrillas, having expected total liberation once the Spanish were driven out, now were organizing an insurrection against the American occupation.

Chair-borne duty, however, proved irksome after eight months as chief of the Bureau of Insular Affairs, no matter how rewarding was his association with Elihu Root. He requested a transfer to active duty in the Philippines, which was granted.

Late in 1899 he sailed for Manila the long way around, via England, the Suez Canal, the Indian Ocean, and the Straits of Malacca. During a stop-off of several weeks in England, he was astounded by the business-as-usual atmosphere while a bitterly difficult war was being fought against the Boers in South Africa. One of the first places he decided to visit was the famous Woolwich Arsenal, which he imagined would be guarded by at least a regiment armed to the teeth, not reckoning with the supreme self-confidence of the British. At the arsenal he strolled through an open and unguarded gateway and soon was looking over "large quantities of military stores" which any Boer agent or saboteur seemingly would have been able to destroy with a minimum of effort.

A guard finally sauntered up and asked him his business. Pershing playfully admitted he had no business there and was evasive in his replies to the guard's questions. "Well," the guard finally remonstrated, "of course you know it's against the rules." Pershing then identified himself as an American officer in mufti, and the guard politely showed him all around the arsenal.

He arrived in Manila aboard the hospital ship *Missouri,* then took a coastal steamer for Zamboanga, on the island of Mindanao. There, in the rebellious southern islands, his future lay. For the best part of the next fourteen years, campaigning against the toughest jungle fighters in the world, he would be tried, trained, and hardened in the harsh school of the colonial soldier.

3. Against the Gong-Maddened Moros

Damn, damn, damn the Filipino,
Pockmarked kodiac ladrone;
Underneath the starry flag
Civilize him with a Krag
And return us to our beloved home.

American soldiers' song to the
tune of "Tramp, Tramp, Tramp"

No longer, deadlier, or stranger war was ever fought by the American
Army, in proportion to the numbers involved, than the intermittent
jungle campaigns between 1900 and 1914 against the Moros of the
southern Philippines. It attracted comparatively little attention in the
United States except when fighting would break out around the Moro
forts in the mountain jungles and stateside humanitarians would protest the "massacre" of native dissidents by American troops indoctrinated with the "civilize 'em with a Krag"[1] philosophy. Though the
Moro campaigns are one of the least-known phases of United States
military history, they served as the proving ground for many of the
leading commanders in World War I, not the least of them John J.
Pershing.

Captain Pershing arrived in the Philippines just as he turned forty
—a trim, energetic, and inobtrusively ambitious officer who had left
important friends in Washington and brought with him impressive

---

[1] That is, with a Krag-Jorgensen rifle, then the standard issue for the
Regular Army.

credentials of service both in staff and line. His first assignment, despite his eagerness to serve in a troop command, was adjutant general of the Department of Mindanao and Jolo, with headquarters at Zamboanga, the recently vacated seat of Spanish military power in the southern islands. The department, known as the Moro Province under civil administration, embraced the islands of Mindanao, Basilan, Jolo, Tawitawi, and many smaller nameless ones in the palm-shaded and coral-shored chain which marked the dividing line between the Sulu and Celebes seas. On August 20, 1901, he was transferred to the 15th Cavalry, again as a staff officer, this time wearing the hats of chief engineer, ordnance and signal officer, and collector of customs at Zamboanga. On October 11 of that year, finally, he broke away from desk duty and was given command of the post at Iligan, on the north coast of Mindanao.

During the irksome months of staff duty he busied himself learning everything he could about the Moros and their customs, applying himself with the same diligence as he had more than a dozen years earlier in Apache country. He learned to speak the Moro dialects and to read Arabic, studied the rambling texts of the Koran, and mingled on friendly terms with the tamer Moros living in the coastal towns. Almost from the outset he saw that if the occupying forces—several thousand troops against more than a half million natives in the Moro Province—tried to suppress certain native proclivities there would be more trouble than a few regiments could handle. Piracy, slavery, and polygamy were part of the Moro's life; slaughtering the Christians or any other brand of infidel was not murder but a passport to the Mohammedan heaven. Barbaric as his customs seemed to the white man, the Moro had established his own kind of civilization in the southern seas dating back six centuries, and it would take more than gunfire, sermonizing, and the lure of indoor plumbing to persuade him to change his ways—if it could ever be done. The best the Americans could hope for was to establish a minimum amount of order and to introduce a more democratic system of law.

Early in his stay in the Philippines, Pershing wrote a rather perceptive description of the Moro character and its resistance to change. "The almost infinite combination of superstitions, prejudices and suspicions blended with his character make him a difficult person to handle until fully understood. In order to control him other than by brute force, one must first win his implicit confidence, nor is this as difficult as it would seem. . . . He is jealous of his religion, but he knows very little about its teachings. . . . As long as he is undisturbed in the possession of his women and children, and his slaves, there is little to fear from him. As a rule he treats his so-called slaves, who are really but serfs or vassals, as members of his family; but any interference with what he thinks his right regarding them had best be made gradually by the natural process of development, which must logically come by contact with and under the wise supervision of a civilized people."

Pershing and other army officers experienced in dealing with native peoples knew that pacification of the Philippines, no matter what people were told back home, would be a long, costly, and patience-demanding project. Since the Spanish fleet had been destroyed and Manila occupied in the summer of 1898, Luzon and the other islands to the north were slowly being brought under control. Emilio Aguinaldo, the leader of the insurrection on Luzon, was not captured until March 23, 1901. On Samar, a particularly vigorous guerrilla leader named Lucban wiped out almost an entire company of U.S. infantry in a surprise attack. Throughout the islands the American troops controlled little more than their posts and garrison towns and their lines of communication; they were surrounded by guerrillas and a population almost entirely sympathetic to them. The Filipinos had decided to resist the decision to replace Spanish rule with a somewhat gentler but not much less irksome American administration.

In a period of little more than three years the American Army in the Philippines was forced to engage in 2811 separate battles and actions. The insurrection slowly flickered out first on Luzon and the northern islands, as civil administrators, doctors, teachers, sanitation and nutrition experts came out from the States by the thousands. A policy of patient instruction seemed to work best. On Samar, for instance, General Jacob "Hell Roaring" Smith decided to take revenge for the massacre of the infantry company at Balangiga and ordered his subordinates, "I want no prisoners. I wish you to kill and burn; the more you kill and burn the better you will please me." He suggested that Samar be made "a howling wilderness" and rounded up thousands of the people in concentration camps. The result was a long drawn-out struggle finally resolved by gentler measures.

The Moro country, being largely Mohammedan while the other islands had been converted by the Spanish friars to the Catholic faith, was a different and more difficult problem. The Moros, like the Taga-

logs, Visayans, and other Filipino peoples, were of Malay stock. Mo-
hammedanism, giving them a fighting creed, made the difference. It
was imported to the southern Philippines in the latter part of the
fourteenth century by adventurers from the Javanese Empire of Ma-
japahit. In 1490, thirty years before Magellan "discovered" the Philippines, Mindanao and the Sulu Islands were ruled by Arab-Malay
nobles from the royal houses of Borneo and Malacca.

When the Spanish came, they were able to subjugate Luzon and the
northern islands after a long and continuing struggle, but in the south
they were confined to Zamboanga, a few other strongly fortified posts,
and a garrison on the mountain-girded Lake Lanao. Even for those
places they had to fight continuously, since Mohammedan missionaries kept the Moro tribes in a constant ferment of resistance. In the
Sulu and Celebes seas, meanwhile, the Moro pirates in their swift
vintas reaped a rich harvest of booty for centuries; the island of Jolo
served as their thieves' market, at which the men they captured were
sold into slavery and the women were parceled out to various Moro
harems.

In their attempt to gain control over the Moro Province without
open hostilities, the Americans negotiated a very tentative agreement
with the Sultan of Sulu and some lesser dignitaries, called the Bates
Treaty, in which the sultanate was defined as a "protected sovereignty"
under the benign guidance of the United States. The sultan was to
receive $250 a month and seven tribal leaders lesser amounts from
the United States. This agreement, however, covered only about a
third of the Moros and did not include the island of Mindanao.

The real ruler of the Moros, as the Americans learned, was not the
Sultan of Sulu at his stronghold on the island of Jolo, but the tribal
chiefs (the datus and panglimas) and the Mohammedan priests
(panditas) who governed their people under a feudal system which
gave them the power of life and death over their subjects. When the
Americans began occupying the coastal towns of Mindanao and other
islands, the less amiable Moros started moving inland, leaving the
coast to the minority groups of Christian Filipinos and a scattering
of pagan tribes who had suffered for centuries from their depredations.

Fiercely independent, warlike on land or sea, the bulk of the Moros
were determined to live their own way—criminal, violent, and barbaric
as it seemed to the Spanish and the Americans, who hoped to instill in
them Occidental law and Christian ethic—and resist any attempts to

impose changes. Their code of laws included the following provisions:

"If a bachelor or widower commits adultery and is killed by a non-Mohammedan, the non-Mohammedan shall be put to death. But a Mohammedan who may kill such an adulterer shall not be put to death.

"If a creditor begets a child of a slave held as security he shall buy the child from the debtor; otherwise the child shall become the slave of the debtor.

"If a married man commits adultery with a free woman, both shall be stoned to death. The punishment of the man may be reduced to imprisonment. The woman shall be buried up to the chest and stoned with medium-sized stones.

"The minimum amount of blood money for a deep stab wound of a Moslem shall be 868¼ pesos; of a heathen or pagan 57¼ pesos.

"If a free man kills a slave, the free man shall not be put to death. If a slave or other servant kills a free man, he shall be put to death."

Slavery was a sacred institution to the Moros, condoned and encouraged in the Koran; piracy was a greatly respected profession; thievery and murder, if directed against non-Mohammedans, were praiseworthy, and polygamy was a decent and moral method of insuring the care and protection of women, always in surplus due to the violent and risky careers of their menfolk. The Americans managed to abolish slavery and break up the slave markets in the relatively small areas under their direct control, but there was no abolition in the mountain jungles, where the tribal chiefs were beyond the application of force.

From their mountain strongholds, the Moros were soon sallying forth and raiding the coastal towns, carrying off cattle and human captives.

Brigadier General William A. Kobbe, then commanding the Department of Mindanao and Jolo, decided that a punitive expedition up the Cagayan River on the north coast of Mindanao would be necessary to show that the Americans meant business. A General Capistrano was reported to be leading the Macajambos of the Cagayan district in their raids. The column of infantry and cavalry, with a few mountain guns hauled on pack mules, was to capture Capistrano, scatter his warriors, and seize his fort on the lip of a mountain gorge.

Since this was the first column to invade the interior, General Kobbe wanted exact and detailed reports on its progress and achievements.

He detailed Captain Pershing, as his adjutant, to accompany the expedition and supply him with those reports.

The expedition took the field on November 27, 1900, moving slowly and laboriously up the Cagayan, cutting a road through the ascending jungle, moving over plains of shoulder-high cogon grass and fields of giant ferns. As they climbed into the foothills, the Americans became aware of the fact that they were being watched every foot of the way and that it would be easy enough for the Moros to ambush them with their blowguns and poisoned darts. The Moros, however, held off their attack, possibly out of curiosity at the sight of these white men toiling so ridiculously at traversing country over which they moved with the ease and swiftness of the animals. The spectacle must have become even more hilarious to the watching Moros as the mountain howitzers had to be unloaded from muleback and hauled by hand over the steep and treacherous mountain trails.

When the American column approached the 800-foot gorge in which their fort was located, the Macajambos finally launched their attack. Some of General Capistrano's followers were concealed in the brush at the bottom of the canyon when the American cavalrymen watered their horses on the afternoon of December 17 and began firing from ambush. The cavalrymen took cover while the infantry went to work. Captain Pershing, although detailed to go with the column as an observer, immediately took a hand in the fire fight. "Pershing took fifteen men on one bluff and I took about the same number on another and poured volleys into the canyon, firing at smoke from the insurgent pieces, silencing their fire," reported Captain James J. Mays of the 40th Infantry. "I think we killed some of them but do not know."

Next day, while patrols from the 40th Infantry guarded the approaches to the fortified village of Macajambos, Pershing crossed the river and joined the mountain howitzer battery commanded by Captain Millar, helping to direct its fire on General Capistrano's stronghold. Terrified by the bombardment, the Moros fled into the jungle and managed to escape Captain Mays's patrols. By the afternoon of December 18, it was obvious that the Macajambos had given up the fight and scattered into the mountains. And that was probably the easiest victory ever won by an American field force against the Moro tribes of Mindanao. Later they would hold to their forts with a bitter courage matched in the American experience only by the Sioux and the Apaches.

The Cagayan expedition wrecked the Macajambos's stronghold and destroyed provisions and ammunition found in the fort, as well as two of the brass cannon known as lantacas. On December 28, near the village of Langaran, a number of insurgents were found to have ventured in from the jungles and occupied a strong position, but just as the Americans deployed to assault it the Moros fled once again.

On February 2, 1901, Captain Pershing wrote General Kobbe that Capistrano, his followers dispersed and disheartened, wanted to come in for a conference with the department commander at Zamboanga and advised that "patrols and expeditionary forces need not be suspended but should be warned to be at special pains not to molest unresisting parties of natives." Capistrano's surrender was followed by the capitulation of a number of his followers.

The suppression of the Macajambos failed to deter other Moro tribes, particularly to the south of Lake Lanao, from contesting the American authority. American soldiers and civilians were murdered and a number of cavalry horses were stolen by the Malanaos, a group of tribes living in the mountains above and on the shore around the lake. After much conferring in Manila and Zamboanga, it was decided to teach the Malanaos a stern lesson, which would take the shape of a large punitive force, a thousand cavalry and infantry troops, to be commanded by Colonel Frank D. Baldwin, who had twice won the Medal of Honor in the Civil and Indian Wars. There were two approaches to the lake district, from Iligan on the north coast, roughly the route taken by the Cagayan River expedition, or up from Malabang on the south coast. Neither was easy, since the lake was 2500 feet above sea level and the intervening country was a tangle of jungle, mountain, and cogon-covered plateau.

While Baldwin's column moved up from Malabang, Captain Pershing was placed in command of the post at Iligan. He had made a number of friends among the Moros of northern Mindanao and was expected to play a semi-diplomatic role. Holding court at Iligan, he encouraged the chiefs of neighboring tribes to come in and talk to him. He explained to each of them that Baldwin's operations were aimed at the Sultan of Bayan and his supporters, not against Moros of the north who were presently keeping the peace.

Pershing's efforts doubtless persuaded many Moros to stay out of the Sultan of Bayan's camp and lessened the dangers of Colonel Baldwin's venture, since there were close to 300,000[2] Moros living in the lake country (according to a Spanish estimate). In due course, Colonel Baldwin assaulted the Sultan of Bayan's stronghold at Pandatahan and carried the place after a hard fight. An estimated 200 to 300 Moros were killed, including the sultans of Bayan and Pandatahan. With evident disapproval, Pershing later commented on this operation, "I think Colonel Baldwin wanted to shoot the Moros first and give them the olive branch afterwards."

An American garrison was established a thousand yards south of the captured fort and preparations were made to bring the whole lake country under control. Pershing was summoned to Camp Vicars in the spring of 1902 to act as Baldwin's intelligence officer and acquaint himself with the command. His superiors had decided on larger responsibilities for Pershing, since General Kobbe was soon to be replaced by Brigadier General George W. Davis and Baldwin was to be promoted to brigadier and sent elsewhere.

There were plenty of senior officers waiting around Manila and Zamboanga to assume the command at Camp Vicars, which ordinarily would have gone to a full colonel—certainly not a junior captain. But his superiors had settled on Pershing for the post, and he had enough highly placed friends in Washington, up to and including President Roosevelt, to override the rigid system of seniority obtaining at the time. General Davis wrote the War Department that the assignment of Pershing to command at Camp Vicars was necessary because "the man to command on the spot should possess certain qualities not easy to find confined in one man: capacity for command, physical and mental vigor, infinite patience in dealing with these fanatical semi-savages, wise discretion, a serious desire to accomplish work set for him, and knowledge of the Moro character."

Captain Pershing's appointment to command Camp Vicars—and whatever punitive forces would be sent from there—was announced on June 30, 1902. A groan of protest went up from the Army in the Philippines, particularly from officers above the grade of captain, as always when sacrosanct seniority was flouted. The appointment was attributed to "pull," and the fact that Pershing had studiously prepared himself for greater responsibility by learning the Moro dialects

---

[2]A short time later, however, Pershing estimated the Moro population around the lake at 80,000.

and acquainting himself with the people while most of his fellow officers were lolling at their ease in cantonments by the Sulu Sea, accepting drinks from native servants bearing brass trays, was disregarded. From then on, a certain amount of professional jealousy evidenced itself during every succeeding phase of Pershing's career, a spiteful quality no less virulent among the military than operatic tenors; he was to be a marked man in more ways than one, and the envy generated by the Camp Vicars appointment was to burst out several years later in a particularly nasty form.

The Manila *Times* took notice of the dissatisfaction in army circles and remarked that the appointment was "very freely discussed in the service, and the men who rank him have been greatly displeased. He is only a captain and the size of his force is out of all proportion to his rank." The *Times* reported that Pershing was the choice of Major General Adna R. Chaffee, commanding in Manila, and General Davis, at Zamboanga, "has not hesitated to continue him in the place." The Manila *American* approved of Pershing as an officer "equipped by nature with a vast amount of patience and a deep insight into human character."

Jack Pershing also had his supporters, few though they may have been, among his fellow officers. Captain Robert Lee Bullard, who had been in the class ahead of Pershing's at West Point and who was then also serving on Mindanao, remarked that Pershing deserved the post because he was "very influential" with the Moros and had won their "confidence and admiration." Bullard also took note of the "adverse criticism of men who were jealous or who disapproved of his thus occupying himself." Bullard believed that "the Americans had inherited the idea that they [the Moros] were irreconcilable, and impossible of civilization. Pershing's influence began to lead them toward the American authorities."

Bullard also noted in his diary that Pershing "was given this duty when there were on the spot other officers many years his senior in age and service. This was accomplished, of course, by a species of military jugglery, but it was amply justified by the conditions. Ill-judged treatment of friendly Moros by an officer of mine had nearly precipitated a general war with the Moros." As Pershing firmly took hold of the troubled situation around Lake Lanao, Bullard wrote that "the more I see of this unusual work the more I am of the opinion that General Davis did right to keep Pershing in charge of these Moros instead of placing in charge some fool officer who ignorantly supposed that he could come and in an offhand manner manage these savages."

Pershing's "unusual work" at Camp Vicars undoubtedly startled his more hidebound fellow officers, who viewed the Moros simply as barbarians to be ignored if they were peaceable or struck down if they got out of hand. Most of the regulars believed they should be ruled at least as firmly, as haughtily, as the British reigned over the teeming masses of India; you had to keep them at a distance, convince them of the white man's superiority, draw an unwavering line between the sahib and the native.

Pershing, however, proceeded to deal with the Moros if not quite as equals, at least as fellow human beings. He spent hours every day receiving their delegations—a datu under a silken sunshade accompanied by a number of retainers—endlessly explaining to them the purposes of the American occupation and pointing out that if they were willing to till their lands peacefully they could make the island one of the most bountiful in the world.

He also contrived to mingle with them on social terms, then and later in his Philippine career, with an ease and lack of condescension rarely attained by other American officers or civilian governors of that period. One of the Moro enthusiasms was for playing chess, which had been taught them by the Arab missionaries. Pershing would squat on the ground for hours studying a chessboard with visiting datus. He also invited 700 of his Moro neighbors to attend a Fourth of July celebration at Camp Vicars in the summer of 1902, encouraging his men to mingle with the guests and show them a common humanity.

In the vigorously colonizing world of 1902, laboring under Kiplingesque delusions of white supremacy, this sort of person-to-person socializing was a radical and possibly dangerous departure from the proper way of doing things.

Despite all his diplomacy and hospitality, a number of sultans in the lake region refused to come in and parley with Pershing. The sultans of Maciu, of Bacolod, of Bayabao, and of Calabui, and the lesser datus and panglimas who sympathized with them, now saw quite clearly that their authority over the tribes would be sharply reduced if they submitted to the Sultan of Camp Vicars. They had no intention of sharing their ancient powers with an American officer. It was time to discourage his attempts to pacify the lake country.

He was not easily dissuaded that peaceful methods would work and even used what must have seemed like white witchcraft to impress the natives. A number of Moro chiefs, on the verge of warring among themselves, were summoned to a peace conference but balked at signing a treaty. Pershing ordered his aides to bring in an Edison "talking machine," which had just been developed and put on the market back in the States. Helen Gould, the daughter of financier Jay Gould, had purchased ten of the machines and presented them to the Army for recreational purposes. One of these had been sent to the Philippines and was passed along, by coastal steamer and pack train, to Camp Vicars.

Pershing played a musical selection, which only bored the Moros, who regarded their own gong, cymbal, and bamboo flute music as superior. Then he put a cylinder titled "A Day at the Farm" on the machine. The sounds of an American barnyard delighted his guests, but they still refused to sign the treaty.

Pershing nodded to another officer, and a moment later two orderlies appeared. One carried a dead pig, the other a bucket of pig's blood. More than anything else, the Moros feared contamination by a pig, which would bar them from the Mohammedan heaven. Pershing scooped up a dipper of the blood, enough to spatter the whole assemblage, then pointed to the treaty. There was no further argument from the chiefs. One by one they stepped forward and agreed to the treaty.

These various techniques, friendly and forcible, proved their value in the hard campaigning ahead. Pershing had only 700 men under his command and could have been wiped out in the coming year of marching and fighting if the thousands of Malanaos in the lake districts decided to rise up against him.

Almost every day, as the summer of 1902 waned, it became apparent that the dissident tribes could not be kept under control without more vigorous measures. As a warrior people, they respected only those who would make war on them. "The inactivity of the command," Pershing noted, "was misconstrued" by the rebellious sultans who "evidently expected the American forces to follow up the battle of Pandatahan with further assaults upon their cottas" and were emboldened by Pershing's peacemaking gestures. At night Camp Vicars was virtually under siege. "We were subjected almost nightly to sniping from a distance, sometimes accompanied by the beating of tom toms, yells of defiance and lusty laughter at our expense. There was not a tent in the camp that had no bullet holes." The Moro attacks grew bolder. Rifles were stolen, the telegraph line to Malabang was cut and a mile of wire carried off, and soldiers coming up the trail from that southern base were attacked.

Admiral Robley D. Evans, the naval hero, came up from Malabang to visit Pershing's headquarters and sat up all night with a rifle in his lap while Moro snipers banged away at the trail camp. He was hardly comforted by the words of a sergeant attached to his escort, "Don't mind them, sir. The Moros shoot at the tents at night, but they don't hit you."

It was all but impossible to keep the Moros from infiltrating the perimeter, particularly on a dark and rainy night, because "in stealth of movement these warriors were more crafty than even American Indians." Pershing told how one of his sentries "saw in a flash of lightning a figure approaching the line of headquarters tents in a crouching position, and in the next flash he fired. The following morning the Moro was found dead with his heavy kris strapped to his wrist." The night of August 11 an American outpost was attacked, two men were killed and two others wounded.

Pershing repeatedly warned his officers to go directly from the camp to the outposts and back on their nightly rounds. A lieutenant who disobeyed this order was shot through the sleeve by a corporal who fired at the officer's silhouette on the skyline.

Pershing sent for the corporal, who was "pale with anxiety" over having shot at an officer, and congratulated him on "the way you carried out your orders. If the lieutenant had been killed, it would have been his own fault."

He decided that the time had come for punitive action and reported to his superiors that "further forbearance might lead friendly Moros also to misjudge our tolerance and take up arms." In mid-September he was given permission to undertake the first of his campaigns in the lake country. Before the campaigning started, however, he assured the peaceful Moros that the military operations were aimed only at the rebellious sultans and datus who "must some day suffer the consequences of their stubborn ignorance."

His command consisted of five troops of the 15th Cavalry, a battalion of the 27th Infantry, a battery of artillery, and a company of engineers (used largely for cutting roads). On September 28 he set out at the head of his column, heading for the stronghold of the Sultan of Maciu, one of the most intransigent of those bent on rebellion. The sultan had reason for confidence, holding a strong position on the southern shore of Lake Lanao. Several hundred of the Maciu tribe, including women and children, who always entered the cottas (forts) of their men and fought at their side, were holed up on a small peninsula jutting into the lake. To reach it, Pershing would have to cross an all but impenetrable swamp or haul boats through the jungle and attack from the water that enclosed the fort on three sides. Pershing decided on the former alternative.

His engineers cut down the huge hardwood trees of the jungle and corduroyed a road through the swamp, a job that took almost two weeks to accomplish.

Then he pushed his assault lines forward, placing them within a few hundred yards of the steep slopes of the cotta and bringing up his battery of mountain guns. The fort itself would be a hard nut to crack. It was surrounded by a moat and had walls ten feet thick. Inside were fighting-mad Moros armed with rifles, wavy-bladed krises, cleaverlike barongs, heavy *campilans* (swords that had to be swung with both hands and could lop a man's head off with one blow), bolos, and brass cannons.

Pershing demanded the fort's surrender, but the Sultan of Maciu responded by unfurling his red battle flags.

Calmly confident, according to a correspondent for the Manila *Times* who had accompanied the punitive force, Pershing prepared to accept the challenge. He had already decided on the tactics necessary for storming a Moro fort with a minimum of casualties: his troops would invest the place, then the howitzers would plaster it with shrapnel, and after that would come the direct assault.

On the afternoon of October 11, Pershing ordered the bombardment to begin. The Manila *Times* correspondent told of interviewing Captain Pershing "as we sat together on a rice dyke a hundred yards from the Sultan of Maciu's formidable stronghold" while the shells arched overhead.

"Will you storm the fort tonight?" the correspondent asked.

"No, we would lose too many men," Pershing replied.

"But aren't you afraid they'll sneak out in the tall grass during the night and get away?"

"That's just what I expect them to do," Pershing said with a "quizzical grin," then explained to the newspaperman, "We'll draw our lines a little closer and when they come out we'll be ready for them."

Assaulting a Moro fort was a hellishly noisy affair. To whip up their courage, the Moros raised an immense clangor with their war gongs, the reverberations almost drowning out the other sounds of battle. "Inside the fort," wrote the Manila *Times* reporter, "the screams of wounded men, the exhortations of the panditti, or Mohammedan priests, and the defiant cries of the warriors mingled with the roar of cannon and the dull reports of muzzle-loading rifles made a din horrid to the ear."

As evening fell and the bombardment ended, Pershing tightened his lines around the fort. F and M Companies, 27th Infantry, to the east, G Company to the west, and C Company to the south, the latter backed up by the battery of mountain guns now loaded with canister for point-blank fire. He warned each of his company commanders to be ready for a wild night attack on their lines.

Shortly before midnight the Moros proved that he had guessed their intentions exactly. "Gong-maddened," as the Manila newspaperman wrote, the Moros came rushing down from their cotta, firing their old muzzle-loaders and swinging their swords. The American infantry was waiting to mow them down. They fired by the volley, perfectly disciplined, as the shrieking, gong-clanging horde swept down on them. The gunners blasted scrap metal at them from close range, firing over the sights of their pack howitzers. Wildly as they fought to escape, the Moros couldn't make a dent in the American lines. In less than half an hour, they called off their attack and crept back into their battered fort, leaving twenty dead in the bloody grass but hauling away their wounded.

Next morning not a sound came from the splintered bamboo palisades of the cotta. With a few exceptions, the Moros of Maciu had managed to escape during the night to the north of the fort, the water side, by wading chin-deep along the shore until they were clear of the American lines.

The exceptions were several white-robed men, who came screaming out of the fort, waving their barongs and trying to cut down the nearest American soldiers. They were shot down before they could harm any of the Americans. These men, according to an old Mohammedan custom, had gone *juramentado,* had run amuck after promising their priests to kill as many white men as they could before they died. A *juramentado* would shave his head and eyebrows, bind his waist, ask the priest for his blessing, and then sally forth on an errand of sanctified murder; in return for killing all the infidels in reach he was promised swift transportation to the Mohammedan heaven and its black-eyed houris. The Moros used *juramentado* as a weapon of terror, which kept the occupying forces, whether Spanish or American, in a constant state of dread. Soon soldiers had to go armed everywhere and be prepared at any time of day or night to fend off such an attack, whether in the towns or out in the country.

Pershing estimated that his provisional force had killed fifty Moros and wounded another fifty in the Maciu operation. The Moros, however, managed to carry off most of their dead and all of their wounded.

During the next week, Pershing marched his troops around the southern shore of Lake Lanao, occupying various villages and showing the Moro chiefs that he could be firm, fair-minded, and friendly all at once. His troops were kept under the tightest discipline, with harsh penalties for any who neglected sanitation in a country where tropical diseases were always endemic, and for those who tried to buy, seduce, or force their attentions on the Moro women. Sentries were instructed to stand up under all kinds of abuse from the natives without firing unless they were physically attacked. Any soldiers who got out of line quickly learned that "Black Jack" was an admirable sobriquet for Pershing.

The Moros were acquiring a certain respect for Pershing. Being a warrior race, they could only admire his conquest of the Maciu peninsula, even though a number of their fellows were killed as a result of it. Aside from demonstrating his ability as a fighter, however, Pershing convinced the Moros that he did not mean to steal their cattle, trifle with their women, or deal too arbitrarily with their customs. The Manila *Times* was particularly enthusiastic over "the Captain's attitude towards the customs of the people. He points out that through the course of centuries certain of them became rooted in the lives of the people and we cannot expect to tear up and destroy them in a day." Dealing harshly with the Moro way of life, the *Times* believed, would "reap a legacy of hatred and ill will."

After his return to Camp Vicars, Captain Pershing settled down to another spell of creating good will in the Lake Lanao district. A cholera epidemic broke out among the natives and 1500 of them died in the space of a few weeks. Pershing sent medicines and instructions for their use to the *rancherías* where the cholera was particularly virulent. Almost at the same time, the new Sultan of Bayan, undismayed by his predecessor's defeat and death only a year before at Pandatahan, was making warlike gestures from his new cotta crowning an almost inaccessible slope. Pershing let it be known that he was preparing an expedition against him, and a few days later Pandita Sjiducimen, the high priest of Bayan, came down the mountainside to negotiate on behalf of the sultan.

Then the sultan himself, accompanied by retainers in tight red pants with gold buttons down the side, appeared at Camp Vicars to talk peace and "see the stronghold of the white chief." Pershing, to the sultan's dismay, announced that he would "return your compliment by visiting you." Disenchanted as he was by the thought of American soldiers being allowed to invade his sanctuary, the sultan was too polite to forbid Pershing's visit.

Accompanied by an escort of infantry and a battery of artillery, Pershing smilingly presented himself at the Sultan of Bayan's craggy headquarters. Since there was no gate in the fort, he and his companions had to climb over the walls on ladders. Once there, he raised the United States flag over the fort and fired a twenty-one gun salute. The Moros were especially impressed with the booming artillery, as Pershing had intended. The sultan, no less impressed, asked Pershing to become the adopted father of his wife. Pershing also adopted four children of the tribe, one of whom he described as "a bright, clean little fellow who has the airs of a Prince of Wales."

Before the visit ended, the sultan and his court decided that an unprecedented honor should be conferred upon Pershing. He was to be consecrated a datu "by the law and rites of the Koran," making him a tribal chieftain, blood relative, and counselor of the Moros of Bayan. Never before and never again would a Christian be made a Moslem prince. With a grave, Moro-like dignity, he submitted himself to the consecration ceremony, possibly wondering what his old Sunday-school teacher in Laclede would have thought of him in that heathen circle.

Pershing, as one of his officers observed, "unflinchingly returned the embrace and kiss on each cheek of the Datu Sadji," even though the datu "had a thick black beard and chewed betel nut . . . and some of the juice thereof had trickled into his beard." There were no comic overtones, however, in Pershing's own account of the Moslem ceremony:

"Each sultan and datu, with his prominent followers in his rear, sat on his heels, the whole forming a circle. The sacred Koran was placed on a mat of native fiber in the center of this circle, guarded by an aged Mohammedan priest, gorgeous in trousers of all colors and a yellow silk upper garment, over whose head a slave held a beautiful silk sunshade. Silver boxes, beautifully engraved, containing betel nut were passed around the circle and then the speechmaking began, each chief in turn giving his opinion. . . . At the conclusion, all the rulers and myself, placing our hands upon the Koran, registered a vow of eternal friendship, allegiance to the United States, and agreed upon a cessation of warfare against each other."

On his return to Camp Vicars, Pershing was so exhilarated by his bloodless victory at Bayan, and more especially by his new rank of datu, that he wrote of his many Moro friendships, "If I should say: 'Go and kill this man or that,' the next day they would appear in camp with his head." From the Manila *Times* he clipped an editorial praising him for "having won the submission of Bayan through diplomacy" and having acquired a "distinction never before enjoyed by an American."

In the more remote western parts of the lake region, however, the Moros were as yet unimpressed by either the diplomatic or military powers of Datu Pershing. Slaving, raiding, and cattle stealing were being pursued without hindrance. Pershing decided that a vigorous campaign would be necessary in the spring of 1903, and headquarters at Zamboanga, where Brigadier General S. S. Sumner was about to succeed General Davis, concurred in his plan.

Pershing was confident that he could cope with whatever forces the Moros of the western lake district might muster against him. "The Moros were like Indians and other disunited peoples," as he later wrote, in considering the success of his expeditions and the factors which enabled them to defeat the warring tribes one by one. "Each group was vain of its own fighting ability and boastful of its bravery." The Moros had neither the weapons nor the tactics to defend themselves against American fire power, particularly the Maxim machine guns and the howitzers packed on muleback. "With our superior arms we could hold or force almost any number of Moros beyond the range of their weapons."

He proposed to march and fight his way all around Lake Lanao, which had never been attempted before.

With 600 warriors ranged in cottas on the mountains overlooking the western shore, the Sultan of Bacolod was in a particularly defiant mood. The Spanish had tried many times to break into his stronghold but always failed. At the approach of the American column the sultan gathered all his followers from the smaller cottas and prepared to defend the fort of Bacolod, which was surrounded by a moat forty feet deep and thirty-five feet wide and presented walls of earth and bamboo twenty feet wide.

Pershing left Camp Vicars with his composite force late in March and on April 6 appeared in battle formation before the fort of Bacolod. The sultan was insultingly brief when Pershing demanded a surrender: "Come and get me if you can."

Inside the fort, taunting them, the Americans could see Moro warriors armored in buffalo horn and brass links, wearing brass helmets copied from the Spanish of centuries ago. Many were equipped with old muzzle-loaders, others with krises and *campilans*. They showered darts and spears on Americans venturing too close to the walls.

The first problem in breaching the position would be to bridge the deep moat. Under heavy fire from the fort, Pershing's engineers cut down trees so they would fall across the wide ditch and filled in the open spaces with brush and native huts uprooted from their foundations. Several such bridges were built under a covering fire from their own men to enable the attacking infantry and dismounted cavalry to engage the defenders on the parapet and in their trenches.

Early in the afternoon of April 8 Pershing gave the signal for the assault to begin. His troops charged across the bridges, over the moat and onto the walls, boosting each other up foot to shoulder or climbing up ropes attached to grappling irons. On the parapet American bayonets parried, clashed, and thrust aside Moro swords. The mountain guns fired over the heads of the American troops into the center of the fort, isolating the defenders on the walls and in the trenches.

For thirty minutes, with approximately equal numbers on each side, the Americans and the Moros fought it out. A bursting shell set fire to part of the fort. The American assault line advanced methodically through the stronghold, doing the job of killing as professionally and mechanically as a McCormick reaper. The Moros rushed at this hedgehog of bayonets with a fanatical courage, but in half an hour it was all over. The bamboo fort was bursting with flame and exploding gunpowder. Many of the defenders fled, or fell, under volleys from the American riflemen. In the confusion no one was able to count the Moro casualties, but as Pershing reported to General Sumner at Malabang by field telegraph, "Sixty dead bodies were counted on one floor of the fort." Three Americans were wounded, none killed. Without any undue modesty he also reported to General Sumner, "Assault carefully planned and perfectly executed. . . . Fort could have been taken in no other way. . . . Troops in good condition. Am preparing to push on this morning. Anticipate opposition at Calani."

The Manila *American,* which favored a conciliatory approach, headlined its account of the battle, BACOLOD MOROS SLAUGHTERED WITH KRAGS, but conceded that "the Bacolodians provoked the fight for they had their battleflags flying defiantly and when the American column approached they opened on it with a volley that dropped two of Pershing's men."

Pershing's column continued its march around the lake, slashing its way through jungle thickets and vast swamps that had to be bridged in places. Cholera struck the command soon after it left Bacolod, and seven men died along the way. At Calani the expected opposition did not materialize, and Pershing telegraphed the base at Malabang, "Moros along route this side Calani turned out in large numbers to meet us and escort us through their *rancherías.* Effect of expedition greater than anticipated." Sharp actions had to be fought at the Iaraca River and at Taraca, however, as the column penetrated country in which the white man, Spanish or American, was only an unpleasant rumor.

At Taraca, where the Datu Ampuan held sway, the fighting was especially bitter. Pershing described it in an afteraction report telegraphed to headquarters on May 5: "Here stubborn opposition was encountered. We attacked the fort of Datu Ampuan which was covered with red flags. Firing on part of Moros began from number of small cottas to our right and left which were promptly taken and destroyed. Right flank of two companies of infantry under Gracie and Shaw was then strung down Taraca River, driving out Moros and capturing cotta on north side, killing 115 Moros, wounding thirteen and capturing twenty-three prisoners.

"First fort in meantime was surrounded and guarded by two troops of cavalry (dismounted) all night to prevent Moros' escape. This morning at daylight Moros surrendered twenty-nine in number, among them Ampuan and a number of datus. Total cannon and lantaka captured thirty-six, some very large cannon, and sixty rifles. Our loss was one killed and seven wounded. I shall push on from here as soon as possible, probably today. Command is in good health, no cholera . . . none reported among the Moros."

Only the Sultan of Anparugano still held out in the lake district, and Pershing concluded his whirlwind campaign around the lake by invading his *rancherías,* capturing ten of his hilltop cottas, and dispersing his warriors.

The completion of the Lake Lanao operations, at a cost of less than a score of American lives, including those who died of cholera, caught the imagination of the people back home. Editorial writers compared his march around Lake Lanao with Jeb Stuart's ride around the Union Army. An interview with Henry Savage Landor, the famous Tibetan explorer and correspondent for the London *Mail,* who had accompanied Pershing on the campaign and told a Hong Kong newspaper that the captain was a "military genius," was picked up and published in many American papers. Landor said that "for pluck and determination few soldiers in the world can compare with the American [Pershing]. . . . The manner in which he conducted the Bacolod campaign entitled him to a high place among the military commanders of the world."

Praise also was showered down on Pershing from his superiors. On May 11, Secretary of War Root cabled General Sumner, "Express to Captain Pershing and officers and men under his command the thanks of the War Department for their able and effective accomplishment of a difficult and important task." General in chief Miles visited Camp Vicars on a last inspection tour of the Army before his retirement that summer and expressed satisfaction over the way Pershing had handled his command. Generals Davis and Sumner, under whom he had served, and Generals Arthur Murray and Leonard Wood wrote letters to the War Department urging his promotion. Secretary of War Root took the rather unusual step of allowing an officer in the War Department to release for publication a letter Pershing had written him describing the victory at Bacolod and the wild melee on the parapet when his troops stormed the fort: ". . . Here they were met with *campilan* and kris," Pershing wrote rather excitedly, "and a bloody hand-to-hand fight occurred—one soldier against two Moros here, another running his bayonet into a fanatic there, Moros plunging headlong into the ditch in their impetuosity and impetus. . . ."

Now that the lake districts were pacified, he was ordered before a medical board at Zamboanga, where a Manila *Times* correspondent reported that "long service in Mindanao has told upon the health of Captain Pershing." He was permitted to return to Camp Vicars, but was soon ordered to duty in Washington. Several years would pass before his return to the Moro country.

On his arrival in the States, he found himself acclaimed a national hero by the newspapers. When he stopped in Lincoln to visit his sister Bessie (Mrs. D. M. Butler), the cadet battalion at the university, now called the Pershing Rifles, turned out in his honor. He also stopped off at Chicago, where his parents were living; his mother had just recovered from an illness so severe that she was not told of his Mindanao campaigns until his force returned safely to Camp Vicars. Then he continued on his way to Washington, where he was to be one of the social lions of the season, a full-fledged celebrity in a society dominated by the hero-loving President Roosevelt, who was to summon him to his office one day solely for the purpose of being introduced to the leading prize fighters of a past era, Jake Kilrain and John L. Sullivan, as "our leading military fighter."

Doubtless he had heard of the statement casually dropped by Secretary of War Root at a social function in New York in the presence of a former classmate: "If your friend Pershing doesn't watch out, he'll find himself in the brigadier-general class very soon."

4. Promotion and Scandal

While Pershing was campaigning against the Moros in the rugged interior of Mindanao, an equally lively if less bloody battle was being waged in Washington to modernize the staff and command system governing the Army. The Cuban expedition and to a lesser degree the Philippine occupation had exposed the moribund condition of the War Department as it sputtered, misfired, and labored to function under the various bureau chiefs. Secretary of War Root, forward-looking and self-assured enough to brave the outcries of those intrenched in the outmoded bureaus and their vociferous political supporters, pushed through a plan to reorganize the Army under a General Staff.

Root had been deeply impressed by a document compiled by the late Major General Emory Upton (subsequently published under the title *Military Policy of the United States*) which analyzed the defects of the United States military establishment and proposed setting up a General Staff such as supervised the German operations against France in 1871. General William T. Sherman had endorsed the Upton proposals, commenting that "the time may not be now, but will come when these will be appreciated, and may bear fruit even in our day." Root seized upon many of General Upton's ideas, including a broader system of military education, which was effected through the establishment of the Army War College in 1900 and the Command and General Staff School in 1901; a program under which officers would be rotated constantly between staff and line duties to produce a more rounded and intellectual soldier; and creating of the office of chief of staff, which would more effectively bridge the gap between civilian control and military administration.

Congress passed the General Staff Act shortly before Captain Pershing's return to the United States, undeterred by protests that the Army was being "Prussianized," that the reorganization was un-American, undemocratic, and would lead to a military dictatorship.

Pershing was assigned to the newly established General Staff first under General S. B. M. Young, then under General Adna R. Chaffee, under both of whom he had served in Cuba and the Philippines. The first General Staff, including three general officers, four colonels, six lieutenant colonels, twelve majors, and twenty captains, was the cream of the Regular Army, as well as the pet project of President Roosevelt and Secretary of War Root.

President Roosevelt's next objective was the reform of the Army's promotion system. At that time the President had the right to promote officers of the rank of brigadier or above, but could not touch the ranks between lieutenant and colonel; he could elevate a second lieutenant to brigadier general, subject to confirmation by the Senate, but the most important grades in an officer's career were closed to him. In those grades, ironclad seniority, promotion by the numbers, was the rule. Many regulars defended this archaic system on the grounds that promotion by selection would be subjected to political influence, that ambitious officers would be prone to devote more of their time to bootlicking than to soldiering, that men of long and faithful service would be victimized by juniors with political influence leapfrogging over their backs.

President Roosevelt called the system the "triumph of mediocrity over excellence" in his message to Congress of December 7, 1903, and asked for legislation to remedy the situation. He cited Pershing to illustrate his point.

The President told Congress: "The only people that are contented with a system of promotion by seniority are those who are contented with the triumph of mediocrity over excellence. On the other hand, a system which encouraged the exercise of social or political favoritism in promotions would be even worse. But it would surely be easy to devise a method of promotion from grade in which the opinion of the higher officers of the service upon the candidates should be decisive upon the standing and promotion of the latter. . . .

"Until this system is changed we cannot hope that our officers will be of as high grade as we have a right to expect, considering the material upon which we draw. Moreover, when a man renders such service as Captain Pershing rendered last spring in the Moro campaign, it ought to be possible to reward him without at once jumping him to the grade of brigadier general."

Congress, however, ignored the President's suggestion.

With the prospects of promotion stymied for the time being, Pershing devoted himself to his professional education as a General Staff officer. He attended the Army War College for a time and served briefly as General Staff officer with the Southwestern Department at Oklahoma City. In-between he pursued a social career with an almost equal vigor. From the summer of 1903 to the end of 1904 the society columns of the Washington newspapers frequently listed him as a guest at various socially important dinner parties, balls, garden parties, and official and private receptions.

During this period of dining out, of being lionized by the Washington hostesses, he met the two persons who were to be supremely important in his private and emotional life. They were Senator Francis E. Warren of Wyoming and his young daughter, Helen Frances Warren. Senator Warren, as chairman of the Senate's Military Affairs Committee, was one of the most influential men in the capital. A native of New England, he had served in a Massachusetts regiment during the Civil War and migrated to Wyoming in 1868. Pioneering in the cattle industry, he made a fortune early in life and turned to politics as a full-time vocation. He was the territorial governor of Wyoming, then governor of the new state, and finally was sent to the United States Senate in 1890.

Since he was a widower, his daughter, whom everyone called "Frankie," presided as his hostess after graduating from Wellesley in the class of 1903. The Washington society columnists described her as "an exceedingly graceful girl," with a lively sense of humor and mischief. At Wellesley her classmates recalled that whenever there had been an outbreak of girlish mischief the school authorities always asked first, "Where was Frances Warren?" Her photographs as a graduate show a pleasant-faced young woman, with features a trifle too generous for conventional prettiness in a time when the Gibson Girl was the shirtwaisted ideal, and strikingly bear out her friends' description of her as "gay, warm-hearted, of blithe originality." A debutante of that season, she was pursued by more than a fair share of the eligible young men of the capital.

Pershing met the Warrens at a dinner given by Senator Joseph H.

Millard of Nebraska and his daughter in their suite at the Willard Hotel. Millard was a friend of Pershing's dating back to his years on the faculty of the University of Nebraska.

From all accounts it was a case of love at first sight between the lighthearted debutante and the middle-aged captain whose hair was beginning to turn gray at the temples and whose face was still marked by the weariness and illness of almost four years in the Philippines. "The fire flew," Senator Warren observed, at that first meeting over the Millard dinner table.

There was a dance at Fort Myer which Miss Warren was to attend later that evening, and she asked Pershing if he were going.

"No," he said, "I have another engagement."

But the captain apparently had second thoughts about that "other engagement." He showed up at the dance at Fort Myer and, with all the enthusiasm of a cavalry charge, monopolized Miss Warren's services as a partner on the dance floor.

At two o'clock that morning Charles E. Magoon, Pershing's lawyer friend from Lincoln who was then serving in the government, was awakened by a banging on his door.

Pershing burst in with the proclamation, "Charlie, I've met the girl I'm going to marry!"

As Magoon told the story afterward, Pershing planted himself on the edge of his bed, disregarding Magoon's yawns and pleas of sleepiness, and "jabbered away" for an hour until the lawyer growled at his smitten visitor, "Jack, if you're in love, I'm not. I want to get some sleep. If you're still in love tomorrow, come around and tell me about it."

Next day Miss Warren dropped around to see the wife of Major General John R. Brooke and very casually inquired, "Oh, Mrs. Brooke, do you happen to know Captain Pershing?"

The shrewd and sharp-eyed Mrs. Brooke replied, "If you think you could stand the life of an army officer's wife, you couldn't do better than marry Captain Pershing."

Pershing was a devoted and insistent suitor, but Miss Warren refused to commit herself for almost a year. In 1904 a girl didn't accept a proposal of marriage, no matter how favorably she looked upon it, without an exhausting period of maidenly indecision. A man had to expect to be kept "dangling," or he might hold her too cheaply. Amiable as she was, Frances Warren was determined that Jack Pershing should serve out his full sentence as a frustrated suitor.

Late in December of 1904, approximately a year after their first meeting, Pershing presented her with what amounted to an ultimatum. He had just been posted to Tokyo as military attaché and lost no time in rushing to her side with the news, pointing out that he might be stationed abroad for years.

"It was now or never," as Miss Warren later told her friends.

Their engagement was announced on January 10, 1905, with the wedding set for sixteen days later because of the groom's immediate assignment to his new post. The newspapers made much of the "Washington romance of the season," and the Philadelphia *North American* heralded it with a rhyming headline:

ARMY'S ONLY DATOO
WINS AT LOVE, TOO

More than 500 guests attended the wedding in the Epiphany Episcopal Church, including President Roosevelt and his family, most of the Cabinet, and a large delegation from Congress, the Senate having delayed its convening time an hour for the occasion. The wedding breakfast at the Willard was equally well attended. Thus, at an age when most men were seeing their children off to college, Jack Pershing had acquired a wife whose background and personality could hardly have been more satisfactory for a rising officer. Mrs. Pershing was attractive, unassuming, well-poised, trained from childhood to take an important place in society, "accustomed to appear at club meetings and afternoon teas when she still wore short frocks." And the marriage, though buffeted by a scandal concocted by her husband's enemies, though their home had to be uprooted a number of times by the exigencies of the service, and though they had to endure occasional long separations while he took to the field, lasted happily for ten years, to the day that multiple tragedy struck. It was also fruitful, and the transient quality of their home life was well-illustrated by the scattered birthplaces of their four children. Helen was born in Tokyo on September 8, 1906; Anne in Baguio, Luzon, Philippine Islands, March 24, 1908; Francis Warren in Cheyenne, Wyoming, June 24, 1909; and Mary Margaret in Zamboanga, Mindanao, Philippine Islands, on May 20, 1912.

Immediately after the wedding, Captain and Mrs. Pershing left for

San Francisco, then embarked for Tokyo. "This is the dearest girl in the world and I the happiest man in the world," he wrote in his diary. The voyage across the Pacific served as their honeymoon, since Pershing had to leave his bride in Tokyo shortly after their arrival. The Russo-Japanese War was then in its final phase and Pershing was detailed to act as one of the American observers in Manchuria.

On land and sea, czarist Russia, her forces dissipated by monstrously incompetent leadership, had been taking a terrible beating. When the war started in the mountainous wastes of Manchuria on February 5, 1904, the rest of the world expected that the island empire of Japan would be crushed like a bamboo hut under an avalanche. As the American war correspondent Frederick Palmer expressed it, "Russia, the mammoth world power with her giant soldiers, against the little fellows who made the pretty lanterns we hung on our lawns for ice-cream parties!" The lantern makers, with their Army modeled on the Prussian pattern and trained by German officers, had surprised the world by turning loose in Manchuria four well-disciplined armies, and their Navy had routed the Russians every time they met at sea. The overwhelming successes of the Japanese, as Major General J. F. C. Fuller (*A Military History of the Western World*) has written, sounded "a reveille throughout the East and Asia began to stir in her ancient sleep"—a stirring which was to result eventually in the attack on Pearl Harbor, the end of colonialism in Asia, and the rise of Communist China. Its significance was little understood at the time; even those who witnessed it, for the most part, regarded it as interesting only from the tactical standpoint.

Captain Pershing joined the other foreign military observers with General Kuroki's First Army on the right wing of the Japanese advance into Manchuria just as the two-week battle of Mukden began late in February on a forty-mile front. By that time the great Russian fortress city of Port Arthur had fallen to the Japanese, and their armies had advanced deep into Manchuria and rolled over the Russians at Liaoyang.

Like the other foreign observers, Pershing found himself in the backwash of the war. Hissing politely, the Japanese kept them in the rear areas and would not permit them more than fleeting glimpses of the actual fighting. The attachés and an equally large group of newspaper correspondents were corralled in separate camps back among the supply trains and ammunition dumps, despite their vigorous and continuing protests. Japanese staff officers would periodically lecture them on the progress of their armies and occasionally take them to a hilltop where they could catch a glimpse of a portion of the distant battle line.

Thus frustrated in their professional concerns, the military attachés of the various countries passed their time in fraternizing with one another and with the neighboring war correspondents, among them Richard Harding Davis, Ashmead Bartlett, Frederick Palmer, and novelist-turned-Hearst correspondent Jack London, who compared the courageous advances of the Japanese infantry with those of "South American peccary pigs in their herd charges."

The foreign observers included the most promising officers of the British, French, German, Italian, and American armies, since this was the first large-scale war to be studied, and possibly to be learned from, since the Franco-Prussian War. Many of them rose to high command in World War I. Before Pershing's arrival, Colonel Enoch Crowder, who was to supervise the draft in 1917, and Captain Peyton C. March, who was to become chief of staff in wartime, were among the American observers. The British were represented by Major General Ian Hamilton, who had distinguished himself in the Boer War and was to command the ill-fated British landing on Gallipoli in 1915, and by Colonel Fowke, who became a lieutenant general and adjutant general of the British Army. Colonel Baron Corvisart was the French observer, and Italy was represented by Major Caviglia, who was to command the armies in northern Italy and become War Minister. Pershing always remembered Major Caviglia best for "waking us every morning singing Italian opera." The German observers were an aristocratic Prussian major named Von Etzel, who would command a division opposite Baron Corvisart on the Meuse one day when Pershing visited the front, and by Captain Max Hoffmann.

By all odds the most interesting member of the foreign military fraternity was Captain Hoffmann, who may well have been the only original genius raised up by World War I on either side. As operations officer under Hindenburg and Ludendorff and later as chief of staff of the German armies on the eastern front, he formulated the battle plans which resulted in the crushing defeats of the Russian forces from 1914 to 1918 and even managed to talk down Leon Trotsky and the other Soviet negotiators at Brest-Litovsk, terminating those endless discussions by sending a German Army into the Ukraine. Hoffmann, a hulking, heavy-jawed fellow with a monocle screwed in one eye, was the antithesis of the stiff-backed Junkers who formed the bulk of his officers' corps. He hated military drill, was a poor horseman and a wretched swordsman, and ridiculed the chivalric pretensions of the proper Prussian officer. "If anyone comes near me with a Nibelung's oath of fidelity and offers to die at my side," he once said, "I shall knock his head off." Hoffmann breakfasted off a quart of Moselle and consumed large quantities of brandy during the day, much to the disgust of Major Von Etzel, with whom he shared quarters.

Other foreign observers politely accepted such Japanese excuses as, "The battle is over for today, the enemy is in retreat," or "The General thinks you would be more comfortable where you are," when their requests to visit the front were turned down. Hoffmann's irritation at being secluded from the fighting often burst the bounds of etiquette. Once he went to General Fujii and requested permission to watch a Japanese attack from a nearby hill, and the Japanese smilingly refused. Hoffmann lost his temper and reminded Fujii that the Germans had taught the Japanese all they knew about modern war. "You are yellow, you are not *civilized* if you will not let me go to that hill," Hoffmann shouted. But General Fujii quietly repeated, "You may not go," and turned on his heel. Later he explained to war correspondent Frederick Palmer that "we Japanese are paying for this military information with our blood; we don't propose to share it with others."

Palmer was Pershing's frequent companion in Manchuria and took many long walks with him over the Manchurian hills. He recalled that Pershing "gave me many surprises in flashes of comment which showed the vast extent of his reading beyond a strictly professional range." They were both amused by "all the European prejudices and racial characteristics that had their reflection in that group of accomplished chosen officers in the pinpricking frustration of their confinement" and by the "caste superiority" of the European attachés of noble birth. Palmer once invited both Major Von Etzel and Captain Hoffmann to dinner and was somewhat surprised when only the major appeared. Next day Captain Pershing, with a slightly malicious grin, explained the matter to Palmer:

"You are not up on the social relations of my German colleagues. Your invitation went to Von Etzel as the senior in rank. So he accepted for himself. Hoffman would not have gone anyway with Von Etzel or Von Etzel with Hoffmann. Can you beat it? The two are living in that little room, sleeping in beds across from each other, and they have not spoken for weeks except when officially necessary. What a life! You'd think they'd have a good bawling out and then make up for convenience's sake, if not their emperor's."

Baron Corvisart was equally entertained by the Teutonic feud. "Even if one Frenchman hates another," he commented, "they have enough *savoir faire* to be polite."

During that dreary winter in the Manchurian hills, amusement was also provided by the mercurial Italian attaché, Major Caviglia, who was outraged by the runty Japanese pony assigned to him by his military hosts. Once Caviglia's pony stumbled, rolled over him, and bent his ceremonial sword into a semicircle. Springing up in a rage, he refused to allow the Japanese officer accompanying him to have the sword repaired. "No," he shouted, "I'll not straighten it. I'll take it to my King so he shall see the kind of horse the Japanese gave his attaché to ride and the insults his attaché has endured!"

The foreign observers were still taking the hindmost when the Japanese armies stormed into Mukden on March 10, 1905, at a cost of 71,000 casualties. Pershing and his colleagues saw the battlefield only after it had been tidied up. But there were striking lessons in fire power and field fortification apparent even after the mopping up. Among these were the first employment in battle of mobile heavy artillery, of large complements of machine guns and intricate trench systems protected by barbed wire. Some of the Manchurian battlefields looked like a rehearsal stage for World War I. "From 1905," as General Fuller has written, "not only had the soldier to obey, but also to think; to know how to live as well as how to fight, not for hours only, but for days on end. This urge to live made the spade as complementary to rifle as once shield had been to sword. . . ."

Captain Hoffmann, in his report to the German War Office, stressed the new problems arising from the widespread employment of the machine gun and the trench system. "The most important thing in the world," he wrote, "is how *not* to mount an infantry attack." But he doubted whether his superiors would see the point, and he was right; one of them, the younger Von Moltke, scoffed at Hoffmann's report, "There never was such a crazy way of making war." General Hamilton's similar views, coupled with the observation that the only sensible thing the cavalry could do in the face of machine gun-mounted positions was to cook rice for the infantry, were also ridiculed by his seniors in the British Army, one of whom commented, "He must have a tile loose somewhere."

From the evidence of the several notebooks which Pershing kept in Manchuria, he did not concern himself overly much with the larger implications of the Russo-Japanese War. He meticulously recorded whatever impressions he could gather of the fighting qualities of the combatants, noting the fact that the Japanese infantry hated to undertake night attacks (an inhibition they lost by the time World War II came around). He also drew sketch after sketch of the Japanese pontoon bridges, of the Russian methods of intrenching and fortifying, of machine-gun positions on both sides, and recorded what Russian prisoners of war told him. He was diligent about reporting what he could learn of both combatants' transport, equipment, and morale. As a mere captain, coming late to the war at that, he did not dwell on the strategic concepts behind the Japanese victory, nor did he see enough of the fighting to be as deeply impressed by the tactical changes wrought by the Manchurian campaigns as Captain Hoffmann and General Hamilton were. His main concern was, in fact, with the individual soldier on both sides, and with how enthusiastically he went to war. He was not at all inclined to overrate the Japanese for their victory over the huge but badly generaled Russian war machine (which was capped in May by the naval disaster inflicted on the Russians in the straits of Tsushima). When Frederick Palmer asked him how the American soldier compared with the Japanese, he snorted indignantly, surprised that the question should be raised, "Better! The American is the best soldier, the best material if well trained."

In his official report on the final operations of the war in Manchuria, which ran to ninety-four pages in typescript, he noted that the "Russian army is in rotten [sic] condition . . . their officers spent their time in drinking." The Russians' artillery was "superior in guns to the Japanese but not so well handled. About seventy percent of the Russian shells fail to burst, probably on account of defective fuses." It particularly interested him that in the Japanese Army "the officers take cover but are not called cowards; no example to the Japanese soldier is needed."

Pershing concluded that the Japanese, encouraged by their successes on the Asiatic mainland, might endanger American interests in the Pacific. "Now it would be a weakness for them to possess the Philippine Archipelago," he wrote. "Yet there is no telling in the years to come if the Japanese rise to power."

Despite years of living under and administrating military discipline, he was still bedeviled by his old failing of tardiness, which neither the switches of his old schoolmaster nor the frowns of senior officers seemed to be able to cure. Close to the end of the fighting in Manchuria, Pershing and other attachés were invited to a Shinto ritual honoring the Japanese war dead. Each foreigner was to place a sprig of evergreen on the altar as a mark of respect and professional condolence.

All the foreign observers but Pershing were present as the ceremony began. The American correspondents, well aware of his habitual tardiness, asked one another, "Will Pershing be on time?" The betting, as Frederick Palmer recalled, was all against it.

Just before the attachés stepped forward with their sprigs of evergreen, however, Pershing appeared "doublequicking with a half minute to spare, looking the pattern plate of military form."

With the conclusion of hostilities in Manchuria, Pershing returned to his young wife in Tokyo, where he was stationed for more than a year as military attaché. Their first child, Helen, was born there September 8, 1906, a few weeks before Pershing was recalled to the United States, and they sailed for San Francisco aboard the *Empress of Japan*.

The Pershings were still en route to San Francisco when President Roosevelt made the announcement that electrified the Army: he was promoting Pershing from captain to brigadier general. Pershing thus was jumped four grades, over the heads of exactly 862 officers who were senior to him. Widespread indignation was expressed in army posts from Governors Island to Manila, and many fellow officers never forgave him the promotion, attributing it to the influence of his father-in-law who, they never tired of pointing out, was chairman of the Senate's Military Affairs Committee. They ignored the fact that President Roosevelt had hinted at the promotion three years earlier, before Pershing had even met Senator Warren or his daughter. They also overlooked certain precedents for the promotion, such as Leonard Wood's elevation from captain in the Medical Corps, Tasker H. Bliss's from major in the Commissary Department, Albert L. Mills's from cavalry captain, all to the same rank of brigadier, all without provoking anything like as much bitterness.

Much of the newspaper comment and many of the younger army officers were favorably inclined to Pershing's promotion. Captain Robert Lee Bullard, who was impressed by his work in the Philippines, was "convinced of Pershing's efficiency, notwithstanding the wide criticism of his promotion, notwithstanding the common assertion that it was due to the senatorial influence of his father-in-law," and wrote him a letter of congratulations. "To which," Bullard wryly added, "I received no answer."

A scattering of newspapers used the Pershing promotion as an issue for criticism of the Roosevelt administration. The Columbus *Sun* commented that "for the extraordinary favor that has been done him, it is not apparent where he has performed the extraordinary service." The New York *Evening Post* published a letter from an army officer, whose name it withheld, saying that "nothing in the history of the army has caused such discontent and demoralization." The Manila *Sun* said his promotion "comes as a surprise to those who knew him and his military record." The St. Louis *Post-Dispatch,* in an editorial, listed as "steps of the ladder of promotion" of an ambitious officer "social pull, service in Washington, good luck in an adventure of doubtful military value . . . and perhaps 'selection in marriage' "—and left no doubt that it was referring to Pershing.

The new general and his wife returned to the United States on October 16, 1906, while the controversy was still going strong. Pershing himself refrained from making any public statements on his promotion, nor did he ever refer to it in any of the diaries and notebooks he kept intermittently at the time. But the bitterness and backbiting which his promotion aroused undoubtedly left their mark on him, particularly the unmistakably antagonistic attitude of many of his brother officers; and quite probably it was reflected a dozen years hence in his ruthless, if necessary, shaking out of human clinkers in the higher echelons of the American Expeditionary Force in France. "Comrades in arms," henceforth, must have been only an echoingly empty phrase to him. It was characteristic that in the many scrapbooks he kept on his career he meticulously preserved all the critical comments as well as the laudatory ones.

With his intensely impersonal attitude, it was also in character that he made no effort to cozen public opinion. While he was in Washington between assignments late in 1906, he came out of a hotel one day and noticed that the doorman was clad in the full-dress uniform of a general officer of the United States Army. Most officers would probably have been more amused than anything else or at least shrugged it off. Pershing summoned the nearest policeman and insisted that the doorman be arrested on a charge of impersonating an officer.

During that waiting period he drew some comfort, perhaps, from President Roosevelt's reply to criticism of his promotion: "To promote a man because he married a senator's daughter would be infamy; to refuse him promotion for the same reason would be equal infamy."

The War Department, meanwhile, was having trouble deciding what to do with its new brigadier. At first it was announced that Pershing would be sent back to the Philippines to command the Department of the Visayas in the middle of the island chain, replacing Major General Jesse M. Lee, who was retiring on January 1, 1907. This command called for an officer of two-star rank, however, and it was decided to assign him to the almost equally important brigade post at Fort McKinley on Luzon.

It was while the Pershings were on their way to Manila in mid-December that the only personal scandal of Pershing's career broke over his head, obviously an outgrowth of the professional jealousy festering over his promotion.

In an article widely quoted and reprinted in the American newspapers, the Manila *American* on December 18, 1906, charged that Pershing, while stationed at Zamboanga a half-dozen years earlier, had "lived almost openly" with a Filipino girl named Joaquina Bondoy Ignacio, that he and the girl had set up housekeeping in a nipa cottage near the post. Pershing, it was charged, had fathered two of Joaquina's children, a four-year-old girl named Petronilla, and another child who died in the cholera epidemic of 1902. Joaquina was now married to an American, a civilian employee named William Shinn, who was quoted as saying that "an emissary of General Pershing approached Joaquina in the spring of this year with an offer of $50 a month as hush money. She refused to accept, saying that Pershing had always been kind to her and that she would not expose him." The Manila *American* story also stated that Joaquina was one of four sisters who operated a canteen patronized by army officers, and that "rumor credits Joaquina with having borne two other children to a Spanish officer before the American occupation."

The charges caused a furor, not only because they involved a high American officer but because mothers and wives of soldiers serving in the Philippines naturally suspected that their menfolk may have been guilty of liaisons similar to the one charged against Pershing. The Chicago *Journal,* reporting from Washington on December 19, only added fuel to their flaming suspicions when it announced that "at least fifty other cases of a similar nature involving army officers" were being investigated and the culprits "may be exposed." Two days later the New York *World* published a chop-licking dissertation (though with a high sociological gloss) on the "querida [sweetheart] system" obtaining among soldiers stationed for two or more years away from their loved ones in the States. "The querida system, officers with experience in the Philippines say, is very popular with some army men and does not throw discredit on the woman concerned. The sweethearts live together as long as they wish and then separate. When Filipino men are one of the parties to this trial contract, they are supposed to care for the children, but when American men break the union the offspring are thrown on the mother."

The *World* subsequently reported that the charges against Pershing "were instigated by jealous officers who hated to see Pershing put over their heads."

In succeeding weeks there were widespread demands that Pershing be cashiered as morally unfit to command American troops, but his friends in high places and some of lesser station came to his defense with vigorous loyalty. His father-in-law, Senator Warren, told newspapermen in Washington that neither he nor his daughter believed there was any truth in the Manila *American's* charges. He explained that earlier that year an anonymous letter had been sent to the War Department containing the same accusations and that it had been submitted to General Davis, Pershing's commanding officer at the time, who labeled the charges false. "Disgruntled persons," said Senator Warren, were responsible for the scandalous charges in the Manila newspaper. The same day, in the Washington *Post,* Elihu Root, now Secretary of State, and William H. Taft, the new Secretary of War, both were quoted as saying there was no foundation to the story.

Two captains, named Swobe and Cloman, who had served in Zamboanga with Pershing came forward to defend him. Both had known him intimately and asserted that Pershing had lived in bachelor officers' quarters on the post, as they did, and that he had not set up any irregular living arrangements with a Filipino. Captain Swobe also told a Kansas City *Star* reporter that he recalled the Bondoy sisters, Joaquina among them, and the joking that went on around the canteen where they dispensed cigars and refreshments to the American soldiers. A number of their children played around the canteen, and when the sisters were asked who had fathered them they would jokingly reply, "President Roosevelt" or "Governor Taft" or "General Wood," or any other officer who came into their minds. That, said Captain Swobe, was the baseless inception of the rumor concerning General Pershing.

The only person who refused to comment was Pershing himself.

As for Mrs. Pershing, she wrote her father a warmly loyal letter from Tokyo, apparently having read of the charges against her husband when they stopped off in Japan en route to the Philippines, and Senator Warren released it for publication. "Dear Papa— If any stories about Jack come to you to his discredit don't believe them," she wrote. "They are not true and you may be sure of it."

The scandal fizzled out after the War Department announced that it had concluded the charges against General Pershing were not even worthy of investigation. It was briefly revived in 1912 when reports were circulated that Pershing was to be appointed the superintendent of the United States Military Academy. The New York *World* somewhat gratuitously recalled the charges against him and pointed out that Pershing "did not demand the usual 'court of honor' to vindicate himself. He ignored the sensational allegations and his wife steadfastly maintained her belief in her husband's innocence." It was entirely in character for Pershing to refuse to comment on attacks against him, unless they were made officially. "Let the record speak for itself," was his invariable reply to suggestions that he defend himself against criticism. He meticulously clipped all the stories concerning the scandal and preserved them in the scrapbooks which are part of the Pershing Papers. In 1912, when the matter was rehashed, he engaged James Ross, a former judge of the Court of First Instance of the Philippines, to gather affidavits and any other information which might refute the accusation, on the possibility that they might be needed. They weren't, so the independent inquiry was dropped. That was the only indication he ever gave regarding his own attitude toward the charges.

Pershing's second tour of duty in the Philippines, despite the controversy and mudslinging which preceded his arrival, began on a note of grace. The man whom he was replacing in command of Fort McKinley, Colonel Henry P. Kingsbury, had been a captain in the 6th Cavalry when Pershing was a second lieutenant. Military etiquette required Colonel Kingsbury to call on General Pershing, his senior in rank if not in service. Before Colonel Kingsbury had a chance to present himself, however, he was surprised to receive a telephone call from General Pershing. The conversation, according to Colonel Kingsbury, was as follows:

PERSHING   "How are you, Colonel?"

KINGSBURY   "I'm all right, General. How are you?"

PERSHING   "You don't like my coming here to command perhaps."

KINGSBURY   "Why, General, I don't see how that makes any difference. You are a general officer. On the contrary, I'm glad you came to the post."

PERSHING   "May I come over and see you?"

KINGSBURY   "I'd be highly honored if you did, sir."

That was the beginning of several pleasant years as commanding officer of Fort McKinley and the brigade posted there. His second daughter, Anne, was born in March of 1908 in the cool mountain air of Baguio, the hill station where officers' wives went during the hot season. Later that year Pershing, accompanied by his wife, was sent to Europe to inspect and report on the efficiency of the European armies. He became mysteriously ill in Paris and was bundled off to Mannheim, one of the spas favored by Edwardians to cure all bodily aches and ailments. The doctors there recommended that he give up smoking, although, as he later told a New York *Times* reporter, "his cigar was part of his life." Pershing thought it over for a day or two and then decided to give up cigars. Breaking the habit was easy enough, he said; "the only hard thing was in making up my mind." The next year, 1909, Pershing was again separated temporarily from his command, this time by illness. He had contracted sprue, a dysentery-like tropical disease which attacked the digestive tract, causing anemia and other side effects. Pershing was ordered to return to the United States for treatment and spent six months at the Hot Springs (Arkansas) Army and Navy Hospital. Mrs. Pershing, meanwhile, gave birth to their third child and first son, Francis Warren, in her home town of Cheyenne, Wyoming.

When the Pershing family returned to the islands, the general was appointed governor of the Moro Province, including Mindanao and the Sulu Islands which formed the tail bone of the Philippine archipelago. The province as a whole was considered "pacified," but Moslem agitators, many of them priests and Arab missionaries, kept the native population stirred up, particularly on the island of Jolo.

Through most of his first year as military governor, Pershing labored to improve the living conditions, the economy, and the morale of his province. In consultation with army engineers he drew up a plan for harnessing the Tumaga River, which periodically flooded the towns along its course, and providing more irrigation ditches in the Zamboanga district for year-round rice planting. The *Voz de Mindanao* commented that "there is no doubt whatever that General Pershing is complying with the promises he made of bettering in every mode possible the condition of the province." From his headquarters in Zamboanga he made frequent tours of the back country and the mountain barrios and traveled continually by navy cutter to keep an eye on conditions in the Sulu Islands extending southeastward toward Borneo.

Under the strain of tropical service and the inbred social life of the scattered garrisons, his own subordinates often distracted him from more important administrative functions. Once it was the suicide of a young lieutenant, another time a sort of Somerset Maugham comedy which, in miniature, exposed the attitudes of the apprentice colonizers. The setting of the latter incident was the island of Basilan; the leading characters were Captain D. and Lieutenant F. (their full names may be found in the Pershing Papers), the captain's wife and a Filipino girl. Lieutenant F., a young Bostonian, had attracted Pershing's attention by studying the native dialects and customs as Pershing had years earlier. In April of 1910 he horrified the small American community on Basilan by announcing his intention of marrying a Filipino girl.

Captain D., his commanding officer, wrote Pershing on April 21, asking for Lieutenant F.'s transfer "because he has become a squaw man, hurting the service in general and us here in particular." When the captain failed to dissuade him, Mrs. D. took up the cause with more emotional arguments of her own, pointing out that the lieutenant's mother had already been saddened by the suicide of another son, and his marriage to a Filipino might be the death of her. Lieutenant F. wept, Mrs. D. wept with him, but all to no avail.

Subsequent letters from Captain D. reported that the lieutenant had married the girl, accepting the fact that he and his bride would be ostracized by the rest of the American community.

The Americans on Basilan were so determined to "cut" the newlyweds that Captain D. and a Doctor W. hacked a new trail through the jungle so that none of the Americans would have to pass their home. In his distress, Captain D. wrote Pershing that "I would beg that he be given a chance to atone . . . by hard work and faithful service, in some other company, preferably one commanded by a squaw captain."

General Pershing, not at all affected by the American colony's social distress, refused Captain D.'s pleas and kept Lieutenant F. at his post. In a few months the Americans learned to accept the situation, and soon Captain D. and Lieutenant F. were leading an expedition into the interior, with the former reporting enthusiastically on his subordinate's abilities as a leader of Moro Scouts. The lieutenant subsequently was promoted to captain and performed excellently as a military administrator in the Lake Lanao district on Mindanao. Before leaving the Philippines for the last time, Pershing, who had benignly watched over the young man's career, took the occasion to "express to you the very high opinion I hold of you as a soldier and as an administrator among uncivilized people."

A decade after the United States moved into the southern islands the everyday life of the Americans was still hazardous, even in the headquarters town of Zamboanga. *Juramentados,* their knives flashing in the midday sun, still ran amuck, cutting down any Christian, man, woman, or child, who crossed their path. Sentries walked their posts around the cantonments twenty-four hours a day, but no one could feel safe until the day his tour ended and a steamer took him north to Manila and home. The letter of a young American woman, the wife of an army officer stationed on Mindanao, described the constant fear and tension under which the Americans lived:

"Last December a Moro attacked a captain, who fired six .38 caliber shots into him. The Moro didn't stop running for a second; he came right on, cut the captain to pieces with his bolo and started on his way rejoicing, when a guard finally finished him with a .45 caliber bullet. That is the size of pistol everyone here carries. I am just beginning to go around without feeling scared to death. Joe says I will give him nervous prostration if I don't stop grabbing him and saying, 'What's that?' . . . I suppose I shall look back on this as a great experience, but just at present I spend my time hoping and praying I won't have cholera or be boloed by a Moro."

Pershing himself described two *juramentado* attacks which took place while he was visiting the island of Jolo in April of 1911, several months before he decided to disarm all the Moros. A young lieutenant of the 2nd Cavalry was strolling through a crowd of natives near the cockpit outside the main gate of the Asturias Barracks when a Moro ceremonially clad all in white approached. The crowd scattered in a panic. Attacking from the rear, the *juramentado* slashed the lieutenant to death with his barong. A few minutes later the guard at the barracks gate caught up with the assassin and shot him to death. Several days later, Pershing wrote General J. Franklin Bell in Manila, two Moros came to the Asturias guardhouse, engaged the sergeant on duty in conversation, then fell on him without warning with their barongs. They killed him before another guard slew them. "The only safeguard against it," Pershing wrote, referring to the terroristic practice of *juramentado,* "is eternal vigilance." He considered that total disarmament was not feasible as yet, explaining, "Until we are in a position to afford protection to all Moros in every part of the Sulu Archipelago, it is idle to talk of requiring them to go about without some means of protecting their own lives."

General Bliss, commanding the Philippine Division, suggested to Pershing on May 23, 1911, that he adopt the methods used by the British in India to deal with Mohammedan fanaticism. *Juramentados,* Bliss recommended, should be buried with the carcass of a pig or encased in a pigskin, which meant to any Mohammedan that he would spend eternity in a state of contamination. "This I think a good plan, for if anything will discourage the *juramentado* it is the prospect of going to hell instead of heaven," Bliss wrote. He recognized that there might be an outcry of protest from humanitarians over such a measure, but "you can rely on me to stand by you in maintaining this custom. It is the only possible thing we can do to discourage crazy fanatics."

Pershing, however, realized that General Bliss's suggestion, while ingenious, might arouse an enduring bitterness among the whole Moro population. The British in India, for all their condign punishments, including the practice of shooting natives out of cannon, had never managed to rule except by the exercise of force, and he was intent on conciliating the Moros to the extent that they could soon be handed over to civilian administrators.

His approach was paternalistic and would probably have seemed to verge on the maudlin to any proper British colonial officer. It was exemplified by a letter he wrote the Moros of the Taglibi district on Jolo: "I am writing this letter that you may know that I want my children to come in and stop fighting. We do not want any more fighting. Too many Moros and their women may be killed. . . . These guns are not worth fighting for. . . . Your people are better off not to have these guns as we can then have peace in the island. The government will pay for all guns. . . . If your people need rice to eat, the government will give it to them. . . . I want to see all of my people and speak to them so that we may forever be friends."

The letter was one of several he collected years later for the memoir of his early career that was never published. "This letter," he later wrote on the top of it, "might be interesting to quote to show simplicity required."

Pershing was an eminently practical man as well as a relatively progressive student of the art of colonization. He had seen and read enough of history to know that the refusal to understand and sympathize with a subject people and the use of naked force as a substitute resulted only in such tragic culminations as the Ghost Dance rebellion of the Sioux, the Sepoy Rebellion in India, the Belgian slaughter of natives in the Congo, the continuing colonial warfare of the French in North Africa, Madagascar, and Indochina . . . and that in the end those methods were self-defeating.

His hope of avoiding an armed showdown with the more unruly Moros was not entirely realized, but he worked endlessly to promote understanding between the native population and the American administration. He established the *Sulu News,* published in Zamboanga in both the English language and the Sulu dialect, to "explain to the Moros the policies of the provincial government." In its first issue, June 30, 1911, Pershing wrote: "I think the most wholesome advice I can give the Moro readers of this periodical is that they devote themselves more earnestly to agriculture. The Moro country still has an abundance of fertile soil which the Moros can plant and own if they wish. In subsequent numbers this paper will explain to the Moros just how they must proceed to obtain a legal title to their farms. . . ."

Early in his administration Pershing also undertook to promote a homogenization of the Moros with Filipinos living in the Moro Province, Christian and pagan alike, since much of the murder and banditry in the mountains and valleys of the interior were directed against the less volatile non-Mohammedan peoples. On the occasion of Secretary of War Jacob M. Dickinson's visit to Zamboango, a mass meeting of the natives was held, with the hope that the Moros and the Christian Filipinos, in particular, might iron out their differences. The meeting, however, soon turned into a first-class row. Christian Filipino speakers demanded that they be domiciled in a separate province, with their own government and their own representatives in the Legislative Assembly. To which the Moro Datu Sacaluran, in turban and full regalia, responded: "I am an old man. I do not want any more trouble. But if it should come to that, that we shall be given over to the Filipinos, I still would fight." Hadji Nuno, a religious leader, took up the refrain: "We are a different race; we have a different religion; we are Mohammedans. And if we should be given over to the Filipinos, how much more would they treat us badly, when they treated even the Spanish badly who were their own mothers and their own fathers in generation? We far prefer to be in the hands of the Americans, who are father and mother to us now, than to be turned over to another people." Secretary of War Dickinson agreed with the Moro position, scorning the proposals of Christian Filipinos that they were "ready and willing to take over the government" of Mindanao.

Pershing accompanied Governor General Forbes on a visit to the Bukidnon district of Mindanao shortly after this unsuccessful effort to ameliorate the differences between the Moros and the Christian Filipinos. Forbes found the Moros of that region "earnest, quiet, modest, and generally pleasing in spite of their ugliness," and peacefully settled in producing honey, gums, rattan, resin, wax, Manila hemp, tobacco, woven cloth and mats. Riding into the town of Tanculan, Forbes wrote, they were "greeted with the most cordial demonstrations by the populace and a ceremonial dance by a warrior who danced backward in front of them, holding a spear with which he made pretended thrusts as he leapt backward purporting to prevent their advance. This seemed a curious form of welcome but it was as a matter of fact performed in all friendliness." They found the streets of the town "scrupulously clean, the buildings neatly fenced from the road, and the yards planted with fruits and flowering shrubs." And the residents of Tanculan had taken up baseball, taught them by American soldiers, as a token of their submitting to Americanization. The young people of the town, in fact, invited the visiting Americans to play ball with them. "Accepting this offer, the Governor General occupied one base, General Pershing another, one of the secretaries caught, while the aides-de-camp were placed in other positions, and a few of the native boys of the town were borrowed for fielders." What a proper British or French colonial officer would have made of American proconsuls playing baseball with the natives is an interesting speculation.

General Pershing, however, was well aware that many of the Moros were still reluctant to lay down their bolos and krises in favor of the baseball bat or the plow. To the War Department he recommended a shifting of forces to "keep down the lawless element among the Moros and pagan tribes." He wrote, "There should be a regimental post on the Island of Jolo, a brigade post in the Lake Lanao division and the regimental post in some point in the vicinity of Zamboanga, besides smaller posts at Fort Overton and Malabang. . . . Jolo is the strategical site for the post in the Sulu Archipelago. From there any point in the Island can be quickly reached and the others of the Sulu group can be easily controlled. It possesses a good harbor and is otherwise well situated as a military station. Mounted troops can go anywhere on the Island and they exert more influence over the Moros than dismounted troops." He also wanted a telegraph line strung to the Davao district to increase the speed of his communications.

Subsequently, Pershing reported even more critically on the state of the military forces in his province. The field artillery, he said, was "below the required standards" and cavalry efficiency had also slipped. He protested giving enlisted men double credit for service in the Philippines and recommended that the strength of infantry regiments be kept to at least 1000 men, 2400 if on active service. The Philippine Scouts, he believed, should be increased. "Considering their low cost of maintenance I believe it is poor policy not to keep them up to the authorized maximum strength of 12,000, reducing the garrison of American troops accordingly." He also suggested the organization of a native cavalry force, "mounted on hardy native ponies which require none of the expensive hay of the American horse." The native soldiery should be provided with canteens dispensing beer and light wines to "furnish soldiers with a club of their own and save many from the grog shops and brothels."

Pershing's concern with the disposition and readiness of his military forces was only natural under the circumstances. He had decided on a disarmament policy for the Moros to be applied with force if necessary, and he knew there were many, particularly on the island of Jolo, who would resist it. The sultans of Sulu and Maguidano, whom the Americans recognized as the nominal rulers of the islands so long as they co-operated with the United States administrators, did not oppose the disarmament. It was the militant datus, the lesser tribal chiefs, who whipped up their people into a furious resentment. On Mindanao, rifles and other arms were turned in by the thousands, even in the remote mountain districts. But the Joloanos were being inflamed to the point of revolt by agitators who pointed out that the Moros were paying American taxes and yet were deprived of slaves and the right to have more than one wife.

On Jolo the flash point of open rebellion was reached after General Pershing issued his order of September 8, 1911: "It is therefore declared to be unlawful for any person within the Moro Province to acquire, possess or have the custody of any rifle, musket, carbine, shotgun, revolver, pistol or other deadly weapon from which a bullet, ball, shot, shell or other missile or missiles may be discharged by means of gunpowder or other explosive, or to carry, concealed or otherwise on his person, any bowie knife, dirk, dagger, kris, campilan, spear, or other deadly cutting or thrusting weapons, except tools used exclusively for working purposes having blades less than fifteen inches in length, without permission of the Governor of the Moro Province. . . ."

Resistance to this order flared up almost immediately on Jolo, with hundreds of Moros "going off the reservation" rather than turn in their weapons. By mid-November it was apparent that a campaign would have to be undertaken against them, and Pershing decided to lead it in person. He particularly wanted to avoid any more charges of "massacre" in the States. Leaving his wife and children, however, was painful, as his letters from Jolo indicated in touching detail. Like many men who marry late in life, Pershing was an exceedingly devoted husband and father. Every morning he and his family went swimming in the Sulu Sea, practically at their doorstep. His wife and children, he wrote, "took to the water like ducklings. But in this I was like an old hen. I was never at ease out of my depth and often fluttered about the shore in dismay when my wife would swim half a mile straight out into the sea." Officers who served with him in Zamboanga related that he often hurried home from his office to have an hour or so with his children before their bedtime. Having been a schoolteacher in his youth, he insisted on hearing their lessons and making certain that, being reared in an exotic and languorous port on the southern seas, they received a proper American education. One decidedly exotic touch to the Pershing children's upbringing was the fact that their playhouse was the former honeymoon cottage of a Moro chieftain. When the Datu Dicky of Jolo, who was two feet three inches tall and reputed to be the smallest man in the world, took a midget bride, Pershing presented them with a tiny house on stilts with furnishings in proportion in which to spend their honeymoon. On leaving for Jolo several months later, the Datu Dicky presented it to the Pershing children.

Pershing's only surviving child, Warren, recalls that just before leaving on the Jolo campaign his father gave him a Philippine pony which he undoubtedly regarded as the suitable birthday present for a cavalryman's son. Warren then was barely able to walk, let alone ride anything on four feet. One afternoon, just as his father was returning home, Warren tumbled off the pony and into the canal which ran in front of the Pershing house. His father hauled him out and took him into the house. "Then," Warren recalls, "the old gent put me to bed and gave me a large dose of castor oil, which was his sovereign remedy for any and all the ailments of childhood."

During Pershing's absence on Jolo, Mrs. Pershing and her three children journeyed to the mountain resort at Baguio, on Luzon, with the hope that he would be able to join them by Christmastime. The affectionate tone of his letters would probably have amazed the men who served under "Black Jack" and considered him a hard-driving, iron-britched old cavalryman without a tender or sentimental fiber in his character. He addressed his wife as "Darlingest," "Dearest Darling," "My Darling Frankie," and "Frances Sweetheart." Often he signed himself "Jackie." He would close his letters with such phrases as "I must say good night to my precious ones" . . . "Good night. Kiss those dear kidlets for me. Their popa. . . ."

His first letters concerning the situation on Jolo were fairly optimistic, reflecting a hope that open rebellion could be avoided. On November 28, 1911, he wrote Mrs. Pershing: "While I do not anticipate anything like a general stampede against us or as some have predicted a 'Holy War' I do not want to be caught napping so I have plenty of troops. The whole 30th Infantry is here, eight troops of the 2nd Cavalry, four companies of Scouts and two companies of Constabulary." Next day, however, he wrote that he was taking reinforcements to the camp at Taglibi which was "attacked last night just as the moon went down and the Moros nearly succeeded in getting in. . . . There were about 200 or 300 Moros in all, so the troops estimate. This is possibly rather high. Thanks to our trenches none of our men were hurt. . . . It is rumored that a strong attack is to be made tonight. . . . You can never tell what the Moros are going to do."

Meanwhile, he was combing out officers whom he considered incompetent or worse. He complained of one senior officer whom he sent back to department headquarters at Zamboanga, "He is loco for sure. I can't run this place with such an old fool as he is. He has got to go. He is a windbag and an obstructionist. He fights with everybody and is a general nuisance." Regarding another high-ranking officer, he wrote, "K—— is a bullheaded bull in a china shop" but "I cannot relieve him now without a scandal."

Pershing hoped that swift action against "the disaffected section east of the town of Jolo" and "a combined movement of five columns to comb the Taglibi country" would prevent a general uprising. "I intend to give them a drubbing," he wrote his wife ". . . I have always said it was an error to sit idly by and let these savages shoot you up without going after them." A few days later he wrote regretfully that "I see now that it is going to be impossible for me to get to Baguio for Christmas. This job is going to keep me here for a couple of months. It is going to be a sad Christmas."

What particularly worried him during the first weeks of December, as it became more apparent that his flying columns would not be able to cauterize all the "disaffected" portions of Jolo, was the probability that the Moros would take to a mountaintop fort with their women and children and an all-out fight would be necessary. "I should dread to think of having to kill women and children," he wrote Mrs. Pershing, and expressed the hope that he would be able to "make a quick night movement and cross the mountain behind them and get between them and the top of the hills they intend to occupy."

Despite all his efforts, however, the dissident Moros, with their women and children, fled to the crater of the extinct volcano, a natural fortress, which was called Bud Dajo. On that craggy height, above the steep flanks of the burned-out volcano, the Moros had fought their most desperate and futile battle in 1906, while General Wood was governor of the Moro Province. The Americans had assaulted the crater without artillery preparation, lost heavily themselves, and killed between 600 and 900 men, women, and children. The outcry in the United States against this bloody by-product of our somewhat tentative venture into imperialism was tremendous.

Even those who favored American custody of the Philippines regarded the killing of women and children an unpardonable crime against humanity. The protestants were, of course, ignorant of the special conditions of combat in the southern islands. A soldier being fired upon in the heat of battle has neither the time nor the inclination, even if he were able to single them out in the smoke and confusion, to differentiate by age or sex whoever is trying to kill him. The only alternatives were to call off the battle (since Moro warriors refused all pleas to release the women and children from a surrounded fort) and give the Moros their way, or to attempt a separation of the men from their families. Pershing tried the second alternative at Bud Dajo and failed. In almost every letter he wrote his wife from mid-December on, however, he reiterated his determination to avoid having the deaths of women and children on his record or his conscience.

As the American columns drew closer to the fortified crater of Bud Dajo and moved up to siege positions, he wrote on December 14 that he planned "no hasty assaults against *strong* intrenchments. I shall use as few men and kill as few Moros as possible. . . . Moros cannot stand a siege. . . ." He avowed that he would force the surrender of Bud Dajo by siege "if it takes ten years to do it." On December 18 he wrote his wife, "I shall *not* kill women and children if I can help it," and on December 19, "Those women and children on Dajo distress me very much. Am going to get them down if possible."

Pershing took personal command of the battle line circling Bud Dajo on December 18; whatever happened, the responsibility was going to be his alone. Under his orders a wide strip of jungle was cleared around the crater so that no Moro could leave the fort for supplies, the rebels having food for only a few days in their fort, thanks to the swift envelopment of the American forces. Pershing disposed a total of 1000 troops on the mountain, half of them U.S. regulars and half Philippine Scouts and Constabulary, and on December 20 wrote that he had completed the job of shutting off supplies, but "I fear we must go in after them."

He could have opened up with his artillery and slaughtered the several hundred "forted-up" Moros without losing a man, but decided to play a waiting game. He put the Philippine Scouts under the capable Major E. G. Peyton in the front lines, with the regulars in supporting positions. Barbed wire was strung up to prevent the Moros from wriggling into his positions and running amuck with their knives. Double sentry posts, one man armed with a rifle and the other with a shotgun, surrounded Pershing's camp. Night after night from then on the Moros made desperate sallies from their crater, with blind head-on fire fights in the darkness. The troops were under a terrific strain, manning their positions during the day, fearful of closing their eyes for a moment on the perimeter at night.

By Christmas eve the Moros were close to starvation and in a state of wild despair. Pershing scrawled a few lines to his wife that night on a field-message pad: "There'll be some fighting tonight. These desperate Moros will make a strong effort to get out. The firing has already begun, and it's heavy all along the line. The night is dark so shooting is a guess. . . ."

Early the next day his message to his wife was even more laconic: ". . . The second Christmas we have been apart. . . . Fighting last night was terrific. . . ."

Later that day, however, Pershing saw his purpose accomplished, a bloodless victory won and a comparatively peaceful Christmas night on Bud Dajo. The Moros decided to surrender, all but forty-seven who fled into the jungle while the others were filing down from the crater under the American guns. The fugitives were captured days later by a pursuing column of Philippine Scouts. On December 29, 1911, Governor General Forbes cabled the War Department, "Pershing reports 300 Moros surrendered; opposition to disarmament practically ended. Consider his management of affairs masterly."

The Moro country was mostly at peace for a year following the surrender on Bud Dajo. Pershing took a breather after that campaign and joined his wife and children at Baguio. During his stay at the hill station he and three other officers made a 400-mile tour of the mountains of central Luzon on horseback. The family returned aboard the cutter *Samar,* resuming their life in Zamboanga, where the fourth and last child, Mary Margaret, was born on May 20, 1912.

Late in the autumn of 1912, Pershing received disturbing reports from Jolo again. The Moros of the Latiward district had retired to Mount Bagsak with their entire population of "6,000 to 10,000 souls." Succeeding events indicated that another campaign would have to be undertaken. Again Pershing's principal concern, as he wrote Governor General Forbes on February 28, 1913, was the lives of the Moro women and children. "The nature of the Joloano Moro is such that he is not at all overawed or impressed by an overwhelming force. If he takes a notion to fight, he will fight regardless of the number of men he thinks are to be brought against him. You cannot bluff him. There are already enough troops on the Island of Jolo to smother the defiant element, but the conditions are such that if we attempt such a thing the loss of life among innocent women and children would be very great. It is estimated that there are only about 300 arms altogether in the Island of Jolo and that these are assembled in Latiward on top of Mt. Bagsak in fortified cottas. It is a common thing among these people to have the women and children follow them into these cottas so that we have there probably five or six times as many women and children as armed men. . . ."

He never believed, Pershing continued, that "the Moros who are now opposing us will all yield without a fight, yet I am not prepared to rush in and attack them while they are surrounded by their women and children as I think most of the women and children can be induced to return to their homes. . . . Coolness and patience are the requisites required. I fully appreciate your confidence in my ability to handle it, and you may rest assured that my best efforts are being put forth to carry out the purpose of our undertaking—disarmament with as little disturbance and as little loss of life as possible."

Pershing spent "months of negotiation," according to Forbes, in trying to persuade the Latiward Moros to cease their defiance of authority. But they could not be coaxed into peaceful disarmament. The Datu Amil and his followers established themselves on the lip of an extinct volcano crowning Mount Bagsak, and Pershing then realized he would have to go in after them.

Early in June 1913 his columns of Philippine Scouts and regular infantry were on the march, drawing a cordon around the Latiward district, then moving on Mount Bagsak itself. "Their forts and trenches on the precipitous side of the crater not only supported each other," Pershing reported to the commanding general at Manila, "but were defended with modern arms." On June 11 five days of battle began as "the Moros fanatically and continuously tried to rush the American lines." He reported to headquarters at Manila that the Moros "were caught unawares with most of their non-combatant followers absent," in a sudden movement which interposed the American forces between the fort and the Latiward villages.

Pershing pushed his lines to within a hundred yards of the Moro fort and ordered a bombardment from noon to dusk on June 15. Shrieking and swinging their swords, the Moros tried to escape the bombardment and rush the Americans, but were thrown back or slaughtered in every attempt. At moonrise, from positions only fifteen yards from the parapet of the Moro fort, Pershing gave the signal for the assault, with Major George C. Shaw commanding the right wing with Company M, 8th Infantry, and the 40th Company of the Philippine Scouts, and Captain Taylor A. Nichols the left wing with the 29th, 51st, and 52nd Companies of the Philippine Scouts, the latter two companies being composed largely of Moros. Captain Nichols was killed, and Pershing himself hurried forward to push the attack. In a few minutes the troops were swarming over the fort, shooting and bayoneting mercilessly; very few Moros survived that slaughter under the rising moon. "A very severe, though well-deserved, punishment was administered," as Pershing put it, citing the fact that many of the fort's defenders were "notorious cattle thieves and murderers."

A Manila *Times* correspondent wrote that "General Pershing was with the troops in the field during the entire time, and was within thirty feet of the last cotta when it was taken. . . . General Pershing has reason to be proud of the conduct of all the officers and men under his command, who engaged in this short but terrific taking of Bagsak. He was on the spot from beginning to end and knows what they were up against."

A Congressional Medal of Honor was proposed for Pershing by Captain George C. Charlton of the Philippine Scouts, who witnessed his un-brigadierlike leadership of the assaulting forces. The general, however, wrote the War Department that he didn't think his actions on Bagsak were "such as to entitle me to be decorated with a Medal of Honor" and that "I went to that part of the line because my presence there was necessary." Pershing's refusal to be considered for the Medal of Honor went through channels and was buried in the War Department archives, coming to light only after World War I.

"Probably there has been no fiercer battle since the American occupation," Pershing wrote to the commanding general at Manila. He listed his own casualties as six killed and seven wounded. Not even an estimate of the Moros who were killed in the crater was given. Newspaper dispatches from Manila reported that Bagsak had been defended by 500 Moros and that most of them had been killed, either in rushes down the slopes or in the crater itself. Back home, however, newspapers gave wide circulation to an interview in San Francisco with John McLeod, a civilian employee of the Army Quartermaster Department who arrived in San Francisco from the Philippines six weeks after the battle. McLeod told reporters that 2000 Moros had been killed, among them women and children "mowed down by the scores" with rifles and machine guns. "The news of the fighting was strictly censored at Manila. . . . Three correspondents who managed to reach the seat of war were arrested on orders of General Pershing. . . . It was believed that every Moro that took part in that battle was killed." The reporters did not question McLeod on the source of his information, and his account, necessarily based on hearsay, was greatly exaggerated. Bagsak, however, was a stern and blood-spattered "punishment," as Pershing himself put it. It was also the last large-scale action fought in the Moro country until the final withdrawal of American authority from the Philippines.

By the time Pershing was ordered back to the States, sailing for San Francisco with his family on December 15, 1913, the Moro Province was so thoroughly pacified that he could be succeeded by a civilian governor. Cameron Forbes, the former governor general, considered that he "exercised the utmost patience in endeavoring to appeal to the reason of the Moro people and in avoiding a recourse to arms." That was one testimonial to his efforts, both corporal and diplomatic; another was that the Moros, on his departure, elevated him to the rank of sultan. It was one thing to disarm and pacify by force, but this was an honor, never given to another white man, which could not be wrested at gunpoint. It was the voluntary homage of the Moros, who felt that Pershing understood them and had treated them sternly but fairly, possibly also a sly recognition that he had a touch of the Moro temperament. Homeward with him went the commendation also of the new Governor General Francis Burton Harrison, "You have restored peace and disarmed the turbulent population, promoted civilization and education, and as rapidly as possible substituted civilian for military control of the districts. It is due to your efforts in that direction that I have been able with perfect confidence to nominate the Hon. Frank W. Carpenter, a civilian, as your successor."

5. The Problem of Pancho Villa

On the homeward voyage General Pershing received an eagerly sought assurance that he was being brought back to the States for an active command. Before leaving Manila, he had cabled the War Department an anxious inquiry concerning his next assignment. A message awaited him in Honolulu that he would be given a troop command rather than the desk in the General Staff's headquarters which he feared might be his lot. Pershing's acquaintance with staff work was not extensive, certainly, but it was enough to give him a distaste for the planning and administering functions of the Army. He realized that modern armies could not be supplied, moved, or directed without a vast amount of staff preparation, of sweating over railroad schedules and warehouse inventories, and theorizing over maps and sand tables. But all the rewards of his profession lay in command, in assuming responsibility, leading men in battle. His scramble up the parapet of Mount Bagsak indicated that he thought more like a cavalry captain than a brigadier general. He had to be in the thick of things.

His new command was waiting for him only a rifleshot from where he and his family disembarked. It was the 8th Infantry Brigade, headquartered at the Presidio. Trouble with Mexico was looming, the possibility of intervention was growing, and the brigade was earmarked for action if the need arose.

The need became apparent early in the spring of 1914, several months after Pershing took command of the 8th Brigade and established himself and his family in the rambling and ramshackle old house allotted the commanding officer at the Presidio.

The situation in Mexico, stated as briefly as possible, was that of a series of revolutions, none of them entirely successful, which had left the country in a state of anarchy. American capital, the most vociferous spokesman of which was William Randolph Hearst with his medieval fief, cattle herds, and silver mines in northern Mexico, wanted the country pacified, by intervention if necessary. But the Mexicans, divided though they were among themselves, were politically united on one subject; they were as hostile to foreign intervention as they had been half a century before when Maximilian and Carlotta were briefly installed as rulers of the "empire" of Mexico in a similar attempt to protect foreign investments. Dictator Porfirio Díaz had been chased into exile, and a long struggle for supremacy began among his would-be successors. Madero, the pathetic idealist, was murdered and succeeded by Huerta, who was addicted to cocaine and treachery in almost equal portions. But Huerta, the corrupt general, could not command a mass following, nor could he summon up the military power to deal with Zapata, the peasant leader in the south, or with the rebels in the north —Obregón, Carranza, and Villa.

In March 1914 came the "incident" at Vera Cruz. A junior paymaster of the American naval squadron was jailed by Huerta's officers while buying supplies. The U.S. State Department demanded that, in addition to his release, the Huerta government order a thirteen-gun salute to the American flag. Huerta replied that he would do so if the American warships would tender a similar salute to the Mexican flag. Washington decided it had been insulted and that Huerta, having favored British oil interests, would have to go. Preceded by naval landing parties, the Army sent an occupying force of four regiments under General Funston to Vera Cruz. Huerta soon followed Díaz into exile.

While Funston was landing at Vera Cruz on April 23, the Regular Army was being mobilized for an invasion of Mexico from the north. The war fever which was to become virulent in Europe that summer of 1914 broke out in the United States several months earlier. The old cry of "On to Mexico City" was heard again.

Among the forces being concentrated on the border were the 6th and 16th infantries under Pershing's command. They entrained from San Francisco, bound for El Paso, on April 25, two days after General Funston's landing at Vera Cruz.

Pershing was uneasy over the departure for personal reasons. His wife had been injured in an automobile collision three days before he left, but the doctors at the Letterman Army Hospital assured him that her injuries were inconsequential and she would be released soon after his departure.

With Pershing riding in an open touring car at their head, the two infantry regiments marched down Market Street to the Embarcadero with thousands of the citizenry cheering them on in a patriotic frenzy. The regimental bands blared a march step, and flags flew from every building. San Franciscans were confident that next thing they heard "their" regiments would be storming into Mexico City. The result was anticlimax. Pershing reported to Major General Tasker H. Bliss, commanding the Southern Department, with his 1800 men; the prospects of intervention on a larger scale fizzled out as Carranza assumed power as the "Constitutionalist" president in Mexico City; and the Army settled down for a long wait on the border. It would be almost two years, in fact, before American troops crossed the international boundary into Mexico.

The Army, having little to do but patrol the long border between Texas and California, decided to woo the Mexican rebel leaders in the north, Pancho Villa in particular. Villa, despite his claims to being "Dictator of Chihuahua," "Lion of the North," and liberator of the oppressed peons, was little more than a bandit chief whose character degenerated with each success, but his personality, his joviality and expansiveness, evidently held a certain amount of charm for Americans. He also had a sense of public relations. During his siege of Ciudad Juárez, across the river from El Paso, in 1911, he held off his final assault for several days after an American newspaperman told him the World Series was about to begin and his prospective victory would be pushed off the front pages. "We shall hold off the attack, boys, until the Americans finish their ball games," Villa told his staff.

With the capture of Juárez and the loot from its banks and storehouses, with money extorted from American ranch and mine owners, Villa began living like a Chinese war lord. He bought five utterly useless airplanes, Pierce-Arrow touring cars for himself and his favorite officers, and a luxuriously appointed special train with a drawing room, barber shop, salon car, and a flush toilet over which he never ceased marveling; at the same time he turned over to his brother Hippolito the bull ring and the whoring and gambling concessions in Juárez. Particularly swayed by Villa's claims that his great mission in life was breaking up the *haciendas* and distributing land to the peons was

Major General Hugh L. Scott, who held the border command before becoming chief of staff on November 16, 1914. General Scott presented Villa with a copy of *Rules of Land Warfare* and gave him fatherly lectures against killing women and children, forgetting that Villa was illiterate and had conquered northern Mexico by throwing the rule books out the window.

Others were less impressed with Pancho's boisterous manner and beaming smile. Timothy G. Turner, an El Paso newspaperman who had been covering Mexican revolutions since Díaz's overthrow, thought General Obregón was the more promising man, "an intellectual type . . . a man who could sit down to a problem and master it." Villa, however, was "passionate, capricious. He lacked the intellectuality to understand anything complex." Still, it was Villa who captured the imagination, who seemed to epitomize Mexico's heroic struggle to liberal-minded Americans and Mexicans alike. One who succumbed to this allure was the aged and disillusioned Ambrose Bierce who disappeared forever after crossing the border to join Villa and leaving a note reading, "If you hear of my being stood up against a Mexican stone wall and shot to rags please know that I think it a pretty good way to depart this life. It beats old age, disease, or falling down the cellar stairs. To be a Gringo in Mexico—ah, that is euthanasia!"

Pershing himself approached Villa more warily and skeptically, regarding him as much the same type as the Moro chiefs he had subdued in the Philippines. He was making friends on both sides of the border, sounding out both Mexican and American opinion, trying to find out what motivated the various rebel leaders. Tim Turner, who discovered that he and Pershing "had a common failing for afternoon tea" and frequently shared a pot with the general at the Hotel Sheldon, recalled that Pershing "spoke Spanish and had a personality that the Mexicans liked, being what they called 'simpático.'"

Thus the comparatively parochial problems of the Mexican border were occupying him when his future colleagues of the Allied High Command were just beginning, in that late summer of 1914, to deal with a continental war. Western Europe had been at peace for two generations, since the Franco-Prussian War, when the statesmen and diplomats suddenly ceased to function and the huge armies of Russia, France, Germany, Austria-Hungary, and finally Great Britain were mobilized. The pressures which built up over the years of peace and finally exploded into a continent-wide war were many and diverse;

the question of "war guilt" was to be debated for a score of years, without either side conceding the truth—there was plenty of it in all camps.

Part of the tension undoubtedly arose from Germany's rivalry with France and England for trade and colonies in Asia and Africa, from the Kaiser's determination to build a Navy as strong as England's, from the French determination to recover Alsace and Lorraine from Germany. In eastern Europe there was a secondary line-up of warring powers. Czarist Russia was eager to expand into the Balkans and toward the Bosporus. Austria-Hungary was determined to resist the Balkan thrust, and the crumbling Turkish Empire would summon up its last resources to keep the Russians out of Constantinople. The Balkans had been in turmoil for years as various nations fought for freedom, fought each other, fought over the European remnants of the Turkish Empire. The series of small but vicious Balkan Wars, Austria-Hungary's seizure of Bosnia-Herzegovina, the blood feuds involving Bulgaria, Greece, Serbia, Macedonia, Montenegro, Rumania, and every other patchwork community of Balkan tribes, the inability of the Hapsburgs to match their fondness for the status quo with administrative efficiency and military power, and finally the larger powers' own selfish interests in that area, all provided enough inflammatory material for a dozen wars.

The point of combustion was reached when England, France, and Russia decided to support Serbia, and Germany mobilized to back up Austria in that late summer of 1914. Then, as Sir Edward Grey said, the lamps went out in Europe, and nothing was ever the same again, particularly for those who were so eager to defend the "old order."

. . . All that was far outside Pershing's province the summer of 1914. He was exerting himself through diplomacy and calculated displays of force to convince Obregón and Villa that it wouldn't pay to trifle with American lives and property below the border. Both rebel leaders crossed the border as his guests on several occasions. He came to the conclusion that Obregón was an "able and sincere patriot," but Villa "was of a different type. He was taciturn and restless. His eyes were shifty, his attitude one of suspicion, and his noticeably bulging coat indicated that he carried a brace of pistols in his hip pockets."

Villa and one of his chief lieutenants, Fierro, were Pershing's guests at a brigade review at Fort Bliss, which was designed to open Villa's eyes to the disciplined power of the American forces. Apparently it did. "When he saw the American cavalry and light artillery do their stunts," Turner wrote, "Villa did not suppress his admiration and astonishment. He sat there rather bashfully, and was still more uncomfortable when, after the review, he was taken to the post commandant's quarters where tea was served. Fierro was so flabbergasted that he forgot to remove his hat when he entered the house, and Villa said in a stage whisper, 'Take off your hat, you brute, you animal!' "

Pershing was popular in El Paso society and dined out frequently, but he missed his family, still living in the commanding officer's quarters at the Presidio in San Francisco. When it appeared that he would be stationed on the border for some time, he began looking for a house but could find nothing suitable. Finally he told a friend, "I'm tired of living alone. I'm having my quarters fixed so my wife and children can join me."

On the morning of August 27, 1915—just about a week before Mrs. Pershing and their four children planned to take a train for El Paso— Pershing appeared early at his office in brigade headquarters at Fort Bliss. He began working on the papers accumulated overnight on his desk—intelligence reports, dispatches from the regiments on border patrol.

Shortly after his arrival, his orderly entered with a telegram. On that slip of yellow paper were contained the bare details of the tragedy which cut his life in two.

Pershing glanced up from his desk and asked that the telegram be read to him.

His orderly, knowing its contents, hesitated.

"Go ahead," said Pershing impatiently.

The orderly, trying to keep his voice steady, read out the news from San Francisco. Hours before, a fire had broken out in the old wooden structure housing his family at the Presidio. His wife and three daughters, nine-year-old Helen, seven-year-old Anne, and three-year-old Margaret, all had been killed. Only his six-year-old son Warren had been saved.

There was a long silence after the orderly finished reading the telegram.

Finally Pershing said, "Is that all? Is that everything?"

His aides said that Pershing took this crushing blow without another word. Not a flicker of emotion crossed his face. Not a word or sound of grief. "Only those who knew him intimately realized the struggle that was taking place within him," the torment contained behind tight lips and frozen features. "For a time it was feared that he would lose his mind. Then once more he got complete mastery of himself." The price of that self-containment was marked on his character from then on; it isolated him from other men and contributed to the general feeling that he was a "cold fish" incapable of human emotions.

Before he left for San Francisco, Pershing received a fuller account of the tragedy. The fire was spotted after midnight by sentries walking their posts as a column of smoke and flame burst through the roof of the two-story building. Apparently it started from a night light left burning in the children's room. Mrs. Pershing and her three daughters were suffocated in their sleep. The Negro butler had risked his life to force his way into Warren's room on the first floor and carry him to safety. Mrs. Warren O. Boswell, a visiting relative of Mrs. Pershing's, also managed to escape from a ground-floor room with her two children. The post fire department found the bodies of Mrs. Pershing and her daughters in rooms on the second floor after extinguishing the fire on the roof.

It could hardly have comforted Pershing, but the San Francisco *Chronicle,* in a front-page editorial signed by its publisher, denounced the housing facilities allotted the officers at the Presidio. The Pershing quarters, said the editorial, were "a flimsy shack built forty years ago, destitute of modern safety appliances and sanitary improvements." The fact that two women and three children had been burned to death in three previous fires at the Presidio "should have aroused the government to the necessity of guarding against the horror which the last accident has brought it face to face with." Scant amends also were offered by the Army some years later: a bronze plaque surmounting a stone block which marks the site of the Pershing family's tragedy.

On arrival in San Francisco, Pershing hurried out to the post hospital where his son was being kept. Doctors and nurses led him, in silence, to the room where six-year-old Warren waited. They closed the door on father and son just as he knelt and took the towheaded little boy into his arms.

Dry eyed and emotionless on the surface, Pershing accompanied the bodies of his wife and daughters to Cheyenne, where they were buried in the Warren family plot. He took his son to Lincoln, where his maiden sister, May, and his married sister, Mrs. D. M. Butler, took charge of the boy's upbringing for the next several years.

He returned to his command on the border, where his officers noted the shocking imprint of the grief which Pershing would not permit himself to display. He no longer looked younger than his years. His face was thinner, almost gaunt; his mouth was tightened to the grim line familiar later in World War I photographs, and his graying hair turned almost white during the several weeks following the tragedy.

Pershing threw himself into his work, the only acceptable anodyne. The Mexican situation was beginning to boil over again, and, according to intelligence reports, Pancho Villa was being financed and goaded into anti-American activities by German agents. The German plan was to involve the United States in a war on its southern border and keep it from joining the Allies, as was to be proved by the intercepted Zimmerman telegram.

He also immersed himself in a study of the war in Europe, based on the newspaper accounts and reports of its observers forwarded by the War Department. If America entered the war, it seemed likely that Pershing would command one of the first divisions to go over, and he wanted to be prepared. By the fall of 1915 the Allies were fighting with their backs to the wall against the Austro-German armies on both fronts. The huge Russian armies had been rolled back along the line stretching from the Baltic coast to the Carpathians, and it was apparent that they could offer little more resistance than their flesh and bone so long as they were led with the most brutal incompetence, supplied so inadequately, and asked to lay down their lives for a distant and bewildered Czar and his corrupt court.

The French and British armies were locked in a stalemate with the Germans from the North Sea to the Swiss border, draining the lifeblood of their nations in futile but repeated offensives which pitted their infantry against the scythelike sweeps of the German machine guns and the pounding of heavy artillery, burrowing into trenches flooded by the autumnal rains but planning more massive efforts at breaking the deadlock. The only inspiring event of the war thus far, from the Allied standpoint, was halting the German drive on Paris at the Marne, which was due as much to a breakdown in the enemy's staff work and command as to the valiant French counterattacks.

As the new year began, Pershing was occupied with more intimate concerns than the European war. Villa and his steeple-hatted guerrilla army were on the move in Chihuahua. In January of 1915, Villa had signed an agreement with the United States, as representative of the

Mexican Government, to halt the brigandage in northern Mexico. Succeeding events, however, gave Villa more than a little cause for a sense of grievance against the American Government. President Wilson had reversed policy and granted recognition to the "Constitutionalist" government of General Carranza, although Villa until then had been fairly co-operative and had the special favor of the United States Army, particularly its chief of staff, General Hugh L. Scott. Scott wrote in his memoirs: "The recognition of Carranza had the effect of solidifying the power of the man who had rewarded us with kicks on every occasion, and of making an outlaw of the man who had helped us. . . . After Villa had given up millions of dollars at the request of the State Department [in expropriated American property] . . . they made him an outlaw. He was a wild man and could not be expected to know the difference between the duties of the State and War Departments."

In September of 1915, President Wilson handed the Carranzistas another precious boon by permitting them to transfer their troops by rail across American territory and fall upon Villa at Agua Prieta, opposite Douglas, Arizona. The Agua Prieta garrison then counterattacked, driving the Villistas away in disorder and reducing Villa's forces from 10,000 to 1500 men. After that, Villa swore vengeance on the United States. There was so much shooting along the international boundary that American border-town hotels advertised themselves as "bullet-proof," and American-owned ranches and mines were at the mercy of roving bandit gangs, not all of them Villista. On January 10, 1916, nineteen Americans were taken from a train near Santa Isabel, Chihuahua, and shot to death. Villa was instantly held responsible for the outrage, but claimed that it had been committed by a renegade former lieutenant.

Four days after the Santa Isabel incident, Pershing was forced to send troops into El Paso when the Anglo-Saxon populace rioted and attacked the Mexican quarters of the city. Martial law was proclaimed after "the arrival here of the mutilated bodies of the Americans" killed at Santa Isabel, as the Associated Press reported, "further inflamed the city."

Early in March brigade headquarters received rather disturbing reports indicating that Villa might be contemplating a raid across the border. The Mexican commandant at Juárez tipped off the American intelligence that his agents had learned Villa was planning a border raid within a few days. On March 7 came reports that Villa's army, numbering between 1000 and 1500 men, was camped on the Casas Grandes River south of Columbus, New Mexico, a desolate little town (population 400–500) two miles north of the international boundary.

Columbus, the headquarters of the 13th Cavalry, Colonel Henry J. Slocum commanding, would make a tempting target with its banks, storehouses, military supplies, and a battery of machine guns which Villa especially wanted to lay hands on. The 13th Cavalry had garrisoned the town since 1911 and had been alerted many times—perhaps too many times—by warnings that the Mexicans were about to attack. It kept the border watch in a routine way, patrolling at irregular intervals the barbed-wire fence which represented the international boundary. Three troops and the machine-gun unit garrisoned Columbus; two troops were stationed at Gibson's Ranch, fourteen miles west of Columbus, and one troop was posted at the border gate, where the United States Customs station was located.

The town itself, lying out on the desert fifty miles west of El Paso, was a dreary, sun-and-sand-blasted place afflicted with windstorms and rattlesnakes; neither electricity nor telephone service had reached it as yet, and its only communications with the outside world were the telegraph and the El Paso & Southwestern Railroad, from whose westbound Drunkards Special every midnight tumbled men who had been celebrating brief furloughs in El Paso.

On the evening of March 7 a Mexican cowhand employed by an American ranch rode into Columbus to report that he and two American riders had sighted Villa's army camped at Casas Grandes. The Mexicans escaped, but the two Americans, he said, were captured and killed by the Villistas earlier that day. Colonel Slocum was prohibited from reconnoitering across the border so he persuaded the Mexican to return the next day to the Casas Grandes and report on the Villistas' movements. The Mexican found that Villa's main body had proceeded east toward Guzmán, while a smaller force of a hundred horsemen split off northward in the direction of Palomas. Colonel Slocum asked the commandant of the Carranza garrison at Palomas to investigate the reports of Villa's movements, but he refused. The pro-Villa sentiment of the Palomas garrison was evident. Colonel Slocum, however, recalled Troop K from the border gate, believing that Villa had probably turned away from the border.

The 13th Cavalry bedded down the night of March 8 without

taking any special precautions against a predawn attack. Lieutenant James P. Castleman took over as officer of the day at regimental headquarters. Sentries walked their posts around the barracks, stables, mess shacks, and guard tent at the camp south of the railroad tracks. The business and residential sections of Columbus were north of the tracks. Soon after night fell the streets were dark and silent— Colonel Slocum's requisition for oil lamps to light the streets had been denied—except for patches of light outside the several saloons and hotels. It was a moonless night.

At midnight everything was so peaceful around the post that Lieutenant Castleman, the sole officer in charge, strolled over to the railroad station to meet the Drunkards Special and welcome back the regimental polo team, which had played in the brigade matches at El Paso. Among the returning players was Lieutenant John P. Lucas, who commanded the machine-gun troop. Both Castleman and Lucas were shortly to spend the busiest several hours of their lives.

In the next few hours, while town and camp slept, Villa's thousand or more horsemen, many of them savage Yaquis from the mountains of Sonora, moved across the border in small bands and took positions for a well-planned attack. On this side of the border they organized themselves into two columns, one of which was to attack from the southeast, the other from the southwest.

The surprise attack began at 4:15 A.M., March 9, with the killing of two sentries in the regimental headquarters area. On hearing the shots, Lieutenant Castleman drew his pistol and rushed out of the officer of the day's shack. Just outside the door a Villista blazed away at him with a 30-30 Winchester and knocked off his hat, to which Castleman replied by shooting him dead. The officer of the day ran across the parade ground under heavy fire and routed out the guard detail at the guardhouse, then Troop F in its barracks, and drove the Mexicans across the railroad tracks. Other troops, though their officers were quartered in town and unable to reach them, organized themselves to join in the fight. The whole business section of the town erupted in gunfire. Mexican horsemen rode up and down the streets, firing into houses and hurling torches into business establishments. The Villistas unwisely set fire to the Commercial Hotel, the flames from which lit up the section and made easy targets for the American riflemen.

In his quarters across the tracks, Lieutenant Lucas was awakened by the clatter of horse's hoofs, looked out the window, and glimpsed the tall sombrero of a Mexican rider. Barefooted and heedless of sand burrs, he hastened to the camp, eluding the Villistas and making his way to the barracks occupied by his machine-gun troop. Lucas and his gunners hurried to the guard tent where the machine guns were kept. The first gun they set up was an old Benet-Mercier of French manufacture, "a very complicated weapon, which required perfect conditions that it might function. The conditions not being perfect the gun jammed after a few rounds, and we left it in position and went after another. . . . By this time the remainder of the troop had arrived and I stationed the guns in what I considered to be strategic positions to fire on the Mexicans in town. Also about thirty men with rifles had shown up, and these I deployed along the railroad track to fire on the same target." The burning hotel in the background "lit up the terrain so that we were able to see our targets very plainly."

Just as dawn broke, Villa's trumpeters sounded the retreat. The streets were littered with the dead, mostly Mexican, and the center of town was burned out. Nineteen Mexican corpses were found in front of the Columbus Bank. Behind them the fleeing Villistas left 215 dead; the corpses were later stacked in a huge pile out on the desert, soaked with oil, and burned. The American losses, thanks to the Mexicans' poor marksmanship, were amazingly small: seven soldiers killed and eight wounded, eight civilians killed and five wounded.

The regiment's senior officers, quartered in town, were unable to join their troops until the Mexicans had been driven off. Without waiting for authorization from higher headquarters, Colonel Slocum decided to drive the Villistas south of the border. Though greatly outnumbered, the American cavalrymen mounted up and began the pursuit. Major Frank Tompkins, with only twenty-nine troopers of Troop H under his command, rode for the border fence at a gallop and found Villa's rear guard holding a hill 300 yards south of the international boundary. They charged with pistols and drove the Villistas back toward their slowly retreating main body. Lieutenant Castleman with Troop F and Captain Stedje with Troop G, from the post at the border gate, joined Major Tompkins in pressing the counterattack.

Fighting mad over having been taken by surprise, the Americans attacked the Mexican rear guard twice more, then flanked the main body, and poured a heavy fire into it. Villa's retreat turned into a rout.

Without food or water, the Americans chased the Villistas fifteen miles south of the border, killing an estimated seventy-five to 100 more. Then, only because their horses were stumbling with thirst and fatigue, they turned back to Columbus.

The American reaction to Villa's raid was swift, although President Wilson and his new Secretary of War Newton D. Baker had often expressed pacifist sentiments in the past. On March 10, the day after the raid, the War Department telegraphed General Funston, now commanding the Southern Department: "President has directed that an armed force be sent into Mexico with the sole object of capturing Villa and preventing any further raids by his bands, and with scrupulous regard for sovereignty of Mexico."

Organization of a punitive expedition began the moment that authorization was received at General Funston's headquarters at San Antonio.

Who was to command it? Secretary of War Baker asked that question of the chief of staff, General Scott, and his deputy, General Bliss.

"Pershing," both replied in unison.

Baker then wired General Funston, "You will promptly organize an adequate military force of troops from your department under the command of Brigadier General John J. Pershing, and will direct him to proceed promptly across the border in pursuit of the Mexican band which attacked the town of Columbus, New Mexico, and the troops there on the ninth instant. These troops will be withdrawn to American territory as soon as the defacto government of Mexico is able to relieve them of this work. In any event the work of these troops will be regarded as finished as soon as Villa's band or bands are known to be broken up."

Only three days after the expedition was ordered, General Bliss saw that chasing Villa would be more than a simple man hunt, and that Pershing's task would be a complicated one. In a memorandum to the Secretary of War, the deputy chief of staff wrote, "They [Pershing and his punitive columns] will soon be beyond assured communication with their home government. They will be in hostile country surrounded by enemies, and they will do as soldiers in the circumstances must do. If they think that Villa and his band are in a certain town and refuse to surrender they must attack that town. If Villa retreats they must follow him; if he breaks up into small bands our people must more or less scatter in order to follow him." Bliss's view, it developed, was remarkably clear-sighted.

The chances for success of the Mexican punitive expedition, no matter what expectations had been raised among the American people, were slim at the outset. Among the handicaps under which Pershing would labor in the coming months were (1) the attitude of the Carranza government, which was opposed to intervention and would prove almost as troublesome as Villa himself; (2) the fact that the United States agreed not to use the railroads of northern Mexico to supply its columns; (3) the sympathy of the Mexicans for Villa; (4) the necessity of hunting down Villa, the national hero, without involving the United States in a war with Mexico; (5) the rugged country in which the American forces would have to operate; (6) the unpreparedness of the United States Army for even such a limited campaign below the border; (7) the inadequacy of communications and methods of supplying the troops in the field—and there were others. Everything had to be improvised on the spot and at the moment. Exactly a week after the Columbus raid, Pershing had pushed his cavalry regiments across the border and sent them southward by forced marches.

Robert Lee Bullard, future army commander under Pershing, who was serving on the Texas border, commented that "all military men know that under the orders he [Pershing] received he had as much chance to get Villa as to find a needle in a haystack. He must have known this before he started, yet nowhere does he seem to have broken over the restraining conditions of these orders."

Pershing's willingness to accept the directives of the government and never to yield to the glory-hunting temptation made him by far the most reliable choice to lead the punitive force. "He will obey his superiors absolutely," Bullard wrote in accurate prophecy. "Had the President searched the whole army over to find a commander of this expedition he could probably have found no other who would be ready so absolutely to obey his instructions and comply with his wishes in every respect." The need for absolute obedience to the government's designs in Mexico was evident: the United States couldn't afford to become involved in a war deep in Mexico at a time when it appeared more and more likely that we would enter the struggle against the Central Powers. Catching Villa would satisfy the national honor but it wasn't a matter of historical necessity.

Pershing was required to salvage a situation manufactured in Washington by inept diplomacy, which had antagonized Villa without winning the support of the Carranza government.

His immediate superior, General Funston, didn't envy him the field command. "John's up against a lot," Funston told a newspaperman on the veranda of a San Antonio hotel. It was the prime understatement of the year.

Four Ages of a Soldier. Cadet — Cavalry Captain — Brigadier — C. — in — C. WIDE WORLD PHOTOS

Brigadier and family man. Pershing and his wife and three oldest children, Helen, Anne, and Warren, outside their quarters at Zamboango, Mindanao. BROWN BROTHERS

Pershing in the Philippines. Second from the left, at the BOQ, Zamboango, on Mindanao. WIDE WORLD PHOTOS

Boyhood home in Laclede. BROWN BROTHERS

Officers of the 6th Cavalry after Wounded Knee. Lieutenant Pershing is second from the right, in the second row. WIDE WORLD PHOTOS

Pershing and Joffre. The A.E.F. commander entertains the hero of
the Marne, now on the shelf, at Chaumont. BROWN BROTHERS

An undying friendship. Pétain and Pershing conferring just before the
western front exploded in the spring of 1918. BROWN BROTHERS

Where's Pancho? A frustrated Pershing, his face lined and weary, reads about the expedition as his columns fan out searching for the elusive guerrilla leader. THE BETTMAN ARCHIVE

Commanding the punitive force. Pershing, right, and his staff beside the Dodge touring car, flying its one-star flag, which carried them deep into Mexico on the heels of the cavalry columns. THE BETTMAN ARCHIVE

Obregón — Villa — Pershing. Just a few months before Pershing
began hunting down Pancho, over Obregón's ultimate objections.
WIDE WORLD PHOTOS

For publicity purposes only. Pershing and aides ford the Santa Maria
across the Mexican border for a Signal Corps photographer. Actually
he traveled south by automobile. But it made a nice picture. BROWN
BROTHERS

Allies and adversaries. Generalissimo Foch and the sometimes difficult commander of his right wing on the western front. BROWN BROTHERS

Architects of victory. General Pershing, Marshal Foch, and Field Marshal Haig, after the war was won. BROWN BROTHERS

6. The Empty Cage for Pancho Villa

A military career is made of many things. Courage, character, and intelligence may be essential, but they don't necessarily bring a man to high command. There were undoubtedly others among the hundreds of career officers in the United States Army who could have handled the vast responsibilities which fell to John J. Pershing's lot; several may well have done better, given the same opportunities. But Pershing had fortune on his side every step of the way in his professional, if not his personal, life. He was always in the right place when the opportunity for achievement arose. Being in command at El Paso, fifty miles from the scene of the Columbus raid, made him the logical choice to lead the punitive expedition, all things being equal; if Villa had struck at some point along the Texas border, another officer might well have led the cavalry columns south. The death of a superior officer a year later cleared the way, inadvertently, of course, for a still greater opportunity.

It didn't hurt, either, that highly placed and well-dispositioned friends in Washington always stood ready to protect him against any intrigues that might threaten to unseat him. His father-in-law was still a power in the Senate, although a Democratic Administration had moved into the White House. And the chief of staff, General Scott, who had dealt with the Indians and the Moros in much the same manner as Pershing, was naturally sympathetic. General Scott, in fact, may well have saved Pershing from being permanently pigeonholed shortly after he began his pursuit of Villa.

Scott recalled in his memoirs that while Pershing was campaigning south of the border someone reported to President Wilson that "Pershing was disloyal to the administration in his remarks about the President's policies." He didn't name the talebearer, and perhaps he didn't know it; that kind of Byzantine maneuvering is generally conducted with guarantees of anonymity. Secretary of War Baker referred the matter to Scott, who asked that nothing be done until he carried out his own investigation. Baker, knowing Scott's reputation for straight dealing and better still his brother's friendship with the President, agreed to leave the matter in Scott's hands. The chief of staff said he wrote Pershing immediately, "informing him that his enemies were working against him."

General Scott said he received a "frank manly letter" from Pershing denying the charge of disloyalty, which was passed along to Baker and Wilson. The President was "satisfied," Scott said, that Pershing was perfectly loyal.

An ill-disposed chief of staff could have handled the matter differently, allowing the distant field commander to remain under suspicion. Pershing's career then would have come to a standstill, Scott believed. "Knowing Wilson as I did I am satisfied that if this matter had not been cleared up, Pershing would never have received the supreme command in France. . . ."

Luck was with Pershing, too, in his Mexican operations—luck, patience, and a sense of discretion nurtured during years of walking the tightrope of a military career, of knowing when to show initiative and when to obey the letter of his orders. One bad break could have ruined him. One flare-up of temper at a crucial moment could have wrecked the preventative purposes of the expedition. Fortunately he thoroughly understood the main objective, which was to stay out of war with Mexico . . . and if possible, and only secondarily, to capture Villa. Just as fortunately he managed to impress his subordinates that it was necessary to turn aside from opportunities for purely military success.

Hastily improvised, mounted within a week after the Columbus raid, the campaign at least had the virtue of simplicity in design. Its objective was to trap Villa between two fast-moving cavalry columns. One column headed south from Culberson's Ranch, the other farther east from Columbus, and both moved on roughly parallel lines. The best information available to the Americans indicated that Villa was holed up in the mountains above Guerrero. Pershing hoped that his cavalry columns would be able to strike fast enough to keep him pinned down there.

The east column included the 13th Cavalry, still smarting from the surprise attack on Columbus, with a congressional committee investigating the conduct of its officers; the 6th Infantry, the 16th Infantry, and Battery C of the 6th Field Artillery. In the west column, which Pershing accompanied, were the 7th Cavalry, 10th Cavalry (the Negro regiment with which he had once served), and Battery B of the 6th Field Artillery. The infantry accompanying the columns, of course, slogged away well to the rear of the mounted regiments. Later the columns were reinforced by other regiments of cavalry and infantry, other field artillery units, and hundreds of supporting troops to maintain the supply and communications lines.

Many of the young officers attached to the expedition, most of them just out of West Point, acquired fame in World War II, including three first lieutenants: George S. Patton, Jr., 8th Cavalry, who was Pershing's aide; Courtney H. Hodges, and William H. Simpson, both 6th Infantry, who were also to command armies in France. Others who later rose to military prominence were Captain Eben J. Swift, Jr., 11th Cavalry; First Lieutenant Kenyon A. Joyce, 6th Cavalry; Second Lieutenant Ralph P. Cousins, 6th Cavalry; Captain Lesley J. McNair, 4th Field Artillery; Captain U. S. Grant, III, 2nd battalion of Engineers; First Lieutenant Brehon B. Somervell, 2nd battalion of Engineers; and three young daredevils who flew with the First Aero Squadron—Carl Spaatz, Millard F. Harmon, and Ralph Royce.

The polo-playing young Lieutenant Patton attached himself to the expedition only through the exercise of a stubbornness equal to Pershing's. A brash, ruddy-faced fellow with a thirst for combat, he camped in the general's front hall for two days and proclaimed a state of siege. Every time Pershing entered or left his quarters, Patton leaped up from his chair and renewed his pleas to be taken along. Each time Pershing bluntly said "no." On the evening of the second day, Pershing wearied of brushing him aside and agreed to take him along. Patton was appointed headquarters commandant and aide-de-camp, and, haring off on adventures of his own, soon exhibited the tendencies which came to full flower when he loosed the armored forces across France in 1944.

Except for a few innovations on the ground and in the sky, the Mexican punitive force closely resembled the expedition which General Miles sent across the border thirty years before in search of Geronimo. The troopers wore khaki instead of the Old Army blue and were armed with .45 pistols instead of carbines and sabers; the commanding general traveled mostly by automobile, instead of horseback, and occasionally a rickety biplane of the First Aero Squadron circled overhead, but the real work of the expedition was accomplished by men and horses struggling over deserts and mountains, guarding against treachery and ambush, just as during the campaign of 1886. Something of the Old West stirred back to life as the columns moved south. As Colonel Toulmin wrote, "The Pershing Expedition placed its reliance on guides, cowmen of the ranges, halfbreeds, ranch bosses, adventurers who had fought either against or with Villa, gunfighters, gamblers—the remnants of the old Indian frontier. This expedition revived old ghosts—life came to the border once more. Once again the great southwest was alive with the United States army in pursuit of ruffian bands."

A surviving unit of Apache Scouts, many of whom had guided the expedition against Geronimo and were now elderly but spry and enthusiastic, were in the vanguard of the expedition. The most reliable of the lot was First Sergeant Chicken, who was serving his seventh hitch with the Army. Equally diligent were Sergeant Chow Big and his brother Corporal Monotolth. The aged Hell Yet-Suey, hereditary chief of the White Mountain Apaches, was especially good at interrogating prisoners; the Mexicans almost died of fright when he approached them, wearing dust goggles, shaking his shoulder-length hair, and baring his teeth. Otherwise, Colonel Toulmin recalled, "Hell Yet-Suey's favorite occupation was to have his picture taken with a captured belt taken from a Villista, his rifle and his trusty automatic, but when there was work to be done, Hell Yet-Suey was absent." Charley Shipp came along in his capacity of tribal judge, but sometimes overindulged in tequila or *aguardiente* and had to be thrown into the nearest available guardhouse. Also among the veterans of the Geronimo campaign were Corporals Big Sharley and B-25.

General Pershing followed his columns in something less than the style and dignity of a commanding general. He wore a campaign hat, boots and britches, a khaki shirt and tie, with a .45 automatic pistol holstered on his hip. The various newspaper and Signal Corps photographs taken of him during the campaign show a lean, fit, sunburned brigadier conferring with his officers out on the desert floor or in a foothill camp; one of the best caught him at the head of a group of horsemen crossing the turbulent ford of the Santa María River at the outset of the campaign. Mostly, however, he traveled in a sturdy Dodge touring car whose only protection against the chill night winds of the desert was isinglass curtains which could be snapped on the sides. His headquarters group was tiny, no staff officers, none of the comforts modern generals were growing accustomed to. It consisted of his aide, Lieutenant Patton; his cook, a Negro named Booker; and four enlisted men who made up the headquarters guard detail—the whole outfit traveling in four Dodges. Pershing had limited his officers to fifty pounds of personal baggage, and himself brought along only forty-eight pounds. Booker had only GI rations—corn meal, coffee, canned beef, and hardtack—to work with. Trailing along in the wake of the four Dodges were a wheezing Model T Ford, with correspondents Robert Dunn of the New York *Tribune* and Floyd Gibbons of the Chicago *Tribune* aboard, and a Hudson touring car carrying the Associated Press contingent, which broke down with a smashed axle eight miles south of the border.

For days Pershing was out of touch with his advancing troops. The Signal Corps strung wires south as rapidly as possible, but telegraphic communications often broke down. The few field radios available had a radius of only twenty-five miles. With more hope than faith, Pershing turned to the First Aero Squadron, which had been ordered to the border from San Antonio, to maintain contact with his forces through courier planes. The expedition was given "eight of the thirteen antiquated tactical planes which constituted our all in aviation," he wrote. Within a month six of the old biplanes had cracked up and the other two were out of commission. "While there were many hairbreadth escapes in Mexico," he added, "fortunately all our fliers were spared to form the nucleus of our World War aviation corps, in which they all served with distinction." Any sort of aircraft would have been invaluable for reconnaissance in that country, but the squadron had to be used as a messenger service so long as it was operative.

That first tentative use of military aviation must have discouraged even its enthusiasts, as the initial report of its operations indicated. On the flight to Casas Grandes, across the border, "one of the planes was compelled to return to Columbus, due to motor trouble. Darkness overtook the other seven planes before they reached their destination, four of them being landed at Ascensión, Mexico, and the three remaining ones . . . at as many different points." One of the three was wrecked on landing near Pearson. Of the four planes which succeeded in reaching Casas Grandes, "misfortune overtook Lieutenant T. S. Bowen . . . who, while attempting to land Airplane No. 44, was caught in a whirlwind. The plane was completely wrecked. . . ." And so it went.

At almost any point along his journey in the tracks of the west column, Pershing and his six-man headquarters, plus the two newspaper correspondents, might have been ambushed and wiped out. "Even the problem of eating was a difficult one and more than once the commander made up his mess from the hoarded supply of the newspaper correspondents who trailed with him," wrote Colonel Toulmin (*With Pershing in Mexico*). "With a canvas bucket for a washtub or a Mexican creek for a bathtub, sleeping in his clothes from day to day out in the open, acting as press censor for newspaper correspondents by correcting their copy on his knee, evading ambush and capture while travelling detached from his troops—these were some of the qualifications of a headquarters commander with the Mexican Expedition. General Pershing took great chances with his personal safety, risking ambush and capture in his efforts to control the rapidly scattering forces in the pursuit."

The country itself was an enemy, wrinkled and tawny as the skin of a dead lion, searingly hot by day, freezingly cold by night. Checkered with alkali flats, the sand and mesquite steppe of Chihuahua stretched to the faint blur of the foothills rising into the Sierra Madre to the west. Three rivers laced the Chihuahuan plain, the Río Casas Grandes, Río Santa María, and Río Carmen, which emptied into Lakes Guzmán, Santa María, and Patos. The National Railway extended from Chihuahua City to El Paso, the Kansas City, Mexico & Orient from Chihuahua City to the Texas border at San Angelo —but neither could be used under the agreement with the Carranza government. The few sizable towns on this vast, thirsty plain were also forbidden to American troops.

Pershing and his rickety motorcade reached Colonia Dublán, which he designated as field headquarters for the expedition; here the two cavalry columns were united, then split up again into three pursuing columns. By March 27 he had pressed on to Casas Grandes, where an advance base was being established, refusing even to consider staying behind at headquarters. The Villa hunters had raised a scent, the 7th Cavalry having flushed Pancho and about 500 of his followers in the vicinity of Guerrero, and Pershing wanted to be in at the kill.

He was guardedly optimistic about the prospects of catching Villa. "Our troops seem to be pressing him," he told the correspondents accompanying him, "but Villa is no fool—it may be that the campaign has just started." A red-shirted scout squatting nearby commented, "As I figure it, General, we've got Villa entirely surrounded —on one side."

Pershing hurried on southward, climbing into mountain snowstorms, finally regaining contact with his cavalry units at San Geronimo on March 30. "Great news," he told the correspondents after a dispatch rider from Colonel Dodd's 7th Cavalry galloped into camp. Dodd's 400 troopers had engaged Villa at Guerrero, captured two machine guns, killed thirty Villistas, and driven them away after a sharp fight. Villa was reported to have been wounded either in that engagement or in a skirmish with Carranzistas the night before, and was believed to be fleeing in a buggy, accompanied by only a handful of his followers. Villa's escape route, the field commanders reported, was boxed in by four different cavalry units scouring the mountains for him at Guerrero, Bachíniva, Providencia, and in the Santa María Valley. Colonel Dodd believed that he had cut the trail of Villa after a seventeen-hour, thirty-mile chase across the Continental Divide.

But Villa made good his escape, and none of his countrymen were inclined to betray his hiding place. The American forces pushed on southward, eventually penetrating about 350 miles into Mexican territory.

On April 1, at Bachíniva, Pershing and his headquarters caught up with Major Frank Tompkins and his squadron from the 13th Cavalry, the same officer who had driven Villa south from Columbus with a handful of troopers.

That evening Pershing sent for Tompkins, and the two men sat before a campfire, discussing the situation.

Finally, and rather unexpectedly, Pershing shot a question at the squadron commander, "Tompkins, where is Villa?"

The major replied, "General, I don't know, but I would mighty well like to find out where he is."

"Where would you go?"

"I would head for Parral and would expect to cut his trail before reaching there."

"Why?" Pershing demanded.

"The history of Villa's bandit days shows that when hard pressed he invariably holes up in the mountains in the vicinity of Parral. He has friends in that region."

Major Tompkins, seeing that Pershing was in a receptive mood, perhaps because the general was growing depressed over the fact that Villa had managed to elude all the traps set for him in more than two weeks of hard campaigning, and the longer the campaign lasted the fewer were its chances of success, ventured a project of his own. He suggested that his squadron, given a few mules for transport, could "move with greater speed and less effort" than some of the larger commands and that "its very size might tempt the Villistas to give battle when with a larger force they would avoid any such issues."

"How many mules would you want?" Pershing asked.

"Twelve," Tompkins replied.

Pershing dropped the subject, but Tompkins had a hunch he would bring it up again after thinking it over.

At noon the next day Pershing called him back. "Go find Villa wherever you think he is," he told Tompkins, without wasting a word. He gave Tompkins twelve pack mules from the 11th Cavalry, which had just joined the expedition, in addition to 500 silver pesos, five days' rations, and his blessings. Less than two hours later Tompkins's squadron moved out.

On April 4, Pershing passed along the telegraphed commendation of General Scott to his command, but added a characteristic footnote of his own: "All officers and enlisted men . . . are cautioned against a feeling of overconfidence as to the final result to be achieved by this expedition."

Pershing's reservations were well founded. The deeper they penetrated into Mexico the more hostility they met from Villa sympathizers and Carranzistas alike, which could only have been expected. The same feeling would have resulted during the American Civil War, had a foreign power invaded the United States, no matter what idealistic and peacemaking intentions it expressed.

Pershing, according to the New York *Tribune* correspondent Robert Dunn, realized that "Carranza would tie up with Villa. . . . And Pershing took it on the chin. He never got a break. I shaved in his mirror, watched him work, but no word, act, mien of his gave away the gyp."

By this time other correspondents were catching up with the advance elements of the punitive force, and word was getting back to the States that the results of the expedition thus far were anything but glorious. Among the newcomers was Damon Runyon, representing the International News Service, who wrote that "Villa has disappeared in a way which, considering the relentlessness of the American pursuit, seems mysterious. The Americans have not encountered any natives who will even admit they have seen Villa."

Pershing stayed at Bachíniva, waiting to hear the results of Major Tompkins's probing operation toward Parral. Ten days later the news came—and it wasn't good. Tompkins and his undersized squadron of two troops entered the town of Parral on April 12. The Carranzista commandant, General Lozano, angrily told Tompkins that the Americans had no right to be there. The populace echoed his sentiments by jeering at the Americans and hurling stones and refuse at them. Under orders from Tompkins, the troopers kept their guns holstered and tried to ignore the demonstration. Tompkins agreed to take his command outside the town to a campsite selected by General Lozano.

As Tompkins's troopers withdrew from the town, the pack train at their rear was fired upon. At the campsite near the railroad tracks the squadron took up defensive positions while several hundred Mexicans, many of them in uniform, massed on a hill to the south. General Lozano sent word that he could control neither his own soldiers nor the townspeople, and the Americans had better leave the vicinity. Major Tompkins, maintaining admirable discipline of himself and his men, decided to withdraw down the wagon road to Santa Cruz de Villegas. Still not satisfied, the Carranzistas tried to cut off the American retreat, upon which Tompkins detailed a rear guard of eight troopers to keep the Mexicans at a safe distance. He could have scattered them any time he wanted to, but recognized that bringing on a battle might have serious consequences for the whole expedition. Two Americans were killed and six wounded as they withdrew under the galling fire, but the tiny rear guard took a toll of forty to fifty Mexican lives as it protected the retreat. The Mexicans followed them for fifteen miles down the road before returning to Parral.

Pershing, according to the correspondents accompanying him, was enraged when he heard the news of how Tompkins's squadron had been greeted at Parral. "Off flew the censor lid," Robert Dunn recalled. "'Nothing, now, should be kept from the public. You can go the limit,' Pershing told us. And when I called the Parral trap 'an ambuscade,' Pershing leaned over my machine on the running board to write in 'treachery.'"

Somewhat annoyed at Pershing's collaboration, Dunn wrote, "Army in full retreat to Salt Lake City. Pershing declares Allegheny Mountains must be defended at any cost."

"How's this, sir?" he asked the general.

Pershing was not amused, Dunn said, and "he only shook his head and walked away when just a chuckle, to my mind, would have made him a great man."

Pershing, however, had every reason to be unappreciative of journalistic humor that day. A fuller report on the Parral affair showed that Tompkins and his command had been given assurances by Carranza officials that they would be welcome in the town and that they had thus been deliberately lured into a trap.

Back in the States people were beginning to realize that what had been a pursuit after an outlaw and his band now was taking the form of an invasion. "Our fast and loose diplomacy with the Carranza government," observed the New York *Tribune*, "sent an undersized American force into Mexico without clear guarantees of friendly assistance." The War Department had no choice but to reinforce Pershing with the 5th Cavalry, the 17th Infantry, and a battalion of the 4th Field Artillery.

Meanwhile, supplying the forces in the field was an increasingly serious problem. At Columbus, the rear base, food, equipment, and ammunition were piling up along the railroad tracks in mountainous stacks while the regiments south of the border were barely subsisting. The Quartermaster Department broke down completely; long freight trains arrived in Columbus with no bills of lading to indicate their contents, which had to be unloaded and sorted out at the trackside. But the real job was getting those supplies south of the border and over the straggling wagon roads and mountain trails along the supply line through Colonia Dublán, Casas Grandes, Galeana, Las Cruces, to the forward base at Namiquipa. Truck convoys of Jeffrey Quads and White one-and-a-half ton trucks were organized, along with mule trains. The truck companies were operated by American civilians under the supervision of army officers. Each convoy carried mechanics to repair breakdowns. After weeks of improvisation, trial and error, the convoy system began to work with a fair degree of efficiency. Meanwhile, the First Aero Squadron had been reorganized and had received new equipment to operate a courier service between Columbus and Pershing's headquarters at Namiquipa. Washington was getting so worried about a deeper and more treacherous involvement in Mexican affairs, particularly after the Parral action, that it wanted to be able to keep in the closest communication with Pershing.

During the last weeks of April, Pershing's columns had several sharp encounters with Villa's bands. The 7th Cavalry, at the Verde River and at Tomachie, killed a number of guerrillas in brief engagements. Since Villa's bands were now operating separately and in widely scattered places, Pershing decided to organize his forces into five different district commands—a system similar to that used by the British Army in India to maintain control of its frontier provinces. He outlined his plan as follows in a general order issued April 29:

"As the result of the arduous and persistent pursuit of Villa by various columns of this command, his forces have suffered losses of approximately one hundred killed with unknown number wounded, and have been broken into smaller bands and scattered to different sections of the State of Chihuahua and elsewhere. The situation has changed to the extent that our troops no longer pursue a cohesive force of considerable size, but by surprise with small, swiftly moving detachments they must hunt down isolated bands, now under subordinate leaders, and operating over widely separated portions of the country. For this purpose the country to be covered for the present is accordingly divided into districts and apportioned to organizations available for such duty."

Each district was to enlist agents and "establish as far as possible its own service of information." Pershing emphasized that "this expedition is operating within the limits of a friendly nation, whose peaceful inhabitants should be treated with every consideration." But he also warned that "experience so far has taught, however, that our troops are always in more or less danger of being attacked, not only by hostile followers of Villa, but even by others who profess friendship, and precaution must be taken accordingly. In case of unprovoked attack, the officer in command will, without hesitation, take the most vigorous measures at his disposal, to administer severe punishment to the offenders, bearing in mind that any other course is likely to be construed as a confession of weakness."

The districts, their troops and commanders, were Namiquipa, 10th Cavalry, Major Evans; Guerrero, 7th Cavalry, Colonel Dodd; Bustillos, 13th Cavalry, Colonel Slocum; Satevó, 5th Cavalry, Colonel Wilder; and San Borja, 11th Cavalry, Colonel Lockett.

Before the district plan could be put into effect, two officials of the town of Cusi came to Pershing's headquarters the evening of May 4 with the news that two of Villa's lieutenants, Acosta and Dominguez, had appeared there with 120 of their followers. The citizens of Cusi wanted protection. A small Carranza garrison in the vicinity, they feared, wouldn't be able to give it to them. Pershing immediately dispatched a provisional squadron of six mounted troops and a machine-gun troop under Major Robert L. Howze.

The squadron arrived at Cusi shortly after midnight and learned that the Villistas had skirmished with the Carranzistas, then retired to the Ojos Azules Ranch for the night. The Carranzistas, regarding their troubles with the Villista band as part of a family quarrel, declined to furnish guides to the ranch. It was six o'clock in the morning, May 5, before the American squadron found the place.

The Apache Scouts, led by First Sergeant Chicken, fanned out ahead of the mounted troops and found Villistas swarming all around the ranch, many of them on top of the buildings, others behind a stone wall on a hilltop to the left.

Howze's troopers charged in, firing their automatic pistols. "Troop A dashed through the ranch under fire from the men on the rooftop," wrote Lieutenant M. S. Williams, "and catching up with the last of the Mexicans commenced a pistol fight which lasted several minutes and resulted in the death of five or six of the enemy. The formation of the attack was with the troop in column of fours, deployment being impossible under the circumstances." The squadron chased the Villistas off the ranch after forty-four were killed, with no casualties among the Americans. "Damn fine fight!" was First Sergeant Chicken's comment.

In the border town of Juárez, Generals Scott and Funston were conferring with two of the leading Carranza generals, Obregón and Trevino, the former being Minister of War. Carranza's representatives demanded the withdrawal of Pershing's forces, claiming that Villa was dead and the purpose of the expedition had been achieved. Meanwhile United States intelligence officers were trying to assess reports that the Carranza regime, encouraged by German agents, was preparing to throw a large force between Pershing and the border to cut his line of communications and then destroy him.

On May 8, Scott and Funston reported to Washington that they believed the Carranza proposals were "redolent with bad faith, that Mexicans are convinced that they are not able to carry out the agreement [to prevent border raids after the American withdrawal] even if ratified and they desire to keep the United States troops quiet until Mexican troops are in position to drive them out of Mexico by force." The meeting at Juárez ended without an agreement.

Washington feared that no matter how circumspectly Pershing and his troops conducted themselves they would become involved in an all-out war hundreds of miles from their nearest American bases. The remaining regiments of the Regular Army—the 3rd, 14th, 21st, and 30th Infantry and the 5th Field Artillery—were sent to the border and the National Guards of Arizona, Texas, and New Mexico were federalized to take over the job of patrolling the international boundary. Calling out the National Guard—a total of 150,000 troops—apparently convinced the Carranza government that it could not afford to attack Pershing, except in isolated actions and ambushes.

A monumental sense of frustration pervaded Pershing's headquarters. All hopes of anything like a success had vanished. There was no chance of capturing Villa so long as every hot pursuit was blocked by Carranza's troops and no Mexican, however opposed to the Villistas' freebooting methods, dared to give information to the Americans without inviting reprisals from his neighbors. About all that Pershing's district intelligence officers could reap was a crop of wild rumors. An American newspaper took sarcastic note of the conflicting reports out of the Mexican interior: "Since General Pershing was sent out to capture him, Villa has been mortally wounded in the leg and died in a lonely cave. He was assassinated by one of his own band and his grave was identified by a Carranza follower who hoped for a suitable reward from President Wilson. Villa was likewise killed in a brawl at a ranch house where he was engaged in the gentle diversion of burning men and women at the stake. He was also shot on a wild ride and his body cremated. Yet through all these experiences which, it must be confessed, would have impaired the health of any ordinary man, Villa has not only retained the vital spark of life but has renewed his youth and strength. He seems all the better for his vacation, strenuous though it must have been."

Pershing was so eager for definitive information about Villa and several of his leading henchmen still at large, particularly Generals López and Cárdenas, the latter the commander of Villa's bodyguard (the "Dorados"), that he yielded to the pleas of Lieutenant Patton to be turned loose on the hunt. Ostensibly on a corn-buying expedition, Patton, with an interpreter and six privates, drove to the village of Las Ciénagas. General Cárdenas's uncle owned a *hacienda* nearby. Patton and his men parked their Dodges a mile from the ranch house, approached stealthily on foot, and surrounded the place. On sighting the Americans, three horsemen rode out with their pistols blazing away. Patton, a crack shot, killed two of them—one of whom was General Cárdenas—and his troopers accounted for the other one. A showman even then, Patton rode back to camp with the dead Mexicans draped over his fenders like slaughtered deer. After that, Patton wrote his wife, Pershing called him "The Bandit." Apparently Pershing was somewhat dismayed by his aide's zeal, for Patton wrote that "there is another bandit here that I wanted to take a try at, but he would not let me."

As summer came to the plains and mountains of Chihuahua, Mexican and American tempers rose accordingly. Carranzista troops began occupying positions along their railroads which threatened the American line of communications. In the vicinity of Ahumada, 10,000 government troops were reported to have been concentrated for an attack, while thousands of others were said to be moving up from the south to Chihuahua City. Messages of Carranzista officers between Ahumada and Casas Grandes were intercepted and found to bear out the suspicion that Carranza was about to declare war.

Then General Trevino, commanding at Chihuahua City, telegraphed Pershing that his government had ordered him to "prevent, by the use of arms, new invasions of my country by American forces and also to prevent the American forces that are in this State from moving to the south, east or west of the places they now occupy. . . . Your forces will be attacked by the Mexican forces if these indications are not heeded."

Pershing fired back his answer the same day: "In reply you are informed that my Government has placed no such restrictions upon the movements of American forces. I shall therefore use my own judgment as to when and in what direction I shall move my forces in pursuit of bandits or in seeking information regarding bandits. If under these circumstances the Mexican forces attack any of my columns the responsibilities will lie with the Mexican government."

The same day the Mexican commander at Casas Grandes warned Pershing not to move his forces in "any direction but north," to which Pershing replied, "I do not take orders except from my own government."

On the following day, June 17, Pershing ordered a reconnaissance of the Ahumada district to determine the strength of the Mexican troops concentrating there—an operation which culminated in the most humiliating defeat suffered by the American forces during the campaign.

Troop C, under Captain Charles D. Boyd, and Troop K, under Captain Lewis S. Morey, both of the 10th Cavalry, were ordered to scout toward Ahumada without bringing on a battle with the Carranzista forces if it could be avoided. Reaching the outskirts of Carrizal early June 20, they asked permission of the town commandant, General Gómez, to pass through on their way to Ahumada. Permission was denied, but Captain Boyd, who was the senior of the two troop commanders, decided to force his way through the town, although Captain Morey protested that they would be exceeding their orders. The Americans, too, were heavily outnumbered, ninety troopers to 400 Carranzistas, and the latter had set up four machine guns and taken up a strong position in a deep irrigation ditch.

When the Mexicans opened fire at long range (as the Americans claimed), Captain Boyd attacked, deploying his men in a dismounted skirmish line which was flanked by the Mexican positions and which had to cross more than 600 yards of flat sandy plain. Captain Morey's troop was supposed to support the attack but was pinned down by machine-gun fire and stayed where it was. Stupid as it was, Captain Boyd's attack at least had the virtue of enthusiasm; somehow his troopers kept going through the cross fire and the ripping swaths of the Mexican machine guns and drove the Carranzistas out of the ditch. The survivors of that charge, however, couldn't hold the position and had to retreat. Captain Boyd and seven others were killed, four were wounded, and eight were taken prisoner. With Captain Morey severely wounded, Troop K also withdrew in disorder, leaving four dead and fifteen prisoners. Pershing had to send out a detachment of the 11th

Cavalry to search the vicinity and bring in wounded and wandering survivors. The twenty-three prisoners and captured American equipment were later turned over at El Paso by the Carranza government under strong pressure from the State Department.

The battle of Carrizal could have been the beginning of an all-out war. Instead, both sides backed away from stepping up hostilities, and the diplomats, who had performed so wretchedly to date, took over the job of finding a way out of the ridiculous dilemma. The United States had no alternative but to pull out, yet had to save face in the process. Mexico faced only a ruinous defeat if it tried to hasten that process unduly and forcibly. The two countries decided to appoint commissioners who would decide how the United States should evacuate.

Meanwhile, Pershing concentrated his forces at Colonia Dublán, far north of the deepest penetrations of his cavalry columns. His troops settled down in camps swept by sandstorms and poorly protected against the desert sun, and here they spent more than six months while the diplomats conducted their interminable discussions. Pershing kept his men busy with drills, maneuvers, and route marches, in the prescribed but unimaginative military tradition. At any rate, they kept healthy, and the general was able to boast to an Associated Press correspondent that his punitive force had suffered only six deaths from disease in five months of campaigning, "a remarkable record for an expedition serving in this sort of country with nothing but field equipment."

Pershing kept himself busy and in good spirits and told correspondent Junius B. Wood that "roughing it has added ten years to my life." Wood wrote that Pershing, who was "easier to approach than many of his younger subordinates," had "smoked his first cigar in eight years," and "after that a box appeared in his tent and the general was smoking again."

Correspondent Wood said Pershing was a tireless worker. "A light may burn in his tent until early morning, while he sits alone reading over reports and planning moves for future days. He may be up at daylight, walking through the sleeping camp and observing with his own eyes. He believes in keeping men busy—officers and privates. 'Don't let them stagnate,' he says. 'If they get out of the habit of working they won't be in condition when they are needed. Idleness has ruined more armies than battles have.'"

The newspaperman marveled at his grasp of detail. He mentioned a camp rumor that fifty horses had been killed by lightning. "That's not quite correct," Pershing said. "Five were killed, one stricken blind and twelve were stunned."

He kept a tight hold on discipline as his regiments suffered through the summer, the fall, and finally the early winter months of 1916–17. "There was no chance to get away from each other and indulge in social relaxation away from the command, so necessary in a soldier's life," wrote Colonel Tompkins. "These men were uncomfortable all the time. In spite of their best efforts, they could not escape the dirt of the dust storms and the swarms of flies." A Christmas barbecue was planned but a storm blew up and "very few men ate at all for twenty-four hours." And as Colonel Tompkins noted, "The slogan 'Villa, dead or alive' was heard no more in Mexico." No doubt Pershing and most of his men would have echoed the sentiments of the New York *Herald:* "Through no fault of his own the 'Pershing punitive expedition' has become as much a farce from the American standpoint as it is an eyesore to the Mexican people. Each day adds to the burden of its cost to the American people and to the ignominy of its position. General Pershing and his command should be recalled without further delay."

Pershing's reputation, if anything, was sounder than ever, despite the disappointments and frustrations of the Mexican campaign. He was promoted to major general in September, and for once there were no public expressions of dismay or insinuations of political influence. "If there is any officer in the army who deserves the honor as much as Pershing," said the New York *Sun,* "we don't know who it is." The Chief of Staff, General Scott, believed that during the Mexican campaign Pershing "made a complete success in the accomplishment of his orders from the War Department." The judgment of history, too, has been almost entirely favorable. Colonel William A. Ganoe, in his authoritative *History of the United States Army,* wrote that "General Pershing's task through this whole campaign was, to speak mildly, awkward. He had to advance with little transportation through the most trying part of a tensely hostile country. He was allowed to attack one party but not the other, while both were equally antagonistic. He was in the position of the man who had to walk into a hungry leopard's cage with orders to beat Mr. Leopard, but under no conditions resist Mrs. Leopard with her cubs. With such a mission, who could have done better?"

Negotiations finally were completed for the American evacuation, which began January 30, 1917. On February 5, the last American troops crossed the border to their own soil. Pershing himself was greeted in El Paso with a parade, a formal banquet, and the presentation of a silver service.

A New York *Globe* cartoon, which apparently amused Pershing and which he clipped for his scrapbook, saluted his return by showing the general hauling an empty cage back from Mexico which was labeled, "For Villa—Dead or Alive."

As for Pancho Villa himself, that rambunctious fellow was stirring back to life even before the American withdrawal. General Pershing had reported, weeks before leaving Colonia Dublán, that Villa was "working south with approximately 1,000 men" and that he was requisitioning horses and cattle in the Santa Clara Valley, preparatory to new forays. (He never again appeared north of the United States boundary, however.) In mid-December of 1916, Villa granted an interview to T. F. Mortensen of the New York *World* in which he boasted about the American troops soon to be evacuated: "I will drive them out or make them fight, and after they are gone I will make a gap between the two countries so wide and deep that no Americans will ever be able to steal Mexican land, gold or oil." On the Columbus raid, he remarked, "I was awake; they were asleep—and it took them too long to wake up."

Whatever the depth of his antagonism toward the United States, whatever his troublemaking owed to the encouragement of German agents, Villa was quite unwittingly the benefactor of the American Army which had chased him through his own country like a skulking fugitive and killed many of his most trusted lieutenants.

His raid on Columbus, and all that followed, as it turned out, was a signal blessing to this country, which two months after the withdrawal from Mexico entered the European war. It awakened the government and the people to the fact that the country was ill prepared for any sort of military action. The unexpected demands of the campaigning in Mexico indicated the need for mobilizing both our man power and our war industries and conditioned the public to the regimentation found necessary when the United States joined the Allies in Europe.

The expedition into Chihuahua was a rigorous field test for almost the entire Regular Army as well as 150,000 National Guardsmen. Without that experience the first divisions sent to France could hardly have performed as well as they did. Even more importantly the Mexican campaign exposed certain serious flaws in the structure of our military establishment. The response of volunteers for the Regular Army had been smaller than expected and pointed to the urgent necessity of a selective service program.

General Scott reported that "recruiting is found so difficult that many of the [National Guard] units have not yet, over three months after the call, been raised to even minimum peace strength. . . . The failure should make the whole people realize that the volunteer muster does not and probably will not give us either the men we need for training in peace or for service in war. In my judgment the country will never be prepared for defense until we do as other great nations do that have large interests to guard, like Germany, Japan, and France, where everybody is ready and does perform military service in time of peace as he would pay any other tax."

The chase after Villa, which eventually called upon the service of almost 10,000 troops in the field against one guerrilla leader and less than a thousand of his followers, also demonstrated many flaws in the composition of the Regular Army. Cavalrymen armed with automatic pistols could no longer be considered the decisive arm in combat, as the war in Europe had shown even more effectively. The insufficiency of our Air Force, which was unable to keep more than a few planes aloft at any time during the campaign, was something to give pause to even the most earthbound generals. In the spring of 1916, while our few planes were carrying dispatches between Columbus and Namiquipa, Great Britain's Royal Flying Corps was employing seventy squadrons on the western front—and the British, French, and German air forces were fighting immense battles in the sky, dropping bombs and strafing trenches, not carrying messages. That summer, while German machine guns were slaughtering thousands around the battered forts of Verdun and along the Somme, the American Table of Organization and Equipment provided for exactly four machine guns to an infantry regiment, and most of them were obsolescent foreign models, no great improvement over the old Gatling guns. The field artillery hardly fired a shot in Mexico, which was just as well, considering the shortage of guns and ammunition. European artillery, meanwhile, was being employed to the extent that a barrage on the western front cost millions of dollars.

In the field of logistics, too, there were striking deficiencies. Obviously motor transport would have to replace the old mule trains which had followed American troops into battle for the preceding half century.

The Quartermaster Department needed a good shaking up after piling mountains of unsorted supplies at Columbus while the men in the field were close to starvation, and the railroads had creaked at the joints when called upon to move whole regiments to the border.

Thanks to Pancho Villa and the dress rehearsal afforded by the Mexican campaign, some realization of American unreadiness was impressed upon the nation and its political and military leaders, not really in time to effect a state of preparedness but time enough to start the job of overhauling, reorganizing, and reinforcing. Without Villa, the American achievements overseas in 1917–18 would probably have been negligible.

Just two weeks after the punitive expedition had cleared out of Mexico, on February 19, 1917, Major General Frederick Funston died of a heart attack, and General Pershing replaced him in command of the Southern Department. Had his heart been stronger, General Funston, with his seniority, his fame as the captor of Aguinaldo, and his record as a fighting general, might well have taken command of the American Expeditionary Force to France. Fate removed him just in time to make way for Pershing.

PART TWO

SOLDIER
ON THE WESTERN FRONT

7. A "Token Force" for France

If there was one word which distilled the hopes of the American people before World War I, it was "progress." Given time, they believed, their leaders would be able to abolish most of the ills which had afflicted mankind since its history was first recorded. Scientific progress would wipe out disease, economic progress would end poverty, progressing civilization would prevent war. It was the generation which regarded *Pollyanna* as the epitome of dramatic art, which esteemed Harold Bell Wright as a literary giant, which believed in the visibility and solidity of the American Dream. In that "age of innocence," people had an almost mystical faith in everything the Twentieth Century would bestow upon them.

When the century was only fourteen years old, however, the assassination of the Austrian archduke was used as an excuse to settle old rivalries—and all those comfortable Edwardian illusions, all that faith in progress, were shattered in one mighty flash of cannon lined up wheel to wheel across Europe. What had happened to the fervent pledges of statesmen that all disputes would be settled before the World Court at The Hague before they reached the flash point of war? They'd evaporated in the threats and recriminations, the demands and counterdemands, the quick step of mobilization that briefly preceded the outbreak of fighting from Flanders to the Masurian Lakes. Obviously the great powers had only been waiting for an excuse to settle their differences, not through arbitration, but by force and aggression.

In America, at first, people were united in a desire for peace, for isolation from Europe's tribal frenzies. Let the war stay 3000 miles across the sea. America would devote herself to trying to end it, to feed the starving children, to plead the cause of humanity. The most idealistic of nations, with its most idealistic President in the White House, wanted nothing for itself but the satisfaction of bringing peace to the world.

Then, slowly, American opinion began to veer in favor of the Allies. Not so much because of what they stood for, and certainly not because of their alliance with czarist Russia, but because of the image of German frightfulness which was becoming sharper and clearer with every passing month of the war. It was an image with many facets: the invasion of neutral Belgium and the partial destruction of Louvain in 1914; the sinking of the *Lusitania,* the use of poison gas, and the execution of Nurse Edith Cavell in 1915; the furious power of the German attacks on Verdun in 1916; and the proclamation of unrestricted submarine warfare early in 1917. Partly through the cunning of Allied propaganda, the poilu and the tommy assumed an heroic aspect, while the German soldier became a brute, a Hun, a throwback to Genghis Khan. Less and less credence was placed in the clamor of the Hearst press that efforts were being made to suck the United States into the war to protect the French and British interests of J. P. Morgan and the financial moguls. Even in the Middle West—the bulwark of the isolationists—sentiment began to turn toward intervention, not for any material advantage or territorial acquisitions which might result from joining the Allies, but to "beat the Kaiser" and those cold-eyed German "war lords" under their death's-head shakos, to "get it over with."

But it takes fear as well as angry passion to drive a people to war. What really propelled American sentiment toward intervention was the apprehension that Germany, once it had defeated the Allies, would turn its ferocious attention on the United States for having been less neutral toward France and Britain than toward the Central Powers. This fear, largely the creation of Allied propagandists, was given a tremendous stimulus by a German blunder which turned out to be fatal. Large numbers of Americans were convinced of Germany's bellicose designs when a coded message from the German Foreign Minister to his legation in Mexico—the famous Zimmermann note—was intercepted by the British. "If this attempt [at keeping the United States neutral] is not successful, we propose an alliance on the following basis with Mexico: that we shall make war together and together make peace. We shall give generous financial support, and it is understood that Mexico is to reconquer the lost territory in New Mexico, Texas, and Arizona. . . ."

The State Department confirmed the contents of the decoded Zimmermann message on March 1. For the next month the war drums sounded from press, pulpit, and every public platform with a quickening beat. None were more urgent in demanding that America go to war than the ministers of God. The New York Federation of Churches proclaimed March 11 "War Sunday." From coast to coast, militant preachers denied that Christ was a pacifist, that war was evil, that killing Germans was any violation of the Commandments. The evangelist Billy Sunday, addressing a throng in Times Square, was only phrasing their thoughts more vividly when he shouted, "If hell could be turned upside down, you would find stamped on its bottom, 'Made in Germany'!"

One of the more violent advocates of war was former President Theodore Roosevelt, who declared, "It has been a war of murder upon us! There is no question about 'going to war.' Germany is already at war with us." Newspaper editorials echoed him throughout the country. "Declare war!" demanded the New York *Tribune*. Other newspapers only picked up the refrain in lengthier and more sonorous phrases.

And still Wilson hesitated. At his second inaugural on March 5, he expressed the hope that "the shadows that now lie dark upon our path will soon be dispelled and we shall walk with the light all about us if we be but true to ourselves. . . ." He was drowned out by the marchers in war parades, by mob action against pacifist organizations, by ranting orators on every street corner.

Finally, on the evening of April 2, President Wilson appeared before Congress to declare that "we shall fight for the things which we have always carried nearest our hearts" and asked that body to "formally accept the status of belligerent which has been forced upon us." Congress cheered. On his ride back to the White House, the people cheered from the sidewalks along Pennsylvania Avenue. The capital throbbed with a febrile rejoicing. But there was no echo of this jubilation in the mind and heart of the President. "Think what it was they were applauding," he told his secretary. "My message today was a message of death for our young men."

Four days later, war was declared.

On May 7, Major General John J. Pershing, commanding the Southern Department with headquarters at San Antonio, was summoned to Washington by the War Department. For a month and a day the United States had been officially at war with the Central Powers. A commander was soon to be chosen for the first American troops to be sent abroad. Furthermore, Pershing's father-in-law, Senator Francis Warren, had telegraphed him a somewhat cryptic query several days before on whether he spoke French, to which Pershing could only reply that he did, somewhat, having grappled with the language at West Point without signal success and having resumed his study during a visit to France in 1908. Putting the query, the summons, and the need for an Expeditionary Force commander together, Pershing was justified in concluding that he would soon be going abroad with new and greater responsibilities.

That day he began keeping a diary which, unlike other journals abandoned after a few days or a few weeks of random observations, covered every day of his life for the next several years. Typewritten and contained in large loose-leaf notebooks, it was a careful record of the people he saw each day, the places he visited, some of the things he said and those said to him. Hardly a twinge of self-pity, only an occasional essay in self-justification, rippled across the dispassionate surface of those thousands of pages. Rarely a quiver of emotion of any kind—except an occasional flash of anger—was contained in that long record. The most momentous days of his career were related with barely a flutter of elation. For all the sense of grandeur or misery it conveys, the Pershing war diary might well have been the journal of some obscure quartermaster. As a diarist he was as grimly reticent as Pershing the commander in chief, close-mouthed and poker-faced in a wartime Paris known to be crawling with spies, agents, and political tattletales. He could no more have bared his emotional life on paper than he could have shouted out military secrets in the Place de la Concorde.

On his journey to Washington he recorded only that he left San Antonio at 11:30 P.M. on May 7 and arrived in the capital on May 10 at 8:30 A.M.

Two hours after his arrival in Washington he was named commanding general of whatever forces were to be sent to France and, in effect, was handed the greatest responsibility of any American officer since General Grant was summoned by President Lincoln in the spring of 1864.

Pershing, however, was able to describe the events of that day in little more than a hundred words: "May 10, 1917—Occupied General George B. Davis' apartment at the Connecticut. Reported to the Secretary of War at about 10:30 A.M. Was informed by the Secretary of War that I was to command the American troops in France; and that I should be prepared to leave for France as soon as possible. In the afternoon had a conference with the Secretary of War, with the Chief of Staff, General Scott, with the Assistant Chief of Staff, General Bliss, and the President of the War College, General Kuhn. Reports relative to the meetings held with French and British officers of the two missions then in America were gone over. Remained at the War Department until about 6:30 P.M."

It was soon apparent to Pershing and his fellow generals that Wilson, the most reluctant of war Presidents, would leave the military details to his experts. The whole aim of his Administration had been to avoid any gestures which might seriously impair neutrality, though its general bias was toward the Allies. In 1916 he had campaigned successfully on the reminder that "he kept us out of war." He had labored endlessly to bring about a negotiated peace during the period when it appeared that the opposing forces were so evenly matched that the war would end in a stalemate. The possibility that the deadlock could be broken arose when the Russian Czar was overthrown; now the Russian armies were falling back and revolting against continuance of the fighting, and German forces would be freed for decisive action on the western front. No longer did the chance for negotiation exist.

President Wilson, finally taking the plunge on the grounds that "the world must be made safe for democracy," had so evident a distaste for military matters, for the mechanics of organizing and operating an Army in the field, that his generals were assured that they would be allowed to work out the problems of confronting a near-victorious Germany without much interference from the White House.

In the month following the declaration of war, it was decided that at least "token" forces were to be sent to Europe, as well as money, supplies, and naval assistance in combating the German submarines. The debate over who was to command the ground forces was brief. General Funston died six weeks before. Most of the Army's senior generals—including Scott and Bliss—were close to retirement. Major

General Leonard Wood, on the other hand, possessed many qualifications: he was an able and magnetic military leader, had performed great service in organizing the Plattsburg officers' training camp, and had acquired more national prestige than any of the eligible generals. But he was also politically ambitious, worse yet (from the Administration's viewpoint) was a Republican and a close collaborator of Theodore Roosevelt's. He could neither keep his mouth shut nor his pen still. He had referred to the "spineless rabbit" in the White House —and the epithet had rankled in Wilson, who was neither spineless nor rabbity, nor incapable of keeping his detractors in their place.

That left Pershing, who could keep his mouth shut and who had proved that he could maintain a respectable state of subordination even when called upon to execute orders such as wrecked whatever chances of success existed for the Mexican expedition. Generals Scott and Bliss both favored him, as did Secretary of War Baker, and President Wilson at least had nothing against him. So Pershing was selected for the command which, it was first thought, would consist of a division of infantry—and which eventually became forty-one divisions, 2,086,000 men, and the gigantic machinery of transport and supply required to usher them into battle.

The question of "how soon and how much" actual fighting assistance the United States would be able to give the Allies on the western front was soon to arise and would be an increasing vexation to General Pershing in the months ahead, since the ignorant and the impatient assumed that mighty America would throw huge forces against the Germans within weeks after entering the war. Little attention was paid President Wilson's statement that the Navy would go into action immediately, having a formidable fleet in being, but that building an army from scratch would take time. As Marshal Ferdinand Foch, the future Allied generalissimo, said, "It was a question of putting on a war footing a country of over a hundred million inhabitants. Everything had to be created. The regular army, maintained on a scale sufficient for the narrow requirements of peacetime, could only furnish a small fraction of what was necessary for the mobilization of the numerous divisions which America had decided to raise. These had to be constructed from the ground up—their staffs, their officers and noncommissioned officers, their troops, as well as the large supply of matériel without which nothing can be done in modern war. An entirely new instrument had to be forged. And not only was it necessary to forge on a vast scale but to forge quickly. The war had been going on for three years; no one can doubt that its very amplitude and intensity rendered its continuance for any great length of time impossible; if America was to make her weight felt in the final decision, she must hurry her forces to Europe with the utmost speed."

Pershing moved into Room 223 in the War Department, across the hall from Scott's and Bliss's offices, and began assembling a staff with which he would take command of the American Expeditionary Force. He was given only eighteen days in Washington during which to familiarize himself with the situation and organize a Headquarters to accompany him to France. Every hour of the normal working day, and much of the night, was crammed with conferences, interviews, and staff meetings. He met Baker and Wilson for the first time. He conferred with staff officers concerned with supplying the A.E.F., whatever size and shape it assumed. He acquainted himself with the views of the French and British missions—the French headed by their former commander in chief, Marshal Joffre, a sleepy old fellow with a mellow disposition and a rather appealing simplicity of manner, the British by General Tom Bridges and Arthur Balfour.

Chief of Staff Scott and his deputy, General Bliss, both of whom reached retirement age later that year, tried to keep Pershing advised of the shifting, often opposed sentiments of the two missions. The French and British were unanimous on the necessity of increasing aid, human and material, but they let their requirements be known gradually as though fearful that their new ally might decide the venture was too costly and withdraw in dismay. Even before Pershing left American shores, the French and British, according to General Bliss's diary, were proposing that American troops be sent abroad as soon as shipping was available, that they forego Stateside training and "join and co-operate with" the Allied armies. The Allies, in brief, were hinting already that what they really wanted was not an American Army, but American troops who would serve as replacements for the battle-thinned Allied divisions.

General Bliss then and later wavered toward the Anglo-French views. On May 4 he wrote General Scott a memorandum stating that "if we want to get into the war with both feet at the earliest possible date, the only way to do it is to follow the recommendations of the two Missions." He also suggested that "all but a small part of our regular army and National Guard and the first 500,000 men" be sent to Europe as quickly as they could be organized, clothed, and transported.

From the beginning, Pershing opposed any such fragmentation of American forces, and perhaps his greatest service as the commander in chief was his unyielding insistence that our divisions fight under their own flag and command. He did not propose to be left in token command of a shadow army, gracefully filling a ceremonial role while foreign generals fought the war with his troops.

Three weeks later when he took over for Scott, who had been dispatched with Elihu Root's mission to persuade the Kerensky regime to keep Russia in the war, Bliss grew somewhat disillusioned with the Allies' maneuverings and informed Secretary of War Baker: "It was not long before they [the French and British missions] said quite openly that we would not feel that we were in the war until we were 'well blooded'; that what we needed was to have a large casualty list telegraphed home and that that would stir our fighting blood. . . . When the war is over it may be a literal fact that the American flag may not have appeared anywhere on the line because our organizations will simply be parts of battalions and regiments of the Entente Allies. We might have a million men there and no American commander." The Allied missionaries, he now observed, no longer talked of "token" American forces to show themselves abroad just for the "moral effect."

Pershing, meanwhile, was pondering the vital question of whom to appoint as his chief of staff. Frederick Palmer, the veteran war correspondent who was to become chief censor on the A.E.F. staff, noted that "there was some concern lest Pershing should give the big plum to a certain classmate who had notably enjoyed his personal friendship." Instead, Pershing was seriously considering a man he knew only slightly, an obscure major then on duty at the War College. His name was James G. Harbord. The two men had met a number of times on shipboard, coming from or going to the Philippines, and in the Islands, but they had never been closely associated. Harbord himself held little hope of a choice assignment for several reasons: he was not a West Pointer, he had come up from the ranks, and he was known as a "Wood man," having served under General Wood for a number of years. Furthermore, at their first meeting Harbord had to confess that he didn't speak French. Pershing didn't tell him what he had in mind but said, "Anyhow, I'm going to take you with me to France." Pershing liked everything he knew about Major Harbord: his excellent service as head of the Moro Constabulary, his quick intelligence, his ability to work with other people, and his firm jaw line (Pershing favored men with strong jaws, like his own). He soon decided to name Major Harbord as his chief of staff—the best appointment he ever made. No more valuable man served with the A.E.F.

The job of fleshing out his staff was complicated by the fact that many of the most capable officers had already been earmarked for other duty—the enormous job of training the draftees and the National Guard divisions, of mobilizing industry and transport and supply facilities, of building huge new camps, and of reinforcing the General Staff itself. He did manage to lay hands on three youngish majors of the Regular Army who were to perform heroic, if relatively anonymous, services on his staff throughout the war. Dennis E. Nolan, who had served under him before, was placed in charge of the G-2 (Intelligence) section. Fox Conner, who had been a cadet at West Point during Pershing's unpopular year there as a tactical officer, an imperturbable and highly educated artillery officer with a year's service in a French artillery regiment, took over the most important section, G-3 (Operations). Hugh A. Drum had caught Pershing's attention during his brief command of the Southern Department by submitting a plan for organizing it more efficiently. He also was attached to the pioneer staff and later became chief of staff of the First American Army.

In the eighteen days before he sailed for France, Pershing collected a group of 187 men to form the vanguard of the American forces. Seventy were enlisted men of the Regular Army, sixty were field clerks and civilians.

A suggestion of the enormity of the task awaiting Pershing's vanguard came from Major Conner, who had been attached to the Joffre mission just before joining the A.E.F. staff. Conner reported that on the eve of his departure from the United States Marshal Joffre remarked that at least 500,000 American troops would be needed in France.

Pershing's directives from his own government were brief, but left no doubt as to where his duty lay. "In military operations against the Imperial German Government," read President Wilson's order, "you are directed to cooperate with the forces of other countries employed against the enemy; but in so doing the underlying idea must be kept in view that the forces of the United States are a separate and distinct component of the combined forces, the identity of which must be preserved. This fundamental rule is subject to such minor exceptions in particular circumstances as your judgment may approve. The decision as to when your command or any of its parts is ready for action is confided to you, and you will exercise full discretion in determining the manner of cooperation."

In the months ahead, the "fundamental rule" preserving the United States forces as "a separate and distinct component" was to be of critical importance. Fortunately, in applying it, in using it as his shield and buckler, Pershing had the firm support of Wilson and Baker. They never once let him down. Their determination to preserve for him the full power of discretion strengthened his hand enormously when the statesmen and generals of France and Britain sought to sway him by every kind of moral, intellectual, and propagandistic pressure.

The Secretary of War's parting words were crisp and unsentimental. "I shall give you only two orders," Baker told Pershing, "one to go and one to return."

The occasionally sardonic Baker did not elucidate, but the ominous inference could be taken that the order to return would be issued if Pershing proved incapable and had to be replaced. Later on, however, Baker said that the possibility of Pershing's relief was never considered through all the vicissitudes of his command.

The departure of Pershing and his headquarters for France was supposed to be the topmost top secret of the War Department. Presumably the people who knew that he was to sail on the *Baltic* May 28 realized that if the Germans learned that the commander of the American Expeditionary Force was on the high seas aboard a certain ship they would make every effort to torpedo it as the liner passed through the danger zone off the British Isles. During the first three months of unrestricted submarine warfare, 844 ships of all nationalities had been sunk by U-boats. German agents were known to be plentiful in the capital and along the New York waterfront, from which the *Baltic* would sail.

Yet the Pershing embarkation was one of the worst-kept secrets of the war. Even before they left Washington for New York, members of his staff had every reason to fear that their mission would end in the icy waters of the North Atlantic. Major Harbord wrote in his diary that the staff was greatly concerned over "War Department bureau chiefs regaling dinner guests with secrets supposed to be sacred; with the Pershing party hiding its heads around the capital for two weeks, avoiding its friends and looking mysterious when Europe was mentioned; with the clever staff departments shipping its supplies to the White Star pier to lie there for hours with 'General Pershing's Headquarters' stencilled in boxcar letters for the whole world to read."

The day before Frederick Palmer left for New York to board the *Baltic* he lunched at the Shoreham and heard Colonel George M. Harvey, editor of the *North American Review,* violent patriot and anti-Wilson partisan, and characterized by Palmer as "chief of the whispering gallery in Washington," sounding off at a nearby table.

"In a voice that could be heard across the room," Palmer said, the vociferous Harvey was telling his guests: " 'I know when Pershing's going and on what ship. It's the *Baltic.*' "

Palmer reflected that it would be "somewhat discomfiting if our first report of Pershing's landing on the other side of the Atlantic had to come to us from the German port of Kiel [one of the chief submarine bases], accompanied by an explanation that while there had been room for him, his Chief of Staff and his aides on the submarine that had sunk the *Baltic,* the rest of the Commander-in-Chief's staff had been left, under urgent military necessity, in open boats on the Atlantic. It was conceivably just such an indiscretion as this that may have informed the Germans that Lord Kitchener was going to Russia on the cruiser that was sunk in the North Sea, tragically ending his career."

Pershing's first and only interview with President Wilson took place at the White House four days before he left Washington. Both men were brief; Pershing because that was his nature, Wilson apparently because, unlike Lincoln, he had no great curiosity about the man who would lead his countrymen into battle. Pershing thanked the President for the honor and responsibility conferred upon him, and Wilson replied, "General, you are chosen entirely upon your record and I have every confidence you will succeed. You shall have my full support."

May 28, 1917, was a gray, rainy day in New York as Pershing and his party gathered on Governors Island for the embarkation on the *Baltic,* which on the journey coming over from Europe had twice been attacked by submarines. Another momentous day in Pershing's life—and again, in his diary, he was laconic, his emotions on setting out on the greatest adventure of his life leakproof as usual. "Breakfast at the Astor," he wrote. "Rained hard during the morning. Went to

Governors Island ferry in civilian clothes with Captain Collins, he stopping at Walcott Hotel to see the Pattons [Captain George S. Patton, Jr., who was to rejoin his staff in France until he transferred to the Tank Corps, and his wife]. Crossed on the 11:15 ferry. Major Bacon in uniform crossed with us. Had chat with General Bell at Governors Island, and left about 12:30 in driving rainstorm for the *Baltic*. The *Baltic* was delayed about an hour in sailing, so we boarded her in the Channel at 3:30, the *Baltic* sailing about 5:15. Lunched as soon as we went aboard. Arrangements generally satisfactory."

Harbord, with his keen eye for the human comedy, was more revealing in his own diary. The A.E.F.'s Chief of Staff recorded that Pershing and his party were ambushed on Governors Island by a forceful and argumentative "female major general" in charge of the women's service camp at Glen Echo (a sort of forerunner of the WAC), who demanded the privilege of accompanying Pershing on the tender which took them to the *Baltic,* as a sort of guard of honor. "The way the General's iron jaw clamped down on the proposition of the ladies to accompany us to Gravesend," Harbord wrote, "confirms my faith in the wisdom of the President in selecting him for France." Blacked out as night fell, the *Baltic* slid down the harbor toward the open sea, and as Harbord said, "There was no inspiring view of the New York skyline, no-Napoleon-on-the-Bellerophon-gazing-at-the-fast-fading-shores-of-France for us, for it was cold and raw, and a fog like a pall settled over the green shores of Long Island."

The *Baltic* proceeded up the fog-shrouded coast to Halifax, with its horns blowing at three-minute intervals. A rumor swept the ship that there was a German waiter, signed on in New York, working in the ship's dining room. An immediate investigation was conducted and quickly ended when it was learned that the suspect's name was Jorgenson, not something more luridly Teutonic. Boat drills were held the first day out, with stern instructions given that the half-dozen women aboard were to be accorded priority in the lifeboats, if it came to that. "When a torpedo strikes and you stroll up to a lifeboat expecting to take a seat in it," Harbord confided to his diary, "it must be very annoying to have your toes stepped on by a lady who beats you to it."

Pershing decided it would be best to keep everyone occupied and let the ship's officers and crew worry about lurking submarines. Beginning the second day out, classes in French were held at 10 A.M.

and 4 P.M. daily by the French-speaking interpreters with Headquarters. Afterward and in-between there were a number of lectures and staff discussions, a Colonel Puckle of the British Army lecturing on supply problems, and even Pershing (as he wrote in his diary June 3) "attended a lecture by Dr. Young on venereal diseases."

There was menace above as well as below the surface of the springtime Atlantic. It was the iceberg season and Harbord noted that the *Baltic* passed "at a comparatively short distance an iceberg as large as the fatal one on which the *Titanic* met its fate" and "it shimmered and shone like glass in the moonlight." The ship's concert was given on the night of June 2, at which General Pershing delivered a "very neat little few minutes' talk, describing among other things the last similar concert he had attended when he and Sir Ian Hamilton were traveling together between Shanghai and Hongkong during the Russo-Japanese War." An opera singer, Helen Juta, closed the program by singing "Keep the Home Fires Burning," "Laddies in Khaki," the "Marseillaise," "America," and "God Save the King."

The night of June 5 the *Baltic* crossed into the danger zone and began steering on the zigzag course recommended for avoiding torpedoes from the ninety to 100 U-boats then reported in the waters adjacent to the British Isles. The sea was calm, the moon was bright, and everything was auspicious for the sudden appearance of a German periscope slitting the water like a shark's fin. All passengers were advised to sleep in their clothes, with a life jacket handy, and to keep a flask of brandy in one of their pockets against the possibility of spending the night in an open boat. Day broke after a sleepless night; then three American destroyers came steaming out from their base at Queenstown to convoy the *Baltic* into the Irish Channel. Interservice rivalry was forgotten as the soldiers on the *Baltic* blessed the Navy with every glimpse of the sub killers plowing ahead and alongside of them.

Palmer, the censor-to-be, recalled a conversation he had with Pershing as the *Baltic* zigzagged under escort through the submarine zone. The general had been reading a book Palmer wrote on the first offensive attempted by the British New Armies, "Kitchener's Mob," along the Somme. Pershing thought it "horrible beyond words that the civilized world should suffer such bloodshed and destruction, horrible that our country should have to join in." He seemed to have considered, for the first time since being thrown into the hurried prepara-

tions for sailing for France, the human cost of joining the Allies on
the western front. "The only way to end it is by force," he continued,
"and we must end it as soon as possible. . . . It will take us time
before we can make our power felt. . . . As I see it now we shall
have to plan for an army of a million in France."

Like the men he was soon to join in commanding armies on the
western front, he was "horrified" by the wastage of human life; also
like them, whether it was Ludendorff or Pétain, Hindenburg or Haig,
Foch or the crown prince of Germany, no solution seemed to have
occurred to him but the application of more and more force, the explosion of more cordite, and the frontward march of more divisions.
But then political leaders had shown a similar aversion for talk of a
negotiated peace—the only possible alternative—whether it came from
the White House, the Vatican, or the Grand Lamasery of Tibet. The
thought of turning back from the slaughter without offering a victory
to their peoples in return for all their sacrifices was too alarming to
contemplate. Revolutionary mobs in Moscow and Petrograd precluded
all contemplation of a peace without victory.

Pershing and his party landed in England June 8 without sighting
a U-boat and spent four days there en route to France. Everywhere
they went there were cheering crowds, massed dignitaries, flowers
strewn in their path, silk hats and gold braid in all directions. The
Allies were intent on putting their best foot forward before the grim
truth of the situation on the western front, necessarily concealed from
their own peoples, was revealed to the American commander. The
façade was impressive, especially with rural England at the height of
its springtime beauty.

The first glimpse of General Pershing seemed to be reassuring to
the people to whom he represented the potential millions of fresh
American troops. At fifty-seven he was still as lean and erect as when
he commanded a cavalry troop. Stepping ashore, hand on sword hilt,
he was the personification of what Europeans expected in an American general, with his jutting jaw, his lancelike eyes under the shadow
of his visor, the straight firm line of his mouth under a close-cropped
mustache, and best of all the air of unalterable self-confidence.

On the dock at Liverpool he was greeted by the lord mayor, the
United States military attaché, British generals and admirals, fifty
newspapermen and newsreel cameramen, and the band of the Welsh
Fusiliers playing "The Star-Spangled Banner." The only moments of

embarrassment occurred when British officers had difficulty interpreting American rank badges. A British colonel deferred at length to Major Harbord under the impression that he was a general officer.

At Euston Station, in London, the turnout was even more impressive. Pershing and his staff were greeted by United States Ambassador Walter Hines Page, Admiral W. S. Sims (the American naval commander in Europe, who had preceded Pershing by two months), the lord mayor of London, and a British military delegation headed by Field Marshal French, who had commanded the British armies in France until he had been superseded by Haig. At Harbord's suggestion—his own sense of public relations was deficient—Pershing shook hands with the engineer and fireman of the train which brought him from Liverpool to London, while the newsreel men cranked away at their cameras.

The British aristocracy seized upon him at once, and the stateliest homes in England were thrown open to him. Brigadier Lord Brooke, the future Earl of Warwick, taking over as his aide-de-camp during his stay in England, kept Pershing's rooms at the Savoy filled with flowers bearing the card, "Compliments of Lord and Lady Brooke." On June 10, the American commander was received at Buckingham Palace by King George V, and that night saw George Robey in *Zig-Zag*, the musical-comedy hit that ran for the duration of the war—a required item on the agenda of all visitors.

Next day Pershing found himself trapped in a social tug of war between General Sir Arthur Paget, commanding the home forces, and the Anglo-American Waldorf Astors. Pershing was supposed to appear at General Paget's country place for tea and dinner, but somehow the imperious Nancy Astor, with the help of Ambassador Page, intercepted him and swept him off to the Canadian Hospital, "a pet of Mrs. Astor's," as Major Harbord noted. It was left to Harbord, who would soon be thoroughly experienced in covering up for his chief's delays and absences, to ease the embarrassment and bewilderment at the Pagets' country home. "It was a rather trying day as far as the tact required to explain our Ambassador and our General was concerned," Harbord confided to his diary that night. Not until shortly after 8 P.M.—more than a half hour late for dinner—did Pershing and his fellow truants appear before their host and hostess.

Next day Pershing conferred briefly with Sir William Robertson, chief of the British Imperial General Staff, who had served in the ranks for eleven years and had never quite lost his Cockney accent. Someone told Harbord how Robertson, when he was designated to replace General Horace Smith-Dorrien during the retreat from Mons, bluntly informed his predecessor, " 'Orace, you for 'ome." On June 12, his last day in England, Pershing accompanied General Paget to Brentwood, the headquarters of the home command, and watched demonstrations of trench attacks, mortar barrages, and the defensive and offensive use of poison gas. He saluted the march past of the 17th Yorkshire, pasty-faced boys from the mill towns. Harbord said he was anything but impressed by the Yorkshiremen, "runts, crooked, undeveloped," nor their officers, who seemed languid and lily fingered and affected the fashionable "Sandhurst stoop," but the Americans would learn that stunted mill boys and slouching officers could handle their share of the fighting. At a state dinner that night Prime Minister David Lloyd George was fifteen minutes late, Harbord observed, but "he can do that sort of thing . . . and our General is no mean imitator."

Field Marshal French warned Pershing and Harbord that on their arrival in France they would be "kissed and cried over," having rather a contemptuous regard for French emotionalism, and recalled that the first time he met Marshal Joffre the latter was sitting in his tent, weeping over the first German flag his army had captured.

A British officer politely inquired of Pershing, "General, is this your personal staff?"

"No," snapped Pershing, "this is my General Staff."

The Pershing party left Charing Cross at 5:40 A.M. June 13, crossed the Channel from Folkestone to Boulogne, and landed in France amid an even warmer and more hopeful welcome than the British had given them. In the Boulogne basin as they docked were tramp steamers discharging Annamite troops from Indochina, Senegalese from North Africa, testifying to the strain on French resources. Pershing towered over the French military and civilian leaders on the dockside cobbles, and Wilbur Forrest, among the war correspondents on hand from American newspapers and press services, thought he was physically the most impressive of all the Allied commanders he had seen. "In physique alone Pershing stood out among commanders, a superb erect figure, a model of military bearing. . . . His European uniforms were for the most part the product of the best English tailors, and they draped his upstanding figure better than those of British or

French generals did theirs. Pershing's very physical bearing told much of his vigor and power of leadership."

Pershing and his officers came to a halt on the dock as a French regimental band played "The Star-Spangled Banner" over and over again, until (Harbord said) "even the General, who stands like a statue, growled over the number of times they were playing it." Then "a dozen fuzzy little Frenchmen came up," each saluting and making a little speech.

Among the French greeters was Lieutenant Colonel Comte de Chambrun, the great-grandson of Lafayette and also brother-in-law of American congressman Nicholas Longworth, who was to be attached to Pershing as a liaison officer and interpreter of French customs. Harbord wryly observed that Chambrun "speaks good English and a great deal of it."

Napoleon reincarnated could hardly have received a more enthusiastic welcome as the Americans proceeded by rail to Paris. Crowds cheered them at every railway station along the way, threw flowers into their cars, and pressed wine on them at every stop. They arrived at the Gare du Nord at 6:30 P.M., when Parisians ordinarily would be off the streets, but there were hundreds of thousands massed around the station who, Harbord reported, "cheered and shouted and wept as only a French crowd can do." Night had fallen when Pershing stepped out on a balcony overlooking the Place de la Concorde and a roar went up from the throngs that seemed to split the sky. Never again, anywhere, would Pershing hear such an outcry. It was the whole French nation saluting the man who represented the only hope that France had left.

For days after the arrival in Paris it went on like that. Pershing and his officers passed through a succession of elegant chambers where the wealth and aristocracy of France stood to greet them as khaki-clad gods of the new world. Pershing was received at the Presidential Palace, watched the fly past of hundreds of planes at Le Bourget airdrome, dined with War Minister Paul Painlevé under Gobelin tapestries with an orchestra playing in the garden. He called on Marshal Joffre at the Military Club and had to appear on the balcony repeatedly until the crowds cheered themselves hoarse. The Chamber of Deputies "nearly went amuck," Harbord wrote, when he paid a call. When he appeared in the President's box at the Opéra Comique, an American woman sang "The Star-Spangled Banner" and a French girl the "Marseillaise," after which the audience sang and cheered for fifteen minutes. "God grant," was Major Harbord's somber thought, "that there may be no reaction in the months that must pass before American flags fly in the trenches."

It was a mass love affair, bordering on dementia, raising expectations on the part of the volatile French to the heights of delusion.

Pershing kept his head while under the focus of this heedless adulation. He could not help being pleased by cheers that rocketed to the rooftops every time he gave the public a glimpse of himself, but he had a clear vision of the difficulties that lay ahead, the disillusionments and differences of opinion that would arise when he and his opposite numbers got down to the business of working out the practical details of military alliance. "Difficult to see how we are to meet the expectations of the French," he laconically observed in his diary on June 14. Who would cheer when the French people realized that it would be many months before any sizable number of combat-ready American divisions could be convoyed across the Atlantic, across France, through training centers and "quiet sectors," and finally deployed for the offensive?

And even while the cheering resounded, there were ominous undertones, audible at least to the perceptive chief of staff of the A.E.F. Under the hullabaloo, Harbord heard "many rumors of French regiments who have recently refused to go 'over the top,'" and reports that "twelve men were shot recently" as examples to the rest. Harbord thought that "there is no doubt that the French morale is waning." But it was worse than that, much worse. It was the reality that underlay the frenzied Parisian welcome of the first American forces to land in France.

8. The War-Weary French

Of all the French military and political leaders, ranging in temperament from the Cossack hetman's personality of Clemenceau to the amiable simplicity of Joffre, the one who captured General Pershing's wholehearted admiration and affection was General Henri-Philippe Pétain, the commander in chief of all troops in the French sectors of the western front.

"My impression of Pétain was favorable," Pershing wrote after their first meeting, "and it remained unchanged throughout the war." After the armistice, Pershing continued to "treasure" Pétain's friendship, as he said, and even during World War II, when Pétain's name was synonymous with treason throughout the anti-Fascist world, he stood by him, confident that his friend's motives were being misunderstood. The friendship, particularly during the war, was more one-sided than Pershing suspected, for Pétain was not above criticizing the American behind his back.

One reason that Pétain attracted Pershing and many other Americans was the fact that he did not look or act particularly French, or at least not in the vaudeville concept of French behavior. Unlike the eloquent and gesticulating Foch, for instance, he was calm, deliberate, and aloof. "There is nothing distinctively Gallic in his appearance," Harbord noted approvingly. "He has blue eyes and looks you in the face when he speaks to you."

The Americans tended to distrust the ebullience of many French soldiers and were reassured by Pétain's plain-spoken attitude, which was more like their own, and what Harbord called his "eminent common sense." Pershing saw him as a man with whom he could cooperate to a degree "rarely attained between men or peoples of different nationalities" because of his "breadth of vision, his common sense and his sound judgment." Unlike other French generals with their arm-waving predictions of the victory to be won with just a few American divisions as a stiffening element, Pétain gloomily "hoped they were not too late" and spoke of Allied prospects with the "solemn seriousness of a sacrament."

Pessimism, in fact, had paradoxically carried Pétain to the highest command. At the start of the war, French officers of the Grandmaison school—"the attack, always the attack"—staked everything on the belief that sheer offensive spirit would sweep aside the plodding gray columns crossing the Rhine from Germany. Pétain had little faith in *élan* as a strategic weapon of war and fought his own kind of battles with emphasis on artillery concentrations, infantry fire power, and taking the defensive whenever possible. Three years of war appeared to have vindicated his unromantic views.

Pétain had always been something of a dull fellow among his gallant and high-spirited comrades of the French officers' corps. At sixty, with his bald crown and his large dreary mustache, his cold and watchful blue eyes, he looked more like the cashier of a particularly conservative provincial bank than the field commander of the French Army.

His prewar career had been undistinguished. He had served as a line officer in the Chasseurs and as an instructor in the Army's special schools, always preaching the necessity for increased fire power and dourly keeping his own counsel, while Foch and his disciples spread the gospel of the grand offensive. When war came, he took command of the 4th Brigade in Lanrezac's Fifth Army, then the 6th Division, as the French armies were driven back to the Marne, establishing himself as a first-rate specialist in the defense. He was one of the first high French officers to realize that the war had turned into a siege and that if France was to endure it must conserve its man power. Promoted to command the XXXIII Corps in the Arras sector, he carefully mounted an attack at Vimy in the spring of 1915 which broke through the German line for two miles—a considerable success in those dismal days—and resulted in his elevation to the Second Army in the Champagne sector.

When the Germans launched their massive offensive at the complex of forts around Verdun early in 1916, hoping to grind the life out of the French Army in the process, Pétain, with his special capacity for holding a position, was the natural choice to supervise the defense. Between February and July that year the French took 350,000 casualties to the Germans' 281,000, a proportion they could ill afford, but losing Verdun would have been disastrous. Pétain had to supply his defending forces of nearly half a million men through a local tramline and the narrow road from Bar-le-Duc, all other routes being under direct fire from German artillery.

Rocklike, always on the defense, Pétain held onto Verdun, and the Army and the nation survived. In April of 1917 he took over as chief of the General Staff. He became commander in chief of all forces in the Zone of the Armies after the failure of the French offensive undertaken that spring just as America entered the war.

For all his successes, mostly defensive in character, and his acclamation as the "Savior of France," Pétain only grew more pessimistic about the outcome of the war. The Germans, he believed, were simply an unbeatable race of soldiers. He shocked Sir Henry Wilson, the British liaison officer with French headquarters, by asserting that three German divisions of nine battalions each were the equal of four French or British divisions of thirteen battalions each. And when it appeared that the fall of the czarist regime would remove Russia as the eastern ally, Pétain told Sir Henry, "If Russia ran out we might have to make peace." That conviction of German superiority, which flowered most fully and disastrously in 1941, apparently did not sufficiently disturb his fellow Frenchmen. Hadn't Pétain always been a gloomy old fellow, even in his youth?

The Americans took this pessimism to be a healthy sense of realism when they confronted it in 1917. There was really very little to be cheerful about. German armies still stood on French and Belgian soil, and all attempts to dislodge them had failed. Italy had its hands full keeping the Austro-German forces north of the Piave. Rumania had almost been knocked out of the war by the Hungarians and Bulgarians. The British attempt to break open the way to the Dardanelles and establish a supply line to southern Russia had failed disastrously, and the Turks were holding on fairly well in Asia Minor. As for the French offensive of that spring, following the blood letting at Verdun, it had brought that nation to the verge of collapse. On April 16, General Nivelle, who had succeeded Joffre as field commander, launched his offensive on the Aisne while the British attacked in the Arras sector. On Nivelle's throw of the dice France had invested most of its available military resources. The French gained ground, but the Germans fell back on a system of defenses in depth that drained the life out of Nivelle's attacks and accounted for almost 200,000 French casualties. The result was that Nivelle and two of his army commanders were sacked; Pétain, the apostle of the defensive, took over the demoralized French armies at the front, and Foch replaced Pétain as chief of the General Staff. The French thereupon decided that if they were to remain at war with Germany it would have to be purely on the defensive; the rank and file of the army had rebelled at all possibility of resuming the offensive.

Soon after Pershing's arrival in Paris, the French made up their minds to inform him of the crisis in the French Army. The extent of its disaffection was undoubtedly the best-kept secret of the war; had it not been so jealously guarded the Germans might well have overwhelmed their enemy and marched on Paris with little hindrance.

On June 22, Pershing was invited to the home of Herman H. Harjes, who managed the Paris branch of J. P. Morgan & Co. His fellow guest of honor was General Pétain, whom he had met for the first time six days earlier at French headquarters at Compiègne. After dinner Pétain took Pershing aside for a very private and confidential discussion. What Pétain told him of French morale, Pershing wrote in his diary, was "disquieting"—a mild word, indeed, considering what had been happening to the French Army, the bulwark of the Allied land forces. "Collective indiscipline"—the official euphemism for mutiny—had spread to fifty-four combat divisions shortly after the failure of the Nivelle offensive on the Aisne. Soldiers were defying their officers and abandoning their positions. Behind the front, gangs of deserters beat up military police and railwaymen, waved red flags, sang revolutionary songs, and uncoupled engines to prevent trains from leaving for the front. A brigade of Russian troops, spurred on by Bolshevik agitators who seemed to have sprung out of the ground, rebelled against further fighting and had to be quarantined.

It was Pétain's first and hardest task to quell the mutiny and persuade the soldiers to stay under arms. This he set about doing with patience and understanding. Courts-martial convened for the more flagrant mutineers brought in 23,000 verdicts of guilty, indicating the scope of the "indiscipline." Of this number, however, only fifty-five were actually shot by firing squads.

Meanwhile, Pétain improved the Army's living conditions, granted furloughs by the thousands, improved the rations, and himself visited many of the disaffected regiments to assure the troops that they would never again be regarded as expendable subhumans. Slowly the poilu began to recover his confidence in the men above him. Pétain's salvage of the Army after the second Battle of the Aisne was an achievement equal to his defense of Verdun. Twice he had saved France, and as the British historian Cyril Falls wrote (in his *The Great War,* best and most recent of the one-volume histories of World War I), Pétain's "personal work" in 1916–17 "should always be remembered when his long and troubled record is reviewed." Perhaps it does much, too, to explain Pershing's lifelong devotion to him.

Not only had there been a collapse of morale among the soldiers at the front; there was a brooding hopelessness to be observed in the ordinary people behind the lines. Paris's great theaters, restaurants, and cafés were thronged with pleasure seekers who had enriched themselves in the war industries, but less privileged citizens were close to despair over the endless casualty lists, the food shortages, and other privations. Pershing remarked on the fact that "one frequently caught a troubled expression among the faces of the people in the streets" —visible even to a foreign general speeding along in the rear seat of a limousine.

"The shortage of food and the continuous air raids at night had a depressing effect," he observed. "From nearly every family some member was numbered among the dead, but there were few women in mourning. . . . The burden of three years of war, with no end in sight, bore heavily upon the people and hidden forebodings filled many a heart." There was also considerable unrest and agitation among the workers in the munitions factories which had been concentrated in the Paris area since the start of the war, some of it an echo of the political turbulence in Russia.

Defeatism verging on treason had infected many of those in high places socially, politically, and financially. A discreet pro-German tendency was becoming almost fashionable in the aristocratic *faubourgs,* and industrialists dismayed at Communist activity among their workers were beginning to wonder whether the violent scenes in Petrograd might not be duplicated in Paris if the war continued indefinitely. Major Harbord recorded that a number of American expatriates in Paris, though largely sympathetic to the French, warned against the corruption prevalent in and out of the government. One of these was James Stillman, the American financier who had lived in France off and on for half a century. "He suggests that we be very careful. Very careful! ! ! !" Harbord wrote of his talk with Stillman, who was referring to the French military and civilian leaders. "He says the Latin mind has kinks and turns in it unknown to ours—and the politics, politics, politics! ! !"

Again, at a dinner at which he and Pershing were guests, Harbord wrote in his diary that "one of the Philadelphia Drexels" had sounded the strongest sort of warning against placing too much trust in the "better people" of France, cautioning that the country had "the most corrupt government on earth; that the power behind the throne was Caillaux [this was just before Georges Clemenceau, Caillaux's bitterest enemy, came to power as Premier], whose wife, you remember, shot a man and figured four or five years ago in a sensational trial for the crime. . . . He controls the banks, and through them the politicians, who nearly all owe him money. Caillaux is intensely pro-German, and perfectly willing to sell France to Germany. . . .

"Our conversation ran to the German secret service, and how they seem to know all that goes on in France, and he told me that since the beginning of the war the Grand Duchess Anastasia of Russia, who is the wife of the Grand Duke of Mecklenburg-Schwerin and mother-in-law of the Imperial German Crown Prince, has lived at the Ritz Hotel here; that he saw her yesterday. She makes periodical trips to Switzerland. . . . Further, that in Geneva recently he himself saw the Princess de Polignac . . . sitting at a table with the German Princess Salm, whom she had come from Paris to visit. . . . Again that a French duchess who before the war was mistress of the First Secretary of the Austrian Embassy, makes periodical and frequent visits to him in a Swiss town, where he is meeting her from Vienna. And yet we wonder why Germany knows movements in France."

Harbord also observed that there was almost a complete breakdown in confidence between the military leaders and their government, that General Pétain "scarcely conceals his contempt for the civil powers."

A.E.F. Headquarters was understandably perturbed by the deplorable security which was supposed to safeguard the movement of the first U.S. troops to France. The First Division was then being convoyed across the Atlantic. Harbord wrote in his diary on June 19,

"Three days ago I was handed a paper which told the date of sailing of our first convoy. I showed it to the Chief [Pershing] and to no one else and locked it in my safe. Yesterday Major Logan, my office assistant, came in from a visit to the French War Office, where he is on very good terms, and said they told him that the convoy had sailed . . . exactly the information I had so carefully put in my safe."

Thus within a month after his arrival in Paris General Pershing and his staff were confronted with the previously unsuspected truth of the situation—that France was close to a military collapse and "there existed serious despondency among all classes," as Pershing later wrote. Much quicker than he had innocently believed on setting out from America, the Allies would have to be bolstered by an A.E.F. in fighting trim, not only to achieve a victory but to prevent defeat. "The map does not tell it all," he was quoted by Major Frederick Palmer, now the chief censor for the A.E.F. "It's the situation under the lines of the map. . . . With Russia in, Rumania in, and all the Allied armies in with their full manpower, they could not win. Apparently there is no hope of increasing Italian manpower, certainly not the French. Look at what is expected of us and what we have to do and what we have to start with! No army ready, no ships to bring over an army if we had one. How will we supply and transport an army across France after it is here?"

He set about answering his own questions and resolving his doubts. A temporary A.E.F. Headquarters was established in a small two-story building at 31 Rue de Constantine, facing the Esplanade des Invalides and close to many of the French Government offices, on the left bank of the Seine. At the same time he moved out of the Hotel Crillon and "after a certain amount of deliberation" accepted the offer of the American financier Ogden Mills to occupy his elegant and spacious residence at 73 Rue de Varenne, where the Napoleonic Marshal Lannes once had lived. Major Harbord, several other members of his staff, and his aides-de-camp moved in with him. The garden, Harbord said, was "as charming and beautiful as a dream of Paradise."

During those first months in Paris, Pershing made himself available to many persons not directly connected with the organization of an army to fight on the western front—even the war correspondents, whom he later kept strictly at a distance. Wilbur Forrest, the United Press correspondent, wrote that Pershing's office on the Rue de Constantine was so cramped that it had room for only a deal table, three chairs, and "a few maps to lend military atmosphere." When a staff conference was held, the doors leading into a small garden outside his window had to be opened to accommodate the overflow.

Forrest approached Pershing with a plan for sending reading material to the troops from America. His suggestion that it be sent post free brought a roar of disapproval from the general. "Hell!" the correspondent quoted Pershing as saying "Give them a chance to send this stuff postage-free and they'll burrow into their attics and send stuff they've been intending to throw out for years, an insult to the intelligence of the American soldier! What did they do when we were on the Mexican border? They sent truckloads of junk no self-respecting soldier would look at. Damned junk—insult to the intelligence of the American army!"

The visiting Americans came in all shapes and guises. One was Dorothy Canfield, now an established writer, whose father had been president of the University of Nebraska a quarter of a century before when Pershing had drilled its Cadet Corps. He took Miss Canfield to breakfast at the Crillon and they talked of the days when "she was my star pupil in mathematics."

Other visitors, who wasted his time with pompous or ill-founded advice, got short shrift in the office on the Rue de Constantine. One day Major Palmer suggested that he should be more diplomatic after terminating an interview "somewhat abruptly." Pershing replied with a sardonic smile, "I didn't know the man with the flowing tie who came in to tell me how to run my army was such an important person. It had been a busy day. He did not look to me as though he had much experience in commanding armies himself, so I was brief."

During July, Pershing was still the darling of the Parisian street crowds, particularly when he appeared at the Fourth of July and July 14 (Bastille Day) celebrations. No doubt the safe landing of the First Division and the appearance of the first American troops on the boulevards of Paris contributed to the continuing warmth of his reception. For the Fourth of July festivities Pershing brought in a battalion of the 16th Infantry, part of the 8th Brigade, which he had commanded at the Presidio and on the Mexican border, and marched them up the Champs-Élysées to the Arc de Triomphe through wildly enthusiastic throngs. Later in the day, at Picpus Cemetery, he laid a wreath on the tomb of Lafayette. The chief spokesman for the Ameri-

cans at the cemetery observance was Major Charles E. Stanton, the
A.E.F. paymaster, who was an orator of the old school and fluent in
French. At the end of his speech, Major Stanton uttered the phrase
headlined all over the world: "Lafayette, we are here!" Pershing then
stepped forward and delivered a few sentences in his undistinguished
oratorical style to the effect that what Major Stanton said went for him,
too. Somehow, Stanton's fervent punch line was attributed to Pershing, perhaps because the American correspondents thought it would
have greater dramatic value coming, though falsely, from the mouth
of the commander in chief. Anyone who knew Pershing, of course,
could hardly have believed that such a ringing declaration could have
been uttered by him, even under the stress of emotion. He was anything but a coiner of phrases, and, according to Major Palmer, whenever public relations experts tried to put words in his mouth, he
rebelled in no uncertain terms, saying, "This is not mine. It is not in
character." Nor was public speaking anything but a torment to him.
Almost apologetically, he told Harbord about his disastrous *Mary
Had a Little Lamb* recitation as a schoolboy and explained how he
"developed a diffidence that still haunts him on such occasions."

At an open house that evening in the American Embassy, Pershing
was less discomfited, Harbord observed, when "bevies of women got
the General into a corner and pawed him over, until it is a wonder
his head is not turned, though I have seen no signs of it." And there
was more flattery at the dinner given by General Foch, the French
Chief of Staff, at Armenonville later in the evening. A French opera
star sang a song which she announced had been composed in honor
of General Pershing, but which Harbord, peeking at the score, saw was
inscribed: "Dedicated to President Wilson." Despite the flattery, the
toasts, and the cheers, Harbord was uneasy over the future, particularly Pershing's future: "It is early to say what the General will do in
the war. It might end before he has a chance. There is always a possible tragedy in the career of every general who starts to serve our
hysterical inefficient people. . . . He has captured the fickle Paris
crowd at any rate, and could be elected King of Paris tomorrow. . . ."

At the Bastille Day celebration Pershing again was the most popular
figure—almost the only one, as far as the crowds were concerned—
among those who sat in the presidential box at the Porte de Vin-
cennes. Again, too, there was a worrisome glimpse of disaffection
and division among the French people, which was particularly notice-

able when the President of France began passing out decorations. A number of French officers present raised a groan of dismay when their President placed the Grand Cordon of the Legion of Honor around the neck of a major general who had been in disgrace since the retreat from Belgium in 1914 and hadn't been entrusted with a command since then. The disgusted officers told Harbord that "this prized decoration . . . was brought about by political influence."

The Americans had more than enough to worry about, however, in connection with their own war effort, if it was not to expire in a vaporing of Fourth of July speeches, toasts to Franco-American amity, and echoing choruses of "Over There." The A.E.F. couldn't make a move toward throwing its weight into the fight until the ponderous machinery back in Washington started turning over, and no one in the War Department had any clear idea of which buttons to push. The problem of how to send an army to Europe had never even been considered by the General Staff, whose function it was to plan for any eventuality. Shortly after his arrival in Paris, a high-ranking French officer had remarked to Pershing that the United States had no General Staff in the European sense, with plans for mobilization, campaigns, and operations already drawn up, and "it takes thirty years to organize a General Staff." Pershing replied in an excess of confidence, "It never took America thirty years to do anything." Now he had cause to wonder.

When General Bliss, the acting chief of staff in General Scott's absence in Russia, "went to look in the secret files where the plans to meet the situation that confronted us should have been found," Pershing wrote, "the pigeon hole was empty. In other words, the War Department was face to face with the question of sending an army to Europe and found that the General Staff had never considered such a thing. No one in authority had any definite idea how many men might be needed, how they should be organized and equipped, or where the tonnage to transport and supply them was to come from."

The War Department seemed to be in a state of paralysis, and it took days, sometimes weeks, to receive an answer to cables with requests or inquiries. Harbord commented harshly on the "long delays attendant on official action—cablegrams consuming six days getting from the office of receipt to the office of action; the Acting Chief of Staff clinging to the short stub pencil of his casemate days and abjuring the use of a stenographer." In his diary, July 10, 1917, the chief of staff described the Rube Goldbergian improvisation necessary when the French General Staff would request information on some point from the A.E.F. staff. "We say we have not yet heard from the War Department. They then cable their Embassy and they send down the Attaché to the War Department, and he finds out things, and wires his people, so that repeatedly we get news affecting us through the French War Office before we get it from our own War Department, and some things we get only through the French. No cable ever reached us about the sailing of our first convoy. Four transports sail tomorrow, according to the French, but we know nothing about them."

Almost every senior officer coming to Paris from Washington had tales to tell of the Stateside confusion. The training camps were overrun, and recruits had no one to teach them the close-order drill which passed as preparation for fighting in the trenches of northern France. Sixty thousand troops, who should have been consigned to the A.E.F., were guarding railway bridges, tunnels, and other installations, so prevalent was the fear of spies and saboteurs.

Presiding over the confusion was the elderly General Bliss, who lacked the ruthless efficiency of a real executive. His habit of slipping papers under his blotter—no matter how urgently they might require a decision—and hiding them there until he made up his mind about them was particularly distressing to his subordinates.

On the evening of July 14, following the Bastille Day celebrations, Brigadier General Peyton C. March, who had come over to take command of the 1st Artillery Brigade, gave the Headquarters mess a graphic description of conditions in the War Department. "He says the Mail and Record Room of the A.G.O. [Adjutant General's office] is piled six feet deep with papers not yet recorded, and that knowing there was a cable from General Pershing asking for him, it took six days to get it from the A.G.O. to the Chief of Staff. He says, and the statement was confirmed by others who were present, that the Chief of Staff writes everything out in long hand and does not use a stenographer at all. Uses a stub of pencil and spends hours over things that ought to be handled in seconds. He predicts the roll of the big steamroller about the day Major General Scott retires. He thinks it will be a clean sweep; if a steamroller can be said to sweep."

Half a year later, as a matter of fact, the incisive and hardheaded General March became chief of staff in Washington and took the wheel of the "big steamroller," the approach of which he so confidently predicted at 73 Rue de Varenne.

Pershing had similar difficulty in obtaining the services of Colonel T. Bentley Mott, who had long been a military attaché in Paris but who was then serving in the War Department, believing his knowledge of French military affairs and personalities would be invaluable. Colonel Mott, in his autobiography, told how he heard a rumor that Pershing had sent for him and went all over the War Department trying to confirm it. Nobody knew anything about the request. The colonel began a search for the relevant papers himself. He finally found the cablegrams from General Pershing, requesting his transfer to the A.E.F. staff, "all piled together (apparently without order or index) in a drawer" of the desk belonging to Captain Phil Sheridan, the son of the Civil War general. Colonel Mott thereupon arranged his own transfer and subsequently was assigned by Pershing to act as his liaison officer with General Pétain's headquarters.

It would be months before the War Department began functioning properly.

Meanwhile, Pershing had the gloomy privilege of studying the latest estimates of the opposing forces, compiled by the French General Staff as of June 30, 1917. These showed that on the western front the Allies had a total of 185 divisions: 115 French, sixty-three British, and seven Belgian. Opposing them were 155 German divisions. Germany, however, had seventy-seven divisions on the Russian and Rumanian fronts, many of which were being or soon would be transferred to the western front with the collapse of the Russian military effort and the disintegration of the Rumanian armies.

The one bright spot in the Allied picture was the success of the convoy system in the Atlantic, an indication of which was the safe arrival of the dozen transports bearing the First Division at Saint-Nazaire. In April, Britain's darkest hour at sea, the German submarines had sunk 545,252 gross tons of British shipping. With the institution of the convoy system, the sinkings decreased to a monthly average of 265,000 tons for Britain alone, and after April 1918 they declined to less than 200,000 tons. The United States Navy threw 400 of its 110-foot sub chasers into the fight against the U-boats. The North Sea Mine Barrage was laid down to supplement the extensive mine laying in the Dover Straits. Troop and cargo ships were armed. Newly developed direction finders were used to triangulate the position of lurking U-boats and send Allied destroyers and sub chasers to dump depth charges on them.

The result, crucial to the formation of the A.E.F., was that eighty-eight convoys, averaging a dozen troop transports, were dispatched from American ports to Brest, Liverpool, or Saint-Nazaire without losing a single soldier to the German submarines.

A less hopeful facet of the Allied war effort was the evidence that Pershing and Harbord noted of friction between the French and British commands on the western front. Three years of war had not only failed to eradicate the historic mistrust and suspicion between Briton and Gaul but in many ways seemed to have increased it. Each was inclined to accuse the other of letting down.

Pershing first met Field Marshal Douglas Haig on July 20 at his Second Echelon Headquarters at Montreuil, ninety miles outside of Paris. Pershing, Harbord, and several other American officers were the British commander in chief's guests at dinner and on a lengthy inspection of the various staff departments. Pershing was particularly impressed with Haig's open hostility toward the French and his comment on "the failure of the French to cooperate fully on various occasions." Haig's remarks, Pershing wrote, confirmed an ominous impression "I had long held that real teamwork between the two armies was almost totally absent." Equally chilling was the report of General Robertson, chief of the Imperial British Staff, who was also visiting Haig's headquarters, that the British Army had suffered 175,000 casualties during the Arras offensive of April and May, which supported Nivelle's attacks in the Aisne sector, and that "preparations were under way at that moment for another attack on Passchendaele Ridge," which would be depressing news indeed to the British infantry.

With the handsomely equine features of the upper-class Britisher and his beautifully trained cavalryman's mustache, Haig made a first-rate impression on Pershing, who believed that the visit established "cordial relations and good understanding" between their two headquarters. Sir Douglas, as various memoirs have since shown, wasn't quite the beau ideal of British chivalry that he appeared to be. Earlier in the war, through his friendship with King George and some of the leading politicians, he managed to undermine the first commander in chief, Sir John French, and supersede him. Contemptuous of the French—he believed that Foch was much too voluble and that Pétain lost his nerve under pressure—he co-operated most reluctantly in any of their schemes. While the Nivelle offensive was being planned, he wrote in his diary that he and his chief of staff agreed that "we would rather be tried by court-martial than betray the army by agreeing to its being placed under the French."

Harbord noted that his chief and Haig had much in common, both being cavalrymen with long colonial service, both with "strong, clearcut features, firmly set jaw and direct gaze which we associate with chieftainship. . . . Each was coldly impersonal and sometimes impassive—the Scot preserving that certain reserve which seems to characterize the high-bred Briton, the American the certain aloofness of his cadet days."

No personal differences arose between Pershing and Haig during the war, none of the fireworks that attended Pershing's relations with many other Allied leaders, partly perhaps because of the physical separation of the British and American forces on the western front, with the French armies between them, but partly also because of the mutual respect that formed with each meeting. Each, perhaps, was also aware of the flintiness in the other's character.

In various diary entries Haig recorded his impressions of Pershing. On July 20, 1917, their first meeting, "I was much struck by his quiet gentlemanly bearing." Subsequently he wrote, "Pershing is a good honest fellow," and "He is a fine type of man, honest, and apparently determined to do what he believes to be right."

About the only thing that Haig found annoying in Pershing was his habitual tardiness. Harbord, the chief sufferer from that trait, wrote on a later occasion that "I was mortified by my General being late for dinner." Sir Douglas would have none of that in *his* headquarters mess, "waited about three minutes and then took us in and we all sat down." Pershing was "nearly ten minutes late" in appearing at the table and "was evidently a little bit startled when he found that Sir Douglas had not waited for him."

On July 26, in Paris, Pershing met the civil head of the British Government, Prime Minister David Lloyd George, who was as eloquently Welsh as Haig was reticently Scottish. Breakfasting with Lloyd George at the Crillon, Pershing listened to a plea that because of the military crisis he should "assume part of the responsibility of deciding the course to be followed by the Allies." Pershing, mindful of the constitutional division of authority between the civilian and military branches of his government, replied that he could "join only in the consideration of the military aspects of the general situation." Later that day he met with Allied military leaders—Pétain and Foch for France, Robertson for Britain, Cadorna for Italy—and listened to even more "pessimistic" talk. Pershing reported to his fellow generals that twenty days earlier he had cabled Washington a recommendation that "at least a million" American troops be sent to France by the following spring. He read the War Department's reply that "twenty-one divisions, comprising about 420,000 men" would be all that the United States could supply by June 15, 1918. Afterward Pershing cabled Washington: "To accelerate participation American forces and provide necessary transport for American army and movements of armies from secondary fronts conference recommends that question of shipping be immediately taken up by Inter-Allied Commission."

The question of shipping, "on which the success of the Allied military effort really hinged," as Pershing said, was to vex the British and the Americans almost until the end of the war. America didn't have nearly enough tonnage to transport its Expeditionary Force, even with a score of German ships which had been in American ports when war was declared and which were recommissioned under the United States flag by the fall of 1917. The British had the ships but intended to use them as leverage—if that is not too mild a word—to get what they wanted out of the United States . . . namely, American battalions to serve under their own command.

But that suavely concealed attempt at extortion was not yet Pershing's problem. The first order of business for the American commander in chief, once he had presented himself to the Allied leaders, learned their views on how his forces should be used, and then formulated his own decision on deployment without excessive deference to those views, was to prepare for his Army to move into the battle line. It was also necessary to organize a line of communications across France from the supply ports to the front. In the meantime, the divisions arriving from the United States must be trained and outfitted for combat, and thoroughly, no matter with what haste the French and British wanted to see them in the battle line.

Major Frederick Palmer recalled a conversation he had with Pershing one evening as he strolled with the general in the garden of the mansion at 73 Rue de Varenne. "He did not mean to let others fool him or to fool himself. In short, J.J.P. knew 'what he was up against'. . . . As the months passed without action by the American army,

French propaganda in America, in its irresistible desire to hasten our blows to aid the French army, would insidiously urge on our public impatience to dissatisfaction which might demand a change of American commanders; another man would lead the victory march of the army he had formed. But he said he would prepare it on such a sound plan as legacy to his successor that he would have fulfilled his mission." Pershing must have been unusually depressed that night; he could never really conceive of being replaced, even through death. As the Secretary of War later learned, he could not be persuaded to nominate a successor in the event he was killed or seriously wounded. The conversation with Palmer sounded very much like that of a man talking to his possible future biographer (which Palmer was).

Certainly there was not a touch of valedictory about the vigor with which Pershing began laying the foundation for the A.E.F.'s entry into battle. The British naturally wanted the U.S. forces to move in shoulder to shoulder with their armies in Flanders, but Pershing decided "we could not be dependent upon facilities already heavily taxed to serve another army," and pointed out that "we would have largely displaced the French armies, whose location was based on the defense of Paris, to which above all things they were committed." Not the least of his concerns over moving in between the French and British armies was the possibility that "we might have found ourselves in a position that would have made it difficult to avoid amalgamation and service under a foreign flag, and that possibility alone was sufficient to preclude consideration of the Channel ports."

Pershing therefore decided to take over the Lorraine front, between the Argonne Forest and the Vosges Mountains and including the Saint-Mihiel salient, which had long been imbedded in the Allied front like an infected appendix. In the final grouping of the Allied armies, the British would operate as the left wing, the French as the center, and the A.E.F. as the right wing.

The most succinct explanation for this deployment was given by Pershing himself: "To the east the great fortified district east of Verdun and around Metz menaced central France, protected the most exposed portion of the German line of communications, that between Metz and Sedan, and covered the Briey iron region, from which the enemy obtained the greater part of the iron required for munitions and material. The coal fields east of Metz were also covered by these same defenses. A deep advance east of Metz, or the capture of the Briey region, by threatening the invasion of rich German territory in the Moselle Valley and the Saar Basin, thus curtailing her supply of coal or iron, would have a decisive effect in forcing a withdrawal of German troops from northern France."

In explanation of his decision to use France's South Atlantic ports to bring in supplies, he wrote, "The British were crowding the Channel ports and the French were exploiting the manufacturing center of Paris, so that the railroads of northern France were already much overtaxed. Even though the Channel ports might be used to a limited extent for shipments through England, the railroads leading eastward would have to cross British and French zones of operation, thus making the introduction of a line of communications based on ports and railways in that region quite impracticable.

"The problem confronting the American Expeditionary Force was then to superimpose its rail communications on those of France where there would be the least possible disturbance to the arteries of supply of the two great Allied armies already in the field. This would require the utmost use of those lines of the existing French railroad system that could bear an added burden. . . . It was estimated that these with the collateral lines available, after considerable improvement, could handle an additional 50,000 tons per day, required for an army of 2,000,000 men. The lines selected, therefore, were those leading from the comparatively unused South Atlantic ports of France to the northeast where it was believed the American Armies could be employed to the best advantage."

The ports of Saint-Nazaire, La Pallice, and Bassens were designated for use of the American Army's supply system, with Nantes, Bordeaux, and Pauillac available in an emergency. "For all practical purposes," Pershing pointed out, "the American Expeditionary Forces were based on the American continent. Three thousand miles of ocean to cross . . . the quantity of ship tonnage that would be available then unknown and a line of communications by land 400 miles long from French ports to our probable front presented difficulties that seemed almost insurmountable as compared with those of our Allies."

To handle the supervision of all these activities, Pershing created five sections of his General Staff at A.E.F. Headquarters, with G-1 assuming administrative functions; G-2, intelligence; G-3, operations; G-4, supply; and G-5, training.

That Headquarters staff, in the summer of 1917, attracted a number of men, many of them expatriates, who were eager for the glamour of a uniform without too much attendant risk. Others felt that their social and lingual qualifications entitled them to a majority or a colonelcy, that the A.E.F. Headquarters needed a certain tone and sophistication that couldn't be supplied by mere soldiers. Pershing would have none of it. He had worked too hard for rank to have it dispensed to every social butterfly that fluttered into the Rue de Constantine.

One of the many applicants was the elegant James Hazen Hyde, whose parties had once been the talk of New York society. One party, in fact, had indirectly resulted in his expatriation. Hyde was the son of the founder of the Equitable Life Assurance Society, in which he inherited the controlling interest in 1899. A cosmopolite and a leader of the porcine playboys of the Edwardian era, he gave his extravagant and fateful masquerade at Sherry's the night of January 31, 1905, with guests and décor a reconstruction of the court of Louis XV, with Mme. Gabrielle Rejane as the centerpiece and Franklin D. Roosevelt among the young stags. The newspapers estimated the cost of the party at $75,000 to $200,000. As a result of that publicity, young Hyde was forced to "mutualize" his insurance company and give up control over its management. The state of New York, meanwhile, began investigating the methods by which the big insurance companies piled up such tremendous profits, their interlocking directorates and other practices soon to be eliminated. Before the investigation ended, Hyde boarded ship for France and there he was still living when Pershing arrived.

Now he wanted a commission in the American Army in the worst way and was able to summon considerable influence on his behalf, but Pershing turned him down.

Three distinctly unmilitary characters who did manage to attach themselves to headquarters were Winthrop Chanler, William Eustis, son of a former ambassador to France, and Richard Peters. They were taken on "by subordinates without Pershing's knowledge," according to Major Palmer, but they more than earned their keep. "These three musketeers were of the same world, with no military experience. Chanler and Eustis were over fifty, and Peters past retiring age. They were in private soldier's uniforms, living at the best hotel, and wearing white armbands with 'Interpreter' in large letters. . . ." One function at which they excelled was taking charge of visiting firemen, who ranged from "the man of political eminence to the woman who wanted to plant flower gardens to beautify the front for the soldiers." They also "heightened the charm of the French countryside" for junketing sight-seers, whose letters of introduction could not be disregarded, such as lady novelists, congressmen, French senators, society women, and in-dustrialists from the States.

Two months after Pershing's arrival in Paris the glamour and ex-citement which had attracted such people to his headquarters, not to mention the cheering of the sidewalk crowds every time he made a public appearance, began to lessen. People were beginning to put a question mark after the refrain "The Yanks Are Coming." In his diary for August 18, Chief of Staff Harbord, now a colonel, re-marked on the "inevitable reaction" from the early enthusiasm over the United States entry into the war, "due to misconceptions of our state of preparedness."

It now appeared that the first American divisions would not be able to move into the line until "at least February . . . midwinter in a severe climate . . . so much participation from America cannot be expected before Spring." Harbord feared that clamor in America and Europe would "force us in before we are ready" and foresaw that Pershing "will have to set hard his projecting underjaw and stand firmly braced." This proved to be anything but an overstatement of the pressure soon to be brought on the American commander in chief.

9. Black Jack and His Nursemaids

Inevitably, under the pressure of responsibility and the necessity for making decisions affecting millions of lives, Pershing became a harder and grimmer man. Those who had known him since his days as a young officer, one of the "Three Green Peas," could see the hardening process develop almost perceptibly in the summer of 1917. He had always been a man of notably firm character, but what had merely been substantial now became granitic. He was to be responsible for the lives of hundreds of thousands of men, and he did not intend to allow human frailty, neglect, or inefficiency—his own or any of his officers' —to interfere with his task. Those closest to him had observed that the death of his wife and three daughters had changed him into a man who rarely thought of anything but his work. The tragedy at the Presidio hit him harder than all but a few persons knew; his only escape from brooding over it lay in the incessant demands of his position, which in that sense were a blessing. His private sorrows, instead of making him more sympathetic to other people's weaknesses, only hardened him.

Perhaps it was the effort to keep his grief and loneliness walled in, dictated by the pride of a man who abhorred any display of emotion, particularly his own, which contributed to making him what newspaper correspondents called a "cold arrogant fish" and his troops "a typical brasshat" (or something a lot more pungent). Pershing simply was unable to trade on his emotions to win the devotion of those who served under him; there was something false and servile about a man who commanded affection through actorish tricks or public heroics, in his view, and a democratic army ought to enter battle as coldly determined to do its duty as he was to do his. The mechanics, not the psychology of command engrossed him.

There were only two discernible occasions on which his façade of impersonality crumbled momentarily and something of his inner torment displayed itself. On both occasions the men with him were close friends, Colonel John G. Quekemeyer, his aide-de-camp, and Charles G. Dawes, an intimate since his University of Nebraska days.

Long after the war, Colonel Quekemeyer told friends of an incident that occurred one night after a grueling and disappointing day when his forces were engaged on the western front. They were driving toward the front. Suddenly Pershing buried his face in his hands, and Colonel Quekemeyer heard him brokenly muttering his dead wife's name, "Frankie . . . Frankie . . . my God, sometimes I don't know how I can go on. . . ."

On an earlier occasion related by Dawes in his diary, he and Pershing were driving across Paris one afternoon when "an instance of telepathy occurred." Dawes's son Rufus had drowned five years before. Each happened to recollect his personal loss at the same time, Dawes wrote, and "each was in tears. All John said was, 'Even this war can't keep it out of my mind.'"

There were other occasions which demonstrated that Pershing had not managed to stamp out all recognition that he shared a common humanity, but they grew rarer in the thinned-out atmosphere of power and intrigue. Frederick Palmer, who had known him since the turn of the century, maintained there was a "warm human personal Pershing" whose facets he had long been aware of but which appeared "less and less frequently as he became absorbed in the machine he created and drove; and, in the lapses, the smile the more quickly faded, the hand drew back more quickly behind the gray stone wall of his West Point training."

With this sort of rigidity of manner, this all but impenetrable armor of reserve and reticence, Pershing was fortunate in his choice of James G. Harbord, an intuitive and understanding man, as his first chief of staff. The relation of a commanding general and his chief of staff has often been compared to a marriage. A conflict of temperaments can ruin it. The commander has the rank and the power—and wins most of the glory—but must depend on his chief of staff, in the wifely role, to keep his house in order and his official family living and working in harmony. Despite the difference in their stations, they have to be able to talk freely, almost as equals. What Harbord called his "native diffi-dence" aside, Pershing allowed his chief of staff to argue with him, talk back if necessary, and give his honest opinions. There was no barrier of rank and privilege between them. When necessary, both men would raise their voices and pound the table—and the fact that Pershing per-mitted this freedom of thought and manner in his junior spoke well for him as a general and as a man.

No man in the A.E.F., with the possible exception of Dawes, got to know Pershing better than Harbord. After three months of close association, this was Harbord's uninhibited opinion of his chief, con-fided to his diary on August 18, 1917:

"General Pershing is a very strong character. He has a good many peculiarities, such as I suppose every strong man accustomed to com-mand is apt to develop. He is very patient and philosophical under trying delays from the War Department. He is playing for high stakes and does not intend to jeopardize his winning by wasting his standing with the War Department over small things—relatively unimportant, though very annoying as they occur. He is extremely cautious, very cautious, does nothing hastily or carelessly. He spends much time re-writing the cables and other papers I prepare for him, putting his own individuality into them.

"He thinks very clearly and directly; goes to his conclusions directly when matters call for decision. He can talk straighter to people when calling them down than anyone I have seen. I have not yet experienced it, though.

"He has naturally a good disposition and a keen sense of humor. He loses his temper occasionally, and stupidity and vagueness irritate him more than anything else. He can stand plain talk, but the staff officer who goes in with only vagueness where he ought to have cer-tainty, who does not know what he wants, and fumbles around, has lost time and generally gained some straight talk.

"He does not fear responsibility, with all his caution. He decides big things more quickly than he does trivial ones. Two weeks ago, without any authority from Washington, he placed an order one after-noon for $50,000,000 worth of airplanes, because he thought Wash-ington too slow, and did not cable the fact until too late for Washington to countermand it, had they been so disposed, which they were not. He did it without winking an eye, as easily as though ordering a post-age stamp—and it involved the sum which Congress voted for National

Defense at the beginning of 1898 just after the *Maine* was blown up, and which we all then considered a very large transaction."

To his chief of staff his greatest fault was a complete lack of time sense. "He is without it, as utterly as a color-blind person is without a sense of color, or a deaf man is without the sound of music. He is most trying in that respect. An American untried major general may not keep a Field Marshal waiting; or be an hour late to an Ambassador's dinner; and those of us around him are forever his guardians and trying to get him over the line on time. He has a similar lack of comprehension as to guests, and with dinner prepared for ten may bring home sixteen."

Pershing's reckless dispensing of hospitality almost drove the chef at the headquarters mess out of his mind, Harbord said, citing a dinner party he had given for "some people who had been kind to us." Pershing announced that the total sitting down to dinner would be fourteen. The following day he was absent from the house at 73 Rue de Varenne but "casting together the number we knew he had invited it developed that nineteen were coming."

Robert Lee Bullard, who had known Pershing since West Point, came over for an A.E.F. command and soon was designated to take over the First Division. Sizing Pershing up at their first meeting in a number of years, Bullard thought him "ambitious, fit, intent upon his purpose, vigorous, firm, thoughtful, discreet, impersonal and dispassionate in demanding obedience, creating and holding confidence by this very efficiency, but nowhere arousing enthusiasm except upon success; not a personal leader; admirable but not magnetic. . . . One of his most marked characteristics was directness and simplicity of action. He has done his greatest deeds as simply and naturally as a man washes his face when he rises in the morning."

The impression of the men serving under him, who saw him, if at all, only from a distance that made him as remote as some visiting maharaja, was closer to Bullard's estimate than those of his staff. The troops glimpsed a beautifully tailored, tough-looking officer with West Point written all over him, whose probing eyes seemed to take in every detail of their uniforms and equipment but had no interest in the men attached to them. One of the sharper memories of the A.E.F. was of whole divisions standing in ranks, in the worst weather, waiting an hour or more for the commander in chief to appear and give them the cold-eyed once-over—and who was Black Jack Pershing to keep thousands of fellow Americans standing on a parade ground swept by winter winds? They didn't know, of course, that he would keep the King and Queen of Belgium, the chief of the French General Staff, and the commander of the British armies waiting the same way, though under more comfortable circumstances. In time, Pershing won the respect of the A.E.F., but he was never beloved.

It was his rather impossible ambition to make every American soldier the model of bearing and discipline, and he expected draftees and National Guardsmen to have the snap and precision of West Point cadets within a few months. In October 1917 he issued an order whose requirements were all but impossible of achievement: "The standards for the American army will be those of West Point. The rigid attention, the upright bearing, attention to detail, uncomplaining obedience to instruction required of the cadet will be required of every officer and soldier of our armies in France."

"Every private a Pershing" seemed to be the commander in chief's motto. In his mind's eye, Pershing saw whole future armies turned out like himself and his West Point classmates of 1886. "When you stumbled upon a lost American doughboy in a God-forsaken hamlet," as Frank Simonds (*They Won the War*) wrote, "his bearing, the set of his tunic, his salute, all authentically recalled the general who sat in Chaumont."

The Sam Browne belt, though purely ornamental, was decreed for all officers in the A.E.F. (And, as a footnote to social history, the women of America had to give up their high-buttoned shoes to conserve leather for that purpose; the kid boot never made a comeback after the war as skirts rose to the flapperish level.) The belt generally was detested, at home and abroad, but Pershing insisted on it for his officers, even after Secretary of War Baker pointedly wrote him that the belt had been abolished in the States and described how officers, including a general, cheered when they were removed on a troop transport on which Baker returned to America. General March, as chief of staff, ordered all Sam Browne belts surrendered at the gangway when returning transports docked in American ports. But, as Baker observed, Pershing ruled over the American forces in France with a dictatorial authority that had never been given any other American general, and Pershing would not be swayed on this issue.

All his obstinacy would soon be needed in dealing with the French and British, both determined to get their share of American troops, with small consideration for Pershing's aspiration to build a separate American Army. It was his opinion and that of most Americans that the doughboy would not fight enthusiastically under foreign command. Many in the A.E.F. had some proportion of German blood and might resent having to fight Germans under French officers; likewise, those of Irish descent, embittered by the ruthless suppression of the Easter rebellion in Dublin, would hardly be eager to serve under British command. Yet it must be noted that American units which served under French and British command showed up quite as well in combat as those directly under American leadership.

The French made their move first. As descendants of Lafayette and the French troops who fought in aid of the American Revolution, they considered that they had a sentimental priority on American gratitude and designated themselves as patrons, mentors, and counselors of the American Army. Patiently and persistently they attempted to infiltrate American Headquarters, and politely and diplomatically they were turned away. First they tried to palm off their revered but declining Marshal Joffre on the Americans, who naturally wondered why he was being wished on them when the French themselves desperately needed all their available talent to revivify their faltering armies. Yet Joffre and his staff were fondly propelled at the Americans with all the persistence of a French matchmaker intent on earning her fee. They were "almost inevitable guests wherever we found ourselves," Harbord remarked. Pershing, he added, had "no thought of engaging any nurse for himself, not even so eminent a one as Joffre."

When the failure to attach Joffre to the American command was apparent, the French attempted to saddle the A.E.F. with "tactical advisers"—planners and instructors, actually—but these, too, were politely brushed off.

Much more subtle were the efforts of General Pétain to guide and influence Pershing. The French commander invited the American to observe the attack of the Second French Army astride the Meuse. En route they stopped to inspect a number of American First Division units billeted in various villages in the Second Army's rear areas. Pershing was so exhilarated by the prospect of visiting the fighting front that he played a small practical joke on Pétain, always a mark of favor among Americans, though Pétain may not have realized it. The two generals had climbed into a haymow to inspect the Americans' quarters in one village. "I happened to stand apart near a neatly made bunk," Pershing recalled, "and in the dim light Pétain mistook me for the sergeant in charge. He asked me how we liked our billets and a number of other questions about our life in France, which I answered respectfully, playing the part the best I could. He did not know the difference until he was told by some of the amused members of his staff after we had descended." At Souilly they stopped at a French military hospital where Pétain conferred the Croix de Guerre on a nurse who had been blinded by a shell splinter and introduced her to General Pershing. The blinded young woman was so overjoyed by the visit, Pershing believed, that she "had entirely forgotten her pain"—a rather common delusion among generals visiting military hospitals.

On August 20, at the command post of the French XVI Corps, Pershing watched the successful attacks on Le Mort Homme and Hill 304, with "the battlefield before us like a panorama." He was particularly fascinated by the Foreign Legion, "in which I had become interested many years before from reading Ouida's *Under Two Flags*," going into action across the Meuse. That afternoon he held a reunion with Major General Corvisart, the commander of the XVI Corps, whom he had met as a military observer in Manchuria a dozen years before. The two men discussed how old friends and acquaintances had been divided by war. Pershing asked about Major Von Etzel, the senior German attaché, and Corvisart replied, "I have just beaten him today. He is commanding a division opposite me."

Pershing considered his trip with Pétain "agreeable" and "instructive." The American, on the way back to Paris, mentioned the fact that an artist named Jonas had just finished his portrait for publication in *L'Illustration*. "Don't let them publish it!" Pétain warned him. "Every officer whose portrait by Jonas has appeared in that journal has been relieved from his command." While denying that he was superstitious, Pershing recorded that he "immediately forbade the publication of the portrait, and to this day it has never appeared."

His chief of staff was not too impressed by the surface amiability between the two commanders in chief. "Both are strong men, ambitious, of the same age; neither of them averse to power; each in a sense ruthless in going to his ends." Harbord foresaw trouble in the French air of superiority in the presence of the American tyros. "For the present the French attitude," he wrote in his diary August 21, just after returning with Pershing from the Second Army visit, "is at times very distinctly patronizing. We are doubtless looked upon somewhat as amateurs, though I believe the average professional level in our commissioned ranks is higher than theirs."

Recently, Harbord said, Pétain had forwarded "several suggestions that have been distinctly patronizing and in which he has played all around the word 'order' without quite using it. He will do well to omit that word from his repertoire. Our General is very cautious, thinks very deeply; takes no false steps; knows his ground, and he knows he holds the whiphand, if one may use that word in speaking of relations with an ally. . . . The General is going to suggest to him that their dealings had better generally be direct and personal instead of by correspondence."

Pershing himself was growing irked by the French practice of taking up matters with the United States War Department when they could not obtain satisfaction from him, and he was none too pleased by Washington's willingness to go along with this procedure. He shot off an angry cable after the French War Office asked for his views on A.E.F. organization, having already taken up the matter in Washington through High Commissioner André Tardieu. "Have replied that my views would always be sent my own superiors through proper channels," he cabled the chief of staff. "Seems unwise that our General Staff should permit such inquiries to be made, at least through a Civil Commissioner." The French, he later commented, had "the idea, at least temporarily, of handling our business directly with Washington."

Pershing was also disturbed by the present necessity of having a considerable portion of his growing forces indoctrinated in the French methods of warfare, which he believed to place an undue emphasis on the defensive. The British training methods, on the other hand, appealed to him "very strongly" because "they taught their men to be aggressive and undertook to perfect them in hand-to-hand fighting with the bayonet, grenade and dagger." His aim was to instill the principles of "open warfare" in his troops, holding that armies burrowed into trench systems might stave off defeat but would never achieve victory.

Some critics termed his beliefs "the cult of the rifle," considering it a throwback to the misplaced enthusiasms of 1914, when generals on both sides hoped to win a quick decision in the field and had to draw back, appalled by the heavy toll taken by machine guns, mobile artillery, and other defensive armament. He was unimpressed by the French and British conviction that "developments since 1914 had changed the principles of warfare" and their outspoken pessimism over whether sharpshooting American riflemen could prevail against the interlocked chains of German machine-gun nests on terrain generally favorable to the defensive.

Somewhat derisively, Pershing wrote that the French could be expected to take an unaggressive view since "nationally, unlike the Germans, they had been on the defensive, at least in thought, during the previous half century." The British also, "to a large extent," had succumbed to a fondness for the defensive. What he heavily discounted, with a newcomer's ebullience, was the fact that France and Britain, not to mention Russia, Italy, and Rumania, had seen whole armies swallowed up in futile offensives earlier in the war. The surviving Allies had then resigned themselves to a static war of attrition in which, presumably, the last living soldier would emerge from the last lice-infected dugout as the victor.

Pershing was determined that his troops should not absorb so much of the trench-bound philosophy of the Allies that they would lack the "aggressiveness to break through the enemy's lines and the knowledge of how to carry on thereafter." As a veteran cavalryman he conceived of a properly conducted war as a decisive clash of arms immediately followed by pursuit of the beaten army. Such a conclusive point could not be reached through one trench system battering at another with long-range weapons, trench raids, and purely local offensives aimed at reducing a salient. Reliance on the rifle would restore the power of maneuver and end the deadlock, he believed. His instructions to United States training officers were emphatic on this point: "All instruction must contemplate the assumption of a vigorous offensive." He never wavered in his conviction that "victory could not be won by the costly process of attrition, but it must be won by driving the enemy out into the open and engaging him in a war of movement." The price would be predictably high, but it must be paid.

It was his determination to train his forces his own way, rather than forwarding them immediately in company and battalion lots to serve beside British and French units in quiet sectors, that brought on his long struggle with the Allied leaders. So far he had managed to contend with Joffre and Pétain. In the fall of 1917, however, he had to deal with two much more accomplished pleaders—General Ferdinand Foch and Prime Minister Georges Clemenceau.

One of the few things that Foch, the Catholic, and Clemenceau, the violent anticlerical, could agree on was that Pershing must be won over. They differed on how this must be done. Foch, the soldier, was inclined to be politic. Clemenceau, the politician, tended to be militant. In this paradox, which should have delighted any Frenchman still capable of appreciating irony, Foch was undoubtedly the wiser man. Any ally should be coerced rather than bludgeoned if his usefulness is not to be impaired. Clemenceau, fortunately, had talents other than the diplomatic.

The history of France glitters with imposing figures, but few have exuded, particularly at his advanced age, the kinetic energy of Clemenceau. More than any other man he roused his country from its trance of defeatism after becoming Premier in the fall of 1917; the whole nation was warmed back to life by his incandescent hatred of the enemy and his determination that France should not slide to ruin in a mass conviction that defeat was inevitable. He had old-fashioned ideas about France's great destiny. While Pétain was completing the restoration of the morale of the field armies, Clemenceau was operating on the body politic, lopping off half-hearted ministers and corrupt bureaucrats. He made the French people believe once again that France was worth fighting for.

As two men who were unalloyed patriots first and Allies second, Clemenceau and Pershing were bound to become adversaries. Clemenceau was continually angered by the way Pershing "kept putting things off" with his "tightlipped smile." Pershing, he thought, merely "owed it to the romantic side of America's intervention to form a self-contained American army." About all that Clemenceau conceded to Pershing as a military leader was an invincible stubbornness, and "the more I insisted the more he resisted. So much so that we often parted with smiles that on both sides concealed gnashings of teeth." The "Tiger of France" had no patience with America's own aspirations on entering the war; its President was a giddy idealist, and its people should be eager to fling a whole generation of its youth into the Allied trenches without asking questions. Pershing and his generals were supremely selfish in withholding their divisions until they were properly trained and organized under their own flag. "The fanatical determination of the great chiefs of the American Army to delay the arrival of the star-spangled banner on the battlefield . . . was costing us, and our Allies too, seas of blood. Their fierce super-patriotism refused to listen, and they wanted nothing less than a heaven-born strategical coup that should enable them to begin and end the war spectacularly with one stroke."

Clemenceau was a man of parts—teacher, physician, author, dramatist, newspaper editor (in which capacity he had vigorously supported the cause of Captain Dreyfus), senator, duelist, above all the perpetual gadfly of French politics, celebrated for decades as the "wrecker of Cabinets." He often expressed "supreme contempt for the human race," and once declared "I am against all Governments, including my own." He spoke English with a strong American accent, having lived in the United States around the time of the Civil War, and General Bullard noted that during a visit to the First Division he tossed off whiskey without grimacing as his companions did. He spoke to Bullard of his great admiration for Andrew Jackson, whom he somewhat resembled, both as a fighter of duels and as an aggressive politician. Clemenceau admitted the resemblance to Bullard, but added with a touch of envy, "Ah, yes, but I never fought a duel on horseback."

When the French Government fled from Paris during the crisis of the first Battle of the Marne, Clemenceau was editing and publishing *L'Homme Libre*. Naturally he stayed in Paris, and his front pages were plastered with denunciations of President Poincaré as a weakling and Premier Viviani as a fool and idiot. The government ordered his paper suppressed. When it was permitted to publish again, Clemenceau renamed it *L'Homme Enchainé* (The Man in Chains), and Paris roared with approving laughter. Thereafter, the government refrained from molesting his paper. Clemenceau was named Prime Minister simply because the desperate situation required a political desperado, and because, as an American correspondent wrote, "he had successively overthrown previous ministries, torn the reputation of every statesman into such tatters that President Poincaré, although he hated Clemenceau just as cordially as Clemenceau detested him, had no choice but to call the old fighter back to power." Few men command the invective to make two enemies in one short sentence, but Clemenceau accomplished the feat when he declared, "Briand knows nothing and understands everything, but Poincaré knows everything and understands nothing."

Pershing first became aware of Clemenceau's capacity as a one-man wrecking crew when, still only a senator, the Frenchman showed up on an inspection tour of the United States First Division, then

commanded by General Sibert. Clemenceau created consternation by
demanding to know why the division wasn't fighting at the front and
insisted "it was not so much a question of troops being ready as it was
of giving relief to the Allies." Senator Clemenceau refused to be impressed with the statement that the division was only partially trained
and "went on to say that America had now been in the war several
months and the French people were wondering when they expected
to take an active part." To Pershing, who would soon have to deal
with Clemenceau as the political leader of France, "it was quite out of
place for M. Clemenceau to make any such demand." He was also
alarmed by the fact that Clemenceau's visit "left the impression that
the French were inclined to dictate what disposition we should make
of our units. In many of their suggestions it was easy to see the possibility of amalgamation lurking in the background."

General Foch, soon to be made a marshal of France, resembled
Clemenceau only in his fiery patriotism and his determination that
the country would not yield to Germany. He was a military monk, who
had devoted all his life and thoughts to the Army and to often grandi-
ose conceptions of strategy. He was a leading apostle of General
Grandmaison's teachings that the French Army should be thrown into
a headlong offensive the moment it was attacked by the Germans, a
school of thought which General Fuller (*A Military History of the
Western World*) has characterized as "rivalled only by the dervishes
of the Sudan." When the war began, he was commanding the XX
Corps of the Second Army and immediately advanced in accord with
his own theories, but was rocked back by a German counterattack.
He subsequently became Joffre's deputy, then commander of the
northern group of armies as the Germans and the Allies raced to extend their lines to the North Sea and the Channel ports. A year after the
war began he was privately conceding that "the violent onset, aiming
at a breakthrough, has not given the results we expected of it." The
bloody but fruitless battles of 1915 and 1916 did little to enhance his
prestige, and by the spring of 1917 he was assigned to take charge
of an officers' school at Senlis—a disheartening comedown for a man
who had commanded a group of armies. At Pétain's suggestion he was
dusted off and appointed chief of the General Staff when Pétain
moved up to commander in chief.

Foch and Clemenceau had never seen eye to eye, although it was
the latter who appointed Foch commandant of the École de Guerre

before the war. Foch, knowing Clemenceau's anticlerical tendencies, told him, "I have a brother who is a Jesuit," to which Clemenceau replied, "I don't give a ——." Clemenceau regarded him as a suspiciously supple and overly intellectual soldier, and remarked that Foch "had the grave defect of being unable to endure the civil power—when he did not need its support."

The American liaison officer, Colonel Mott, who knew both generals well, considered that Pétain operated behind an "impenetrable mask" and "habitually screened his intense timidity behind a silence which often became uncomfortable" but that Foch had "a wider vision. . . . He belonged to no epoch; he would have been as much at home maneuvering the army of Caesar or Hannibal as he was in a campaign where aeroplanes soared and artillery fired at ten-mile ranges."

Whereas Clemenceau was inclined to bluster at Pershing, and Pétain to work on him through the friendship that had formed between them, Marshal Foch, in his efforts to explain the French viewpoint on absorbing American troops, was both gentler and more honest. Foch, according to Colonel Mott, who acted as interpreter at many of their sessions, "would try Pershing out on different lines to get his reaction and find the best approach. As time went on he came to understand the fire and generosity that were hidden beneath a grim exterior which, at first, had seemed to him, as to many others, like an unrelenting obstinacy." There were "heartbreaking difficulties," said Colonel Mott as they tried to understand each other over the barrier of differing languages. "Their minds could haltingly get into contact, but their souls would be groping in the void."

No matter how much good will was mustered on both sides, or how patiently they strove to understand each other, Pershing had to fight continuously for a self-contained American Army almost until the day of armistice. He had to endure a conflict of wills with the French, and later the British, at the same time he was laboring to train, organize, and supply the A.E.F. and then direct it in battle. It has been remarked that Pershing did more fighting in the months before the First American Army moved into the line than during its several months of actual combat as a unit. Much was made of his occasional bursts of temper over the Allied conference tables. The wonder was that they occurred so seldom.

The problem of supply, with bottlenecks at both the American and

French ports, with purchasing boards running rampant, with co-ordination applied only after the failure of various conflicting procurement systems had proved disastrous, was a constant vexation. The breakdown of supply was well illustrated by the fact that Pershing intended to have a ninety-day reserve of food and equipment in his depots and warehouses but soon was forced to settle for a forty-five-day reserve. If the Americans were amateurs at war, as Europeans maintained, they were even more innocent of knowledge on how to supply an army on another continent.

In the early months of the A.E.F., supplies piled up on the docks of French ports partly because there was little native labor available for stevedoring and partly because the American quartermasters simply didn't know what to do with them. Along the line of communications northeastward from the supply ports there was chaos resembling that across the Isthmus of Panama when construction was started on the canal. Back home it was just as bad. Hoboken looked like Tampa in 1898, with the lack of shipping causing a mountainous pile-up on the docks.

Pershing and his staff inevitably made many mistakes in ordering supplies, in countermanding orders, in asking for the unusable and forgetting to requisition what was needed. A classic example of the confusion was the matter of ordering unloading equipment for the French docks. On July 14, 1917, the A.E.F. ordered sixty gantry cranes. The order was then canceled by one purchasing board, but confirmed by another. Eight of the cranes were on their way before the cancellation arrived in the United States, were installed at the port of Bassens and found to be highly useful. The other fifty-two were left lying on various docks or at the plants where they were manufactured. On August 18, 1918, the A.E.F. cabled for the fifty-two abandoned cranes, plus sixteen more, and the war ended before everything could be straightened out.

On the other hand, Stateside purchasing and procurement were even more wildly erratic, having more men and money to confuse the situation. Forty-one million pairs of shoes were bought for 4,000,000 soldiers. Twenty-one million dollars' worth of horse-ambulance harnesses were acquired, although most ambulances had been motorized. Washington ordered 965,000 saddles for only 86,000 horses in the remount stables. A Chicago firm received $171,687 for producing exactly ninety-eight kitchen utensils ordered by the Army, and a Pittsburgh company got $3,000,000 for chemicals never delivered. A Massachusetts shoe manufacturer showed unfinished contracts totaling $6,000,000 when the war ended and received $1,300,000 by way of compensation.

Pershing complained that there was "ample evidence of great confusion at home due to lack of efficient supervision, even in New York Harbor, where experts should have been easy to find. Ships were seldom loaded to their full capacity; supplies greatly needed were often left behind; non-essentials were being sent over; many things were broken due to careless loading; and troops were often shipped to one port and their equipment to another. The Washington bureaus oftentimes followed blindly some out-of-date supply table drawn up under a former regime by an antiquated desk soldier long since retired and forgotten."

One shipload of oddities whose bills of lading were shown Pershing as an example of the useless items being sent over provoked the following angry cable from Pershing to the War Department:

"Recommend no further shipments to be made of following articles . . . bath bricks, book cases, bath tubs, cabinets for blanks, chairs except folding chairs, cuspidors, office desks, floor wax, hose except fire hose, step ladders, lawn mowers, refrigerators, safes except iron field safes, settees, sickles, stools, window shades. Further stop orders will follow soon."

In a subsequent cable, October 10, he cited a number of regimental units which had come over with only their combat equipment, medical detachments arriving without supplies or transportation, other units dispatched with their equipment and supplies loaded onto other ships, and added, "Manner in which these regiments come to France does not indicate much improvement over conditions Spanish-American War."

Human material for the A.E.F., particularly senior officers who would command brigades and divisions, had also become a matter of concern, and Pershing wrote Secretary of War Baker in a confidential letter: ". . . I fear that we have some general officers who have neither the experience, the energy nor the aggressive spirit to prepare their units or handle them under battle conditions as they exist today. . . . A division commander must get down into the trenches with his men, and is at all times subject to severe hardships." Few of the general officers coming over had "the vigor and alertness to inspire our men with confidence," he warned. "The French Army was filled with dead timber at the beginning of the war, and many French failures are due to this fact. General officers must be fitted physically and mentally, must have the go and initiative to fill positions fraught with such momentous consequences to the nation and which involve the lives of thousands, perhaps hundreds of thousands of our men. All the officers referred to [he had appended a list of officers whom he considered unfit physically and professionally] are friends of mine, but that should count for nothing. . . . There is one thing more, if you will pardon me. An army is a better fighting unit if it is a contented army. All other things being equal, this can best be produced by giving the most efficient officers merited recognition. Always having high efficiency as a guide, I believe promotions could safely be made from various arms on a basis of length and service and experience. . . . Any high class officer who has made good with troops in one arm very soon grasps the duties of another arm."

Pershing seldom, if ever, allowed friendship to influence his judgment of personnel. Aside from purely patriotic considerations, he was too ambitious to allow his own career and record to be jeopardized by men who were incapable of doing their jobs efficiently. Many old friends tried to get their sons or other relatives commissioned under his command, but they were almost invariably turned aside. One of his few exceptions was obtaining commissions for two of Theodore Roosevelt's sons—both of whom more than proved their worth in combat—and this was undoubtedly due to their obvious potentialities as well as to the fact that their father had given Pershing the key promotion of his career.

The only personal friend whom he plucked out of regimental obscurity and raised to a high place at A.E.F. Headquarters was Charles G. Dawes, whose experience as a Chicago banker and as comptroller in the McKinley administration he regarded as invaluable in straightening out the Army's procurement difficulties in France. Before Pershing went overseas, according to Dawes, he arranged for his friend from Lincoln days to be commissioned over lunch at the Metropolitan Club in Washington—the scene of more high-level politicking in the capital's history than any congressional cloakroom—at which their mutual friend, Charles E. Magoon, former governor general of Cuba, was also present. Dawes, joining the 17th Engineers, had gone off to war in style. He and his commanding officer took a private car to the base at Atlanta and lived aboard it with their wives while the regiment was undergoing its training. Herbert Hoover had tried to snatch Dawes back into civilian life as head of the grain price-control agency, but Dawes had successfully protested the proposed transfer as "unfair and cruel." Like many men of middle age he wanted the reflected glamour of war and the stimulant of whatever small risks attended the work of the rearmost headquarters.

As it turned out, Dawes not only performed splendidly as general purchasing agent for the A.E.F. and head of its ten-man General Purchasing Board, which represented all procuring departments of the Army as well as the Red Cross and the Army Y.M.C.A., but fulfilled another role as no other man could. He was Pershing's confidant, the man with whom the commander in chief could relax completely—even to mourning over their dead children—without losing face. Dawes's amiable personality and sense of humor undoubtedly helped Pershing over many rough spots.

Colonel Dawes was probably the only man in uniform who could get away with poking fun at the military formalities which Pershing held so dear. Harbord observed that Dawes "satirized" army custom by "exaggerating the customary military amenities." Once when Pershing made a surprise appearance at the château near Tours where Dawes and his staff had established themselves, an orderly rushed into the dining room to inform them of Pershing's arrival. Dawes and his companions had been chatting over coffee and cigars. They hurried out to line up and salute the general. Dawes, however, had forgotten to remove the cigar from his mouth and, in saluting, he showered himself and Pershing with sparks and ashes. Later Pershing took him in a corner and said, "Charlie, I might suggest that the next time you salute you put your cigar in the other side of your mouth."

For his part, the future vice-president of the United States recorded in his diary that "I have never worked in greater accord with anyone than Pershing," and regarded him as "the strongest character I have ever known." As Pershing's closest confidant, he reported in his diary that (as early as September 3, 1917) Pershing predicted the war would end by Christmas 1918 and foresaw as the greatest problem to be met by the Allies the working out of co-operation, somehow, between the United States, France, Britain, and Italy. "John is the master of his great place," he wrote on October 12. "It has not affected his perspective or changed him in any way. He has the proper mixture of caution along with his tremendous initiative and executive capacity. He thinks a thing out, and then acts without indecision."

His admiration for Pershing never quite inhibited his teasing the general in public. Once, dining at the home of Herman Harjes, the Morgan partner now serving on Pershing's staff, Dawes leaned back in his chair during a lull in the conversation and playfully announced, "General, I know Mrs. Harjes will be interested if you tell her about the old Spanish nobleman, Don Cameron, who used to entertain us in the same way in the old days." Unflustered, Pershing turned the tables on his friend by explaining "in detail" to their companions how he and Dawes had dined nightly at Don Cameron's ten-cent lunch counter in Lincoln, then "entered upon a forcible statement of the impossibility of properly militarizing an old friend."

In the fall of 1917, the A.E.F. moved its General Headquarters from Paris to Chaumont, which was closer to the sector its forces would occupy, removed Pershing and his staff from the intrigue and harassments of the French capital, and gave them a place where they could work out their problems in a thoroughly Americanized atmosphere. When necessary, Pershing could reach Paris by train or automobile in a few hours. Furthermore, he was provided with a château, seemingly an historic necessity for all generals fighting on French soil, whether they had been welcomed there or not.

Chaumont, a city of 16,000 and the capital of the Department of the Haute-Marne, was located in the beautiful rolling country of the Upper Marne and long had been a name place in history. It was the meeting ground of three feudal domains, standing where the frontiers of Burgundy and Champagne had touched on Lorraine. A century ago Francis II of Austria, Alexander I of Russia, and Frederick William of Prussia had signed a defensive alliance against Napoleon in its castle. The A.E.F. Headquarters was located in town, at the Damremont Barracks, the long stone buildings of which were grouped around a quadrangle. Pershing's office was a large, sparsely furnished room whose appointments discouraged visitors from tarrying. The light from the barracks-square windows shone over his shoulder and right in their faces. There was a row of straight-backed wooden chairs, no rugs, no wall decorations except a huge map of the western front on the wall to the left of his desk. The only other furnishings were a lamp and a telephone.

His residence, which his classmate General Avery D. Andrews

called "somewhat over-furnished," was the Château des Escholiers, built in the seventeenth century, four miles south on the winding road to Langres. He took over a suite under the baronial tower in the southeast corner of the second floor. In the east wing a collection of armor, medieval halberds, helmets, and ancient family portraits were moved out and another office established for the commander in chief. Here was his famous "night desk," where he received late reports from the front and disposed of matters left hanging fire from the daytime proceedings.

Chaumont still wasn't far enough from Paris to discourage ceremonial visits and junketing delegations. Among those received in the next twelve months, some with genuine warmth, others with whatever amenities the situation required, were the Prince of Wales (presently the Duke of Windsor), Lord Northcliffe, Hilaire Belloc, the Japanese Marquis Saito, Herbert Hoover, Franklin D. Roosevelt, E. H. Sothern and Julia Marlowe, Margaret Wilson (the President's daughter), Walter Damrosch, Elsie Janis, Dwight Morrow, Samuel Gompers, William Allen White, and countless American, French, and British politicians. President Wilson and his wife paid a brief visit there shortly after the war ended.

One particularly keen-eyed caller was Colonel Repington, the celebrated London *Times* military expert and intimate of Field Marshal Haig. On his visit to Chaumont on October 11 he was somewhat taken aback by the fact that only water was served in the G.H.Q. mess. Furthermore, he observed that the American staff officers "know very little of practical soldiering. One came in one day when I was in Wagstaff's [Colonel Cyril Wagstaff, the British liaison officer] office and said, 'Say, Colonel, when you have to move troops by rail what do you do?' Wagstaff had to explain the whole process from A to Z." General Pershing, however, "inspires me with complete confidence. He is naturally reserved, but frank, clear-headed, wise, uncommonly determined." Colonel Repington also observed that "Pershing and Harbord have an intolerable number of people to see and an overwhelming mass of administrative matters to attend to apart from all their difficulties with the French. The Americans do not yet understand what a General Staff means. It has been ignored or snubbed in the past, and, having become academic, it stands apart from the troops and is not, Pershing says, too popular with them."

Soon after the move to Chaumont—one of those "difficulties with the French"—it became apparent that the senior ally was still intent on supplying the A.E.F. with what the Americans called "nursemaids." The French kept sending missions to Chaumont in various watchful and tutorial capacities, and unlike the British liaison officer they were not inclined to sit in their offices and wait to be asked for advice or information. Pershing, in fact, felt it necessary to make tracks for General Pétain's headquarters to "enlighten him on their respective functions and powers," as Harbord wrote in his diary, "and incidentally to discourage his mission-creating tendencies." Pétain suggested that he send one of his best generals to Chaumont as an adviser. "Figuratively his Mission would warm the milk for our General, and do their best to see that he was taught his business. . . . I suspect, though, that he bumped into Pershing's projecting chin, for no Mission is to be established by him."

One visitor who was received with a sort of kindly impatience was Marshal Joffre. His staff demanded ceremonial flourishes for the visit, and the Americans had to turn out a guard of honor, complete with trumpeter, to lend tone to his arrival on October 15. "Personally," Harbord wrote, "I think that the simple-minded kindly old soul would prefer to be left at home to admire the goldfish and attend his geraniums, and think of the triumphs of his American visit, but the staff can see him sliding out of the public mind, completely ignored officially, without influence and power, and only for a moment regaining the limelight in the occasional exchange of visits with General Pershing."

It was rather a pathetic lesson in how quickly military glory can fade, once a man has been placed on the shelf and told to stay there until it comes time to grace some ceremonial occasion. One wonders whether Pershing himself ever recalled the rather tolerant and condescending politeness with which the old "Hero of the Marne" was received. He might well have, a quarter of a century later, when another world war had broken out and he himself ached for some sign that he was not forgotten.

"After dinner," Harbord wrote, "and we had said the usual banal things which people who are trying to learn each other's language say to each other, Boyd [Pershing's interpreter] was told to tell the old Marshal that he was no doubt fatigued and wished to retire. And he was and he did."

Joffre was pleased with the visit, even though he had been packed off to bed like an elderly child, and told Harbord that "we showed him the first soldiers he has seen in eight months."

Another eminent French soldier, still on the active list and commanding the quiet sector west from the Swiss frontier, also came to pay his respects. He was General Marquis de Castelnau, whom many considered to be the best of the French generals, but royalist and Catholic and therefore suspect. The Americans were highly pleased with Castelnau, partly because of his soldierly aversion to oratory. "Good old Castelnau," Harbord said, "confined his remarks to the raising of his glass and hoping that we might water our horses together in the Rhine, which I took to mark him of cavalry origin, but it turned out that he was an infantryman."

It was still necessary for Pershing to make frequent visits to Paris on inter-Allied matters. On one of his early commuting trips he and his aides stopped their automobile for a picnic supper along the roadside near a section house not too different, perhaps, from the one in which he was born. A half-dozen youngsters, thin-faced and hungry-eyed but hanging back at a respectful distance, gathered around to watch. Pershing, whose fondness for children was one natural instinct he did not attempt to suppress or dissemble, coaxed them until they shyly joined the picnic. On every motor trip to Paris after that, unless he was in a great hurry, he stopped the car at the section house and dropped off a box of candy, a cake, or a food parcel. His public relations officers might have worked up a much-needed human-interest story about those stops, except that he insisted they be kept secret. Apparently they served as a sort of talisman, a contact with simple reality, an antidote to the pomposity and egocentricity that filled his days.

Perhaps it was just as well that he had removed himself from the superficialities of Paris. He was especially irked by the numbers of Americans coming over to dally on the fringes of war and demand guided tours of the training camps. His wrath at idlers and curiosity seekers exploded over at least one innocent head, and a very pretty one at that. Mrs. Theodore Roosevelt, Jr., the daughter-in-law of his prime benefactor, had come over to Paris and busied herself with Y.M.C.A. work, partly, of course, to be closer to her husband, who had been commissioned on Pershing's recommendation.

She met Pershing at a reception, and the general was very pleasant, as always in feminine company, until "suddenly a thought struck him."

With his face "set like the Day of Judgment," Mrs. Roosevelt recalled, he demanded in a harsh voice:

"How do you happen to be here anyhow? No wives are allowed to come overseas. Where are your children? Your place is with them, not here. I think you ought to be sent home."

The young lady was mortified. Pershing's voice had carried across the crowded room; "it was as if the angel Gabriel had blown his horn." Causing a scene of any kind, particularly one that would embarrass a lady, was totally out of character for Pershing and testified to his exasperation with his junketing countrymen. Apparently he soon realized that he had taken it out on the wrong person. A few weeks later he apologized to her as handsomely as possible. His peace offer evidently was accepted. An entry in his diary read, "Had Mrs. Theodore Roosevelt Jr. to dinner with others."

10. The "Valley Forge Winter"

In the fall of 1917 one of the United Press war correspondents in France was an eager and ambitious young man named Westbrook Pegler. He was one of a dozen newspapermen domiciled at the A.E.F.'s press camp at Neufchâteau in the valley of the Meuse, not far from where the First Division was in training, at Gondrecourt, or the General Headquarters at Chaumont. One day when the other correspondents were herded off to visit the First's artillery camp at LeValdahon young Mr. Pegler decided to attempt a coup of the first magnitude—an exclusive interview with General Pershing. He drove over to Chaumont and, with the brashness acquired in the knockabout school of the police reporter, bluffed his way past guards and aides until he found himself in Pershing's office at the Caserne Damremont.

The interview, as Pegler told his colleagues that evening, was neither lengthy nor informative.

"General Pershing," he announced to the scowling figure behind the desk, "I'm Pegler of the United Press. Can you give me a statement on the general situation?"

"Pegler, get the hell out of my office," was the general's full and considered reply.

For most correspondents, the exceptions being those who had known Pershing before or were accustomed to dealing with the Regular Army, that seemed to epitomize the commanding general's attitude toward the press and its responsibility for gathering and disseminating the news. Not unexpectedly, therefore, the press regarded him as a ruthless disciplinarian, an overactive censor, a khaki-clad dictator, and often portrayed him as such for the people back home. Criticism had to be conveyed subtly, of course, or the correspondents risked having their credentials snatched away; they were treated much less liberally than during World War II, when a horde of public relations officers was assigned to cozening the press.

The conflict of interest between the press and the military was inevitable, the correspondent's job being to transmit all the information he could gather, favorable or not, and the soldier's to suppress a large portion of it on grounds of patriotism and/or military security. Generals had always tended to regard any newspaperman who told unpalatable truths as a potential traitor. During the Civil War, General Sherman had solemnly proceeded with plans to hang a correspondent until deterred by higher authority.

Pershing was never impelled to consider the firing squad for any of the correspondents attached to the A.E.F., but as a rule he kept them sternly at a distance. The newspapermen, accustomed to a certain deference from public figures, were affronted by his cold demeanor during their few and brief initial contacts with him. Nor was there any growth of sympathy when he finally submitted to a mass press conference at Chaumont. He tended to lecture rather than accede to the give-and-take which newspapermen expected of a confrontation with a government official. With sixteen accredited correspondents present, he tried to explain his reasons for demanding strict obedience of all his troops, to show that discipline would save their lives in battle. He added that he didn't want his soldiers to be turned into automatons but to learn and think out for themselves the purpose of their presence in Europe. They were learning the fundamentals of trench warfare under French instructors, but he wanted them also to learn to rely on the rifle and the technique of fast-breaking infantry attacks. He was preparing the A.E.F., he emphasized, for battles of maneuver which would break the deadlock on the western front.

An Associated Press correspondent suggested that Pershing might want to reconsider that last statement, since Allied generals of greater experience than his had reiterated publicly that the trench line could not be broken by any means. Would it not sound like boasting for an American newcomer to proclaim, without having fought a battle, that he had the recipe for victory? Pershing stared coldly at the A.P. man and replied with a rasping edge to his voice: "Of course the Western Front can be broken. What are we here for? We and our allies together are going to break it. You may quote me as stated."

Some may have been impressed with his confidence, but most of the correspondents were repelled by what they considered his arrogance in claiming that he had discovered the secret of victory. They little understood the complexity of the problems confronting him—the pressure from the French and British to parcel out his forces, the difficulties in setting up a supply line across France, the backbiting and confusion in Washington—and few took the trouble to wander afield from the press camp and explore them. The journalistic reaction to Pershing from then until the end of the war was as hostile as the general himself seemed to be toward the press. Their opinion was summed up by Herbert Corey, the correspondent for Associated Newspapers, in a letter to Henry W. Suydam at the American legation at The Hague: "The West Pointer promises to be the biggest joke of the war. He is ignorant, arrogant and in advanced state of mental decay. The younger officers may grow out of it. The older are, I think, hopeless. Our staff is viciously incompetent and is covering up the incompetence which it may suspect by a huge pretense of desk-slamming and cursing."

The most caustic journalistic appraisal of Pershing's stewardship of the A.E.F. was written by a lumbering young man who represented the New York *Tribune* in France during the fall of 1917 and then returned home before Christmas to deliver his opinions and observations beyond the range of army censorship. Few more telling pieces were written than those of Heywood Broun, who didn't like the Army, viewed all forms of military life with something close to horror, and detested most generals. He described the boredom of the troops, the petty tyranny of their officers, the general atmosphere of homesickness and frustration.

His comments on Pershing naturally reflected his attitude toward the seeming inhumanity of most military leaders:

"Nobody will ever call him Papa Pershing. He is a stepfather to the inefficient and even when he is pleased he says little. . . .

"His interest in detail is insatiable. He can read a man's soul through his boots or his buttons. . . ."

On a trip through a training camp, "we found him talking about onions to a cook," and he minutely inspected the sewage system, the kitchens, and hayloft billets.

On Pershing's strictness, a young officer was quoted as saying, "I think that his favorite military leader is Joshua, because he made the sun and the moon stand at attention."

Pershing, he thought, was learning the "value of a pat on the back given at the right time" but "still lacks a little of the French feeling for the dramatic in the doing of little things."

Broun observed with amusement Pershing's technique—or lack of it —in accepting the bouquets that were presented to him in every village along the way. "The donor was usually a French girl and a very little one. . . . General Pershing began by patting the little girls on the head, but he realized it was not enough and after a bit he began to kiss them too; only once or twice he got tangled up in their hats and found it hard to maintain military dignity. He handled the flowers gingerly. He seemed to regard each bouquet as a bomb which would explode in five seconds."

The habitually disheveled Broun could only marvel at how Pershing could emerge from a muddy trench or drill field without a spot or smudge on his boots and uniform, and his intense dislike of "rust, dust, dirt, round shoulders and hands in pocket."

Broun accompanied Pershing and his aides on a tour of American-held trenches in a quiet sector of the front, the general stomping along with a Romeo & Juliet cigar stuck in the corner of his mouth. They came to the dugout of a company commander who, they later learned, had spent fifty-two sleepless hours settling his nervous and apprehensive troops in the line.

The captain was just dropping off to sleep when Pershing banged on the door of his dugout and shouted, "Is this the company commander?"

"Yes," bellowed the captain, "and what the hell do you want?"

"I'm General Pershing!"

Broun noted, however, that Pershing "permitted himself the shadow of a smile" as he confronted the weary company commander in his dugout and listened to his stammered apologies.

The average West Pointer's attitude toward his men, Broun observed, was "generally speaking the same as that of General Pershing" and "I was inclined to believe that the men from the academy handled men better than reserve officers. They are strict, it is true, but at the same time they have been trained to look after the needs of their men closely."

Pershing's staff collected Broun's articles for the general's inspection, incensed particularly by the prediction that the troops would never call him "Papa," obvious though it should have been that he was hardly striving for popularity with his men. They drew up a statement charging that Broun had broken faith, having signed a pledge not to write anything without submitting it to censorship by the A.E.F., and presented it to Pershing for his signature. His chief censor, Major Palmer, argued against it. Broun, he pointed out, was "a good deal of a genius" and the regulations governing censorship should not always be applied "so literally." Pershing wisely agreed with Palmer and tossed the statement aside. Broun's credentials were revoked, however, and the $1000 bond posted by the *Tribune* was seized by the government on the grounds that Broun had violated censorship.

Pershing's views on press and propaganda were understandable enough to Major Palmer, but his natural aloofness prevented him from sharing them more widely. The general thought a lot of talk issuing from Chaumont would only be harmful. Disregarding the appetite for information in a democracy, he told Palmer "his army would speak for him when he had it in action. It ill became him to talk when as yet it was only in training, and he was protecting it from French pressure to infiltrate our troops into the French army." And there was an even more urgent reason for clamping the lid on optimistic statements from G.H.Q. He "did not want our own public or the French public to be deceived by false promises. . . . Our first hundred thousand were not to wonder, as Kitchener's did, if the war would not be over before they reached France; our people must realize they would have to put their backs into it until their withers were wrung and the French that they had to keep on having their withers wrung for a long period."

As for propaganda, Pershing tended to underestimate its potentialities and obviously did not devote a great deal of thought to the subject. The only psychology that interested him was his soldiers' morale; what happened on the home fronts, friendly or enemy, was beyond his sphere of responsibility. He told Palmer quite emphatically that he wanted to "avoid a propaganda of hate" toward Germany and the Central Powers, that he was determined that the Americans would "fight cleanly for the principles which had brought us into the war." (Doubtless, many of his Allied confreres would have regarded that statement as a fair sample of American naïveté.) As to the atrocity stories ground out by Allied propagandists—the tales of crucified

Canadians and violated nuns—he simply said, "Let's see if we can not get on without it." There was little hatred in his system for the Germans as men; he had a professional soldier's sense of detachment which tended toward a reluctant admiration of the enemy when he fought well. "Look at what the German army has done to the Allies," he told Major Palmer. "It has blown a balloon into their lines. It is a great army. I have some German blood in my veins and we will give them as good as they send, German against German, and better." He referred to the large number of German-Americans in the A.E.F. and the as yet unrealized hope that they would perform nobly against the German-Germans.

. . . The October rains came, and with them the cessation of major campaigning on the western front. Behind the lines the pace of work was necessarily accelerated. Almost every day the signs multiplied that American forces would be needed much more quickly than Pershing believed advisable. He now saw the war as ending in 1919, but many of his colleagues wondered if Allied morale would hold out that long. Russia had completely dropped out of the war, fully occupied with its internal problems. At the end of October, Italy suffered a crushing blow when the German Fourteenth Army broke through at Caporetto, took 275,000 prisoners, and was halted seventy-odd miles away on the Piave.

It was the beginning of what the Americans called, with some exaggeration, their "Valley Forge winter."

Pershing worked twelve to sixteen hours a day, sometimes holding as many as twenty conferences in his offices at Chaumont or in Paris, traveling constantly to the French capital and to his various training and supply centers. As his chief of staff recalled, the pressure around General Headquarters often caused tempers to crack. Colonel Harbord, even-tempered as he was, sometimes found Pershing more than a little trying. "It was not easy to read General Pershing, nor to know how seriously to take his first utterances on a subject. Sometimes they were thrown out to provoke discussion or were trial balloons or smoke screens. He took practically nothing on faith . . . and 'had to be shown.'" When Harbord told one hard-working staff officer that Pershing had queried him on just what the officer was doing, he was somewhat taken aback by the reply, "Hell, does he expect me to run and tell him every time I do anything?"

A "rather difficult period," Colonel Harbord called it, and the supply situation alone would have made it that. The chief of staff recorded in his diary how peculiarly the A.E.F. was being supplied. ". . . Caterpillar tractors where motorcycles are needed; kalsomine instead of paint; birdshot instead of bullets; mothballs instead of shrapnel, etc. Hundreds of well-intentioned suggestions, scores of self-advertising Americans, newspaper correspondents on every ship. . . . Wagon bodies without wheels, motor trucks without engines . . . mules without harness . . . forty-seven porcelain-lined bathtubs for the Aviation School. Trucks for these Headquarters, standing on the Hoboken docks on June 8, have not yet arrived. Ships coming over here loaded have to go back in 'ballast' as we sailors say. Last trip over one of them took 800 tons of sand. In the whole world just now, from our standpoint, there is no material thing or entity so valuable as shipping space to bring over material, men and munitions. Yet that ship was allowed by an intelligent Quartermaster Department to haul 800 tons of St. Nazaire sand back here on its return trip. Think of the shoes, the toothpaste, cartridges, socks, etc., etc., crowded out by that 800 tons of French sand. Wow-wow, and then wow!!!"

Several of the more energetic American correspondents began investigating the supply situation and found it deplorable. Item: 400 ailing soldiers of the Rainbow Division were being cared for in haylofts while hospital space was sought for them. Item: the few ambulances available to the United States Medical Corps had papier-mâché sides which disintegrated in wet weather. Item: elements of the First Division moving into the quiet sector near Arracourt were short of rations, soap, candles, and their American-made gas masks did not function properly.

The correspondents wanted to tell this story and applied to Pershing personally to have it sent through censorship. Pershing immediately cabled the War Department, asking permission to release their accounts of the supply shortages. ". . . Suppressing these dispatches subjects us here to charges of keeping back information which press reasonably claim American people is entitled to know. Such news must undoubtedly reach public in some manner. . . . As criticism seems inevitable, probably best not wait until it is published from hostile sources but accept it from friendly sources instead. Recommend therefore release to correspondents here articles involving temperate criticisms on supply departments where they are known to be well founded. Early action requested." The War Department rejected his disingenuous request immediately, pointing out that the stories "might be construed as criticisms by you through the press"—which, of course, was exactly what they would have been. It was a shrewd retort, bearing the hallmark of Secretary of War Baker's agile mind.

Pershing's chief consolation during the month of October was the news that the United States Senate had passed an act approving his promotion to full general, the first since General Sheridan. Otherwise it was not a heartening month. He cabled the War Department on October 21: "During the past week the water-soaked ground in Flanders and on the Western Front has prevented further development of offensive movements. . . . Next year must see two offensives, continuously maintained throughout the summer, if decisive result is to be obtained. This can only be secured through aid of effective United States Army on this side."

In his continual round of visits to American training centers, many of them under supervision of the French, he was depressed by the emphasis on the use of the hand grenade and trench-digging tools and kept pointing out that "in the American army the rifle has always been the essential weapon." At his insistence the American troops were taken out on the rifle ranges as frequently as possible. He kept a firm hold on all his units farmed out to the French and British armies for instruction. As General Bullard noted, "It was his requirement, at least with the commands which I exercised under the French, to keep a special wire from the commander of American troops to his own headquarters and to require full reports therefrom daily of what was passing—of all orders and operations."

Late in October the first American shots of the war were fired after four battalions of the First Division, on October 21, moved into the line east of Nancy with the 18th French Division. On October 23, First Lieutenant I. R. McLendon, Battery C, 6th Field Artillery, pulled the lanyard on the first American gun at 6:05 A.M. Seven days later a platoon of Company F, 2nd Battalion, 16th Infantry, was struck by a German box barrage and a trench raid by 250 storm troops, in which three American soldiers were killed. The A.E.F. was now officially "blooded." The trench raid, which acquainted many Americans with the sudden terror of fighting on the western front, was feelingly described by General Bullard. "It is a short, terrible, crashing fight, a thing of a few rods and a few minutes, filled with danger and death. It is preceded and followed by a tornado of artillery fire [the box barrage] that drives men into the earth as the only safety, from which they may not emerge at all—or emerge to death and capture. Its suddenness, its hand-to-hand deadly encounters, its carnage at close quarters with daggers, pistols, and fearful explosives, its shattering, bloody, merciless action, make it terrible to both raiders and raided. Well that it lasts but a few minutes; it cannot last more."

Pershing himself appeared in the front-line sector held by elements of the First Division when it planned to undertake its first trench raid. The raid was a complete fizzle. A long tube of explosives, called a Bangalore torpedo, was brought up to tear a gap in the barbed wire, but it was broken while being carried to the jump-off position. A half-hour delay ensued while the men tried to bring up another torpedo. By the time it was found, all hope of surprising the Germans was gone, so the raid was sensibly called off.

Pershing witnessed a much larger operation when the French Army Group of the North, under General Franchet d'Esperey, launched its offensive on the Chemin des Dames. It was a limited success. While the guns thundered across the Aisne, Pershing "enjoyed a menu that would have done credit to any restaurant in Paris," as he wrote, during a luncheon given in his honor by the French commander in a chamber of the old Fort Condé. With the battle hanging in the balance, General d'Esperey, with the ultimate in nonchalance, provided his guests with a long account of how he had crossed Iowa several years before during a local experiment with prohibition and could not slake his thirst with even a glass of wine. "To have heard him describe how he suffered while in Iowa," Pershing commented, "one would have thought he was telling of a trip across the Sahara Desert."

Continuing his whirlwind tour of France late in October, Pershing returned to Paris en route to Saint-Nazaire, where he was to inspect the docks and other supply facilities. For a man with his capacity for detail, he became quite helpless when confronted with the intricacies of a timetable and other aspects of travel. His aides and staff officers, including Colonel Harbord, were driven frantic by his talent for wrecking their arrangements. The party was supposed to leave the Gare Quai d'Orsay at 7 P.M. on October 27 for Saint-Nazaire. An hour before traintime his aides learned that Pershing would be delayed. His portrait was being painted by a young French artist, Mlle. Micheline

Resco, in whom he was taking a great deal of interest,[1] and he had loaned her his hat and belt to allow her to fill in those details in time for an important exhibition.

With considerable misgivings the rest of the party proceeded to the railroad station while the general, one aide, and a driver waited for Mlle. Resco to return the missing items of his uniform. When she failed to appear, Pershing finally consented to borrow his aide's hat and belt. By then the main body of his party was using every possible argument with the French railroad officials to hold up the train to Saint-Nazaire. Pershing finally showed up, fretting over the disgusting fit of his aide's hat, and the train was allowed to depart. Next morning, in Saint-Nazaire, his staff had to scurry around until they found a hat of the proper size. Colonel Harbord overheard his chief "pointing with evident satisfaction to the fact that his size was one-eighth larger than that of any of his party—to which I was tempted to reply that none of the rest of us had quite so much reason to have a large hatband. . . ."

Colonel Harbord was also afforded a certain amount of grim amusement by the struggle for favor between Pershing's two French aides-de-camp, Colonel Chambrun, Lafayette's descendant, and Captain the Marquis de la Ferronays, who would "sometimes almost push the General to the wall trying to snuggle up to him." The Americans had to arrange for the two Frenchmen to take turns sitting next to him; otherwise, as Harbord somewhat rudely observed, "someone might get slapped on the wrist, or they might start a duel with hairpins."

Through the orchards and hedgerows of Brittany, Pershing and his staff hurried on their inspection of the A.E.F.'s alimentary canal. They found little to applaud. The port of Saint-Nazaire was congested and the stevedoring situation was "worse even than had been reported." At the port of Bassens the construction of new docks was held up by an alleged shortage of long timbers for piling; the French, jealous of their forest reserves, wanted the Americans to bring the required timbers from the Pacific Coast, but Pershing remembered seeing tall trees in the Vosges Mountains and insisted that they be procured in France. At Coetquidan, where the artillery of the 26th Division was being

---

[1] Further details of Pershing's relationship with Mlle. Resco may be found in later chapters.

trained under French supervision, Pershing was displeased by the over-crowded condition of the camp.

All this was nothing compared to the disgust he registered on visit-ing a camp at Le Corneau, which the Americans marked down as a possible site for one of their infantry training centers but which was now occupied by the brigade of "disaffected" Russians who had to be removed from the battle line after raising the red flag and murdering their officers. The Russians had plundered the countryside; yet the French hesitated to disarm them, and a sort of armed truce prevailed between the Russians—"a heavy, stupid-looking lot," Pershing called them—and their nominal custodians. The camp at Le Corneau was the "vilest and most unsanitary place I have ever seen," Pershing said, and decided to let the rebellious Muscovites keep it.

Confronted by the disaster of Caporetto, which essentially was caused by the lack of co-ordination among the Allies and the ability of the Germans to transfer their forces quickly on interior rail lines, the Allies finally decided that their military efforts must be given a central direction. Unity of command was supposed to be the first prin-ciple of strategy, but until now the Allies had relied upon more or less voluntary co-operation between their commanders in chief. It simply hadn't worked. Haig and Pétain, in fact, avoided each other as much as possible.

Now the military situation demanded a change. Even with the Americans in the war, an Allied victory appeared anything but prob-able. Up to January 1918 the war of attrition in which the French and British high commands had invested their last desperate hopes was going against the Allies. On the western front, Germany had inflicted 5,800,000 casualties on her opponents, while France and Britain had inflicted a combined total of 3,349,000 on her, and even at Ver-dun, where the French fought mostly behind their complex of fortifica-tions, the Germans suffered fewer casualties of all kinds. "Germany," commented the caustic General March, soon to be United States chief of staff, "could have gone on forever under the system of attacks pur-sued by the Allies."

Three steps had to be taken to insure that the Allies would not con-tinue this slide toward military bankruptcy: the creation of a Su-preme War Council, the appointment of a Supreme Commander, and the formation of an Inter-Allied Reserve.

But the idea of unified command so affronted national interests and so provoked the professional jealousies of the generals that it had to be pursued with the utmost tact and caution. Only the Americans, among the military, seemed to have no fixed prejudice against the idea. The Allied chiefs of state, Wilson, Lloyd George, and Clemenceau—none of whom were inhibited by any great awe of their military leaders—were fortunately unanimous in favoring the scheme.

It was a critical moment in the political and strategical war that was waged endlessly behind the fighting fronts. The whole foundation of future campaigning under new conditions—Russia out, America in, Germany regrouping for a decisive effort in the West—had to be constructed under depressing circumstances. Whatever hopes the Allies still had of winning rested on whether the United States could fill the military vacuum created by the Russian withdrawal—and that did not now seem likely. The only possible way to take up the slack was to employ the Allied forces with greater effect and skill, which meant, first of all, that a Supreme War Council must be agreed upon. Toward that end the Allied leaders began gathering in Paris early in November under gray dripping skies and the pall of depression which hung over the wartime capital. Prime Minister Lloyd George came over from London; the United States was to be represented by Colonel House, President Wilson's plenipotentiary, and General Bliss, still acting chief of staff but soon to retire and become the American representative of the War Department.

Lloyd George, eager to sound out American opinion on a Supreme War Council, invited Pershing to breakfast November 4. Brisk as always, Pershing told him the idea didn't go far enough. "No council ever won a war," he snapped. "We must have a Supreme Commander."

The Briton, however, didn't think the Allies could agree on such a radical (though logical) step. The French would insist on a Frenchman for Supreme Commander and his own generals "might not like that."

Meeting three days later at Rapallo, the Prime Ministers of France, Britain, and Italy announced the formation of the Supreme War Council, which was to sit permanently in Versailles with General Foch representing France, General Wilson for Britain, General Cadorna for Italy, and General Bliss for the United States. It was resented bitterly by the field commanders to the end of the war, although they had only themselves to blame for it. Pershing believed that if the French and British commanders had "seriously undertaken to pull together," the Supreme War Council would never have been imposed upon them.

Many civilian as well as military leaders were opposed to the council, Pershing observed. "Military commanders were afraid it would result in undue interference with the conduct of operations and it was often referred to in derision as the 'Soviet.' The British Army viewed it with considerable suspicion, thinking it might substitute politicians for professional soldiers as directors of the strategy of the war. A stronger central control was advocated by influential French newspapers in the fear that their Government might not have so much say in Allied affairs as heretofore. . . . The action of the Prime Ministers was a step in the direction of unified command, which was no doubt one reason why most British as well as French officers, and a considerable number of those in high civil positions, were lukewarm toward it; yet not a few who spoke against the Council at the time said later that they had always been in favor of unified control."

Pershing himself was suspicious of any homogenized decisions that might come out of the council, having the old-fashioned idea that wars could not be directed by committees, that any practical and effective plans could be conceived in only one brain. Allied strategy would drift, he believed, until one man was placed in supreme command. Without that unity, he said, the French and British "made plans independently and any advantage gained was purely local, with little material effect upon the final outcome."

To Pershing, as he wrote Secretary of War Baker on November 15, the decision of the Rapallo conference showed only an "awakening" to the approaching crisis at the front. "Hitherto, each nation considered only its own interests, thus enabling Germany to beat her enemies in detail. It may not have been possible to have avoided the Russian collapse or to have saved Rumania, but as has been pointed out, it does seem that with a unified control the Italian failure might have been avoided."

Later that month the Inter-Allied Conference met in Paris. The American attitude toward it reflected a growing cynicism. Just before the conference met at the French Foreign Ministry, Colonel House called a meeting of the American delegation, along with Pershing and Harbord, at the Hotel Crillon. House made "a baldly cynical little speech," according to Harbord, and "in substance" told his countrymen: "We are going to meet this morning. Nothing will be done more than to go through the form of an organization. No speeches, for someone might blunder on to the subject of Russia, and some of the little fellows might ask disagreeable questions. It will be our business to be pleasant and sympathetic with the small nations. Listen to what they have to say. Do not promise them anything. Be pleasant. It is our day to smile. Just circulate among the little fellows and listen to their stories. Be kind and agreeable." A strange contrast, indeed, to the American propaganda pouring out of Washington about freeing the smaller nations from age-old tyrannies and "making the world safe for democracy."

Harbord had to concede that House's prediction was correct and "nothing was done" at the conference.

Pershing thought its only accomplishment was to agree that "the study of various subjects should be left to committees composed of Inter-Allied representatives"—the creation of more debating societies, in other words, as a substitute for action. He also noted that "everybody was looking to America to provide the additional manpower needed to give the Allies superiority."

General Bliss, who also attended, foresaw quite accurately that "the difficulty will come with the political men. . . . They do not fully realize that *now* the only problem is to beat the Central Powers. They are thinking too much of what they want to do after the Central Powers are beaten."

It would not be the last time an American registered such a complaint of his allies.

His British colleagues found at least one useful aspect to the conference, that of sizing up Pershing. Major General Sir Frederick Maurice, later a distinguished military historian, decided that the American was stubborn and standoffish, "singularly naïve and lacking in understanding." Sir William Robertson, the British chief of staff, found that he could also be sharp-tongued and incisive. Robertson had been expanding on the critical situation of the Allied armies in Europe when Pershing abruptly inquired why the British were undertaking an offensive in Palestine if they were so concerned about the security of the western front. Perhaps that kind of tactless question persuaded General Maurice that Pershing was "lacking in understanding." From the British standpoint, the truth was, Pershing understood all too well.

While the statesmen and the generals deliberated and formed committees, the lesser ranks suffered through a cruel winter. The winter of 1917–18 was the most severe of the war years, and the largely unheated billets of the A.E.F., the heavy snows in eastern France, and the shortage of firewood for stoves added to the general misery. "The gloom of short days and long nights in the isolated and largely depopulated French villages can hardly be described," Pershing wrote. The uniforms supplied American soldiers were lightweight and shoddy. Emergency purchases had to be made from the British Army, leading to near-rebellion in a regiment composed mostly of Irish-Americans who furiously objected to buttons bearing the English coat of arms.

Pershing himself did not allow the bitter weather to interfere with keeping in condition, which was almost an obsession with him. During fair weather he went riding every morning, with Harbord as his customary companion. Now he took his exercise afoot. Colonel Dawes, visiting Chaumont just before Christmas, found the château so inadequately heated that he dressed in front of a wood fire in Harbord's room. He glanced out the window after dressing, "and there was Black Jack, clad only in pyjamas, bathrobe and slippers, his bare ankles showing, running up and down in the snow outdoors."

But a chill wind of pessimism was circulating among even the comfortably quartered senior officers of the A.E.F. One divisional commander was so gloomy over the A.E.F.'s prospects that Major Palmer, at G.H.Q., arranged the tours of important visitors to avoid his headquarters.

Temporarily, at least, one of the pessimists was General Bullard, commanding the First Division, whose diary entries for the early winter months were drenched with gloom. He wrote of attending a *lycée* for senior officers of General Castelnau's army group at which high-ranking French officers "frankly faced and acknowledged that there was almost no chance of victory." At home, he noted, the chairman of the Senate Military Affairs Committee had charged that the War Department was so bogged down it had "ceased to function."

Bullard complained of "the growing rottenness" wherever he went in France. "Germany was plainly acquiring friends, spies and helpers in France. . . . Communication with the enemy was growing through Switzerland. French government officials were involved in the weakening and the preparation to yield . . . more, I believe, than was ever proved or than Frenchmen will ever admit. . . . Whatever may be the spirit or complexion of the Government, France is not going to fight any more in this war." (Somewhat more tempered but similar impressions were gathered by General Pershing at the same time. He said that the possibility of a negotiated peace was being considered by "not a few influential men" in England, and that in France the same idea was being propagated on the grounds that German and Austrian troops released from other sectors would reach the battle line in northern France before American troops could bolster the Allies.)

Bullard had long been an admirer and supporter of Pershing, back to the days when many other officers were enraged and embittered at his rapid promotion, but now his confidence in the commander in chief had ebbed away completely. On December 3 he wrote in his diary: "Our General Pershing is not a fighter; he is in all his history a pacifist and, unless driven thereto by the A.E.F., will do no fighting for France for many a day. Now let's see if this doesn't turn out so. I have had some (perhaps better than others) means and opportunity, in the Moro Country and the Philippine Islands, of observing and judging him. He is a worldly-wise, extremely ambitious and confidence-inspiring man, but not a warrior."

On publication of his diary some years later, Bullard appended the somewhat apologetic footnote that this entry showed "my depressed state of mind at the time." Bullard, a first-rate soldier, soon recovered from his moodiness. Had he not, it may be presumed, he would have found himself at the "canning station" at Blois, where misfit officers were gathered for reassignment, usually to a lesser command.

. . . If many of his officers were turning a critical eye on their commanding general in their understandable dismay over the progress of the war, Pershing was looking them over with an increasingly judicious and not entirely happy scrutiny. Within the next several months the first American divisions would be going into battle, and he was determined above all else to make sure that they would be led bravely and skillfully. In that determination, he never hesitated to relieve officers who faltered even momentarily, even though they were old friends or classmates.

He kept a particularly watchful eye on the division commanders and instructed the inspector general of the A.E.F., Major General Andre W. Brewster, to do likewise. The first to fall under the ax was General Sibert, who had commanded the First Division since its earliest days in France. Sibert was an engineer who had worked on the Panama Canal. In late November, General Brewster inspected his division and found its discipline far below the standards Pershing demanded and recommended that Sibert be relieved. Pershing sent him home immediately. On assigning General Bullard to take over the command, Pershing stressed the necessity of "being an optimist over the conditions existing." Bullard was also pointedly informed that another reason for Sibert's relief was "too much acceptance from the French of only defensive trench methods of warfare." His optimism may have evaporated once or twice, but he trained the First in Pershing-style, free-wheeling methods of attack. By war's end, the division was First in more ways than one.

The War Department began sending over groups of major generals who had been training divisions in the States, the first lot of seventeen arriving in mid-December. They were to tour the training camps and the battle front, ostensibly to gain some idea of what they would be up against if they brought their divisions overseas, but more importantly to be looked over by General Pershing. By then, Pershing had sent home a second division commander, Major General William A. Mann, who had arrived at the head of the 42nd (Rainbow) Division but who was nearing the retirement age and was characterized by Harbord as "a politician always."

Among the visiting generals was Hunter Liggett, who, as former head of the Army War College, was regarded as a "military highbrow." He was also one of the most capable officers in the Army. Harbord noted that he had "a tremendous waist measurement" and Pershing, with his belief that every officer should be as lean and tough as a young cavalryman, initially marked him down as "probably unfit" for service in France. Both Harbord and Pershing, however, were impressed with Liggett's determination to lose weight by going on morning-long walks. Bullard neatly described him as "a tremendously big man, bulky stout, of good-humored, non-worried, cheerful face. His great bulk might impress you as a physical weakness. It was not. He was active enough; he went when it meant anything to go. He was strong and hard; I have seen a big horse fall with him, pitching him a great distance on a hard, rough road, from which he rose without sprain or injury. . . . Liggett had the valuable faculty of seeing what was important and what was not. . . . Faster and with less concern (yet without offending) than any other I know, he could dismiss trifles . . . he just good-humoredly but effectively passed over them without notice, no matter who brought them up. . . ." Fortunately for himself and for the American Army, Pershing decided to keep Liggett in France and gave him command of I Corps as soon as it was organized. He became one of the most valuable of Pershing's lieutenants, ranking in that respect with Harbord, and eventually succeeded Pershing in command of the First American Army.

Two of the division commanders, Leonard Wood and J. Franklin Bell, were former chiefs of staff and Pershing's seniors in service. Both of them had been his superior in the Philippines, and both, for different reasons, presented vexatious problems. He simply didn't want Wood, regarding him as a troublemaker and a publicity seeker; yet consigning him to the dustbin would stir up a political storm. The case of General Bell was more grievous in a personal way. Pershing was very fond of him and owed him a debt of gratitude as one of the sponsors of his own success, but he was obviously too old for the trenches and was a diabetic besides. Pershing listed him among the "unavailables" in a confidential list compiled for the War Department. Bell returned to the States "a very heartbroken man," according to Secretary of War Baker. The latter appealed to Pershing on behalf of Bell, suggesting a training command in France. Again Pershing said no. Bell died a short time later, confirming Pershing's diagnosis if not his reputation as a good fellow.

Ridding himself of Wood would have been much more difficult had the ex-Rough Rider not talked his way into temporary oblivion, saving Pershing the trouble.

On his way to France, General Wood stopped over in London to renew his many old friendships in high political circles. He particularly charmed Lloyd George by agreeing that the American high command ought to pay more attention to British advice. He made no secret of his opinion that he could serve the Allied cause better than Pershing. Even the beguiled British must have remarked on his lack of discretion. If not, two of his high-ranking colleagues certainly did, and they made the most of it. Both Pershing in Paris and Bliss in London, uninhibited by any professional comradeship, tattled on him immediately. Pershing, in one of his "confidential" letters, wrote Baker that Wood was denouncing both the A.E.F. leadership and the Wilson administration and was showing an enormous appetite for personal publicity. General Bliss was even more specific in detailing Wood's indiscretions to Baker:

"I have heard repeated to me from all sides many reckless remarks

made by General Wood in regard to our military situation. The sum
and substance of it seems to be that he has done his best to discredit
the United States here in Europe. . . . I think I can already see the
evil effect produced on the minds of British officials here. It is going
to make it difficult for us to negotiate about getting aid in shipping if
people here believe that whatever sacrifices they make to give us additional tonnage are only for the purpose of bringing over an unorgan-
ized and undisciplined mob. From what I am told as to his sayings in
France, I should think that it would add very much to the difficulties
of General Pershing's position. . . .

"He knows that the British and French want us to do certain things
which I am afraid the American people will be very loath to approve.
He can tell their commanders and the heads of their governments what
he would do were he in control, leaving them with the conviction that
he would do exactly what they wish. I would not be surprised if you
were to find a quiet movement initiated through diplomatic channels
to substitute him for General Pershing. I learned yesterday that Mr.
Lloyd George had inquired at our Embassy whether General Wood
had returned from France, and had expressed an earnest desire to see
him as soon as he arrived."

Even while striving to replace him through currying favor with
Lloyd George and bringing British pressure to bear on a change of
commanders, Wood's manner with Pershing while visiting France was
most ingratiating. If he failed to replace Pershing, he still wanted to
come over as a division commander and make himself readily available. Pershing, however, refused to be charmed. When Wood told him
that the War Department was not supporting him to the best of its
ability, Pershing curtly replied that he was quite able to look after his
own troubles.

That chilly interview at Chaumont was not the least of Wood's mis-
fortunes during his French tour. He was struck by a mortar fragment
while watching a demonstration at the French school of automatic
arms. (GENERAL WOOD WOUNDED IN ACTION AT THE FRONT, read the
headlines back in the States.) On recovering from that wound, Wood
announced that he intended to stop off in London on his return home,
but Pershing insisted that he travel straight from Bordeaux to New
York. His bold attack on the Administration before a Senate committee cost him still more supporters in the government. "We have
piled mistake on mistake," he said, "but the American people are

aroused. This is their war now, and mismanagement cannot prevent them from bringing the full weight of their power to bear against the enemy."

Obviously General Wood would have to be scrapped. But it would not be easy. He would resist bitterly and would be echoed by his large political and journalistic following. Secretary of War Baker realized that sacking Wood would "cause almost as great a controversy as McClellan's relief from command of the Army of the Potomac." The War Department first tried to have Wood relieved on physical grounds —he had suffered a head injury in Cuba years ago, had been operated on for a brain tumor, and still walked with his left leg dragging—but a medical board unobligingly certified him fit for duty. The War Department then summarily and rather brutally ordered him to hand over his command just as his 89th Division embarked for France. (One of those saddened by his comeuppance was Colonel Harbord, who remembered his willingness to debate with younger officers on "terms of intellectual if not military equality," although conceding that Wood was not "notably discreet.")

Wood fought back as best he could, undismayed by a letter from Baker charging that "it is very difficult, if not impossible, for you to be subordinate." He demanded an interview, at which he was visibly shaken when Baker informed him that Pershing had said, "There is not room in France for both Wood and me." In his conversation with Baker, Wood apparently referred to Pershing in a rather threatening manner. On June 5, 1918, Baker wrote him, "Since you refer to our conversation of May 27, I take the liberty of pointing out to you another incident in it which left an unpleasant impression in my mind. I refer to the suggestion made by you that, because you had protected General Pershing's personal reputation in some way in the Philippine Islands, he ought now to feel himself under the obligation to take a personal, rather than a military, view of the possibility of your service in France." Just how Wood had "protected" Pershing, as he claimed, was not revealed. It was undeniable, however, that Wood had done his best in Cuba and the Philippines to promote Pershing's career.

No great admirer of Pershing's, General March, by then chief of staff, put the final damper on Wood's hopes for a combat command with a characteristically caustic comment that "it seems high time that meddling political generals be put where they can do no harm." Furthermore, March wrote Wood, "No backfire on General Pershing will be permitted, and you should understand, as a military officer of high rank and experience, that we must either support General Pershing or relieve him, and we don't propose to relieve him." After that, Wood stayed quietly on the shelf. A later and necessarily Republican Administration sent him to the Philippines as governor general. His greatest failing was not knowing when to keep his mouth shut; Pershing, who knew very well, rose above him with no great edge in ability and a great deal less persuasiveness—a lesson which might be emphasized in every military academy's curriculum.

It may seem from the above that Pershing had his own way entirely in matters of high-echelon personnel. On the contrary, he was balked on several such issues almost as important to him as the case of General Wood. He wanted to have General Liggett named United States representative on the Supreme War Council instead of General Bliss, but, as General March said, "That recommendation got nowhere." Nor did he want March as chief of staff in Washington. When Scott and Bliss both went into retirement, General John Biddle, a former head of the Army War College and ex-commandant at West Point, was named acting chief of staff on Pershing's recommendation. Biddle, however, failed to make much headway in clearing up the muddle and confusion in the War Department. Apparently he had acquired his predecessors' fatal habit of trying to deal with everything personally. Once Secretary of War Baker found him laboring over a pile of charts and making computations on a pad at two o'clock in the morning. "You ought not to be doing that," Baker told him. "Your part is to do the thinking."

Somehow Baker was convinced that General March was the one officer in the Army who had the energy, the ruthlessness, and the executive ability to straighten out the War Department. He kept cabling Pershing almost wistfully seeking March's services, and Pershing would reply that March was too valuable in his artillery command to be spared. On January 26, 1918, close to despair, Baker finally sent Pershing a peremptory cable: "Can Major General Peyton C. March be spared to return to this country as Acting Chief of Staff? If he can, direct his immediate return. I feel it urgently necessary to have him. Please reply." That pried March loose from his post as Pershing's chief of artillery. The latter's reluctance to let him go back to Washington may have been compounded in almost equal parts of his high estimate of March's ability as an artilleryman and a well-founded suspicion that he and March would find it difficult to get along. And Pershing was dead right; he and March kept butting heads from then on, and two harder heads could not have been found in the service.

Between March and Pershing there was no sympathy and little understanding, perhaps because they were too much alike in character. Both were ambitious, strong-willed, incisive. "I wish March were a little more human," Pershing was quoted as saying by Major Palmer, ignoring the fact that many complained of his own air of chill reserve.

March was a trim, energetic, hard-driving man who started out his day with dawn tennis matches and was as obsessed with fitness as Pershing. He was ruthless with men less robust and sharp-witted than himself and his prescription for a lagging or work-worn officer was "Send him to the Philippines!" as Pershing's was "Send him to Blois!" Secretary of War Baker recalled in later years that he had learned from General March that "when the moment comes to strike, a vigor and intolerance of position that amounts to ruthlessness may be necessary. I used to say to General March that he wasted a substantial part of my time and he would ask how; and I would tell him that I had to go around with a cruse of oil and a bandage to fix up the wounds which he had made." A less appreciative subordinate said of him, "His corpuscles are steel filings." But, as Bernard Baruch observed, "nine times out of ten his decisions were right."

With his neat, peculiarly suitable spade beard and his razorlike gray eyes, General March stalked the War Department, tracking down inefficiency, blasting a clearance of its paper-clogged channels, and ruining its gentleman's-club atmosphere. He was just as hardheaded as Pershing about dumping venerated senior officers. While acting as Secretary of War during Baker's absence from the country, he issued an order relieving General Scott, his own predecessor as chief of staff, as commanding officer of Fort Dix, believing a more active officer was needed. He did this, knowing that Scott's brother was a professor at Princeton during Wilson's presidency of the university and that Wilson himself had suggested General Scott for the post. Wilson did not interfere, nor did Scott protest.

One of General March's first objectives was to reduce Pershing's all but dictatorial powers as commander in chief in France. He told Colonel House, Wilson's "gray eminence," that Pershing's "primary duty was to command the American Forces in France; that he ought not to be allowed to undertake diplomatic work of any kind, and that he was peculiarly unfitted for it; that he ought to be freed from anything which would militate in any way against his actual command of the fighting forces there." He complained endlessly of and to Pershing. Many of his cables to A.E.F. Headquarters were phrased so peremptorily that they produced a mutinous reaction at the other end.

The issues between the two men ranged from the matter of the Sam Browne belts, which March detested, to Pershing's demand for cavalry regiments, which he thought ridiculous. Pershing wanted eight regiments of cavalry despite the experience of the French and British that cavalry was practically useless on the western front. It was a sort of boyish foible, March believed. "It must be remembered that he was a Cavalry captain before he was a general officer, and naturally would have a predilection for that arm."

March did not propose to humor the A.E.F. commander in this regard. He pointed out that the regular cavalry was patrolling the Mexican border, that sending mounted regiments to France meant fitting out additional transports with horse stalls and would necessitate space-consuming shipments of hay, straw, oats, and grain needed to sustain the animals. In opposing any sizable cavalry force for the A.E.F., March pointed out that the French had ten idle cavalry divisions and that the British had "135,000 cavalrymen eating their heads off" in reserve. He also believed that supporting a huge cavalry army had weakened Russia to the point of collapse. "The Cavalry arm was a gigantic incubus on the neck of the proletariat of Russia which finally drove it to the breaking point." He could not agree with Pershing's theory that cavalry might be employed as the pursuit arm even in open warfare.

That he succeeded in balking Pershing on this score was not the least of March's services. It took some doing, for almost to the end of the war Pershing kept riding his pet hobbyhorse. He also maintained a close inspection of the horses being sent to France for transport and hauling guns, much to March's annoyance. "I will not dwell," March acidly remarked, "on Pershing's cable bitterly protesting that the horses shipped him were not roached, or other minor eccentricities of the day's work."

It was the chief of staff's overriding ambition to impress the fact that, according to the regulations, he was the A.E.F. commander's superior.

Pershing, in the opinion of Major Palmer, admired March's qualities as a "driver," but even this tempered enthusiasm was not requited. March's tongue "had no less sharp an edge with his stenographer at his elbow, writing a cable to the commander in France, than it had when he had an officer on the carpet for castigation." Even though his temper "momentarily flamed," Pershing never would allow a "reply in kind to March." Much of the rub may have come from the fact that March was nominally, but only nominally, Pershing's superior as chief of staff, although he had been Pershing's subordinate as the A.E.F.'s chief of artillery. The two men were never able to agree on a clear division of authority between them, which made it necessary for the Secretary of War, as the superior of both, to act as referee and arbitrator.

March, in his memoir, *The Nation at War,* made no secret of his belief that a better commander could have been chosen for the A.E.F., nor that he himself might well have filled that role more capably. He claimed that Pershing's disrespectful attitude toward Marshal Foch was simply a symptom of his fear of men of greater ability. "Pershing tries to tell us that Foch was a mere strategist, as if the knowledge of strategy were a disqualification. . . . General Pershing's differences with Foch during the war were accentuated by a profound ignorance of the French military policy, curious in a regular officer of such high rank, and peculiarly unfortunate in one whose position, which brought him into daily association with the French military leaders, demanded the most exact knowledge on his part of every phase of the French military effort and character." March blamed Pershing's blind spots on his jump from captain to brigadier, because if he had advanced through the grades like most officers "his experience in handling larger bodies of men would have increased with his increase in rank. . . . He lost all this training as a soldier by being jumped over all those grades, and this experience is the very foundation of a complete knowledge of the art of war and of the command of men." General March chose to ignore the fact that Pershing had commanded formations of all sizes and varieties in the West, in the Philippines, and in Mexico, and that he had been chosen to lead the A.E.F. precisely because he had succeeded in every command, whether it was a cavalry troop or a division.

Harbord, who was frequently caught in the cross fire between Pershing and March, credited the latter with "tremendous driving force, notably in getting men and munitions to Europe," Pershing with being "too good a soldier" to allow March's abrasive temperament to "sway his official attitude of scrupulous punctilio." To March's claims for a larger share of the credit for the eventual victory, Harbord supplied a coolly judicious footnote: "No successful war has ever been fought commanded by a staff officer in a distant capital."

Pershing, at any rate, was fortunate in having such a shrewd and politically adept man as Newton D. Baker in the office of Secretary of War. Baker knew that both men were needed where they were. He also realized that March hoped to take Pershing's place as commander in chief in France. The Secretary of War killed off that ambition by informing March that he would never be sent to command the A.E.F., no matter what happened, and that his career was bound up in his success or failure as chief of staff in Washington. Nor would Baker be influenced against March by hostile emanations from Chaumont. March claimed that on August 17, 1918, Pershing wrote Baker "behind my back" that "while we seemed to have sufficient energy it was badly directed, and better results would be obtained if an officer from his own staff were put in charge of the War Department General Staff. He wanted a rubber stamp for Chief of Staff at home, so he could be entirely independent of any supervision or control." March said he didn't learn of the letter until after the war or "there certainly would have been a showdown." Baker, in any case, ignored Pershing's suggestion, as he must have ignored similar jogglings from March.

As the fateful year of 1918 began, Pershing seemed to be foundering under the strain of increasing responsibilities. Late in December Sir William Robertson reported in a memorandum to the British War Cabinet, following a conference with Pershing, that the American looked "older and rather tired." Pershing must have felt the way he looked to the British chief of staff because from January 12 to 15 he had a series of thorough physical examinations. The debility must have been superficial. The doctors, he wrote in his diary, with more elation than that with which he recorded the armistice, "found me in excellent condition and said my heart and arteries were as good as a normal man of thirty-five" and that his eyesight was as clear as that of "an eighteen-year-old boy" except that he needed "some correction for astigmatism." After that he wore glasses occasionally, but only in private, since he regarded the slightest physical flaw with intolerance.

The general's sense of humor, perhaps almost as important as his health under the circumstances, was also in working order. Just after the New Year, while visiting the Belgian front, he journeyed to Adinkerke to pay his respects to the King and Queen of Belgium. The train arrived ten minutes early, and Pershing, as usual, was about ten minutes late in his preparations.

Pershing and his orderly were still struggling with the general's left boot when the train stopped and his aide, Colonel Boyd, came to the compartment to announce that royalty was waiting on the platform. Pershing said he knew it only too well, as the royal band outside was "playing the 'Star-Spangled Banner' in the usual mournful cadence common to foreign bands." Colonel Boyd went away but returned a few minutes later to announce, "Sir, the King is out there standing at the salute."

The situation of a balky boot keeping a sovereign waiting was so ludicrous that "for an instant all of us, including the orderly, who rarely smiled, were convulsed with laughter."

Pershing finally conquered the boot and hurried out to the platform, buttoning his coat with one hand and saluting with the other, at which the band "ran through our National Anthem rather more vigorously, cheered up no doubt at last to see me in evidence."

He said that both Their Majesties joined in the laughter when he explained the situation and that the luncheon a short time later was "quite gay, especially when I became bold enough to air my dreadful French."

King Albert indicated that Pershing, whatever his lapses in punctuality, came off a lot better than the visiting American congressman who had recently slapped the king on the back and exclaimed, "King, you're the right sort of fellow and everybody in America admires you."

11. The Great Gamble

In the early months of 1918, General Pershing took one of the most prolonged and coldly calculated gambles in military history. It was a paradoxical role for a man of his character. Nothing in his earlier career, certainly, would have indicated any fondness for gambling on the grand scale. All his life he had played it safe; he had never taken chances with his professional career, but was a typical Regular officer to whom the regulations had a Biblical authority, who lived and acted "by the book," accepted and welcomed the safe bounds of prescribed doctrine. With no "book" to fall back on, he was now taking risks laden with historic consequence: virtually on his authority alone the American Army was to be withheld from the battle line until it was organized to fight as an independent unit. The French and British, seeking to absorb the troops coming from the States battalion by battalion, infantry and machine-gun units only, were warning that the war might be lost if he continued to hold out. Washington was weakening in its determination to uphold its commander in chief in France. His only legal prop, in fact, was a few words in the presidential directive—"the forces of the United States are a separate and distinct component, the identity of which must be preserved."

By the time the scarlet poppies covered the fields of northern France, the German armies might have an overwhelming superiority over the French and British. Pershing himself estimated (in a letter to the Secretary of War, November 13, 1917) that the Germans could mass 265 divisions, including forty-eight Austrian, on the western front, against a total of 169 Allied divisions. General Ludendorff, the Germans' presiding genius in the west, was then congratulating himself that "as in 1915 and 1916" Germany could return to planning on "deciding the war by an attack on land."

If Pershing held out too long, in other words, the Allies might be overwhelmed and the A.E.F. would have to be evacuated without having fought a battle. Pershing could then be charged with having lost the war.

On the other hand, he could have agreed to the French and British claims on his forces, citing the clause in his directive that "until the forces of the United States are in your judgment sufficiently strong to warrant operations as a separate command, it is understood that you will cooperate as a component of whatever army you may be assigned to by the French Government." In that case, the A.E.F. would probably never have existed except as a hollow shell of command, operating in an administrative vacuum; and whatever Americans accomplished militarily in the war would have been submerged entirely in the jealously competing French and British propaganda. Or Pershing could have thrown the whole problem back to Washington, refusing to assume such an immense responsibility himself. In the Mexican campaign, after all, Washington had called all the shots, and Pershing had not made a move without authorization. No one had criticized him for refraining from taking the initiative then. On the contrary, he was praised for possessing a fine sense of discretion.

But if the responsibility was his now, he was not going to shirk it or share it or shove it off on someone else. He was sustained by his undiminished self-confidence, which Frank H. Simonds (*They Won the War*) defined as the ability to "believe in himself without thinking of himself" and which possessed dimensions far beyond mere egotism. Several other factors also bolstered his determination: 1) his conviction that the Germans would fail to achieve a break-through, 2) his confidence that an American Army could be organized in time to tip the scales in favor of the Allies, 3) the fact that most Americans wanted their forces to serve under their own flag and command, and would have strongly resented their being used as replacements in battle-worn French and British divisions, 4) his belief that American methods of breaking the trench deadlock, of following the "fire and movement" pattern, would prove decisive.

The Allies had appeared to accept Pershing's program for an all-American Army that summer, when he made it plain that was the only way the A.E.F. would go into battle, but with the approach of spring and the crushing offensives which could be expected from the Germans they were obsessed, soldiers and statesmen alike, with the necessity of getting every Allied soldier into the line or the reserve positions just behind it. Only a wall of human flesh, they seemed to think, would stop the enemy's onrush; they had given up hope of outwitting and outmaneuvering him. Undoubtedly if Pershing had been able to organize an autonomous army by then, nine months after the United States entered the war, the Allies would have been willing to hand over a sector for its employment—they could hardly have done otherwise. In midwinter, however, Pershing could muster only four complete divisions in France, with only the First expected to be combat ready by spring. Many more were coming, but the shipping shortage slowed their movement overseas.

Thus Pershing was working toward victory in 1919, while the Allies pointed to the increasing possibility of defeat in the spring or early summer of 1918. Between these two conceptions, it was obvious, adjustments would have to be made. In pursuit of such accommodations, the Allies began an interminable series of meetings in Paris, London, Washington, and at various military headquarters in France.

To his face and behind his back, the Allied leaders maneuvered to obtain control of Pershing's forces. The British had now entered the game, having what they regarded as a pair of trumps, the theme of Anglo-Saxon solidarity and the control of the shipping which would bring the American forces to France. They had professed sympathy for the American determination to form a separate army, but now their generals were piping a different tune. Sir William Robertson, in a memorandum to the British War Cabinet, observed that Pershing had so many administrative problems that he was "unable properly to train or command his troops." In the present state of affairs, Robertson emphasized, "America's power to help win the war—that is, to help us defeat the Germans in battle—is a very weak reed to lean upon." Haig was still proclaiming his sympathy with American views to Americans but, home in England on leave, he confided to Colonel Repington, the London newspaper oracle on military affairs, that he "wants the Americans to come to us, and he wishes gradually to build up American divisions under our wing and instructions. . . . Haig would like to make good our deficit with American recruits. . . ."

The British then cautiously began advancing their own proposals for employment of American troops. Haig suggested that United States battalions be used to round out British brigades, now down to nine battalions from the standard twelve. The British furthermore wanted the Americans to trim the size of their divisions—which were "quadrangular," with four regiments and a total of about 27,000 men, more than twice the size of the French and British divisions—to something closer to the Allied standard. Pershing, of course, resisted. The argument that America's entry into battle could be hastened by bringing its troops over on British ships and inserting its battalions into the British brigade structure was now pressed upon General Bliss, the United States representative on the Supreme War Council, who obviously was a more reasonable man. And Bliss, whose concern for American interests was the equal of Pershing's but who was beginning to share the Allies' fears of what would happen in the spring, began leaning toward the British views. In a memorandum of December 18, Bliss already gave indications of this, writing that amalgamation with the British was "greatly to be desired" if "the French could be brought to look upon the Anglo-Saxon union as having no ulterior object, other than a certain defeat of the enemy." Baker, to whom this memo was directed, wrote Pershing a week later a letter reflecting this opinion:

"We do not desire loss of identity of our forces but regard that as secondary to the meeting of any critical situation by the most helpful use of the troops at your command."

General Bliss also believed that "our line of military action" should be changed to "bring us in closer touch with the British." He added, with evident approval, that the British held a "very strong conviction" that the "war must finally be fought out by an Anglo-Saxon combination," and that Haig "even said that he would give command of these mixed organizations to American officers."

The pressure on the Americans to yield rose to new heights, and, as Colonel Harbord wrote, "High dignitaries of Allied Governments appealed to the unofficial ambassador, Colonel House, as he tiptoed in and out of Europe. General Bliss . . . was constantly besieged on the subject. Every device known to advocates and parliamentarians was brought to bear. Every argument—except, perhaps, the one that amalgamation of our men in Allied units and the failure to put an integral American Army in the field would obviate the necessity of our country having to appear at the Peace Table." The British plan to bring over American infantry and machine-gun units, omitting the artillery and the supply trains which would make their organization into a division, "was not in the general Allied interest," Harbord believed, "—otherwise, why had it not been offered before?"

Now the French entered the lists again, with their new champion, the incomparable Clemenceau. It was the aggressive French Prime Minister's apparent design to eliminate the problem of Pershing's intransigence by getting rid of Pershing himself; the method was to suggest to Washington that Pershing couldn't get along with Pétain.

Pershing thought he had convinced Pétain that American troops should be trained his way, but according to Colonel Harbord the French commander "had not thought it improper to give Colonel House the impression that according to his ideas our training was not proceeding as it should." (That Pétain was going behind Pershing's back on more than one occasion was confirmed by an entry in Haig's diary the day of a conference at Compiègne [January 24, 1918] when he wrote that Pétain "told me that he is tired of the Americans, who are doing very little to fit themselves for battle." In Pershing's presence, however, Pétain was invariably courteous, sympathetic, and bleakly charming.)

The differences between Pershing and Pétain, Harbord believed, were "carried to America as an evidence that we were not in accord with our Allies, and synchronizing as it did with all the flubdub about the Supreme Inter-Allied Council, it was made to appear as but another evidence that soldiers cannot get along with each other, and thence to the easy Lloyd George reasoning that politicians ought to run the war."

In line with this objective, Clemenceau cabled his Ambassador Jusserand that Pershing and Pétain were at odds and Jusserand, as intended, passed this information along to the War Department, which immediately and rather sternly suggested that Pershing make amends. Pershing replied that "the French have not been entirely frank, as unofficial information indicates they really want to incorporate our regiments into their divisions for such service in the trenches as they desire." This charge evidently was based on information gathered by his chief of staff, for Harbord wrote in his diary at this time: "A French officer assured me that while ostensibly training was the object in General Pétain's mind, what he really wished to do was to reinforce his depleted divisions with American regiments. The loss of our national identity in the war, the absence of training to our higher command, meant nothing to him."

And now Marshal Joffre, shelved though he was by his own people and perhaps dimly resenting it, stepped creakily forward to bolster Pershing's determination. Pershing called on the old marshal on January 26 and found Joffre willing to speak frankly on the differences between America and its Allies. Joffre, Pershing said, confirmed "my objections to amalgamation," whether with the French or British armies, and told him that the French could effectively flesh out their divisions by rounding up *embusqués* (men who had avoided service on one pretext or another) and calling up the class of 1918, thus having no real need for American replacements. He also opposed absorption by the British on the grounds that "orders might be given by a British general or his staff that would be resented by Americans, but the same orders would be accepted without question if given by an American commander. In case of a reverse, there would be the tendency to place the blame on the Americans." Joffre also pointed out that the British had never dared to incorporate their own Commonwealth troops in the imperial forces. The marshal expressed himself so freely, even indiscreetly, Pershing said, "as an act of friendship." It was probably also an act of malice, an old man's resentment at the way he was being ignored.

Secretly supported by the senior French general, Joffre having insisted that his advice and opinions be kept confidential for obvious reasons, Pershing now proceeded to confront Clemenceau on the issue of intriguing against him through the French Embassy in Washington. He wrote the Prime Minister:

"May I not suggest to you the inexpediency of communicating such matters [as the dispute with Pétain] to Washington by cable? These questions must all be settled here . . . and cables of this sort are very likely, I fear, to convey the impression of serious disagreement between us when such is not the case."

Unabashed at being found out in his devious maneuver, Clemenceau replied that "contradictory responses" from Pétain and Pershing caused him to "seek an arbitration" through the latter's superiors. He insisted, however, that he had not authorized Jusserand to intervene with Secretary of War Baker, though "I do not disavow anything I wrote." Clemenceau ended his letter with the barbed promise to "exercise all the patience of which I am capable in awaiting the good news that the American commander and the French commander have finally agreed upon a question which may be vital to the outcome of the war." The upshot was a limited concession by Pershing: American regiments would serve in quiet sectors with French divisions until "sufficiently experienced," then be reunited under American command.

In advance of the meeting of the Supreme War Council at Compiègne on January 24, the three Allied commanders sat down together for the first time. It was not a moment too soon. Until then, wrote Major General Henry T. Allen, who had served with Pershing in Mexico and was to command the 90th Division and later the occupation forces, there had been much talk among the Americans because "Pétain, Haig and Pershing have never been in the same room together. . . . Pétain has stated that Haig is *un imbécile* . . . he does not rate Pershing's military talents at all high." Foch and Robertson joined the three field commanders at the Compiègne conference, and a general disagreement soon developed. The two French generals could not even agree between themselves. Pétain stressed the necessity of organizing a defense in depth to meet the German offensives expected in the spring. Foch, having recovered his faith in a more aggressive posture, argued in favor of a powerful counterstroke and expressed the opinion, displeasing to Pétain as the First Hero of Verdun, that "the German offensive at Verdun was stopped not by our resistance there but our offensive on the Somme." Both Allies professed to be astonished when Pershing reported his difficulties in obtaining supplies, rail transportation, and trans-Atlantic shipping. They proposed no solution for his problems, nor did they achieve "real unity of action," as Pershing had hoped they would.

Between then and the crucial meeting of the War Council, General Robertson finally spelled out just what the British wanted: 150 battalions of American troops. They would ship, billet, and supply them while they were serving in British brigades. Eventually they would be grouped into regiments and returned to American command. Just when, Robertson refused to say. Pershing therefore bluntly rejected the scheme.

General Bliss, however, viewed Robertson's plan with an enthusiasm that surprised and probably infuriated Pershing. The latter immediately took Bliss aside for a private conference, at which each general defended his views with vigor. Bliss finally suggested that since they couldn't agree, "each of us would cable his views to Washington to ask for a decision."

"Well, Bliss," Pershing replied (according to his own account), "do you know what would happen if we should do this? We should both be relieved from further duty in France and that is exactly what we should deserve."

Pershing hammered away at his senior until Bliss finally conceded, "I shall back you up in the position you have taken."

At the January 30 meeting of the Supreme War Council, Field Marshal Haig chilled the marrow of his confreres with the prediction that "calculating on half a million casualties . . . the British would in nine months be reduced by thirty divisions and the French by fifty-three divisions." The British commander also asserted, with a dogmatism equaled only by the inaccuracy of his forecast, that "the American army could not be trained sufficiently to operate in divisions this year," meaning that for the next year American troops could serve the cause only by fighting under foreign command. Under such dire prophecies Pershing had to concede that the British should have the 150 U.S. battalions but insisted that artillery and auxiliary troops must also be shipped, hastening the formation of American divisions once the infantry completed training. Bliss, keeping his bargain with Pershing, "made it as clear as possible that the permanent use of American troops . . . would not be permitted."

Pershing thus had yielded some ground to both the British and the French because the A.E.F. could not move without British shipping and could not fight without French-made guns, tanks, and planes, but he would not yield on the principle of turning troops over to the Allies for their permanent employment. In admiration of his lonely stand, Colonel Dawes wrote, "The President of France, the British authorities, Lloyd George, General Bliss—all arrayed against John—mean nothing to him except as they present reason. . . . John Pershing, like Lincoln, 'recognized no superior on the face of the earth.'"

Pershing believed his attitude toward the Allies was justified by what he divined of their real purpose, which was to engorge whatever American troops came under their control. He learned that Allied officers attached to A.E.F. Headquarters were secretly advising their superiors to "make every concession in order to get control of American units. . . . Among these there was one British officer who suggested to his superiors that they should aid us ostentatiously in building up a corps, which he thought would quiet the American people, especially if we were permitted to wave the flag hard enough."

Apparently he was unaware of a report by General Rageneau, chief of the French mission with the A.E.F., which supported Pershing's position. General Rageneau warned his government that insistence on combining American troops with the French "would only develop a useless tension." He also emphasized that all Americans were "unanimous on this point, from the Commander-in-chief to the lowest officer who discusses it. They do not wish to hear any talk about an amalgamation in which the American army would lose its personality."

For the time being, the integrity of the A.E.F. seemed to be assured, and Haig's attempt to have the Americans take over a sector next to his armies rather than in Lorraine, on the other side of the French, had been fended off. To maintain this balance between Allied demands and American military independence, to bear what Harbord called the greatest responsibility ever placed on an American commander, Pershing had to summon up all his energy and self-discipline. "The wear and tear on the man was something enormous," wrote Colonel Mott, his liaison officer with the French. "The tension lasted eighteen months without one day's respite." Only through this expenditure of energy was the A.E.F. able to pass something like a miracle—considering that there were only four organized U.S. divisions, plus the components of another, in France early in 1918—by throwing a force of 1,200,000 men into the Argonne that fall.

During the seven weeks between the Supreme War Council meeting of January 30 and the opening of the Germans' spring offensive, Pershing was constantly on the move between Paris, Chaumont, the supply centers, and the training areas of the five divisions now in France, traveling by automobile and a special train called the Headquarters Special which was completely outfitted for living and working, had telegraph and telephone communication, and had its accommodations supervised by a former Chicago hotel manager. Random notes in his war diary indicated the vigor of his watch over the A.E.F. On February 10 he sprained a tendon in his calf while leaping a ditch in his eagerness to get on with the job of inspecting the 2nd Division's training center. A week later he was back on his feet and descending on the 26th Engineers at Montigny-le-Roi, handing out "one hour's drill per day" to the regiment because "men going about the street presented a very slovenly appearance." In the base hospital at Savenay he was pleased that the nurses "stood at attention like men."

He avoided Paris as much as possible to keep the swarm of propagandists, Liberty Loan orators, and foreign military missions at a distance, and possibly also to stay away from the politicking and intriguing of the "Versailles Sewing Society," as his staff called the Supreme War Council. Only a week before the German armies started their big push for Paris, Harbord said, the A.E.F. Headquarters was overrun with missions which should have consisted of three or four officers but had swollen to sixty and "every excuse seems seized to create places that will justify the detail of officers away from troops." He was also disgusted with a flood of propagandists from the States who came over with the mission of "convincing the gallant French of the justice of a cause that they have given more than a million lives to defend." Of seven Liberty Loan orators who had arrived that week to seek inspiration at the source, only one of them was a man "of more than average intelligence, who eats with his fork, is not angry because the *petits pois* are round instead of square, and who seems to have heard of the places he is visiting before he came. Only one. The others are second-rate businessmen. . . ."

Secretary of War Baker and a large entourage arrived in France on March 10 and were taken on an extensive tour of the A.E.F. Pershing and Baker dined near the front at Baccarat, with the roar of German artillery shaking the silverware on the table, with Major General Charles T. Menoher, commanding the 42nd (Rainbow) Division, and his "very good-looking" chief of staff, Colonel Douglas MacArthur. They also visited the command posts and training camps of the First, 26th (Yankee), and 32nd (Michigan and Wisconsin National Guard) divisions. If a mere five divisions seemed a paltry effort after the United States had been in the war for eleven months—and it must have, no matter how much the various personages reassured each other —they could comfort themselves with the thought that another forty-five had been organized back home and were awaiting shipment.

On their return to Paris, German planes conducted a night bombing raid on the capital while Baker and Pershing were conferring at the latter's residence in the Rue de Varenne. As the two men watched the flashes and heard the distant crump of exploding aerial bombs from an upper window of the mansion, it occurred to Baker that even commanders in chief were mortal and were subject occasionally to such dangers as long-range artillery and enemy bombers. Had Pershing given any thought, Baker somewhat morbidly inquired, to a successor in the event of his death?

Pershing, a trifle startled, replied that he hadn't considered the matter but would do so.

He never brought up the subject himself, Baker said, but the Secretary of War reminded him of it just before leaving France. Pershing replied that he hadn't been "able to make a selection." This was quite probably true: it was inconceivable to Pershing that anyone else would lead the American forces into battle, and to that extent he was unwilling even to consider the possible claims of mortality. The doctors said he was in fine shape for a man of fifty-eight, and though he claimed not to be superstitious he had a firm belief that the Pershing luck would protect him against any stray shrapnel, strafing German planes, or automobile accidents.

Since Pershing never got around to making a selection, Baker decided that if the eventuality arose he would make a choice among three men: Hunter Liggett, Charles P. Summerall (an artilleryman soon to fulfill his great promise), and James G. Harbord. After a second visit to France, during which interval Harbord had given further proof of excellence both as a staff officer and a field commander, Baker decided that the A.E.F.'s first chief of staff was the best man to replace Pershing, having exhibited the "poise, initiative, judgment and perspective that fitted him for the command of the whole."

The morning of March 21, Pershing drove to General Pétain's headquarters at Compiègne, and the two generals discussed what measures might be taken to contain the imminently expected German offensive. One measure that would not be taken, although everyone agreed it was essential, was the creation of an Allied General Reserve, which would have allowed the reinforcement of any strongly threatened section of the front. It was agreed that thirteen French, ten British, and seven Italian divisions were to be contributed to the reserve, but the British had recently announced they would be unable to spare any of their divisions. Instead, Haig and Pétain were to support each other by mutual agreement. In other words, the Allies again were relying on the illusion of "co-operation."

While the two generals were talking, they heard a low rumbling noise coming from the north, the direction of the battle line. It sounded like someone shifting large pieces of furniture in a nearby house. The maps on Pétain's office walls fluttered from the vibration. Pétain's desk furnishings were joggled as the rumbling noise increased slightly in volume. Was it the long-awaited bombardment signaling the start of the German offensive? They listened anxiously, all considerations of strategy drowned out by the distant booming of the guns. In a few minutes their apprehensions were confirmed as the telephone lines from various army headquarters started ringing. The greatest crisis of the war was at hand. Between the Oise and the Scarpe, on a forty-mile front, the Germans were attacking the British Third and Fifth armies in a "maneuver of rupture" which they hoped would crack the Allied front wide open.

For months Ludendorff and Hindenburg had been planning to strike a decisive blow before the bulk of the American forces could arrive. The east had been secured by the Brest-Litovsk Treaty with Soviet Russia and by the occupation of the Ukraine. Their greatest obstacle to complete victory was the 4,000,000 men raised by the United States. At the moment Germany had a slight superiority in troops on the western front, and Ludendorff believed this advantage must be exploited before summer. He concentrated 192 divisions in the west—considerably less than the 265 Pershing had predicted, since he called on the Austrians for only a few divisions—and planned a series of triphammer blows to crack the hinge between the French and British armies, drive the British forces out of Flanders, and capture the Channel ports which were their life line to the home islands. Hoffmann, now commander in the east, was amazed that Ludendorff did not concentrate all his forces on one overwhelming blow and bluntly told Ludendorff, "Your Excellency, any cadet who tried to solve the problem in such a way would flunk his examination." Gambler though he was, Ludendorff couldn't be persuaded to risk everything in a one-shot effort. He wanted to pick up half a dozen victories, hoping they would add up to an Allied catastrophe. Hoffmann's prescription would probably have won the war for Germany; it was the Allies' good fortune that the brandy-fumed but clear-thinking brain of Hoffmann was never employed on the western front.

In a dense fog on the morning of March 21, two German armies, including many of the sixty-four divisions which Pershing said were specially trained in the mobile-warfare tactics he had been advocating for his own army, launched their attempt at a break-through. They were preceded by a hurricane bombardment supervised by an elderly artillery colonel named Brüchmuller, who had been brought out of retirement by General Hoffmann and whose uniquely ferocious technique of concentrating his guns in a short but shattering explosion of effort had been eminently successful on the eastern front. The bombardment wrecked the British forward positions. German infantry overran the first lines of the British defense and tore a huge gap in the Allied lines. In succeeding days the Germans gouged out a salient forty-five miles wide and fifty-five miles deep, wrecking Gough's Fifth British Army and taking 90,000 prisoners.

Now the front was ruptured, with the German assault divisions heading for Amiens and beginning to drive a wedge between the French and British armies. Paris itself was brought under bombardment by huge cannon (the "Big Berthas") with a seventy-mile range.

The Allied reaction, especially from the French side, was anything but bold or decisive. Now was the time to counterattack on the flanks of the German salient, but Pétain moved eleven divisions toward the gap in the British line so slowly and deliberately that it was obvious he was more concerned with covering the approaches to Paris than succoring his allies, and he was not up to the bold gesture of a counterattack. The Germans halted in their advance toward the vital nerve center of Amiens largely through a loss of momentum; there was little else to stop them, and if they renewed their attacks quickly the French left flank would be torn from the British right.

Pershing couldn't understand "why the British and French should not have had a larger number of reserve divisions within easy reach of the point of juncture. . . . Certainly it seemed logical that the enemy would endeavor to separate the two armies by attacking at that point. . . . The French staff seemed to fear that their front might be the German objective, and this might account for the lack of French reserves near the junction of the two armies."

But the Allies weren't asking for Pershing's advice. When he went to Pétain's headquarters to offer whatever help he could, the French commander, who "wore a very worried expression," hesitated over how the American forces might be employed and said, in effect, he would think it over. Meanwhile, Pétain tried to cheer up his armies with an appeal to hold their ground. "Our comrades," he proclaimed, meaning the Americans, "are coming. All together you will throw yourselves upon the invader."

The need for co-ordination of the Allied defense was so painfully obvious five days after the beginning of the German offensive that the Allied leaders held an emergency meeting on March 26 at Doullens, behind the British front. Present for the British were Lord Milner, the new Secretary of State for War; General Sir Henry Wilson, who had superseded General Robertson as chief of the Imperial General Staff the month before; and Field Marshal Haig—and for the French, Clemenceau, Foch, and Pétain. The Americans were not invited to attend. The main order of business was a document, signed by the participants, which read, "General Foch is charged by the British and French Governments with the coordination of the action of the Allied Armies on the western front. He will make arrangements to this effect with the two Generals-in-Chief, who are invited to furnish him with the necessary information." This was the first step toward making Foch the Supreme Commander. It was grudgingly taken. The minds of the generals who were to be subordinate to Foch swarmed with inner reservations.

Haig, in his diary, expressed his distaste for Foch's expansive theorizing on the virtues of the offensive, which he believed were impractical because "we have not the forces." He also noted that neither Clemenceau nor Pétain were very keen on the voluble little man. "It was evident that Pétain thought little of Foch, and that there is considerable friction between them." Haig also overheard Clemenceau "rather bitterly" congratulate Foch on obtaining "what he had always desired," and Foch's unawed retort, "A fine gift! You give me a lost battle and tell me to win it."

Pershing himself had always been in favor of a Supreme Commander, although his liaison officer with French headquarters, Colonel Mott, said that "Foch could never produce in Pershing the feeling that he was no longer a French general but solely an Allied commander-in-chief." He may secretly have preferred Haig or Pétain for the post, but Foch was the inevitable choice, having impressed the Allied statesmen particularly with his grasp of strategy.

Two days after the Doullens conference, on March 28, Pershing repeated his offer of all his resources to the Allies, but this time in a more resounding voice and dramatic manner. This time he saw to it that, unlike his offer to Pétain, it would echo throughout the Allied world. He set about staging his gesture of annunciation with all the care of a theatrical producer. The scene at Clermont, the headquarters of the Third French Army, was minutely described in his diary, almost as though it were a stage setting. He related how he and his aide, Colonel Boyd, waited in the garden for Foch, Pétain, and Clemenceau and "admired a cherry tree which was in full bloom. . . . There was not a sight or sound that would make one realize that not more than thirty kilometers to the northeast the French were at that moment counterattacking furiously. . . ."

Pershing took Foch aside a few minutes later and recited what was evidently a carefully prepared statement in French, worded in the somewhat grandiloquent, neo-Napoleonic style that Americans fancied would appeal to their mercurial allies:

"I am here to say that the American people would hold it a great honor for our troops if they were engaged in the present battle. I ask it of you in my name and in that of the American people. There is at this moment no other question than that of fighting. Infantry, artillery, aviation—all that we have are yours to dispose of them as you will. Others are coming, which are as numerous as will be necessary. I have come to say to you that the American people would be proud to be engaged in the greatest battle in history."

Fine, stirring words, and Pershing quoted in his diary the compliment of his aide that "under the inspiration of the moment . . . I out-Frenched the French."

Foch responded with Gallic enthusiasm, more apparent than real as it turned out, and "rushed across the lawn, holding me by the arm as he went. He told them [Clemenceau and Pétain] quickly what I had to say. M. Clemenceau showed a buoyancy and a gleam of fire in his face that made me realize why they call him 'Le Tigre.' General Pétain, who has a very unchangeable face and manner for a Frenchman, reflected the appreciation of his comrades. They were all manifestly touched. . . . I left a few minutes later with a distinct feel of admiration and sympathy for the French generally and in particular for those men."

Pershing was so gratified by the attention his offer received that he pasted *Le Matin's* front-page story in his diary, with the blaring headline:

UNE SPLENDIDE DECLARATION
DU GENERAL PERSHING

It was a regular Franco-American love feast, that scene in the garden at Clermont, but it produced nothing except headlines and visions among the French people of those stalwart young Americans, whom they saw standing in trucks or marching through villages, going into the line to relieve their own war-weary men. What Foch wanted was not the few available American divisions in the line, taking over their own sector under their own I Corps headquarters, but those hundreds of thousands of troops which were to be shipped over that spring and summer. The western front was cracking, but Foch was looking to the months ahead and the dissensions of the peace table, when it would be preferable to deal with the British alone over the spoils and vengeances of what was, after all, the European war.

In explaining his refusal to use the American divisions, Foch wrote in his *Memoirs* that France and Britain would not be able to replace their infantry losses out of their own resources and "what was needed, above all, was that during several months the United States should send only infantry to the exclusion of other arms." Foch thus revealed his intention of using the military crisis as a means of forcing the Americans to agree to the Anglo-French plan for absorbing most of the American troops. "It remained to convince General Pershing, who was full of the idea of commanding a great American Army as soon as possible, although he was not, it is true, fully aware of the urgency of our present necessities."

If Pershing was not "fully aware" of the urgency of the situation, he could hardly be blamed when the French were politely shrugging off the opportunity of deploying a full American corps in the battle line.

On April 3, the Allied High Command gathered again, this time with both Lloyd George and Clemenceau present. This time, too, the Americans were invited to attend and were represented by Generals Pershing and Bliss.

The meeting at Beauvais, forty miles north of Paris, was convoked to settle on General Foch's exact functions, none of the Allied statesmen being satisfied that the soldiers could be entrusted with submitting to Foch's "co-ordinating" until his directive was spelled out and agreed upon by all parties.

Pershing arrived an hour early for the conference and, though not ordinarily addicted to Baedeker he strolled around Beauvais with

Colonel Boyd, admiring the thirteenth-century architecture of its cathedral.

Then, at the Hotel de Ville, the amiable-looking but sharp-tongued Lloyd George opened the proceedings with the demand for a "better understanding" of Foch's powers to compel co-ordination. Always skeptical of the willingness of soldiers to co-operate with one another unless it was to their own advantage, he told his confreres:

"During the last year we have had two kinds of strategy, one by Haig and another by Pétain, both different, and nothing has been gained. The only thing that was accomplished was by General Nivelle when he was in supreme command. The Germans have done exactly what General Nivelle tried to do."

These initial remarks caused much inward consternation among the French and British military men, who regarded the Nivelle offensive as one of the great blunders of the war, an operation which, like Gallipoli, was inadequately supported and could have succeeded only with the utmost expenditure of men and matériel.

Lloyd George continued: "The Supreme War Council that met in February adopted a plan for handling a general reserve, but through the action of those concerned nothing has come of it. It is a nullity. What has happened recently has stirred the British people very much and must not happen again, as the people will demand why it has happened and somebody will be called to account. They want some sort of unity of command. . . ."

The British Prime Minister then asked the Americans to state their views, probably because he knew they supported his position more fully than the French or British military leaders.

Pershing, brief to the point of acerbity, said there would never be any semblance of unity until a Supreme Commander was named. "Each commander-in-chief is interested in his own army and cannot get the other commander's point of view or grasp the problem as a whole. I am in favor of a supreme commander and believe that the success of the Allied cause depends upon it. I think the necessary action should be taken by this council at once. I am in favor of conferring the supreme command upon General Foch."

It was virtually the only time during the war that Pershing and Lloyd George publicly admitted seeing eye to eye on any issue.

"Well put," commented the long-maned Welshman.

His own chieftain was less approving. As far as unified command was concerned, Haig said, "We have had it." In support of this amazing view, he added the even more astonishing claim that "General Pétain and I have always worked well together."

Pétain, agreeing with Haig for once, also thought that the Allies could operate efficiently with a co-ordinator rather than a Supreme Commander.

The conference, however, took a second reluctant step toward naming Foch the generalissimo of the Allied forces. This time his function was officially defined as "strategic direction of military operations." But his powers were to be anything but supreme. Tactical control would remain in the hands of each commander in chief, who would have the "right of appeal."

Thus the French would be allowed to maneuver as they saw fit to cover Paris, for instance; the British could concentrate to save the Channel ports, no matter what was happening on the rest of the front; and the United States could battle for the preservation of the integrity of its forces, come what may.

No mention was made of the American Army in the original draft of the Beauvais agreement, which caused Pershing to protest against its exclusion because "it will soon be ready to function" as an independent force.

General Pétain rather ungraciously pointed out that there was no United States Army in being "as its units are either in training or are amalgamated with the British and French."

"There may not be an American army in force functioning now but there soon will be, and I want this resolution to apply to it when it becomes a fact," was Pershing's forceful reply. "The American Government is represented here at this conference and in the war, and any action as to the supreme command that includes the British and French armies should also include the American Army."

He won his point, on this score, but he was not at all satisfied with the powers given Foch. Long before Haig and Pétain, he saw that the war could hardly be won without a Supreme Commander; his colleagues would not be convinced until other crises arose because, as he said, "in this case national pride entered to an unusual degree."

For most of the ensuing weeks, while the Germans renewed their pounding at the Allied trench wall, striking next against the British on the Lys River near Armentières and breaking through but failing to destroy the defending forces, Pershing did all his fighting across the conference tables, both in France and England. From then until a week before the armistice he would be involved in a constant struggle to form and hold onto an independent American Army.

It seems almost incredible now that only slightly more than forty years ago the United States should have been rated so low among world powers that its armed forces could almost be cannibalized by its allies. Had they succeeded, it may be questioned whether the United States would have reached its present eminence. The fact that they didn't can be credited only to Pershing; at Versailles and in Washington there was a tendency to yield under the Allies' pleas of "urgency," and several times Pershing himself was forced to retreat a little, but he refused to envision anything but a self-contained American Army.

American troops were not going to be fed into foreign armies and their lives frittered away in the deadlock of the trenches; they would fight under their own flag, and only when their efforts and sacrifices would result in ending the war. Clemenceau and others found his concept almost incredibly naïve; how could anyone guarantee victory by any means, when so many proudly proclaimed methods had fizzled in disastrous futility? Undismayed, Pershing clung to his one idea: that the war could still be won by overwhelming blows launched by unjaded troops. Anything but a visionary, with a brain which many rated as no better than a first-rate post commander's, with his schoolboyish distaste for theorizing and distrust of military intellectuals, he was the man who saw most clearly what the war and the peace would be like without an independent United States Army in the field. . . .

In the midst of such high-level concerns, Pershing could still fret over a button. Colonel Dawes, woefully unmilitary as always, accompanied him to a conference with General Foch in mid-April. Foch had just been named—at long last—the Supreme Allied Commander. As Pershing and his staff lined up outside Foch's headquarters, Dawes noticed on the general's face the look of "mingled friendliness, admonition and concern which characterizes his expression during some of my interviews with his better-disciplined military associates." Dawes then became aware of the fact that several of his overcoat buttons were undone. Pershing muttered something to his chief of staff, and Harbord solemnly went over to Dawes and buttoned up his coat for him, whispering, "This is a hell of a job for the chief of staff—but the general told me to do it."

On April 21, Pershing journeyed to England for another go-around on the question of troop shipments. The British, understandably dismayed at their losses in bearing the brunt of the German attacks thus far, were going to almost desperate lengths for reinforcements. Furthermore, Lord Reading, the British ambassador in Washington, working constantly on President Wilson and the State Department, had obtained Wilson's agreement that for the next four months 120,-000 American troops were to be shipped monthly on consignment to the British Army—infantry and machine gunners only—just what Pershing had been opposing so staunchly for so long.

En route, Pershing and his chief of staff received depressing news of the action at Seicheprey, where elements of the 26th (Yankee) Division were hit hard in their supposedly "quiet" sector east of Saint-Mihiel. The division had suffered 634 casualties, of which 130 were prisoners taken by the Germans. A box barrage had isolated a forward battalion, which was driven out of Seicheprey, and partly due to disrupted communications there had been poor co-ordination between officers and troops. The disproportionate number of men captured indicated both poor leadership and dispirited troops. It was not the kind of news a commanding general liked to hear at a time when he was trying to defend the integrity of American arms.

He was definitely out of sorts when he arrived in London. The night before the conferences were to begin he and Harbord dined at the Savoy amid the gleam of white shirt fronts and bejeweled bosoms. Later he wrote in his diary of his "annoyance" when the band struck up "The Star-Spangled Banner" to grace his entrance and "everyone stood up and made me feel conspicuous"—as though an American general with four stars on his shoulders, whose photograph had appeared on the front pages for months, could have failed to attract attention even from well-bred Englishmen. The Savoy, he conceded, was "a very gay place and little like any I have seen in France—people very dressed up and no signs of food shortage. We had oysters, soup, salmon, chicken, asparagus and soufle [sic], all on a regular menu card."

All that nourishment gave him needed strength for the often acrimonious meetings with Lloyd George, Lord Milner of the War Ministry, and the chief of staff, Sir Henry Wilson. The British attitude, as Lloyd George wrote in his *War Memoirs,* was summed up as follows: "General Pershing, fighting fiercely to ensure the corporate unity of the

American forces in France, had been successful in defeating every proposition which seemed to him to entail a possible threat to that unity. . . . The ultimate formation of intact American divisions was facilitated as a result of his stand. This would have been poor compensation had we in the meantime lost the war." The British Prime Minister conceded that Pershing was no worse than the other generals. "Pershing wanted to fight his own battle and win his own victories with his own army. Haig wanted his own offensive on his own front, ending in his own breakthrough. Pétain wanted to make certain of beating the enemy on that part of the front for which he was responsible."

Lord Milner, according to Harbord, was equally tough-minded. Milner, he wrote in his diary, "was born in Germany of British parents and seems to have acquired a little of the blood and iron. At least he is the most difficult person to bring over that my General and I have attempted. He wants all infantry and machineguns, and while protesting that they all look forward to the day when we shall have our American Army on the line as such, is demanding the things that will make that impossible, at least before 1919." Harbord's opinion of General Wilson, echoing that of most of his colleagues, was that he was "a good deal of a politician."

Harbord was distressed by the fact that Washington had given in to Lord Reading's arguments, and "worst of all they commit themselves to the agreement and do not tell us about it." He wondered "if the President realizes what it will mean to get a division or two annihilated under the British flag with Ireland in arms against conscription and our people none too warmly inclined to the British alliance, and our equally strong obligations to our other Allies, the gallant French."

In the end, as Harbord phrased it, Pershing's "straight back bent just a little." The Americans and the British bargained with the ferocity of a Levantine market place. Right off, Pershing took the bold stand that the British claim to an agreement between Wilson and Lord Reading on shipping six divisions of infantry and machine gunners was not conclusive. He thus indicated that he did not consider himself bound by the constitutional commander in chief of the United States armed forces, which was just the sort of defiance of civil authority that particularly infuriated Lloyd George about his own generals. Undoubtedly Pershing took this stand purely for bargaining purposes. As a result, each side gave a little, and they finally succeeded in hammering out an agreement among themselves. Briefly, the new compromise provided that the six divisions soon to be shipped would include various headquarters and auxiliary troops, and would cover May only, not the four months the British wanted, and that shipments from June 1 on would be subject to further negotiation.

No one was pleased with the Pershing-Milner agreement, neither the participants nor the French, who insisted on their rights to half of all U.S. troops brought over.

More rancorous disputation was to arise in the next few weeks. At times the war itself, the roar of thousands of cannons across trench-scored valleys and blasted forests, the desperate drives of the German infantry toward Paris, the stubborn defense of the heights of the Lys and the Aisne, seemed to be only the rattling of an off-stage thunder sheet compared to the battles of the Allied conference tables.

12. Cantigny . . . Belleau Wood . . . Soissons

In the spring of 1918 the western front was a ditch of blood running from the North Sea to the Swiss border, drifted over with cordite and poison gas, in which a whole generation was killing itself off because neither a means of victory nor an acceptable formula for peace could be found on either side.

The warring world was living a nightmare, the depth and horror of which can be recaptured only by those who lived through it. Not the worst part of it was the numbing certainty in everyone's mind that it would go on forever, even as it was generally comprehended that the offensives and counteroffensives—each heralded with a glorious burst of communiqués—would result in nothing decisive. All attempts to by-pass the western front, with operations on the North Sea coast, at Gallipoli and Salonika, or through northern Italy, had failed.

"There are not two armies fighting each other on the western front," as a French writer epitomized the feeling of hopelessness. "There is one great army committing suicide." The people of the Allied nations and of the Central Powers resigned themselves to the slaughter of their youth and to the semi-starvation of their children through the mutual blockades. Only a few of the wilder optimists could conceive of the war ending, one way or another, by the end of that year. It could go on endlessly; perhaps it was only the start of another Thirty Years' War.

Meanwhile, their leaders were fighting on two fronts, against the Germans and against each other. With the ebbing away of the successive German offensives, the Allied leaders were getting a whiff of hope for the first time since 1914. More than 100,000 spring-heeled young Americans began arriving in the French ports each month. Peace and its rewards might soon be in their grasp. They had to look ahead to *how* the war would be won, to ensure that their own peoples would be comforted, in whatever small and illusionary measure was possible, by its results. The British and the French each wanted the victory for themselves, naturally, with the oncoming Americans representing the force that could tip the balance their way, if only the A.E.F. command would not insist on delaying matters by organizing a self-contained army.

Polite and judicious historians generally minimize the acrimony of that Anglo-French-American struggle over the conference tables, saying it is bound to arise under the stresses of a military alliance, it happens in all wars, it is a small insignificant part of the mutual war effort. The statesmen and the generals, in their memoirs, were not inclined to shrug it off as part of the game or minimize its historic effects. Nor did they temper the bitterness, even when they wrote of their recollections a decade or more later in the shady peace of retirement. Lloyd George wrote of Pershing that "he could see no further than the exaltation of his own command, the jealous maintenance of his own authority." Pershing was a rebel against the civil authority, refusing to accede to the decisions brought about in Washington by British diplomatic pressure. "It was President Wilson's first experience of just the same kind of professional egotism as we had frequently experienced in dealings with our own army heads." What really irked him was that "Lord Reading told me that the attitude in Washington was much more sympathetic to our demands than that displayed by Pershing."

As for Clemenceau, he distrusted his own military leaders almost as much as he suspected the British postwar plans; Pétain, because he "foresaw the worst and contemplated withdrawals, of which it was dangerous to show troops a possibility" and Foch, because of his expanding ambitions; he regarded Haig as a typically stolid and unimaginative Britisher, and Pershing as a stubborn fellow of doubtful and untested competence as a commander, someone to be shouted down or, if he could not be bluffed, replaced through protests to his superiors. Clemenceau and Lloyd George could agree on one principle at least: the war must be taken out of the fumbling hands of the generals.

They saw that Pershing was the only real stumbling block to their separate designs and so renewed their attacks on his position a few days after his return from the London conference. Foch, tackling him first, told Pershing, "I hope that America may send over as much infantry as possible during the next three months. The other arms to complete your divisions can come afterwards. What do you think of that plan?"

It was, of course, the same old plan that Pershing had been rejecting for months.

"I cannot commit myself to such a proposition," he curtly replied. "If nothing but infantry and machine gunners are brought over . . . it will be October or November before the artillery and auxiliary troops could arrive and we could not foresee the formation of an American army until next spring."

Foch entered an eloquent plea on the theme that "we are in the midst of a hard battle" and warned that the British might be pushed back to the sea, the French back to the Loire while the American Army "tries in vain to organize on lost battlefields over the graves of Allied soldiers." But Pershing could not be swayed; it was rhetoric such as that which convinced him that Foch was largely a man of words and gestures and which attracted him, by contrast, to the disenchanted Pétain, with his pale sunken eyes and his pessimistic practicality.

Several days later, in the conference at Abbeville on May 1, the Allied campaign to bring Pershing around to a less parochial attitude rose in pitch and volume. A whole table of opponents confronted him in unison; Clemenceau, Foch, Lloyd George, Lord Milner, and Orlando of Italy showering him with their demands and arguments. In his war diary, Pershing noted with his customary restraint, "Everybody at high tension. . . . Discussion at times very lively."

General Bliss also attended but uttered hardly a word. He "sat absolutely silent and gave no support to Pershing," wrote Lloyd George. "I heard privately that he has expressed to his colleagues complete disagreement with Pershing's attitude." Since the Allies did not hesitate to spy on each other when deemed necessary, Lloyd George's information on Bliss's attitude may have been correct.

The conference opened with a blast from Clemenceau denouncing the London agreement on immediate troop shipments "in which it appears none are to go to France." To which Lord Milner angrily replied, "We had no intention of depriving France of any American troops. I do not know that anything has been said regarding their allotment on arrival in France. We simply wanted to hasten their coming." Lloyd George pointed out that ten British divisions had been "so severely handled that they cannot be reconstituted"; the whole Fifth British Army, as a matter of fact, had been destroyed. "They must be replaced by new units," the British Prime Minister said, meaning, of course, the Americans. Foch, however, insisted that the Americans shipped in June should go to the French Army, adding, "I am sure that General Pershing, with his generosity and his breadth of view, will grant the fairness of this and will extend for June the agreement decided upon for May."

Listening to the Allies quarreling over his army—or what he intended to be his army if it was not snatched out of his hands, battalion by battalion, on arrival—Pershing was not at all inclined to be "generous."

With cold anger, he told Foch: "I do not suppose that we are to understand that the American army is to be entirely at the disposal of the French and British commands."

He insisted that the American Army "must be complete under its own command. I should like to have a date fixed when this will be realized. I should like to make it clear that all American troops are not to be with the British, as there are five divisions with the French now and there will be two more in a short time."

He added that he had explained to both Milner and Foch "why I do not wish to commit the American army so long in advance. If need be, I shall recommend the extension into June. I can see no reason for it now."

Foch tried to pacify him by saying, "Nobody is more for the constitution of an American army than I, for I know how much more an army is worth when fighting under its own commander and under its own flag." Even so, he spoke in favor of extending the May program, adding that as Allied commander in chief "I believe it is my duty to insist on my point of view."

Unity of command forgotten for the moment, Pershing reminded himself that "no authority to dictate regarding such matters has been conferred upon General Foch." Thus, like Pétain and Haig, he had decided that he could stand just so much co-ordination. He was not at all dismayed when "all five of the party attacked me with all the force and prestige of their high positions."

He raised his voice almost to a bellow as he declared that the war could not be saved by "feeding untrained American recruits into the Allied armies."

He slammed his fist on the table, startling his august colleagues, to emphasize his point.

Hoping that a more personal appeal might work, Foch and Milner took Pershing into an adjoining room, away from the three Prime Ministers, their aides and secretaries. But Pershing only restated more forcefully his opinion that the Allied scheme would "neither relieve the situation nor end the war."

With all the theatricalism at his command, Foch asked, "You are willing to risk our being driven back to the Loire?"

"Yes," Pershing retorted, "I am willing to take that risk. Moreover, the time may come when the American army will have to stand the brunt of this war, and it is not wise to fritter away our resources in this manner. The morale of the British, French and Italian armies is low, while as you know that of the American army is very high. It would be a grave mistake to give up the idea of building an American army in all its details as rapidly as possible."

Lloyd George, Clemenceau, and Orlando then rejoined the other three, and Pershing overheard Lord Milner, "in a stage whisper behind his hand," tell Lloyd George:

"It's no use. You can't budge him an inch."

When the Allied leaders renewed their demands that he yield on the troop issue, he brought the first day's session to a close by getting to his feet and announcing, "Gentlemen, I have thought this program over very deliberately and will not be coerced."

Then he stalked out, his cavalry boots clattering defiantly over the parquet floor.

Next day Lloyd George was even more vociferous, if not insulting in his remarks, and was quoted by Pershing as saying that "if the war is lost it would be lost honorably by France and England, as they would have expended their last for us in the struggle, but that for America to lose the war without having put into it more than Belgium would not be in compatibility with American pride and American traditions." Foch spoke ominously of hoping to hold out until August. In his cool, almost contemptuous reply, Pershing reminded them that "America declared war independently of the Allies and she must face it as soon as possible with a powerful army . . . the morale of our soldiers depends upon their fighting under our own flag. America is anxious to know where her army is. The American soldier has his own pride, and the time will soon come when our troops, as well as our Government, will demand an autonomous army under the American High Command. . . . That is all I can agree to at present. . . ."

The Supreme War Council, confronted by Pershing's blunt refusal to compromise, had no alternative but to produce an agreement that "an American army should be formed as soon as possible under its own commander and under its own flag." Pershing had it in writing now and would never let anyone forget it. The Allies also conceded that the U.S. troops serving as a blood transfusion to the French and British armies were to be "withdrawn and united with their own artillery and auxiliary troops into divisions and corps at the discretion of the American commander-in-chief after consultation with the commander-in-chief of the Allied Armies in France." That clause, too, would be recalled by Pershing on more than one occasion.

The Abbeville agreement as a whole, however, turned out to be another of those "scraps of paper" scattered like confetti over the history of World War I. Only two days after it was signed, Lloyd George was cabling Lord Reading in Washington: "Difficulty arises over fact Pershing given no definite instructions, only agreement on general principles." He admitted the conference "couldn't move Pershing beyond the point of six divisions in May and June" and added that "Foch, who is much the greatest Allied general, was intensely depressed and disgusted." In a few more days, working through their ambassadors in Washington, France and Britain were renewing their campaign behind Pershing's back to nullify the Abbeville agreement and increase the priorities on U.S. infantry and machine-gun units.

Haig, meanwhile, was plotting his own raid on the A.E.F.'s resources. Thus far, the British commander had allowed the politicians to conduct the negotiations for American troops, perhaps out of delicacy of feeling for a fellow soldier whose command was being nibbled away, perhaps out of sympathy with a comrade in the subtle resistance movement against the Supreme War Council. Clemenceau wrote that when Haig himself was presented with the idea of a Supreme Commander and the necessity of submitting himself to foreign dictates he had "jumped up like a jack-in-the-box" and proclaimed, "I have only one chief, and I can have no other. My King!"

Now, quite willing for Pershing to forget his own more diffuse loyalties, Haig wrote the American commander a one-paragraph letter asking him for the loan of 10,000 artillerymen as casually as a housewife seeking to borrow a cup of sugar from a neighbor. Concealing his irritation, Pershing offered a mere six batteries to be "trained and employed by complete units." That wasn't at all what the British wanted; their demand was for Americans in job lots, 10,000 or a 100,000 at a crack, and they would not be fobbed off with smaller packets made up according to Pershing's wishes. The offer was declined.

On May 30, preceding another session of the Supreme War Council, Pershing was taking a less enthusiastic view of the Briton than he had previously held, noting that Haig "showed a disposition to criticize the French for their unsuccess in meeting the German offensive between Soissons and Rheims. . . . He admitted that criticism on his part was not quite in place and that he was only saying this to me and that he was going to play the game and do what they told him because he realized the importance of this." Pershing thought Haig's carping "rather remarkable" considering the "events that took place two months ago on the British front."

The meeting of the War Council, largely occupied with demands for more American troops, was as Pershing said "very erratic." The French and British, incredible as it may seem, could not even agree on how many divisions they had at the front, Foch claiming the total was only 150, Milner vehemently ticking off 169. They finally decided the 162 Allied divisions were in the line. Was it possible that the Supreme Commander had actually lost track of twelve divisions, the equivalent of a whole army? Undismayed by the faultiness of his arithmetic, Foch presented the council with a scheme for bringing over 250,000 troops in each of the months of June and July, although Pershing objected strenuously to drawing on men with "only one month's training." To the unimpressed Pershing, General Foch was overdoing the dramatics. "General Foch flung his hands in wild gestures and kept repeating, 'La bataille, la bataille, il n'y a que ça qui conte.'" After two days of wrangling, a compromise was reached whereby Pershing would determine the composition of about one fifth of the 250,000 troops to be shipped over in June, 110,000 of the 250,000 in July. And again neither party to the agreement was pleased with it. . . .

For both Foch's excitability and Pershing's confidence in council there were good reasons. The Germans' third offensive was aimed at the French, and they were reeling back in confusion and defeat. The Americans, on the other hand, were meeting the test of battle in their first large-scale engagements.

The first two German offensives, across the Somme and the Lys, had gained considerable ground, smashed the Fifth British Army beyond repair, and placed the British in a critical situation, but they had not been decisive. The third blow fell on the French, and they were poorly prepared for it. In attempting to meet it, the Allies, for all their intelligence and reconnaissance apparatus, failed miserably at divining where it would be directed. Haig thought it would strike the British on the Arras front, Foch that the Montdidier-Noyon area would be the target. A reserve officer at A.E.F. Headquarters, Major S. T. Hubbard, Jr., the Americans' expert on the German order of battle, repeatedly warned Pétain's headquarters that all signs indicated the Germans would attack in the Aisne sector, on the Chemin des Dames, but Foch was so convinced that the offensive would not be launched east of Soissons that he sent three battle-worn British divisions to hold that part of the line and rest "in a quiet place." The French were so complacent about that sector that they failed to conduct trench raids or order aerial mapping of the enemy positions, even though Major Hubbard's study of the movement of German reserve divisions showed a strong build-up in that area.

On May 27 the enemy attacked with forty-two divisions, spearheaded by tanks, and was astonishingly successful. Sixty-five thousand French surrendered; the others fled so precipitously that bridges over the Aisne were left intact for the German advance. Three days later the Germans reached the Marne—again. The war had retrogressed, from the Allied standpoint, to 1914.

A day after the German offensive began, the American First Division went into action at Cantigny.

It was the Americans' first offensive action of the war, and Pershing was determined that it would be successful. The operation had to succeed, partly as a boost to morale back home and in the A.E.F., but most of all to convince the Allies that the American combat efficiency was not mere boasting (and there had been plenty of that wherever Americans congregated). Pershing had sent the First, the best-trained of all his divisions and the longest in France, to the front some weeks before, after assembling its officers and giving them the kind of inspirational address that came unexpectedly from the tight-lipped man they called "Black Jack." In essence, his speech was a reminder that they were to fight as Americans, without remembering too much of their foreign indoctrination, and he concluded, "In your training you have been made by my orders to adhere to American traditions and methods. You must hold to these in your fighting and in all your future action against the enemy. They are ours, right, sane, reliable, and will win."

The First Division, attached to the First French Army, was assigned to capture the fortified village of Cantigny opposite its lines at the apex of the Amiens salient. The objective was important because the village stood on high ground and gave the Germans excellent observation of the Avre River valley; the enemy had spiked it with machine-gun nests and covered its approaches with reserve artillery concealed in the woods to the rear of Cantigny.

After an hour's barrage from both French and American artillery, the division's 28th Infantry attacked on a front a little more than a mile long, charged on through heavy fire, and captured the patchwork of shattered houses which then comprised Cantigny.

The German reaction was swift and furious, the enemy pouring in two immediate counterattacks, but the Americans were ordered by Pershing to "hold on at all costs" and stood their ground. A transcript of a telephone conversation between a German staff officer at G.H.Q. and the chief of staff of the corps in the Cantigny sector indicated how seriously the enemy took the breach in their lines.

STAFF OFFICER   The failure of the counterattack at Cantigny is very depressing.

CHIEF OF STAFF   Our infantry had to get out again.

STAFF OFFICER   New attacks must be carefully prepared.

CHIEF OF STAFF   The counterattack has now been slated for June 6.

STAFF OFFICER   Why delay so long? The counterattack must take place as soon as possible.

The 28th Infantry, reinforced by a battalion from the 18th, held onto Cantigny despite heavy bombardments from the enemy artillery. They dug in so stubbornly, in fact, that the Germans called off any plans for an all-out counterattack, realizing it would cost more than Cantigny was worth to retake the battered village. Pershing visited the First Division's command posts a short time later, and General Bullard, the division commander, recalled that he was "on his mettle over the American success but still burning inside over the aspersions cast on the American willingness to fight." They discussed their relations with the Allies at length.

Bullard, in his memoirs, quoted Pershing as asking him, "Do they [the French] patronize you? Do they assume superior airs with you?"

"No, sir, they do not," General Bullard replied. "I have been with them too long and they know me too well."

"By God, they have been trying it with me," Pershing said vehemently, "and I don't intend to stand a bit of it."

Pershing's touchiness about French attitudes came to the surface several other times that spring. When M. Tardieu, the head of the Franco-American Committee on supply procurement, ventured criticisms of the American General Staff system at a conference, Pershing rounded on him and suggested with more than his usual abruptness that Tardieu had better worry about his own army. And on a tour of American forces in the Belfort area, he visited the headquarters of General Paulinier, commanding the XL French Corps, and General Pichet, 10th French Division, at Valdons, and expressed his annoyance because both generals "seemed quite surprised that the Americans should know anything at all." (Pershing was equally displeased with some of his regimental commanders on that tour, recording that the colonel of the 127th Infantry "had spots on his clothing and did not have very much grasp of his real duties," the commander of the 307th Infantry "answered in vague terms questions concerning his sector," and the commander of the 128th Infantry "didn't seem to have much grasp of his functions." Vagueness and sloppiness were two faults that Pershing couldn't abide; sharp of eye and tongue, he soon weeded out such officers, often on the basis of a very short interview, and packed them off to Blois.) Later on, he told off General Tom Bridges of the British Army, who had been head of the British mission in Washington the year before and apparently regarded himself as the godfather of the A.E.F., for suggesting a number of major changes in his army. "He has been trying to advance his ideas on a machinegun corps, and thought of meddling with repartition of the line on the Western Front," Pershing wrote in his diary. "I told him that I did not propose to have any more instruction with the Allies; that I consider some of the instruction which we had received from the British to be a positive detriment; that I do not care to have the British instruct my men as they instruct their own. . . ." He was particularly distressed, he explained, by the British practice of attacking a strongpoint rather than flanking it, which he regarded as "behind the times."

The amount of "instruction" offered by the Allies soon diminished under the pressure of events.

On May 30, alarmed by the depth and speed of the German penetration, Pétain asked for American reinforcements in the region of Château-Thierry, on the Marne. Four French divisions and three British had been shattered, the entire French reserve had been committed, and Pétain was desperate for reinforcements to plug the gap. Pershing immediately handed over the 2nd and 3rd divisions, which had been in training near Chaumont.

The immediate danger point being Château-Thierry, General Dickman of the 3rd Division rushed his 7th Machine Gun Battalion to that town in a truck convoy the afternoon of May 31, while the infantry and engineers boarded trains that night for the front and their supply train moved more deliberately over the crowded roads leading to the Marne. The Germans were throwing all their resources into forcing a Marne crossing, probing for a weak spot and hitting the highroad for Paris. Retreating French troops crowded the roads and byways. Yet the Americans moved confidently forward through the backwash of a defeated army.

Arriving at Château-Thierry late in the afternoon of May 31, the machine-gun battalion was ordered into action at once. The Germans already held the northern half of the town, on the other side of the Marne, and were trying to force a crossing over the two main bridges.

Under orders from the French commander on the scene, the Americans set up their machine guns and covered the approaches to the railway bridge and the main wagon bridge. Next day, all seventeen guns hammering away every time the German assault units approached the bridges, the battalion repulsed every attack. That day, also, the 3rd Division's infantry battalions came up on the double and reinforced the French positions for ten miles east along the Marne. Château-Thierry and its bridges were secured.

The German thrust in this sector, as it developed, had been a feeler rather than an all-out attack. Thanks in part to the American machine gunners' furious resistance, the enemy had been persuaded to probe elsewhere for a weak spot. It was a job well done, though not the salvation of France, as the first dispatches of U.S. correspondents proclaimed and U.S. schoolbooks persisted in maintaining.

The 2nd Division, taking its orders from Sixth French Army Headquarters, moved into battle more ponderously but with greater impact.

Sent to the front in trucks and buses, the division commanded by General Omar Bundy took up positions to defend the Paris-Metz highway, once trod by the soldiers of Caesar and Napoleon, against the German advance from the northeast. Now commanding its highly professional Marine Brigade was Brigadier General James G. Harbord, who had departed as Pershing's chief of staff in mid-May. Pershing hated to part with him, valuing not only his superior abilities but his tact and amiability, but he knew that Harbord needed experience with a line command to advance his career. Harbord was considerably more cheerful at the parting than his chief, writing in his diary the day of his severance from G.H.Q.: "It is fine to be able to know that your duty lies in certain established lines, and that your meals will be served when the hour comes, etc. I admire General Pershing more than any other officer in the army, but his utter lack of consciousness of time and his irregular habits are extremely trying." Harbord was replaced by Major General James W. McAndrew, a West Pointer who had been two classes behind Pershing, whose personality was best summed up by his nickname of "Dad." McAndrew performed ably in that post to the end of the war.

As the Marine and Regular Army brigades hurried forward to interpose themselves between their allies and the onrushing Germans, the French appeared to Harbord to be utterly demoralized. "We passed a great many French officers and men, but all going from and none towards the front. All afternoon they passed, that motley array which characterizes the rear of a routed army." The French, he said, were pulling back at the rate of one to ten miles a day, depending on the pressure from the enemy, and "no unit along their whole front had stood up against the Germans." The 2nd Division took on the job not only of halting the German offensive in its tracks but retaking positions which had been occupied by the enemy. It moved into line under circumstances that would have been disheartening to more experienced troops, deploying across the Paris highway near Lucy-le-Bocage June 1, taking the place of two French divisions which then fell back through the American positions.

Harbord was intensely disgusted with the French, who failed to supply the American command with maps of the tangle of rain-soaked forests in which his troops were deployed because neither the Deuxième Bureau (Intelligence) nor the Topographical Section could agree on which was responsible for mapping the region. "It will be a wonder if we do not feel as much like fighting them as the Germans before the war is over," Harbord groused in his diary.

On June 4 the German spearheads began battering at the 2nd Division, but the Americans stood firm under alternate pounding by the enemy artillery and fierce assaults by the infantry. Two days later the Americans went over to the offensive and in six days of fighting at Vaux, Bouresches, the Mares Farm, on Hill 142, they drove the Germans out of Belleau Wood, wrecking four enemy divisions in the process. Harbord wrote that his men individually charged German machine guns, killed their crews, and kept on going, and "literally scores of these men have refused to leave the field when wounded." In return, the division took almost 10,000 casualties.

After a solid month of fighting, the 2nd consolidated its positions on high ground captured from the enemy and was relieved by the 26th Division.

The 2nd and 3rd divisions were only two of the forty-five Allied divisions engaged in blunting that third German offensive. Their feats were somewhat exaggerated in the U.S. press, which insisted that they had "held" the Marne and "saved" Paris, but there was real significance in one factor of the Americans' first large-scale appearance at the front: they showed a combativeness well above the current Allied level. The Germans recognized this when Ludendorff, on June 8, ordered that "American units appearing on the front should be hit particularly hard," and his intelligence officers conceded that the 2nd Division "may even be reckoned a storm troop." There was no higher praise in the German lexicon.

Among the French, the third German offensive produced a profound crisis. Retreating troops and terrified peasantry clogged the roads to Paris, and the French Cabinet was considering another evacuation to Bordeaux. There was something like panic in the higher councils of the government over charges that Foch had blundered in failing to anticipate the attack, in allowing the Germans to assemble a huge force behind the Chemin des Dames without trying to break it up. The former Prime Minister Barthou told General Harbord at Marine Brigade Headquarters of a secret session of the Chamber of Deputies at which it was stated that "if Caillaux were made Prime Minister and General Sarrail given command of Paris, the war would end in three weeks."

Pershing never admired Foch and Clemenceau so much as he did in those critical June days when they alone seemed to be determined to keep France in the war. On June 9, Pershing wrote in his diary, Foch assured him that the French would continue fighting even if Paris fell and quoted Clemenceau as saying, "Above Paris is France, and above France is all the civilized world to save." Pershing was not given to emotional gestures, but confessed that "I was inspired to jump up and shake hands with him right then and there."

The next day he cabled the War Department a warning that "the possibility of losing Paris has become apparent," and there was a danger that the Clemenceau government might be replaced by "a Ministry in favor of peace."

In the minds of many Frenchmen, by then, the war was all but lost. Even before the third German offensive, General Pétain was convinced that his forces would not be able to hold the line. Foch complained to President Poincaré that "Pétain is intolerable with his pessimism. . . . Would you believe it, he said something to me which I would not tell any other living being. This is what he said: 'The Germans are going to defeat the English in the field, and then they are going to defeat us.' Should a general talk or even think like that?"

Looking at the situation from a purely military standpoint, Pershing refused to be similarly disheartened. He saw quite clearly that the Germans would be unable to exploit their successes and renew their drive on Paris unless they were able to capture enough of the railway net to supply their troops. Thus the enemy launched his fourth offensive June 9 in the direction of Compiègne, hoping to open up the great trunk lines running from Cologne, but the French stopped them with slight ground gains and heavy troop losses. Pershing cabled the War Department on June 11 that without the rail and road centers of Soissons and Rheims "the enemy will be confronted with difficult transportation problems, involving the use of motor trucks on sixteen roads, for the most part cross-country roads, now available to him. . . . The enemy's transportation situation cannot be satisfactorily adjusted until he has taken Rheims; hence the recent heavy attack on this important center." He could envision a turning of the tide by the end of summer; already there were seven American divisions in the line, and forty-six should be available by October.

The Americans had proved themselves so eminently battleworthy in their first confrontals with the hard-pressing Germans that Foch wanted an American regiment attached to each French division as a stiffening element. Pershing would have none of it. Nor would he allow the British to attempt the same maneuver. On July 2 he learned that General Bell had assigned ten companies of his 33rd Division to go over the top with British units to the north. "I disapproved the whole scheme," he wrote in his diary, but the next day he found out that the British were planning to conduct the July 4 operation as scheduled. He had a member of his staff telephone Haig's chief of staff immediately to have the American participation canceled.

His own officers also got the rough edge of his tongue, sometimes without good reason, as he bustled up and down the western front on the Headquarters Special or in the khaki-colored sedan flying his four-starred pennant, which subordinates frequently thought might as well have flaunted the skull and crossbones. On June 21, for instance, he swooped down on the 42nd (Rainbow) Division at the railhead of Charmes as it was marching back from heavy duty at the front. The Rainbow was returning from eighty-two days in the lines under British command, having suffered 2014 casualties. It had marched sixty kilometers after being relieved, and the uniforms of the men were filthy and ragged, their transport muddy and battered, their horses gaunt and stumbling with weariness.

About two o'clock in the afternoon, according to war correspondent Frazier Hunt, Pershing and his staff descended on the division's chief of staff, Colonel Douglas MacArthur, as he and an aide were supervising the loading of the troops and horses up the ramps of the marshaling yards.

Pershing immediately began chewing out MacArthur in a voice that carried to hundreds of grinning soldiers. "This division is a disgrace," Pershing roared. "The men are poorly disciplined and they are not properly trained. The whole outfit is just about the worst I have seen."

MacArthur was so dumfounded that he couldn't speak. Didn't Pershing know that the men had just come out of the line?

"MacArthur," Pershing continued, "I'm going to hold you personally responsible for getting discipline and order into this division. I'm going to hold you personally responsible for correcting measures with the officers at fault. I won't stand for this. It's a disgrace!"

"Yes, sir!" was all that Colonel MacArthur could find to say.

For weeks after that, headquarters at Chaumont sent inspecting officers to rake over the Rainbow Division and incessantly find fault. Finally one day a colonel on the inspector general's staff showed up at divisional headquarters with another niggling list of complaints. MacArthur ordered him out of his office and told him he'd shoot him if he ever showed up in the division's area again. There was no more harassment from Chaumont after that.

Pershing was determined that his senior commanders should not linger in comfort well behind the lines but should have at least a minimal acquaintance with the hardships of the men at the front. He ordered that divisional commanders were to visit the trenches in their sector at least once a week, a requirement that did not sit well with some of the more sedentary generals. Major Palmer heard one disgruntled division commander growl that "I would like to tell the damned fool at headquarters who wrote that order what I think of him"—but he pulled on his boots and set out for the front.

With all his burdens that summer of 1918, a certain amount of testiness could be expected in Pershing. He was not only keeping a watchful and jealous eye on his divisions fighting under French and British army commanders but struggling constantly to prevent Foch, Haig, and Pétain, not to mention the Allied statesmen behind them, from making permanent use of them. His behind-the-scenes war against the Allies consumed as much of his energy as the war against Germany, and it did not even end with the armistice. In addition, there was his war with Washington, particularly General March, and the smaller wars within his own command. In a man with a less formidable arterial system, apoplexy would have been inevitable.

Not the least of his administrative worries was the Air Service of the Signal Corps, as the A.E.F.'s air arm was then titled, nor the least of his vexations its chief of Air Service, Colonel William Mitchell, brilliant, unorthodox, unawed, and already conscious of his role as the prophet of American air power. Imbued with the ideas of Douhet and Trenchard and looking to the day when air armadas would be decisive in war, Billy Mitchell was not the sort of man to win the entire trust of a commander in chief who hardly knew a joy stick from an aileron and was still dreaming in off moments of delivering a paralyzing blow with horse cavalry. Pershing would never be the patron saint of American military aviation, whose pioneers were more inclined to view him as the man who wanted to strangle it in its cradle.

The Air Service had plenty of trainees at its own and the Allied airdromes, but American industry had failed to produce the planes to carry them into action. General March, the chief of staff, blamed this on "the fact that General Pershing was constantly altering his requests for planes. We did not know from day to day where he stood. As soon as we got going on the construction of a type which he had stated was necessary, a cable would come from him, saying that he did not want that type and asking for something else."

Mitchell blamed it on the earthbound officers of the military bureaucracy, both at home and in France, and wrote in his diary: "The General Staff is now trying to run the Air Service with just as much knowledge of it as a hog knows about skating. It is terrible to have to fight with an organization of this kind, instead of devoting all our attention to the powerful enemy on our front." Whoever was responsible, the Americans had to take to the air in planes of foreign manufacture.

In trying to hasten the development of the Air Service, Mitchell had "many heated talks," he said, with General Pershing. Often there was "much pounding on the table on both sides." Apparently impressed with Mitchell's drive and aggressive faith in his branch of the service, Pershing named him a member of the seven-man board responsible for formulating an aviation program for the A.E.F. Washington, however, ignored its recommendations and sent missions over to junket around France and select training centers for the Air Service without consulting Pershing. Colonel Mitchell was so disgusted with the roving missions that accomplished nothing, the procurement agencies that procured nothing, and the A.E.F. bureaucracy that decided nothing, that he quoted with approval the jape of a subordinate equally disgusted with the endless talk: "A conference is a collection of human beings of almost superhuman unintelligence, gathered together for the purpose of passing a series of resolutions based on their combined ignorance of a particular subject. Every conference has a main bore, an auxiliary bore or other bores stationed at strategical points. When anybody ventures an original idea it is the duty of the main bore to head it off. He usually succeeds."

The considerable publicity given the various "aces" and the highly romantic accounts of the "chivalry" of air warfare, helped along by the fact that there were some first-rate writers and publicists among the fliers, began to annoy Pershing. Air Service propaganda irked him to the extent that on February 28, 1918, he cabled Secretary of War Baker: "Newspaper clipping from United States received here to effect that U. S. has thousands of fliers in Europe and that thousands of American aeroplanes are flying above the American forces in Europe today. As a matter of fact there is not today a single American-made plane in Europe. . . . Emphatically protest against newspaper publicity of this nature and urgently recommend drastic steps be taken to stop publication of such articles." Earlier he had insisted to Baker that pay increases for "engaging in aerial combat" must be rescinded because flying "involves nothing like the hardships endured by troops that occupy the trenches." This made him popular with the infantry but contributed to the feeling in the Air Service that, next to Baron von Richthofen, Pershing was the American airman's worst enemy.

Colonel Mitchell's pet scheme was to have hundreds of Americans trained at French aviation schools and equipped with French planes, then sent to the front immediately, long before the arrival of the infantry. Pershing undoubtedly saw this as a bold maneuver to reap publicity for the Air Service to the detriment of the A.E.F. as a whole. It led to those table-pounding sessions which Colonel Mitchell reported with relish in his diary.

He also wrote that "one time he [Pershing] told me that if I kept insisting that the organization of the Air Service be changed he would send me home. I answered that if he did he would soon come after me. This made him laugh and our talk ended admirably."

Actually Mitchell had allowed himself to be lulled into a false sense of security. He thought he had Pershing's number—typically crusty old fellow who was sick of being yesed all the time and valued somebody who'd stand up to him. Otherwise, why could he be cajoled into laughing at himself? But Pershing wasn't as simple as the cartoon character Mitchell had in mind. The longer that Harbord, as chief of staff and in other capacities, knew him the more he was impressed with the fact that "canniness" was one of the strongest traits of his character (as he remarked in an address before the Army War College in 1933). In France, Pershing learned to deal with men more subtly, less forthrightly, than in earlier days; it was the almost inevitable result of having to handle all kinds and nationalities, of divining human motives in the mass of self-seeking, intrigue, and ambition that naturally was attracted to his headquarters by centripetal force.

He must have stopped laughing the moment Mitchell left his office, naïvely convinced that he had charmed the Old Man into an agreeable humor.

In a very short time Pershing announced a reshuffling of the Air Service command which amounted to Mitchell's demotion. He had decided that he wanted that branch of the service operated as part of the Army, not an independent force of airborne guerrillas who would go bounding off in their own picturesque way. To head up the whole operation he picked General Mason Patrick, an Engineer officer who had been at West Point with him and who had almost as much distaste for newfangled machinery as the commander in chief himself (Pershing did not even know how to drive an automobile). In tactical command of the Air Service would be General Benjamin Foulois, with whom Pershing had worked in Mexico. Colonel Mitchell was shuffled down to No. 3 man on the totem pole, taking over as commander of I Corps' Air Service under General Liggett, who happily shared Mitchell's views on the importance of air power. Liggett and Mitchell made a perfect ground-air team, a model of co-operation for a later war.

Mitchell still kept an eye on the Air Service command headquartered at Chaumont, which was soon staffed with non-flying old Regulars who thought of war as a pursuit of guerrillas through an island jungle. It takes a radical change in perspective to realize now that the A.E.F. was built on the foundations of the little army that was trained to keep order in the Philippines and chase Villa into the Mexican interior. Widening its professional horizon to take in the frightening demands of a continental war required a painful wrench, particularly for the older officers, many of whom never really made the transition and would always look back on the fighting in France as a kind of aberration. Mitchell, himself trained in the Philippines, had only scorn for them and wrote in his diary: "It was bad enough having this crowd down in Paris but to bring them up near the line was worse. It reminded me of a story told of old Major Hunter of the Cavalry, when General Otis, in command of the Philippines, had taken him to task for not accomplishing more. Major Hunter replied that he had two hundred men who had never seen a horse, two hundred horses that had never seen a man and twenty-five officers who had never seen either. This was the state of the entourage with which General Foulois had surrounded himself."

In July of 1918 friction also arose between Pershing and the War Department over the Services of Supply in France. Supplies had continued to clog up along the rail and road arteries from the ports of entry to the front. Major General Francis J. Kernan worked himself almost to the point of a nervous breakdown trying to cope with the huge and hastily improvised establishment under his command, but he was too much of an Old Army specimen, in the opinion of many subordinates, to make an efficient executive who could cut red tape and get things moving. Pershing had been too absorbed in the more active phases of command to give the S.O.S. much attention, but he had to agree that General Kernan "has not all the qualifications necessary for success."

On July 6, Secretary of War Baker sent him a long and very tactful letter on the subject, suggesting that Major General George W. Goethals, the builder of the Panama Canal and a somewhat overbearing personality, be appointed to take over the S.O.S. in a status equal to Pershing's. Baker wrote in part:

"As the American troops in France become more and more numerous and the battle initiative on some parts of the front passes to you, the purely military part of your task will necessarily take more and more of your time, and both the President and I want to feel that the planning and the executing of military undertakings has your personal consideration and that your mind is free for that as far as possible.

"The American people think of you as their 'fighting General,' and I want them to have that idea more and more brought home to them. For these reasons, it seems to me that it would help if some plan were devised by which you would be free from any necessity of giving attention to Services of Supply; and one plan in that direction which suggested itself was to send General Goethals over to take charge of the Services of Supply, establishing a direct relationship between him and Washington.

"Such a plan would place General Goethals in a coordinate rather than a subordinate relation to you, but of course it would transfer all the supply responsibilities from you to him, and you could then forget about docks, railroads, storage houses, and all the other vast industrial undertakings to which up to now you have given a good deal of your time, and as you know, we all think with superb success. I would be very glad to know what you think about this suggestion. . . . The President and I will consider your reply together, and you may rely upon our being guided only by confidence in your judgment and the deep desire to aid you."

Baker also suggested that Pershing's work load could be "somewhat lightened by a larger use of General Bliss as a diplomatic intermediary," which would simplify "the presentation of inter-Allied questions to the President."

Pershing was willing for Bliss to assume more of the diplomatic burden, but the thought of having the abrasive character of General Goethals in a "coordinate" position, co-dictator of the A.E.F. in effect, was thoroughly alarming. Pershing was jealous of his powers and yielded up fractions of them only under the inexorable pressure of circumstances or still greater authority. He immediately sat down in his office at the Damremont Barracks in Chaumont and wrote out a cable to Baker, with "RUSH . . . RUSH . . . RUSH . . . RUSH" scrawled in block letters at the top:

"I very much appreciate your desire to relieve me of every burden that might interfere with the direction of military operations. However, there appears to be an exaggerated view concerning the personal attention required in handling details of administration of this command. . . . The whole must remain absolutely under one head. Any division of responsibility or coordinate control in any sense would be fatal. The man who fights the armies must control their supply through subordinates responsible to him alone. The responsibility is then fixed, and the possibility of conflicting authority avoided. This military principle is vital and cannot be violated without inviting failure. . . . When it becomes necessary for me to be constantly at the front I shall retain control through the General Staff. . . ."

Pershing was, of course, absolutely right about the principle of retaining the Services of Supply as his responsibility. No modern army has ever attempted to make the supply chief co-equal to the commander. The risk of their working at conflicting purposes—particularly in the case of Pershing and Goethals—was enormous. Baker and Wilson soon saw that such a risk could not be taken.

It was obvious to A.E.F. Headquarters who the prime mover behind the Goethals scheme was—General March, the chief of staff in Washington.

General Harbord produced evidence that March not only conceived of the idea of sending Goethals to France, as a means of chipping away at Pershing's authority and bringing him more under the control of the chief of staff, but had told Goethals that he was going. In his memoir, General March wrote almost tearfully of Goethals's heartbreak and disappointment at learning that Pershing had rejected him. He also wrote with the bitterness of his own disappointment that "General Pershing's refusal to have Goethals and Wood as part of his command, his sending General Sibert back to the United States, and his attempt to get rid of General Bliss as the American representative at the Supreme War Council at Versailles, showed clearly a marked fear of men whom he recognized as men of great ability." There was a shred of truth in the charge that Pershing was wary of men whose reputations and capacities might prove a challenge, but Wood and Sibert had wrought their own downfall and Pershing never actually tried to "get rid of" General Bliss, annoyed as he sometimes became with the older man's tendency to sympathize with the French and British points of view on absorbing U.S. troops. March avoided the real issue, which, as Harbord stated it, was: "A divided control here in France would mean nothing but disaster."

In any event, Pershing solved the problem of straightening out the Services of Supply most adroitly. He called in Harbord, now commander of the 2nd Division, although he knew that his former chief of staff wanted to stay with the troops. Exhibiting what Harbord called his "great native charm when he chooses to exercise it," Pershing told his former chief of staff that he was "the only officer to whom he could turn in the emergency" and cited his fine combat record and the "liking which the Secretary of War had taken for me." And what was more, but left unstated, Pershing knew he could trust Harbord not only to do the job but to subdue any yearnings for a "coordinate" status, to remain a loyal satrap administering the vast military corporation which was the Services of Supply.

In July, meanwhile, the Allies began to inflict severe losses on the Germans, whose offensive potential had been drained away in the four earlier offensives of that spring. The German Army had shot its bolt, but Ludendorff lacked the moral courage to admit his gambler's try at total victory had failed. He couldn't resist one more toss of the dice: on July 15 he sent fourteen assault divisions across the Marne. This time Pétain fell back on a skillfully organized and elastic defense. Long-range artillery and aerial bombing wrecked the Germans' bridges and prevented them from supplying their advancing divisions. The fifth and final German offensive stumbled to a halt within three days, when it became noticeable that the vaunted German infantry, though still obeying orders, was going forward with only the fatalistic fortitude of veterans, not with the surging hope that wins battles.

On July 18, Foch launched his well-timed counterstroke to reduce the Marne salient and retake the important rail center of Soissons. He called on the Americans to spearhead the attack. General Bullard's III Corps, including the First and 2nd divisions, was rushed from rest areas to join General Mangin's Tenth French Army on the western face of the salient. Since Bullard's headquarters had not yet been organized, the two American divisions were thrown in with the First Moroccan Division to form the XX French Corps, although four fifths of its troops were American. The frontward movement of the First Division, under General Summerall, and the 2nd, still under Harbord, who had not yet been summoned to take over the S.O.S., was accomplished under the most excruciating circumstances.

All the night of July 17–18, on trucks and on foot, the divisions struggled toward their jump-off positions through the darkness and rain, over unmapped roads and through dense forests west of Soissons. The French again had neglected to supply maps or guides. The machine gunners of the Marine Brigade had to carry their heavy weapons across twelve miles of plowed fields. Only the heroic labors of the 2nd Division's military police kept traffic moving along the Paris-Soissons highway through the forest of Retz. Seven hours before zero (4:35 A.M., July 18) only the artillery was in place. "It rained hard," Harbord recalled; "the forest was plutonian in darkness; the road, beyond words to describe; trucks, artillery, infantry columns, cavalry, wagons, caissons, mud, MUD, utter confusion." The Americans had neither food nor water, nor had they slept for the previous two nights, yet they reached their positions by zero hour. One battalion, in fact, had to run the last several hundred yards to its position, reaching it just as the barrage started, but Colonel Paul B. Malone, commanding the 23rd Infantry in the 2nd Division, reported they "met the enemy in an intrenched position with no other weapon than the rifle; yet they were completely and overwhelmingly successful."

The Germans were caught by surprise as the Americans' assault battalions, supported by light tanks, advanced behind their rolling barrage toward the enemy positions in a series of ravines which scored the Soissons plateau. Flanking the Moroccan division in the center, the First and 2nd divisions plunged into wheat fields on the plateau which gave cover to the enemy's machine gunners and intrenched infantry, tore apart the Germans' forward positions, and broke through their zone of light artillery. At noon the XX Corps had captured half of the Soissons plateau. Just before nightfall the 2nd Division overcame strong resistance around Vierzy, took the town in a bayonet charge, and seized the heights of the Crise River; the First Division, meanwhile, was storming into fortified farmhouses and finally captured Missy-aux-Bois in the murderous twilight.

German resistance stiffened overnight, but the American-Moroccan corps continued to advance doggedly, fighting for every yard of ground gained, during the next two days. By July 21, the 2nd Division had advanced six miles from its jump-off position, captured 3000 prisoners, and taken eleven batteries and hundreds of machine guns; it had also suffered 5000 casualties in its headlong attacks. The First had taken 3500 prisoners and sixty-eight guns and suffered 7000 casualties. Allied guns now commanded Soissons, and the Germans were retreating from the Marne. In other sectors of the Marne salient, American divisions including the 26th, 4th, 3rd, 32nd, 42nd, and 28th also had pushed forward under French army commanders.

Largely through the initiative of American troops willing to take heavy losses, considering the short period in which they were engaged, the Allies had managed to throw the German war machine into reverse at last. In those several days of campaigning, wrote the German Chancellor von Hertling, "even the most optimistic among us understood that all was lost. The history of the world was played out in those three days." Field Marshal von Hindenburg was equally downcast and recalled in *Out of My Life:* "From the purely military point of view it was of the greatest and most fateful importance that we had lost the initiative to the enemy. . . . How many calculations had been scattered to the winds!"

Congratulations were rained down on the A.E.F. "You rushed into the fight as to a fête," exclaimed General Mangin of the Tenth French Army. Pétain told Pershing that "all French commanders were enthusiastic over American troops."

All very pleasant, but Pershing did not forget for a moment that his divisions were still fighting under French and British command. The Allies would obviously like to keep everything the way it was, with American divisions and even smaller units folded into their own forces. Pershing was more annoyed than flattered by the way Haig, for instance, clung to the 33rd Division . . . "fine big men," as the British commander wrote in his diary, "reminded me of tall Australians." Haig thought their officers, however, were "all very ignorant of military ways and arrangements and tactics," which their British mentors, of course, would remedy in due time. It was just as well that Pershing could not then read Haig's joyful entry that the 33rd's commander, General Bell, "was very pleased with the way the English looked after him and his division. . . . The Americans had not treated him so well. . . . Bell is distressed that General Pershing won't let him take part in our offensive battle. . . ."

Perhaps Pershing divined that Haig was still hoping to hang onto his American protégés. Colonel Mott, who accompanied him on a visit to Haig's headquarters just after the successful actions of mid-July, recalled that he congratulated Pershing on having been made a Grand Commander of the Bath by King George, who was also at Haig's headquarters, which led to "one of the worst breaks I ever made with the General."

Colonel Mott jocularly remarked, "Well, I suppose I can call you Sir John now."

Pershing, he said, "jumped on me like a tiger."

Many Americans were not too happy with their other Allies, either, Bullard citing bitterness among his countrymen brigaded with the French Sixth Army during the Aisne-Marne counteroffensive which was "due very largely to the Americans' belief that the French would not stand beside them in front of the enemy. . . . Attacks would start in due form, but the French troops had the wisdom always to stop before annihilation. In this they were most skillful. Long experience had taught them how to save themselves. American troops, doing the same thing beside them, lost twice as many men."

On July 24, Foch and the three commanders in chief met at Bombon to consider the generalissimo's plans for pursuing eventual victory. In brief, the first phase of his program was to drive the Germans out of the Marne, Lys, Amiens, and Saint-Mihiel salients and reestablish the rail communications needed to supply the Allied armies for the final drives toward the Rhine. The second phase would consist of a general offensive designed to end the war in the summer of 1919.

The answers of the three commanders in chief to Foch's question regarding their readiness aptly summed up the moral and physical potential of each:

MARSHAL HAIG   "The British army, entirely disorganized by the events of March and April, is still far from being re-established."

GENERAL PÉTAIN   "The French army, after four years of war and the severest trials, is at present worn out, bled white, anemic."

GENERAL PERSHING   "The American army asks nothing better than to fight, but it has not yet been formed."

Pershing emphasized to his colleagues that he was strongly concerned that—with 250,000 Americans now arriving monthly—five U.S. divisions were fighting under the British and the rest under the French. He was assured that the formation of an independent American Army was "contemplated," and that the reduction of the Saint-Mihiel salient, as one of the initial steps toward taking the general offensive, would be an exclusively American assignment.

Allied "contemplation" of his demands was no longer good enough, now that his troops had proved themselves in battle.

He pointed out, before the conference adjourned, that until an independent American Army was formed "our position before the people at home" was anything but "enviable."

He couldn't wait any longer; it was time for a declaration of independence, and let Foch and the others try to nullify it.

That day, on returning to his headquarters, he issued a general order announcing the formation of the First American Army, effective August 10, with himself—inevitably—as its commander.

13.   The Jaws of Saint-Mihiel

On leaving Pershing's office after being ordered to take over the enormous task of straightening out the Services of Supply, General Harbord had ruefully remarked, "Here I had a first-class fighting division. Now see what my general has done to me." Few officers would admit to being willing to give up a combat division in exchange for an administrative post, even though the latter was the second most important in the A.E.F. There would be little headline glory in supervising the S.O.S., even though the combat efficiency of the whole Expeditionary Force depended upon its efficient administration. Harbord may well have risen to a corps or army command had he stayed with the troops, but in the end he had little to complain about. His performance as supply chief later obtained for him one of the most prized executive jobs in American business.

Four days after the Bombon conference, he and Pershing set out on an inspection of the S.O.S. facilities, indicating the latter's concern over the supply situation. Among the officers accompanying them were General McAndrew, the A.E.F. chief of staff; Colonel Avery D. Andrews, Pershing's classmate and now assistant chief of staff, G-1; and Major Edward Bowditch, an aide who had been secretary of the Moro Province when Pershing was its governor.

What they saw on that quick-step tour was not particularly encouraging, considering that in six weeks the clotted arteries of the S.O.S. would have to pump forward the supplies for an army of 600,000 engaged in battle.

Perhaps the worst problem was the French railway net, burdened as it was with moving 700,000 tons of American supplies monthly in

addition to the requirements of the French Army. The French, Harbord complained, were "in the early Victorian days of railroad management . . . cramped and provincial . . . with continual jealousy
and bickering between local officials and the big central control in
Paris." As a result, he said, "every side track in France seems to lodge
empty cars which are more precious to us than jewel caskets." Harbord
was also harshly critical of the "boneheadedness and inefficiency which
allowed some thousands of cars to fall into German hands in the
March and May advances from mere failure to run them back before
the German advance." He decided to make the railroad operation's
shake-up his first objective and commandeered a special train for himself which allowed him to proceed immediately to wherever a bottle-
neck occurred.

At Tours, Pershing took time out for a sentimental pilgrimage to
the pension where he had "spent two happy months" with his family
in 1908. "The beautiful garden, the shade trees, the swing, the children's sandpile, all were the same, but the management had changed
and I was a stranger."

Pershing and Harbord gave particular attention to the docks on the
Gironde River, at Bordeaux and Bassens, and the vast marshaling
yards at Saint-Sulpice. Conditions at Bordeaux were so unsatisfactory
that they decided to replace the commanding officer, Harbord noting
that "there seemed to be more attention paid to what would now be
called 'public relations' than to hustling freight off the ships and ex-
pediting their turn-around." In the same area they inspected the storage depot at Saint-Sulpice, where the last of 107 warehouses were
under construction, the tank farm at Gièvres where 2,000,000 gallons
of gasoline were stored, and the largest refrigerating plant in the world,
which required 20,000 men to operate. At Saint-Nazaire they trotted
hurriedly around the great port depot of Montoir, with its 2000 square
acres of installations serviced by 200 miles of railroad track. Pershing paused at Saint-Nazaire, much as he hated speechmaking, to
address the hundreds of Negro stevedores who gathered around him.
He had always been rather sentimentally inclined toward Negroes—
with more than a hint of condescension, perhaps, by today's standards,
but his affection was nonetheless genuine—and spoke of "my service
with a colored regiment and how proud we were of its conduct in the
Spanish-American War." As though conferring a boon, he announced
that they might have the "honor" of serving at the front later on—a

suggestion which the stevedores received with something less than enthusiasm.

Pershing and his party motored up the Loire to the classification depot at Blois, one of the functions of which was to sort out officers who
had somehow failed in their duty—a "human salvaging plant" as Harbord called it, "the grave of buried ambitions, the temporary home
of the homeless." Blois was the scrap pile of hundreds of personal
tragedies, but undoubtedly the rehabilitation system established there
was more humane than the sacrificial "Company Q's" to which
blemished Civil War officers were consigned. "Officers of all grades
from brigadier down came here for a sizing-up, some to find duty in a
different unit from that in which they failed, others to stay away permanently from combatant troops, confessed failures," Harbord wrote.
But it was still a shameful place, and Pershing did not mention it except
in passing when he compiled his account of the trip with Harbord; instead, he wrote approvingly of a German officers' prison at Fort Pen-
field, near Pontanezen, where "it was everywhere noticeable that
whether in prison or at work the German soldier always retained his
military bearing and his excellent discipline."

On returning to Paris from the inspection tour, Pershing cabled the
Secretary of War that on the whole the S.O.S. was in working order
and would "be able to provide for the needs of our expanded program." And he repeated his view that "all must be under one head to
insure success," just in case Washington was still wondering whether
the supply chief of the A.E.F. should have "coordinate" status.

The French and British, during most of August, were engaged in
reducing the various salients thrust into their lines by the German
offensives. The British pinched out the Amiens salient in successful
attacks between August 8 and 15, and between Soissons and Arras,
August 18 to 29, the French and British together forced the Germans
back to prepared positions in the Battle of Picardy. Toward the end
of August the enemy began evacuating the Lys salient. All along the
line the Germans were falling back, shortening their front, preparing to
offer the most desperate resistance to the heavier blows expected from
the Allied armies that fall. A number of American units participated
in those actions under French and British command. The Allies had
not yet given up hope that Pershing could be dissuaded from carrying
out an all-American operation designed to eliminate the Saint-Mihiel
salient; the most determined attacks on his plan were still to come.

Happily unaware that the Allies had not reconciled themselves to his program or that they were maneuvering behind the scenes to delay the formation of the First American Army, Pershing went ahead with his plans at his new headquarters at La Ferté-sous-Jouarre. Much of his time was spent going over reports on the performances of his various divisions, particularly the fifteen earmarked for participation in the Saint-Mihiel offensive, and the competence of their senior officers. He was interested not only in the evidence of their capacity to handle their present responsibilities but to "grow up to" larger ones. In the expanding A.E.F. he had to be searching constantly for men with the talent and outlook elastic enough to move up the ladder of command. Major Palmer recalled that he would ask one of his staff, "What is the matter with so and so?" The officer would reply, "He not only does not see the forest for the trees, but he is digging himself a hole under the roots of one tree." And Pershing would comment, "Why I considered him one of my broad-minded ones. Haven't you met any of my narrow-minded ones?" To one rather surprised officer he recommended a reading of Tolstoy's *War and Peace* to "develop your imagination." Of another he complained, "He has not yet gone as far as Caesar's *Commentaries* in studying the history of war since he forgot the history he learned at West Point."

General Liggett, as commander of I Corps, was living up to the great expectations held for him and proving, as he said, that fat "doesn't matter if it does not extend above the neck." General Bullard, commander of II Corps, had demonstrated the kind of drive and self-assurance that was essential in executing the kind of fast-breaking offensives with which Pershing hoped to break the German line. Now another man had come along and proved, in the space of a few months, that he also had the capacity for high command. He was Major General Charles P. Summerall, recently elevated to command of the First Division, now known as "Pershing's Darlings." Many historians have designated him as the only original genius raised up by the A.E.F. Originally an artilleryman, his strong point was promoting teamwork between the artillery and the infantry, using his guns to cover and clear the way for the ground forces. "No attack of the World War before 1918," he said, "was supported by half enough artillery to protect the men."

Summerall, who was descended from a long line of preachers, and himself intended for the pastorate, was a fifty-one-year-old West

Pointer. He had won distinction during the Boxer Rebellion when Reilly's battery was trying to batter down the gate to the Forbidden City. Summerall dashed up to the gate under heavy fire from the Boxers, chalked up a big cross as an aiming point, and returned to his guns as they blew the gate down. Later he served for many years in the Philippines.

In December of 1917 he succeeded General March in command of the 1st Artillery Brigade and built a strong communications net, stringing wires from the forward positions of the First Division through the switchboard at artillery headquarters direct to his batteries. On March 19 his system met the test when the Germans threw in a storm-troop battalion behind a box barrage. Summerall's guns went into action immediately in the Toul sector, killing all of the assaulting battalion's officers and half of the men before they had advanced halfway across No Man's Land. During the First Division's attack at Cantigny, Summerall reinforced his batteries of French 75s with a collection of old fortress howitzers of limited range but heavy caliber and kept plastering the German positions around the clock for four days, until a captured officer complained, "My God, your artillery must be crazy. All they do is shoot. My men couldn't get any rest or work on the trenches or lay their guns properly."

Summerall kept pounding away at his credo, "Artillery exists only to protect and support the infantry," and insisted that the machinegun deadlock on the western front could be broken by a more perfect co-ordination of artillery and rifle fire.

He was one of the few high-ranking A.E.F. officers for whom the troops demonstrated any considerable enthusiasm. General Bullard said his subordinates "both feared and loved him. . . . He possessed the quality of giving the severest reprimand in the quietest words. . . . He never coddled, he sometimes even treated soldiers with a calm, uncompromising harshness, but the soldier that did something under Summerall was never forgotten."

General Summerall was a fervent teetotaler, which alone distinguished him from most of his brother officers. On an inspection tour in the Toul sector one night he asked a company commander his usual question, "Is there any drinking in your command?" "Some drinking, sir," the infantry captain replied, "but no drunkenness." Just then the company cook staggered out of his quarters and lurched toward Summerall with a glad cry of, "My old captain from the Philippines," and collapsed in the snow at the general's feet. Summerall, putting aside his convictions in favor of sentiment, immediately claimed him for his headquarters mess.

Among the divisional reports that Pershing studied with particular interest in those late August days were those of the 32nd and 42nd, which had been engaged in heavy fighting. The 32nd was composed partly of National Guard troops from Wisconsin, mostly German-Americans, who were not expected to take kindly to the idea of fighting under French command. In the forests of the Vosges, however, they had distinguished themselves in some of the bitterest hand-to-hand fighting of the war. The 42nd (Rainbow) Division's toughest outfit was the 165th Infantry, as the old "Fighting 69th" had been renamed. The regiment had been recruited largely from the Irish-Americans of the Hell's Kitchen section of New York, and their sentiments also were suspected of being less than lukewarm. On the Ourcq that summer they had shattered the counterattacks of four German divisions, including the crack Fourth Prussian Guards. The reports on the 32nd and 42nd divisions only confirmed Pershing's belief that Americans would fight in the national interest, regardless of who the enemy was or who their allies were. . . .

On August 29, Pershing moved closer to the front and established his battle headquarters at Ligny-en-Barrois, which was twenty-five miles southwest of Saint-Mihiel. The French handed over command of the Saint-Mihiel sector with considerable ceremony. Dress trousers of red and sky-blue tunics, which had gone out of fashion at the front in 1914 when they proved attractive targets for enemy machine gunners, adorned the French general and his staff. His chief of staff made quite a ritual of turning over two large volumes, one the Offensive Plan and the other the Defensive Plan for the Saint-Mihiel salient, each numbering about 150 pages. Pershing sardonically pointed out later that he had brought along his own plans, which ran to a total of only fourteen pages, and which he said "showed the difference between planning for trench warfare, to which the French were inclined, and open warfare, which we expected to conduct."

American troops were already moving into position for the offensive two weeks hence, the I and IV corps replacing the Second and Eighth French armies in the sectors from Void to Souilly and Void to the Moselle River.

Pershing's plans were made; the First American Army, which would also include the II French (Colonial) Corps and the American V Corps, with three divisions in Army Reserve, would go over the top on September 12.

That was the situation on the afternoon of August 30, everything moving like clockwork, everyone looking forward to a smashing success against the Germans, convinced that the Allies had finally yielded to the idea of an integrated American Army.

That evening, however, Generalissimo Foch appeared at Ligny-en-Barrois, bearing with him a new plan of operations. Foch's proposal, as Pershing summed it up, was that "the objectives in the St. Mihiel operation should be restricted and the attack made on the southern face only, and that upon its completion two other operations be undertaken by combined Americans and French, a number of our divisions going *under French command*." [The italics were Pershing's.]

The British, it later developed, were particularly active behind the scenes of this latest maneuver, foremost among them Sir Henry Wilson, the chief of the Imperial General Staff, who had little sympathy for Pershing's yearning for independence. Haig was also in favor of the revision, but more on tactical than on political grounds. On a visit to British headquarters earlier that month Pershing should, perhaps, have been forewarned. King George, also in attendance, had spoken to Pershing of his desire to have as many Americans as possible serve under the British command, emphasizing that "their presence has an excellent effect in stimulating the morale" of the British units to which they were attached.

Unmoved by the royal compliment, Pershing later that day gave Haig the news that he would have to withdraw three of the five American divisions serving with the British to build up his own army for the Saint-Mihiel operation. Haig argued that he had "understood that the American divisions had been sent there to be trained and to serve on the British front and that now, just as they had become useful, it was proposed to take them away."

When he saw that Pershing was adamant, Haig said, with every appearance of good grace, "Pershing, of course you shall have them. There can never be any difference between us."

In London they were less inclined to be sporting, Lloyd George cabling Clemenceau that he wanted American divisions to form a reserve group behind the British armies, and reminding him that "the greater part of the American troops were brought to France by British shipping and that because of the sacrifices made to furnish this shipping our people have the right to expect that more than five divisions of the twenty-eight now in France should be put in training behind our lines."

Even more vociferous, though not publicly so, was General Wilson, who was convinced that his country was bearing the heaviest burden of the war, that "the French are not fighting at all and the Americans don't know how." An adept at political and military intrigue, he had opposed the plan to assign the reduction of the Saint-Mihiel salient to the American Army—and he was accustomed to getting his own way sooner or later. Few of his colleagues were willing to pay him any high personal or professional regard. Sir Andrew Macphail (*Three Persons*) wrote of him: "A creature with the characteristics of separate species is abhorrent; it has the worst features of both. The dog, the ape, the man, the politician, the soldier are as God made them. Sir Henry Wilson was politician and soldier at the same time."

On August 27, pushing harder for revision of the campaign plan, Field Marshal Haig wrote to Marshal Foch that the direction of the American offensive should be changed "in such a way as to make possible the launching of a concentric movement against Cambrai and, starting from the southwards, against Mézières. The actual direction taken by my attacks will bring me to Cambrai, provided the pressure exerted against the rest of the enemy's front be constantly maintained." Haig, in other words, wanted the American attack to veer toward his own objective, making both offensives more difficult for the Germans to counter. Pershing, on the other hand, had proposed to attack in a more easterly direction and bring more direct pressure to bear on the enemy's vitals. As General Harbord pointed out, Pershing's plan would have been "perhaps less expensive of life and equally effective in ending the war. . . . It was the shortest line to the enemy's line of supply and communications. It might have looked a bit more like an American victory ending the war than the Franco-American effort west of the Meuse."

Harbord, undoubtedly reflecting his chief's views, believed that between August 24 and 30 Foch "must have had counsel from some source which disposed him to the frustration of the hopes of the Americans and the disorganization of their First Army." There is little doubt that Wilson and Haig were that source.

When Foch appeared at his Advanced Headquarters on August 30, Pershing, listening to this new scheme, must have thought back to the marshal's assurance of several weeks before that "I am going to be more American than you are" in pushing the organization of an American Army.

The new proposition, Pershing wrote in his diary later that night, came "dropping out of a clear sky without the slightest warning."

Foch, always hopeful of finding Pershing in a mood to say yes for once, asked his opinion of the new plan.

"Well, Marshal," Pershing replied, "this is a very sudden change. We are going forward as already recommended to you and approved by you, and I cannot understand why you want these changes. Moreover, I think that to make an attack in the salient with limited objectives would cost little less than to carry out the original idea, which would put us in a much better position."

Foch remarked that he had hoped to avoid dividing the American Army, now barely organized, but didn't see how it could be done. He also suggested that two French generals, Degoutte and Malcor, be assigned to presumably influential positions on Pershing's staff. "This was only a roundabout way of attempting to assign General Degoutte to command our forces," Pershing maintained, adding that many Americans who had served under Degoutte when he commanded the Sixth French Army considered that "because of his orders American troops had been unnecessarily sacrificed."

He rejected the suggestions at once, then by way of conciliation told Foch that he would be willing to accept the limited objectives if the secondary attack from the western face of the salient could be retained in the plan of operations. He also made it plain that he would not consider any plan in which the American First Army would be broken up before it was given a chance to fight.

The conversation then became quite heated.

"Do you wish to take part in the battle?" Foch demanded.

"Most assuredly, but as an American army and in no other way."

Foch explained that his timetable would be upset if Pershing's plans were not changed in line with his suggestions.

"If you will assign me a sector," Pershing said, "I will take it at once."

"Where would it be?"

"Wherever you say."

The marshal pointed out that the Americans lacked artillery and other supporting elements to carry out a large-scale operation, to which Pershing retorted that the United States had concentrated on shipping infantry and machine-gun units on demand of the Allies, who had promised to supply the auxiliary forces.

Foch clung so stubbornly to his new proposals that Pershing finally told him:

"Marshal Foch, you have no authority as Allied Commander-in-Chief to call upon me to yield up my command of the American army and have it scattered among the Allied forces where it will not be an American army at all."

"I must insist upon the arrangement," Foch reiterated.

"Marshal Foch, you may insist all you please, but I decline absolutely to consider your plan. While our army will fight wherever you may decide, it will not fight except as an independent American army."

Thereupon Foch gathered up his maps and papers and turned toward the door. He was ten years Pershing's senior, and his face was pale, lined, and weary from the tension of the interview. Pershing noted, not without satisfaction, that Foch looked "utterly exhausted" from the ordeal. He paused at the threshold and handed Pershing a memorandum listing his proposals and expressed the hope that the American, after considering them in writing, would change his mind.

After the weary generalissimo departed, Pershing decided that Foch had "allowed himself to be persuaded that after the reduction of the St. Mihiel salient [the American Army] should be split up. . . . With the added support of American divisions, making the Second [French] Army largely American, Foch's advisers no doubt thought that the French themselves would then be able to push forward and cut Germany's vital line of communications."

He looked over the memorandum Foch had left, which included these proposals:

"a) An attack between the Meuse and the Argonne executed by the French Second Army reinforced by a few American divisions (4 or 6), to be prepared at once and launched as soon as possible after that in the Woëvre [that is, the Saint-Mihiel salient].

"b) A French-American attack extending from the Argonne to the Souain road, to be prepared also without any delay so that it may be launched a few days after the preceding one. This attack will be executed by: On the right, an American army acting on each side of the

Aisne—on the left the French Fourth Army extending its action to the Souain road."

It seemed to Pershing, pacing his office that night, that Foch "has some brilliant ideas but many of them are, unfortunately, not possible of execution." Aside from the question of breaking up his army and submitting to further "coordination" by the French, it would have been all but impossible to reduce the Saint-Mihiel salient, then proceed with two other operations immediately afterward "with forces which don't exist."

Undoubtedly Foch's proposals of August 30 bore all the earmarks of hasty improvisation; they had been concocted in a last-minute effort to forestall any independent operations by the American Army, presumably with postwar political objectives in view. There hadn't been time to draw up a well-considered plan of operations. The sketchy memorandum submitted by Foch was the result.

Next day Generals Pershing and McAndrew and their operations officer, General Conner, drew up a strongly worded reply which read in part: "I can no longer agree to any plan which involves a dispersion of our units. . . . Briefly, American officers and soldiers alike are, after one experience, no longer willing to be incorporated in other armies, even though such incorporation be by larger units. The older American divisions have encountered so much difficulty in their service with the French and British that it is advisable to consider the return of such divisions to French or British control. The same is true of our corps staffs." Pershing added that he was willing to make a concession in changing the direction of the American attacks toward Mézières "even though it complicates my supply system and the care of sick and wounded," but "the American army must be employed as a whole, either east of the Argonne or west of the Argonne. . . ."

On September 2, Foch and Pershing met again, this time with General Pétain present, at Foch's headquarters at Bombon. Again there was sparring between Foch and Pershing, with Pétain as referee, but an agreement was finally reached. Pershing wrote that Foch, "though assuming a very bluff air," was more conciliatory than on the evening of August 30. But the Supreme Commander still drove a hard bargain. The Americans were to undertake the Saint-Mihiel offensive, then in the brief space of two weeks transfer their forces for a much larger operation on the Meuse-Argonne front. The movement would entail lifting 600,000 troops and 3000 guns, plus all the other equipment and supplies, from the Saint-Mihiel battlefield and depositing them on the new front sixty miles away, over three roads that could be used only during the night hours.

The French and British had long been carping about the deficiencies of American staff work, yet now were handing them an enormously complicated problem in logistics which would have taxed the ingenuity of the most experienced staff in military history. Mounting an offensive of that scope usually took months of preparation. Not even the logistically brilliant Germans tried to work that fast. Even so, Pershing said, "it was a relief to have a decision"—by which he meant a decision acceptable to himself.

The objective of the American offensive was a triangle of ground between the Moselle and the Meuse rivers, about eighteen miles deep and thirty miles across the base. Since the earliest months of the war, it had been a wedge driven into the Allied front, cutting the Paris-Nancy and the Toul-Verdun railroad lines and posing a constant threat to the rear of the defenses of Verdun. For years Allied strategists had been staring at that wedge called the Saint-Mihiel salient and shaking their heads; the Germans had made full use of their tenure and created a powerful defensive position.

On the western face of the salient were the heights of the Meuse, extending along the eastern bank of the river. Beyond the heights was the broad plain of the Woëvre, covered with lakes, marshes, and woods which had been heavily fortified by the Germans. Running through the salient from its base, flowing northeast and emptying into the Moselle, was a small stream called the Rupt de Mad. During the rainy season, generally beginning in mid-September, the Woëvre plain was flooded and often its roads were impassable. The salient, Pershing said, was "practically a great field fortress."

It had been German real estate since September of 1914, when the enemy tried to cut off Verdun, and it had been developed with their accustomed skill and thoroughness. With excellent observation from the heights of the Meuse and the hill of Montsec near the apex of the triangle, the Germans commanded the western face of the salient with their massed artillery. Their main defenses included an outpost system, the Wilhelm position paralleling the front, the Schroerer position about five miles to the rear, and finally the Michel Stellung, part of the

Hindenburg Line, behind which the enemy hoped to hold out against the general offensive.

To the rear of the salient, certifying its strategic importance, was the fortress city of Metz with its converging rail lines and the nearby Briey iron mines which were the sole support of the German war industries. Metz was the most sensitive spot on the German war maps. Any movement in its direction was regarded as critical. From the moment of its seizure the Germans had decided to settle in the salient permanently. A doughboy in the 42nd Division observed that in the salient "the graves of German soldiers are not marked by rude little wooden crosses but substantial and sometimes elaborate monuments in stone."

The German commander on that section of the front was General Max von Gallwitz, whose army group included Army Detachment C, charged with the defense of the salient, and the Nineteenth Army, covering the defenses of Metz. From then until the end of the war he was to be Pershing's chief opponent. He was sixty-four years old, the son of a Breslau tax collector promoted from the ranks during the Franco-Prussian War. The fact that he had risen to high command in an Army dominated by Prussian aristocrats testified to his competence. He was a steady and iron-nerved, if not brilliant or inspired, commander—something like Pershing in temperament. As commander of the Guard Reserve Corps, he captured the fortress of Namur August 1, 1914. On the eastern front he had commanded the Twelfth Army, then had returned to the west and command of the Second and Fifth armies until September 1918, when he was promoted to army group commander. In the salient itself, General Max von Fuchs directed the operations of Army Detachment C.

To crush the enemy forces in this salient, Pershing and his staff worked out a plan for double envelopment, the jaws of which would close on the base of the triangle and trap as many as possible of the defenders. With forces greatly outnumbering those of his opponent, Pershing wanted an overwhelming victory because, as he wrote, "anything short of complete success would undoubtedly be seized upon to our disadvantage by those of the Allies who opposed the policy of forming an American army." To this end he mustered fifteen divisions with four in reserve. Opposed to them would be only nine enemy divisions in the front line and one in reserve—and the German divisions then were much smaller than any of the Allied, especially the American. The Germans, however, had the advantage of their experience and of fighting a defensive battle on ground they had been fortifying for four years.

The American order of battle was as follows: I Corps under Liggett (the 82nd, 90th, 5th, and 2nd, with the 78th in reserve) and IV Corps under Dickman (the 89th, 42nd, and First, with the 3rd in reserve) on the southern face of the salient. In the center, assigned to a holding operation, the II French Colonial Corps (the 39th, 26th, and 2nd Cavalry dismounted, all French). On the western face of the salient, V Corps under Cameron (the 26th, the 15th French Colonial, and the 4th). In Army Reserve were the 35th, 33rd, 91st, and 80th.

Moving his divisions into line and bringing up their supplies in the brief time allotted to preparing for the operation was a tremendous job in itself. The army engineers had to build forty-five miles of standard-gauge and 250 miles of narrow-gauge railroads, a 200-foot bridge at Griscourt, and fifteen miles of road. Every day 1,200,000 gallons of water had to be provided. The Medical Corps brought up 15,000 beds and arranged for sixty-five hospital trains for those who would be wounded. Nineteen railheads had to be established to furnish the daily requirements in food, clothing, and equipment. The Signal Corps set up a central switchboard at Pershing's headquarters at Ligny-en-Barrois with thirty-eight circuits for corps and auxiliary headquarters and separate nets for the units in the field.

Pershing now commanded the largest and most powerful army ever raised under the American flag, consisting of 550,000 Americans plus four combat divisions, aviators, tankers, and gunners supplied by the French for the occasion. Of the almost 3000 guns brought up in their support, none were of American manufacture. An air fleet of 1481 planes under command of Billy Mitchell, including 600 French aircraft and the British Independent Bombing Squadron led by General Sir Hugh (Boom) Trenchard, was also to be thrown into the fight. It was the largest air force ever assembled up to that time. None of the planes had been manufactured in the United States.

Despite the overwhelming superiority of the army compared to its opponent, Pershing was still not complacent about his prospects. Under his orders an elaborate plan to deceive the Germans on the site of his offensive was concocted, not only to draw off enemy troops but to achieve the tactical surprise he believed necessary to its success. Major Omar Bundy, commanding the VIII Corps, was ordered to establish himself and his staff at the Grand Hotel du Tonneau d'Or in Belfort, near the Swiss border, which was a rendezvous and clearinghouse for secret agents. Bundy and his staff rather ostentatiously began drawing up plans for an invasion of Alsace through the Belfort Gap.

Almost immediately the hotel began to fill up with overly nonchalant tourists, commercial travelers, Swiss businessmen, roaming artists, and other impostors who bribed the waiters for scraps of intelligence overheard in the dining room and bought the contents of wastebaskets from the chambermaids. Fragments of operational plans were among the scraps of paper bought by German agents, encouraging the enemy intelligence to decide that an attack on Mülhausen was being prepared for mid-September. The German High Command fell for the deception and moved three divisions to the Alsatian sector from the front covering Metz.

Now everything was ready; the First American Army would go into action on the morning of September 12.

On the evening of September 11–12, a heavy rain began pouring down, flooding the flat fields and marshes of the Woëvre, but fortunately it soon tapered off to a persistent drizzle. During that night the infantry moved up to its jump-off positions. The main attack on the southern face of the salient was to begin at 5 A.M., the secondary attack to the west at 8 A.M.

Four hours before zero the massed Allied artillery opened up, pounding away at the dense thickets of German barbed wire, the enemy machine-gun nests, and the forward positions of its infantry. The barrage was one of the most terrific of the war. On the First Division's front, General Summerall, the perfectionist in artillery, was more selective in his fire patterns than the steamroller barrage preceding the other divisions in the line. He had ordered "one heavy or two light guns" to fire on each enemy machine-gun nest until his infantry could bring it under direct assault. His guns were employed so skillfully, at each stage of the advance, that the First Division was enabled to cover the most ground in the least time.

Long before dawn, Pershing and several of his staff officers motored to old Fort Gironville on a height commanding the battle line from the south and watched the bombardment. Fog and drizzle covered the wooded plain before them, and they could only hope that the autumnal rains would not begin in earnest until the battle was over.

The sky was flaming with a thousand explosions as Pershing and his officers watched the spectacle over the salient. Shells exploded with sharp bursts of flame and steel fragments in the dark woods held by the enemy. Star shells soared into the misty sky, lighting up the terrain for the alarmed defenders, and colored signal lights were rocketed heavenward all along the twenty-five-mile front. Villages caught in the bombardment behind the German lines went up like torches. Enemy ammunition dumps touched off by direct hits rocked the earth with their multiple explosions. A dozen years later Pershing could recall the "exultation in our minds that here, at last, after seventeen months of effort, an American army was fighting under its own flag."

Meanwhile, unseen by their commander, hundreds of thousands of infantry waited to go over the top, men from every state in the Union huddled in their trenches, waiting for their sergeants to blow the whistle or fire the flare gun as the hands of their watches raced toward 5 A.M. Only a small proportion of them had actually been under fire, and, as a British observer commented, they were full of "boldness and dash" and their worst faults "arose from over-keenness, such as carelessness about liaison, overstepping of boundaries, overrunning the barrage."

They waited in their muddy trenches and rifle pits, under their saucerlike helmets, in the cramped and uncomfortable work clothes of the doughboy, with tight-fitting tunic, high choking collar, and troublesome puttees, only the trench-coated officers adequately protected against the rain. They were loaded down like pack mules, since Pershing and his officers regarded government property as sacred and would not let it be abandoned under any circumstances. Heavy packs, cumbersome gas masks, intrenching tools, bayoneted rifles or their allotted section of a machine gun or mortar burdened each man. Silently they waited in the mist and fog, listened to the guns, and wondered what was waiting for them in the wet woods and deep ravines ahead.

A few minutes before five o'clock the lighter guns began firing just over their heads; whistles blew and flares exploded; the sergeants yelled their blasphemous slogans; and the doughboys clambered out of their trenches, following the rolling curtain of their barrages. Tanks rumbled up to join the advance, and the battle was on.

Three hours later, on the western face of the salient, the three divisions of the V Corps jumped off as scheduled and stormed through the woods on the heights of the Meuse.

Foul as the weather was, Billy Mitchell's two attack brigades of 400 planes each took off to bomb and strafe the German communications at the base of the salient. For the next three days the Allied fliers —French, British, and American—kept up a constant air assault on the German rear, shooting up every troop movement and dropping explosives on all visible installations. Mitchell "used his 1,481 airplanes as cavalry itself had once been used, as an active arm in itself, "as Quentin Reynolds (*They Fought for the Sky*) has written. A few weeks later Mitchell was promoted to brigadier and given command of all the A.E.F.'s air forces at the front.

By 9 A.M., when Pershing returned to his headquarters at Ligny-en-Barrois from Fort Gironville, it was apparent that the attacks were succeeding at all points. On his way back to headquarters he passed groups of German prisoners being marched to waiting stockades. Studying the first action reports from his unit commanders, he saw that the initial German resistance was crumbling and his forces were advancing, for the most part, ahead of their timetables. The southern force was to pivot on the Moselle and make a right wheel toward Vigneulles, its seven divisions swinging in a twelve-mile radius. One division of the western force, the 26th, was to drive ahead to meet the First Division of the IV Corps at Vigneulles and close the trap on the Germans in the salient. When those pincers closed, the battle would be won. All that day Pershing sat at the telephone, ordering his corps and division commanders to drive on, exceed their first day's objectives and get the fighting done with. Late in the afternoon aerial observation confirmed what Pershing already suspected—the German forces compressed in the narrowing space between his southern and western wings were crowding the roads through the forest trying to get away with their artillery and supply trains. The French Colonials took the village of Saint-Mihiel and were beginning to follow up the retreating enemy.

The Germans, it was apparent from their action and situation reports and war diaries, as translated from the Potsdam archives after the war by United States Army historians, were hard-pressed to keep their retreat from turning into a rout. They had been expecting an attack in the salient since September 1, when Hindenburg's headquarters forwarded intelligence summaries indicating that a converging offensive against Metz could be expected, and on September 7 Von Gallwitz and Von Fuchs worked out a plan to hit first and get the jump on the Americans. They dropped the plan hurriedly when they learned that the Americans were closing in on both sides of the salient. The enemy commanders were surprised not so much by the attack but the force and violence with which it was launched. The army group's war diary for September 12 expressed alarm at the "rapid launching of the enemy attack against the west and south front of the Army Detachment." Von Gallwitz had already asked permission to withdraw his forces to the Michel position and had started moving back some of his units and heavier equipment. "The enemy's advance," his headquarters' war diary added, "has to be stopped under all circumstances so as to protect the left pivot of the Michel movement" [back to the main positions of the Hindenburg Line]. For six hours the Germans fought to maintain their front line, but at noon orders went out from Army Detachment C Headquarters to begin a graduated withdrawal.

Fragments of radioed and telephoned messages from German forward units to their various headquarters provide a graphic picture of the fury with which the Americans attacked, scattering everything before them, then heading for the next line of resistance. "Despite repeated requests our infantry does not indicate its positions. . . . Battalion staff of the 15th Pioneers has just arrived at the Brigade command post. Companies scattered, only one in hand. . . . Left flank in bad shape—Grusdorf cannot hold out any longer—batteries have no ammunition at the present time. . . . Line of riflemen seen advancing on the other side of the Grisières farm. . . . Retrograde movements at the Grisières farm. . . . Sixth Regiment thrown back—entire 47th in retreat—1st Battery of the 56th destroyed. . . . Enemy tanks at Rambucort—70 to 80 tanks observed to the southeast preparing for heavy attack. . . ."

Those messages, gasped out over the German radio and telephone nets, told the whole course of the battle. The Germans were accustomed to the methodical attacks of the French and British and could move methodically, sensibly, to forestall them. These Americans, however, came on like wild Indians, swarming over everything, rarely pausing to regroup, ignoring all the sane and logical patterns of warfare.

And later that night the situation reports of the mauled and disorganized divisions were even more alarming. The log at army group headquarters noted that the 192nd Infantry Division had reported that "it will not be able to offer stubborn resistance and that the forces are no longer sufficient for any kind of organization in depth." Unfortunately for the enemy, the troops caught in the American nut-cracker were not top drawer, mostly war-weary and middle-aged Saxonians, Bavarians, Württembergers, and Austrians.

By then, at Ligny-en-Barrois, Pershing had flashed orders to all his commanders to disregard the original plan to advance by stages, keep on attacking, and close the gap at Vigneulles before the bulk of the German forces could escape. With the enemy in full retreat, the old cavalrymen at headquarters thought they saw a chance to prove that the mounted arm was not yet completely useless, as the footsloggers, the airmen, and the tank enthusiasts maintained. Pursuit was supposed to be the cavalry's job and someone at G.H.Q.—it may have been Pershing—remembered that three troops of the 2nd Cavalry were right behind the advancing infantry. Here was one last chance to send the horse cavalry in, before the tank took over its historic role in warfare.

Orders went out for Troops D, F, and H, 300 troopers altogether, to reconnoiter the German line of retreat and try to cut the railroad at Vigneulles, where the First and 26th divisions were supposed to join hands. If the cavalry got there first, it might prove a point in Pershing's wrangle with Chief of Staff March over shipping two cavalry divisions from the States. The lesson of Carrizal, where four Mexican machine guns had chopped up two troops of the 10th Cavalry, seemed to be forgotten.

That brief cavalry action on the road to Vigneulles is seldom mentioned in histories of the war, yet it was the final footnote to the record of the American cavalry, which had played a decisive role in three previous wars and the conquest of the Indians.

What happened in that last charge, which must have further convinced the Germans they were dealing with lunatics, sounds like a page from a military satire. According to Thomas M. Johnson, the New York *Sun* correspondent, the three troops of the 2nd Cavalry were in poor shape for any kind of endeavor, let alone attacking the battle-hardened professionals of the German Army. They were mounted on the sorriest horseflesh, culled only three weeks before out of the veterinary hospitals. Many of the troopers were cavalrymen in name only, with no more than ten days' training on horseback. All were armed only with pistols. They lacked everything but courage.

Troops D, F, and H trotted down the road in obedience to orders until their scouts spotted the rear guard of a column of the Michel Group heading back to a new position. Confident as their forerunners under the guidons of Stuart or Sheridan, they deployed, drew their pistols, and charged. A few seconds after recovering from their surprise at this quixotic gesture, the Germans unlimbered their machine guns and cut loose.

At the first rattle of gunfire the 2nd Cavalry's mounts reared, unseated many of their riders, and galloped off, but the dismounted troopers stayed to fight. When the skirmish was over and they straggled back to Nonsard, five miles behind the front, they found they had won themselves a small victory. One trooper had been killed and another captured, but ten bewildered Germans were brought back as prisoners of war. In modern war it appeared that the horse was simply unwilling to co-operate. The cavalry raid, as such, had failed to achieve its purpose. It must have been a dismal hour at Ligny when the old cavalrymen learned what had happened on the road to Vigneulles. However, the frustrated "raid" served a purpose, in that it discouraged Pershing from demanding further shipments of cavalry.

All during that night of September 12–13 the Americans kept pressing to close the trap on the Germans. Since the auxiliary services had a hard time keeping up with the advance, German prisoners were employed to carry the wounded of both sides back to the dressing stations and incidentally to absorb a lesson in democracy. A soldier in the Rainbow Division wrote that white-gloved German officers were forced into an acquaintance with manual labor for the first time in their lives. "It seemed to do these enemy enlisted men good to see their officers thus reduced to their own plane." The prisoners, in fact, had cheered up considerably after finding that "they weren't going to be scalped as they had been led to believe these aboriginal Americans were wont to do."

Next morning Pershing arose after a few hours' sleep and at daylight heard the news he had been waiting for. The First and 26th divisions' leading elements had just met in the ruins of Vigneulles. Saint-Mihiel salient was in the bag. The whole front then moved forward to the line Noroy-Hattonville-Fresnes, which included all the objectives originally staked out. Several counterattacks were repulsed, and the line again was advanced, to Haudiomont-Doncourt-Vandières, where it was stabilized. Almost 16,000 prisoners and 450 guns had been taken, and the Germans were forced back into their last ditch, the Hindenburg Line.

It had been an easy victory, helped along by the fact that the Germans had already started to withdraw from their forward positions. Liggett's I Corps, in fact, had reached its second-day objective only seven hours after the offensive began. One of his brigadiers strolled out on a personal reconnaissance, unescorted, and not a shot was fired at him; not an enemy soldier was to be seen. He sent a cocky message back to corps headquarters, "Let me go ahead, and I'll be in Metz, and you'll be a field marshal." Liggett, always shrewd and cool-tempered, reasoned that Metz could have been taken in another bound forward "only on the supposition that our army was a well-oiled, fully coordinated machine, which it was not as yet."

Other field commanders, watching the Germans frantically throwing up field works along the incomplete Michel Stellung, were convinced that with reinforcements the First Army could have pushed on and broken the Hindenburg Line, taking the Briey iron fields and threatening the German line of retreat by slashing the enemy's communications in Lorraine. "We could have gone on and taken Metz," mourned General Summerall. General Dickman expressed it even more strongly: "The failure to push north from St. Mihiel will always be regarded by me as a strategical blunder for which Marshal Foch and his staff are responsible. It is a glaring example of the fallacy of the policy of limited objectives."

The victory was secured on Pershing's fifty-eighth birthday, September 13, with President Wilson cabling his "warmest congratulations on the brilliant achievements of the army under your command." Marshal Foch, who had the generosity of a great man in such situations, telegraphed Pershing that the American First Army "has won a magnificent victory by a maneuver as skilfully prepared as it was valiantly executed." Even more flattering, perhaps, was the fact that Pétain sent a large number of observers to the battlefield of Saint-Mihiel a few days later to learn how the Americans had cut through the fields of barbed wire so quickly (by smothering the enemy artillery and allowing men with wire cutters to work undisturbed). One French officer seriously expressed the opinion that Americans could better cope with the wire entanglements than his countrymen because they had longer legs and bigger feet.

Yet the Battle of Saint-Mihiel was not a total success, principally because the Germans had managed to withdraw so many of their troops. General Bullard, who did not participate, believed that it "was given an importance which posterity will not concede. . . . Germany had begun to withdraw. She had there chiefly weaker divisions, young men and old, and Austro-Hungarians." In the larger picture of the western front, it was rated a "local success."

Its real significance rested on the fact that the American Army had fought and won its first battle as an independent force and, despite the use of Pershing's more aggressive tactics, at a cost of only 7000 casualties, the same number the First Division alone suffered at Soissons. Undoubtedly it could have pushed on and attained a major victory, but was stopped in its tracks by the conflicting demands of Allied strategy, one of the inevitable hazards of fighting a coalition war.

Ahead, in the tangled forests and fortified heights of the Meuse-Argonne, lay the real test of American arms.

14.   The Longest, Toughest Battle

In the ten days between September 16 and 26, an enormous feat of logistics had to be performed. To change the direction of the American attack from Metz to Mézières, switching the center of gravity from the Saint-Mihiel sector to north of Verdun and the western edge of the Argonne forest, it was necessary to move out 220,000 French troops then holding that section of the line and replace them with 600,000 Americans. This had to be done secretly, if possible, which necessitated night movements on foot, by rail, and by truck. The facilities for accomplishing this miracle of transportation were scant. There were only three standard-gauge railroad lines behind the new battle front and three roads leading toward it through Varennes, Avocourt, and Esne, each assigned to a corps. Nineteen railheads and eighty supply depots had to be established. Forty thousand tons of artillery ammunition alone had to be stockpiled behind the lines before the zero hour. And all this had to be worked out by Americans whose staff work had been under constant criticism.

The burden of planning and executing this quick and secret movement of the First American Army fell upon a youngish lieutenant colonel who until then had been working in the sacerdotal obscurity of the General Staff. He was George C. Marshall, Jr., only thirty-eight years old and not even a West Pointer. A graduate of the Virginia Military Institute, he had been commissioned a second lieutenant and sent to the Philippines early in 1902, served with the infantry on Mindoro, and in the years leading up to the European war had acquired a promising reputation as a staff officer. He went overseas with the first convoy and was assigned to the First Division as operations officer.

His first encounter with General Pershing, when the latter was inspecting a two-battalion maneuver in October 1917, was not particularly auspicious. Pershing's criticism of the way the troops were handled was harsh.

Marshall rather boldly pointed out that the field problem had been set up only the day before, coincidental with the announcement of the general's coming, and that the troops "should have had two weeks preparation for a complicated maneuver like this." Pershing glared. Contradictions by a junior staff officer are seldom welcomed by a four-star general. Finally he said, "Yes, you're quite right," and stalked away.

Marshall next came to Pershing's attention as the planner of the Cantigny operation. Pershing, looking over his plans, not only approved of them but marked down their author as a highly promising man. With the organization of the First Army, Marshall was moved up to operations officer on that staff under General Liggett and his chief of staff, General Hugh A. Drum. He was a quiet, sandy-haired man, imperturbable under the terrific pressure of those September days when the First Army was changing front.

On September 21, Pershing moved his headquarters from Ligny-en-Barrois to Souilly, on the road from Bar-le-Duc to Verdun, down which millions of Frenchmen had marched in 1916 and 1917, hundreds of thousands of them never to make the return trip. Headquarters was in the corner room of the shabby little town hall where Pétain had proclaimed, "They shall not pass," and where Nivelle had planned the recapture of Fort Douaumont. Down the hall, in a small front room cluttered with maps, General Drum and Colonel Marshall grappled with the problem of bringing their forces into the line before September 21.

Marshall, who was now referred to as "the wizard," stationed officers at check points along the roads to report on the hour-by-hour movement of troops and supplies, keep breakdowns from tangling traffic, and make certain each division kept to its march tables. His calculations were based on this formula: each truck could carry twenty-four men, it took a thousand trucks to move one division, which occupied about four miles of road (not counting the baggage trains), and there were fifteen divisions to be moved.

The complications arising from this movement were neither foreseeable nor preventable, and trucks broke down, horses foundered in exhaustion, and columns could become snarled because tractor-drawn artillery could travel at only eight kilometers an hour while another lot could make fifteen in the same time. By telephone and dispatch rider, and often in person when a bad traffic jam developed, Marshall supervised the movement and kept it flowing. Marshall was able to report that "despite the haste with which the movements had to be carried out, the inexperience of most of the commanders in movements of such density, the condition of the animals and the limitations as to roads, the entire movement was carried out without a single element failing to reach its place on the date scheduled, which was, I understand, one day earlier than Marshal Foch considered possible."

General Pershing considered it a "stupendous task and a delicate one" to engineer that transfer without arousing the suspicions of the Germans, indicating "the smoothness and precision with which it was calculated and accomplished." He gave all the credit to the "able direction" of Colonel Marshall and quoted with approval the comment of Colonel Repington, the London *Post's* military writer, that "it was a fine piece of Staff work and no other Staff could have done it better." It was, in fact, one of the greatest achievements of the war. From then on, almost to the day of his death, Pershing was the prime mover, patron, and protector of the modest and quiet-mannered Marshall's career.

While his troops were moving into position, Pershing was speeding around the circuit of the various Allied headquarters in his sedan with the four-starred pennant. Co-ordination with the French, in particular, had to be worked out since their Fourth Army was to attack on the Americans' left flank. He formally assumed command of the Meuse-Argonne sector on September 22. That day, only four days before the offensive was to begin, he had to straighten out a misunderstanding with Pétain. He wrote in his diary that Pétain somehow had understood him to say that there would be no preliminary bombardment on the American front. "Certainly I did not say to General Pétain that there would be no artillery preparation by the Americans. . . . This is a matter which I will decide myself when the time comes to decide." The language barrier, even between two men who knew each other as well as Pétain and Pershing did by then, was formidable. Everything had to be interpreted or translated, then checked back on to make certain that a precise understanding had been reached, particularly when French and American units were fighting side by side;

and in addition to different languages there was a different way of thinking and of acting on thought; the matter of liaison was always delicate, taxing, and vexatious.

A clear understanding, however, had been reached on how each ally was to participate in the general offensive, how the converging armies were to make the grab for victory immediately rather than wait until the summer of 1919, which as late as July 24 Foch had envisioned as the climax of the war. The American First Army and the French Fourth were to drive forward on September 26, the British First and Third were to attack in the direction of Cambrai the next day, the Flanders group of armies (British Second and the Belgians) were to take the offensive September 28 between the Lys River and the sea, and on September 29 the British Fourth and the French First were to join in the movement on Cambrai.

Confronting this array of armies from the Meuse to the Channel, 217 divisions in all, were 193 German and four Austrian divisions. The enemy's morale was sinking, not only because of the series of defeats which had been inflicted since midsummer but the privations of the soldiers' families on the home front and the increasing talk of a soldiers' and workers' revolution. Ludendorff's nerves were cracking and Crown Prince Rupprecht of Bavaria, commanding the German army group of the north, was writing that peace must be arranged by winter, no matter how hard the Allied terms. But the German armies were still capable of bitter resistance, knowing that the harder they fought the more favorable the peace terms that Germany could secure. They had the shelter of the belt of field fortifications called the Hindenburg Line, and their High Command hoped that by holding the prewar, permanently fortified line between Metz and Switzerland they could conduct a graduated retreat to the Rhine, taking an immense toll of the attacking Allies while their diplomats negotiated from a position of comparative strength. The German defense was organized in depth, with six separate zones: the outpost line, the forward battle zone held mostly by machine guns and single field guns, the main battle zone, the greater battle zone which was the main line of resistance, the rearward position, and the rearward battle zone. In between these zones were placed large numbers of machine guns.

Nowhere were the Germans stronger and more determined to make a fight of it than in the Argonne, which for four years had been considered impregnable by the Allies.

The Argonne was designed to be the sinkhole and deathtrap of any army rash enough to attempt a penetration.

Everything favored the defense. The two rivers trisecting the front were the Meuse, which was unfordable, and the Aire, which could be forded only in places. The Argonne, lying between the Aisne to the west and the Aire to the east, greatly resembled the Wilderness of Virginia, where the Union and Confederate armies all but destroyed each other in 1864, just as the Battle of the Argonne greatly resembled the epic struggle of Grant and Lee; there were the same density of forest and scrubby undergrowth, the same lack of roads and settlements, the same dark and forbidding air of desolation. Nothing on earth can be gloomier than the heart of a forest where the sun rarely penetrates to the carpeting of rotten leaves, the scummy ponds, and the lost little streams. As a military obstacle the Argonne and the terrain eastward to the Meuse, with their steep hills and deep ravines, was more formidable than the Wilderness, where the ground was fairly level and roads could be built. From the heights of the Aire on the left and the Meuse on the right the Americans could expect a terrific cross fire from the German artillery along the twenty-five-mile front. They would also have to force their way over three sizable barriers—the heights of Montfaucon, of Cunel and Romagne, and finally the ridges of the Bois de Barricourt and the Bois de Bourgogne.

The natural defenses of the region, Pershing reported, "were strengthened by every artificial means imaginable, such as fortified strongpoints, dugouts, successive lines of trenches, and an unlimited number of concrete machinegun emplacements. A dense network of wire entanglements covered every position. With the advantage of commanding ground, the enemy was peculiarly well located to pour oblique and flanking artillery fire on any assailant attempting to advance within range between the Meuse and the Argonne. It was small wonder that the enemy had rested for four years on this front without being seriously molested. He felt secure in the knowledge that even with few divisions to hold these defenses his east and west lines of rail communication in the rear would be well protected against the probability of interference." This was the most sensitive section of the German front, considering Ludendorff's plans for a step-by-step withdrawal, since it covered the vital rail line between Metz and Mézières. Loss of that line before the Germans could pull back in northern France and Belgium would mean the ruin of their armies. They pro-

tected the Meuse-Argonne sector with four lines of defense, the lightly
held forward positions, the Diselher Stellung, the Kriemhilde Stellung,
and the Freya Stellung, all comprising a part of the Hindenburg Line.

Against the narrow but heavily fortified sector between the Meuse
and the western edge of the Argonne, Pershing was prepared to channel the initial attacks of his 600,000 troops. Before he was done, twice
that number would be thrown into the fighting. The First American
Army's order of battle for September 26 included the III Corps (Bullard) on the right, the V Corps (Cameron) in the center, and the I
Corps (Liggett) on the left. In addition, the IV Corps (Dickman) and
two French corps were holding the line between the Moselle and the
Meuse. Other parts of the A.E.F. were still serving under French and
British command. The crack Second Division was soon to go into
action with the French Fourth Army when its attack bogged down.
The whole II Corps (Read) was participating in the British Fourth
Army's offensive.

Rather than leading off the Allied general offensive, less than two
weeks after the Saint-Mihiel operation, Pershing might well have taken
a little more time with his preparations, considering his hope and expectation that the Meuse-Argonne line might be broken with one tremendous rush. It would have been a good time to make a stand against
Foch, once again, and let the other Allied armies open the offensive
while German reserves were drawn off and his own divisions prepared
themselves more thoroughly for an assignment which the cautious
Pétain believed to call on a "more than human" effort. Pershing, however, wanted to make good his boast to Foch that he could wipe out
the Saint-Mihiel salient, then switch over to the Meuse-Argonne and
attack again, all within exactly two weeks' time; and perhaps the easy
success at Saint-Mihiel had made him overconfident. He knew that the
Argonne would be tougher to crack, but he seems to have been ill-
prepared psychologically and militarily for the forty-seven-day ordeal,
the unending nightmare that encompassed the Battle of the Meuse-
Argonne. It was the longest, toughest battle ever endured by an American Army. Another few days of preparation might have lessened the
prolonged agony. But Pershing, "canny and cautious" as Harbord said
he was most of the time, was also capable of taking the most audacious
risks. He was a gambler, as all great commanders must be, and like
a gambler he believed in the Pershing luck, which had never failed
him. And luck, it has been said, is a part of genius.

At 5:30 A.M. on the designated day, the nine American divisions jumped off, preceded by a three-hour bombardment, a rolling barrage, 189 light French tanks, and 800 French, British, and American planes. Opposing them on that day were five German divisions, the enemy commander, General Von Gallwitz, having concentrated most of his reserves to the east in the expectation that Metz rather than Mézières would be the direction of the American attack.

Pershing was making his headquarters on his train drawn up on a spur concealed in the woods near Souilly. For most of the forty-seven anxiety-ridden days ahead he would sleep there and work in his office car for several hours during the morning, then spend the rest of the day and often much of the night in an endless round of his corps and division headquarters. He spent most of his time, in fact, at the various command posts, raising hell with commanders who were not driving ahead fast enough, shaking up his command structure when he felt his officers weren't pushing ahead to the limit of their capacities, even lending encouragement on occasion. But Pershing was more of a driver than a coaxer; he spread more acid than balm in his constant round of his commanders' posts. Whatever the outcome of this fight, Pershing would take the full responsibility and he demanded the full extent of his generals' skill and determination. The Meuse-Argonne was fought in its larger detail on Pershing's direct orders. Colonel Mott of his staff wrote that before and during the battle "every move of every corps and almost every division was ordered by one officer— General Pershing."

Both the driving energy and the lack of finesse with which the First American Army hammered, at high cost to both itself and the enemy, at the Meuse-Argonne sector derived from its commander. The Army operated on the "Combat Instructions" which Pershing circulated shortly before the campaign began and which were designed to encourage initiative in every unit down to the platoon. His kind of fighting, he pointed out, was marked by "irregularity of formations, comparatively little regulation of space and time by higher commanders, the greatest possible use of the infantry's own firepower to enable it to get forward . . . brief orders and the greatest possible use of individual initiative by all troops engaged in the action. . . . The infantry commander must oppose machineguns by fire from his rifles, his automatics and his rifle grenades and must close with their crews under cover of this fire and of ground beyond their flanks. . . . The success of every unit from the platoon to the division must be exploited to the fullest extent. When strong resistance is encountered, reinforcements must not be thrown in to make a frontal attack at this point, but must be pushed through gaps created by successful units, to attack these strong points in the flank or rear."

By following the fire and movement pattern with which the American infantry had long been indoctrinated, Pershing hoped to force his way quickly through fortified lines which the Germans had prepared at their leisure for four years. He had neither the time nor the inclination to work out complicated plans using the newer weapons to the fullest extent of their present efficiency; the terrain was miserable for tanks and the plane was most efficient, in his view, as an observation platform for the artillery.

A step-by-step account of the Meuse-Argonne battle would take a full volume, even concisely written. A whole book has been compiled on the ordeal of the so-called lost battalion. The following, therefore, is a ruthlessly compressed account of a battle which deserves the utmost elaboration. The confusion, the despair, and the agony may be found in the various unit histories and the recollections of the participants; for those who weren't there the result has tended to mute and conceal the sheer ugliness of the whole affair. From beginning to end, the battle, more than most, rested on the willingness of the men to stick it out, climb the next slope under a cross fire of artillery and machine guns, hit the next machine-gun nest, head into the next gas-shrouded woods. It was the common soldiers' fight; the generals had very little to do with it. Pershing, foreseeing this lack of contact between the commanders and their troops once the battle began, had painstakingly directed their whole training at being able to fight without constant and precise orders. When their will faltered, the campaign came to a stop; when it was renewed through rest or reinforcement, it ground forward again.

Hardly a worse place to fight an offensive battle could have been found. A single theme with a thousand dissonances dominates all the eyewitness accounts of the fighting—the damnable difficulty of campaigning in that country—the shell-pocked terrain, the mined roads, the mud and rain, the difficulty of hauling guns over abandoned trenches and brush-covered shell holes, the broken bridges, the embankments sideslipping into swamps, the all but hopeless tangles of trucks, caissons, staff cars, and tractor-drawn guns trying to make their way frontward over rutted roads, the rolling kitchens that didn't roll, the lack of food, shelter, and dry clothing for days on end, the eternal buck passing and the brass-hat stupidities. And there was no escape from this sodden hell except death, a wound, or certifiable shell shock —the cordon of military police behind the front line, on Pershing's orders, were ruthlessly efficient about herding stragglers back to the front.

The battle opened encouragingly enough. Pershing's plan was to drive two salients into the German line, one to the east of Montfaucon and the other to the west, the V Corps in the center then taking the dominating heights by storm. In the first day's fighting, the enemy's forward positions were carried and his defenses on the whaleback of Montfaucon were brought under fire. The night of September 26, Pershing wrote in his diary that he was pleased with the initial advances but foresaw trouble in keeping the offensive rolling. "The most serious problem of the day was mending the roads across what had been No Man's Land. This was a very difficult proposition because all of this ground has been fought over since the beginning of the war and absolutely every trace of the former roads there was lost." He was also troubled by less than satisfactory performances by the 37th, 35th, and 28th divisions. "They were new, their staffs did not work particularly well, and they generally presented the failings of green troops."

Next day his three advancing corps cracked the Germans' second position, the Giselher Stellung, and stormed into the ruined village of Montfaucon on the heights dominating the center of the Meuse-Argonne sector. Pétain had told Pershing that the First Army would get no farther than that ridge before winter closed down the fighting.

On the third day of fighting, September 28, German resistance stiffened as the enemy reserves moved into position and rather elderly but casehardened Landwehr troops, who had taken up almost permanent residence in the Argonne and knew every wrinkle of the forested hills, gave the raw American troops a rough handling, particularly the 28th Division climbing the eastern spurs. Driving ahead into the enfilading fire of light artillery and machine guns, the less experienced American units outran their own artillery and suffered severe losses.

That night Pershing visited each of his corps headquarters and was "dismayed by evidence of bad staffwork." He also noted in his diary that General Traub, commanding the 35th Division, and General

Muir, the 28th, both of whom were engaged in the I Corps attack, "had to play to a certain extent the role of regimental commander" because of the inexperience of their subordinates. Since the 28th had a particularly rigorous mission and General Muir complained of a breakdown in the function of his headquarters, Pershing immediately loaned him the services of General Dennis E. Nolan, his G-2 (intelligence) officer at Chaumont, and Colonel A. L. Conger, his order-of-battle specialist, to keep the division rolling. "I gave orders for the advance to be resumed," he wrote that night in his diary, "and certainly have done all in my power to instil an aggressive spirit in the different Corps headquarters."

That last line indicated a foreboding, and it was well justified. In the first four days an average advance of eight miles was registered and the line of Bois de la Côte Lemont-Nantillois-Apremont was reached. But the impetus was gone, and by October 4 it was necessary to move more experienced divisions into line and withdraw the 37th, 79th, and 35th. They were replaced by the comparatively veteran 32nd, 3rd, and First divisions.

In that pause before the general attack was renewed, Pershing would have been less disappointed if he had been able to peer into the mind of General Ludendorff, who later wrote, "Between the Argonne and the Meuse the Americans had broken into our positions. They had assembled a powerful army [estimated at eight to one] in this region, and their part in the campaign became more and more important."

The British armies, meanwhile, were attacking on a broad front across the Canals du Nord and de Saint-Quentin, and by October 4 had smashed through the third zone of the Hindenburg Line. Their success, both in ground gained and in prisoners captured, was far more spectacular than the Americans' or the exceedingly deliberate advance of the French Fourth Army. The British deserved every bit of their success and the praise accorded it, but it was also true that the American effort not only was directed against more difficult objectives but was striking the Germans in a vital spot. The enemy, that is, could afford to yield space in Flanders but would be ruined by a breakthrough between the Meuse and the Argonne.

From then until the end of the month the American advance was slow but steadier as more experienced troops were fed into the line and the greener outfits began to learn their business in the freezing cold, amid trackless forests where a chill fog tufted every tree. Pershing confided to his diary that Foch "seems to have become restless because of the temporary stop in our advance." For the outside world, America in particular, the desperate nature of the fighting on the American front was symbolized and perhaps overdramatized by the plight of the mixed battalion of infantry of the 77th Division commanded by Major Charles Whittlesey. It had pushed forward too eagerly, and German units had craftily cut in behind it and demanded its surrender. The battalion exhausted its food, water, and ammunition, but not its courage, and held out until relieved by other units of the somewhat embarrassed division. By then the struggle of the lost battalion had attracted more headlines and more thunderous journalistic prose than the whole U.S. battle line, of which it was a minuscule part; it was the one combat of World War I with which all Americans have some familiarity.

While the Americans struggled to get their offensive rolling again, the French, in the person of Generalissimo Foch, were conducting another raid on A.E.F. Headquarters. Foch's narrow-eyed little General Weygand appeared at Souilly to present a scheme by which the general offensive would be "accelerated." The French Second Army would be inserted between the French Fourth and the American First and would take over those U.S. divisions engaged in the Argonne, while Pershing would be left with the remaining forces from the Argonne to the Moselle. Pershing suspected the new attempt to chip away at his authority was prompted by Prime Minister Clemenceau. He said no loudly and firmly.

Pershing was still indignant several days later when Foch agreed that the command setup would remain as it was "provided that my attack should be resumed at once." Pershing thought that "the Marshal quite overstepped his bounds of authority. . . . His functions are strategical and he has no authority whatsoever to interfere in tactical questions. Any observations from him as to my way of carrying out my attack are all out of place. I will not stand for this letter which disparages myself and the American army and the American effort. He will have to retract it, or I shall go further into the matter. . . ."

Those last three weeks in October were the most trying of his whole career. If ever Pershing came close to cracking, aside from the days following the death of his wife and daughters, it was during that period when it seemed that his army might be bogged down all winter midway through the German defense zones. During the battles of the

Wilderness, General Grant had suffered a similar crisis of the spirit and will, had retired to his tent, looking a broken man, and emerged to announce several hours later, "It is all right . . . we shall go forward."

One night during the second phase of the operations against the strongest position of the Hindenburg Line, Pershing appeared unannounced at the headquarters of the 90th Division, commanded by his old friend, General Henry T. Allen, who had served with him in Mexico and the Philippines. Pershing had never looked so downcast in all the years Allen had known him. He sat down heavily and confessed, "Things are going badly. We are not getting on as we should."

General Allen, in his war diary, said that Pershing also told him "our advance here had not been as the Allies had anticipated, nor as he had anticipated. . . . He told me of the failures of some of our divisions and their commanders, and emphasized certain points which he was very keen to have me impress down through all grades in the division."

Much of the trouble, the generals agreed, lay in the difficulty of commanders in maintaining contact with their units. Allen cited a brigade commander who "had no knowledge of his left regiment" and asked that he be relieved, to which Pershing agreed.

Apparently Pershing, in the course of that conversation, talked away much of what was troubling him. Before leaving his old friend, he squared his shoulders and said: "By God, Allen, I was never so much in earnest in my life, and we are going to get through."

It was almost an echo of Grant in the Wilderness. But Grant at least had no allies to contend with. During that period, Pershing was troubled by a letter from Secretary of War Baker, who had finished his second tour of France and was returning home. Just before his departure, Baker dined with Lloyd George in Paris and was advised that the British Prime Minister still staked claims on U.S. troops. Lloyd George bitterly complained that "for all their pains and sacrifices for training our troops and equipping them they had gotten no good out of them whatever, and that the American troops had not been of any service to the British." He also entered an eloquent plea of "intermingling our soldiers" in the interests of Anglo-American solidarity, and charged that "some influence was at work to monopolize American soldiers for the assistance of the French and to keep them from the association of the British." Baker, however, managed to fend off

Lloyd George, and Pershing concluded that "no American general in the field ever received the perfect support accorded me" by the Secretary of War.

Between October 4 and 11, the American First Army slowly fought its way toward the Kriemhilde Stellung, the main German defensive position, and the Romagne Heights on which it was based. The 4th, 80th, 3rd, and 32nd divisions pushed their way through the Bois de Fays, the Bois de Peut de Faux, the Bois d'Ogons, and the Bois de Cunel. The First Division, dependable as always, drove a deep wedge in the enemy's line paralleling the wooded heights of the Argonne. At the same time the enemy resistance was stiffening. Alarmed at the Americans' progress, the German High Command was rushing divisions to the Meuse-Argonne from other sectors of the western front and by October 8 had twenty-seven facing the American First Army with seventeen others in reserve . . . the firmest of all indications that the enemy regarded the American offensive as the most dangerous to the security of its field armies.

The hard-driving attack of the "Big Red One" which was designed to clear space along the Aire River, so that the rear of the enemy's positions in the Argonne forest could be struck a mortal blow, was especially important. The First, with its artillery firing off the map at 1200 yards to give the infantry perfect cover in accordance with General Summerall's doctrine, had taken the whole complex of the enemy's defenses on the slopes of Montrefagne and the Arietal Farm. It was one of the crucial operations of the whole campaign, and recognized as such by the Germans. General Von Gallwitz sent in the German Army's toughest outfit, the Prince Eitel Friedrich Division of the Prussian Guards, to drive the First back. The Guards and a Bavarian division counterattacked, and there was a morning-long fight on the slopes of Montrefagne, one of the rare hand-to-hand combats of the war, with pistols, grenades, bayonets, knives, and clubbed rifles. Summerall's troops held on while Von Gallwitz poured in three other divisions, until the U.S. 82nd came up and helped drive the Germans back to their Kriemhilde defenses. The vaunted Prussian Guard Division was so badly shot up that it was valueless during the rest of the war; whole battalions had been wiped out to the last man. Saturated with mustard gas, its groves shattered to the stump, cratered with shell holes, the crest of Montrefagne, dominating the terrain for miles around, was now firmly in American hands.

On October 11, the second phase of the battle ended and another halt was necessary before the Kriemhilde Stellung could be brought under direct attack.

This second halt was seized upon by Premier Clemenceau to make the boldest attack so far on Pershing, culminating in an all-out attempt to have him removed as commander in chief of the A.E.F. The smell of victory was in the air now, wafting sweet and clear through the clouds of poison gas, the gun smoke, and the reek of decaying flesh that hung over the western front. On October 6 a new German Government, with Prince Max of Baden as Chancellor, had assumed power and had immediately appealed through Switzerland to President Wilson: "To avoid further bloodshed, the German government requests the President to arrange the immediate conclusion of an armistice on land, by sea, and in the air." Emboldened by the prospects of peace, Clemenceau could not resist the temptation to make one more try at having Pershing removed. He had been stewing over what he considered Pershing's inefficiency ever since late the previous month when he went up to look over recaptured Montfaucon and was caught in the jam of First Division trucks headed frontward for the relief of the 35th Division. The Premier of France, in fact, was trapped in the traffic jam for eight hours, his notorious temper boiling to the point of apoplexy, and never did get to Montfaucon.

After his return to the capital, the knowledgeable circles in Paris, in which nothing was safe or sacred, buzzed with rumors that Clemenceau was determined to have Pershing removed. On October 4, Colonel Dawes noted in his diary: "While John is at the front, an attack is being made on his management of the rear. If he cannot advance his army farther because his rear is disorganized, they say, then why not let the French and British take over more of his troops in their sectors." Several days later Dawes wrote, "His [Pershing's] attack of October 4 silenced the French military critics. Now they are beginning again."

Another good friend of Pershing's who was troubled by the rumors was Daisy (Mrs. J. Borden) Harriman, a blonde and comely society woman who had come over to work with the Red Cross Motor Corps (and who later was United States Ambassador to Norway and a reigning hostess in Washington for many years). Mrs. Harriman often visited Pershing at his headquarters or dined with him in Paris. She attended a luncheon at the Ritz at which General Tom Bridges, the

The President in France. Wilson and Pershing review the troops at
Chaumont after the armistice. WIDE WORLD PHOTOS

Homecoming in 1919. General March and Secretary of War Baker
welcome Pershing as he arrives in New York Harbor. WIDE WORLD
PHOTOS

Just before retirement. In his last year as Chief of Staff, Pershing watches President Coolidge sign a bill on the White House lawn. WIDE WORLD PHOTOS

Guidons of the old 10th Cavalry. Pershing, at Fort Myer in 1932, reviews the Negro regiment with which he served as a lieutenant and charged up San Juan Hill. WIDE WORLD PHOTOS

The rare dimpled smile. Pershing grins with delight as his mount
breaks into a trot along the parade route. BROWN BROTHERS

Arch of triumph. Pershing leads the crack First Division down Fifth Avenue, New York, in its proudest moment. BROWN BROTHERS

Armistice Day 1942. Pershing hears President Roosevelt promise an Allied victory over the Axis at the tomb of the Unknown Soldier at Arlington. WIDE WORLD PHOTOS

Aid the Allies. Pershing, in 1940, submits to a rare interview at which he urged that planes, arms, and other supplies be sent overseas. WIDE WORLD PHOTOS

Eightieth birthday. President Roosevelt, with Secretary of War Stimson, has just decorated Pershing with the Distinguished Service Cross. WIDE WORLD PHOTOS

The A.E.F. staff — Eighteen years later. Gathered at a West Point reunion were, left to right, Generals Nolan, Conner, Harbord, Pershing, Connor, McCoy, Moseler, Andrews, and Colonel James L. Collins, his former aide. WIDE WORLD PHOTOS

The general at seventy-seven. Just before his near-fatal illness, Pershing attends a rodeo. His strong-minded and devoted sister, May, is at the right. WIDE WORLD PHOTOS

No road back. The funeral ceremony for General Pershing in amphi-theater at Arlington. WIDE WORLD PHOTOS

Sleep, soldier, sleep . . . Sergeant Charley Wycoff blows taps, as Pershing had requested. WIDE WORLD PHOTOS

Britisher whose suggestions for the A.E.F. Pershing had rather harshly rejected, "began telling all his guests about the dreadful mistakes that were being made and how if Pershing had followed British advice, everything could have been averted," and a French official told her that Clemenceau was "furious" and that Pershing was "certainly going to be recalled." That night, at a British general's house in Paris, a "very high British official" told her Pershing would be "replaced in a very few days," upon which Mrs. Harriman bet him 800 pounds that the A.E.F.'s commander in chief would not only hang onto his post but would be elected President of the United States. Later that night she wrote in her diary (apparently there was hardly an American who went overseas who didn't keep a diary): "If one woman can run into so much malice against Pershing in one day, what a terrific amount of propaganda the French and British must be making against him, and all because he very properly refused to continue to brigade our troops with theirs. To be tolerant of wartime hysteria or not to be——"

Political considerations, of course, bulked large behind the assaults on Pershing's competence to command. On October 7, Clemenceau, Lloyd George, and Orlando had met secretly to plan how to undermine President Wilson's idealistic Fourteen Points program for peace and substitute a harsher scheme. The hardheaded Pershing, obviously, was another obstacle to be cleared from the Allies' path to a peace on their own rigorous terms; he represented not only the 1,700,000 American troops now in France but the United States' share in the prospective victory. General Bliss, as United States representative on the Supreme War Council, warned the War Department that France and Britain would "attempt to minimize the American effort as much as possible. They think that they have got the Germans on the run and they now do not need as much help as they were crying for a little while ago. I think I told you some time ago that I had heard a gentleman in high position here say that the United States was building a bridge for the Allies to pass over; that the time for the United States to secure acquiescence in its wishes was while the bridge was building; that after the Allies had crossed over the bridge they would have no further use for it or its builders."

Luxuriating in the assurance of victory, it might be added, the French were hardly keeping pace with the British and the Americans in the general offensive and were hardly in a position to criticize Pershing for his difficulties. Marine General John A. Lejeune of the

314 SOLDIER ON THE WESTERN FRONT

U.S. 2nd Division, which was spearheading one of the French Fourth Army's attacks, telegraphed Pershing's headquarters that the French units on his flanks had let him down so badly that he would resign his commission rather than fight again under French command. The British military historian Liddell Hart (*The Real War*) has written of this tendency on the part of the French: "With shrewd strategic sense the French in the center appreciated that decisive results depended on the rapid penetration and closing of the pincers [by the British and American armies on the left and right], and so did not unduly hasten the retreat of the Germans facing them. In their skilful advance they usually kept a step in the rear of their allies on either flank. . . . If their commanders had been slow to learn how to economize life, they, and still more their men, had learnt it now. Perhaps a shade too well."

Pershing apparently was too deeply involved in the shooting war to realize the extent and seriousness of the rearward campaign against him, although he noted after a conference with Marshal Foch at Bombon on October 13 that Foch "sees but will not admit that we are up against a tough proposition" in the Meuse-Argonne.

This wasn't quite fair to the marshal, who during that highly critical period was actually Pershing's stanchest defender. Foch stood up for Pershing even as he realized that inept tactics were responsible for many of the Americans' difficulties. The trouble, as Foch saw it, was that Pershing tried to remedy his situation simply by the application of greater force, by shoving in more divisions on his narrow front, which "only intensified the difficulties, and resulted in a complete blocking of his rear and the bottling up of his communications." He considered that the results obtained by Pershing were "inferior to what was permissible to expect."

But he did not lose faith in Pershing, and he risked his own career to support him in the face of his Prime Minister's attacks. "I am not under your orders," he had told Clemenceau when the latter demanded action against Pershing. To which Clemenceau replied, "I have much good will for you, but, if I have any advice to give you, it is not to try that game."

Unknown to Pershing, Foch also protected him from the machinations of his fellow commanders in chief on the western front. He forbade Pétain to submit a report which concluded, "If General Pershing perseveres in his present line of conduct, it can only end in disaster."

At almost the same time, in mid-October, Haig asked him to requisition two American divisions to reinforce his own advances to the north, showing scant sympathy for Pershing's difficulties in the Argonne and even less comprehension of how much annoyance such a request would cause at A.E.F. Headquarters. Foch kept stalling on the British request, until Haig went over the Supreme Commander's head and appealed to Clemenceau, who was only too pleased to urge compliance. Foch, however, refused to harass Pershing with the unfeeling British request.

On October 21 he received a letter from Clemenceau which, as he said, proposed "nothing less than to effect a change in the chief command of the American Army."

"One does not have to be a technician," Clemenceau wrote, "in order to understand that the immobility of your right wing [that is, the American First Army] cannot possibly be a part of your plan and that we have lost—no matter how favorably other things may have turned out—the benefits of movements which, through lack of organization, have not been effected. I am aware of all the efforts you have made to overcome the resistance of General Pershing; indeed, it is because you have omitted nothing in the way of persuasion that I cannot shirk the duty of asking myself whether, after the failure of fruitless conversation, the time has not come for changing methods.

"When General Pershing refused to obey your orders, you could have appealed to President Wilson. For reasons which you considered more important, you put off this solution of the conflict, fearing that it would bring reactions of a magnitude which you thought it difficult to gauge.

"I took the liberty of differing with you. . . . You wished to prolong the experience. . . . I think it will not take long for you to make up your mind on this subject. If General Pershing finally resigns himself to obedience, if he accepts the advice of capable generals, whose presence he has until now permitted only that he might reject their counsels, I shall be wholly delighted."

In demanding that Foch arrange for Pershing's dismissal, Clemenceau overestimated the extent of the marshal's powers as Allied commander in chief. In his memoirs, the Premier revealed that only Pershing's "passive resistance" irked him more than Foch's reluctance to command rather than persuade, than his arguments that "you have to know how to lead the Allies. You must not command them. . . . I have to *persuade,* instead of *directing.*"

Foch, in any case, refused to go along with his irascible chief, and two days later sent Clemenceau a memorandum showing that of thirty U.S. combat divisions ten were serving with the French and British armies, the remainder in the American, and tried to placate him by promising that he would vary the proportions, "increasing the ten and diminishing the twenty, whenever operations being prepared permit it." The generalissimo later wrote that "having a more comprehensive knowledge of the difficulties encountered by the American Army, I could not acquiesce in the radical solution contemplated by M. Clemenceau." To Foch there was "no denying the magnitude of the effort made by the American Army," and no matter how unsympathetic he had seemed to Pershing he realized that the Americans were operating "over particularly difficult terrain and in the face of serious resistance by the enemy." It was not the least of the occasions on which Foch demonstrated that he could act fairly and reasonably as co-ordinator, arbiter, and generalissimo of all the Allied forces.

The French President Poincaré, on reading Clemenceau's letter to Foch, was shocked at the Premier's tirade against Pershing and demanded, "Is it M. Clemenceau's business to concern himself with what Marshal Foch does as commander-in-chief of the American Army? In that capacity is not Marshal Foch responsible rather to the American government?"

When the news of Clemenceau's aborted maneuver reached the Americans, their reaction was understandably indignant, particularly since Pershing's removal was being touted on the threshold of victory and peace. Clemenceau's proposal thus seemed all the more vindictive and senseless. Harbord thought that he was "writing about things of which he had been ignorant even in his splendid prime." Secretary of War Baker commented that "it would be a long time before any American commander would be removed by any European premier." In Pershing's opinion, Clemenceau's proposal was an attempt to "discredit our accomplishments" and a "political gesture designed to minimize America's prestige at the peace conference."

During the days in which Clemenceau was attacking from Paris, Pershing was regrouping for the decisive thrusts against the German rail complex in Lorraine. He had called a halt October 11 and shook up the structure of his forces, rested and refitted until October 14, when the offensive was resumed against its toughest objectives with still greater force and power. During that interval he extended the front of his attack and created the Second American Army; corps, division, and brigade commanders who had not pushed hard enough in the first two weeks of fighting were demoted or relieved of command. In the process, Pershing became an army group commander, like Pétain and Haig, though that was not the expressed purpose of the realignment.

On resumption of the offensive, the First Army was to be commanded by General Liggett, the Second Army by General Bullard. The Second, with three U.S. divisions, was to take over the sector from Port-sur-Seille east of the Moselle to Fresnes-en-Woëvre southeast of Verdun and eventually attack in the direction of the Briey iron fields. Its principal function was to distract the enemy while the First Army continued to pound away at the Hindenburg Line and break through to the lateral railroads which even now were within the range of heavy artillery. Pershing had been advised that Germany had asked for an armistice, but did not intend to allow the enemy to strengthen his defenses while bargaining for peace. "There can be no conclusion to this War," he said, "until Germany is brought to her knees."

In the command shake-up, Summerall had been promoted to command of the V Corps, Hines to the III Corps, Muir to the IV Corps, and Dickman shifted to I Corps. Cameron had been demoted from V Corps to command of the 4th Division. Three major generals and three brigadiers were relieved of their commands, including General Clarence Edwards of the 26th Division, an exceedingly popular commander whose relief brought a roar of protest from the New England states from which most of his troops were enlisted. There were many who thought that sending General Edwards home was as brutal and unnecessary as Pershing's dismissal through the machinations of Premier Clemenceau would have been, but the commander in chief considered that Edwards had not been vigorous enough in handling his division.

Pershing now concentrated his forces for the final drives over the wooded and fortified heights beyond which lay the Metz-Mézières rail line, the city of Sedan with all its tragic significance to French history, and victory. Men were being rushed to the front as replacements straight from the troopships, a matter which caught the critical eye of General March, the chief of staff in Washington. March, in his *The*

Nation at War, condemned Pershing for insisting on too much training for American troops, claiming that the "keen edge of the enthusiasm" was dulled by too much drill. Pershing refused to accept his views, March said, "until the tremendous Argonne battle compelled all his theories to vanish, and he had to shove men into the fighting just as fast as he could get them." The hypercritical March, of course, chose to ignore the fact that Pershing insisted on thorough training only until it became a luxury he could not afford when the heavy fighting in the Meuse-Argonne began. General March also condemned Pershing's demand for a 100-division army in France, pointing out that "near the end of October we passed in strength the entire British force operating in France and Belgium, and with the advent of the eighty-division program, we would have a larger force in France than any of the Allies."

Great and growing as its strength was, the American Army's operations were marked by a wastage of men and material, by necessarily hasty improvisations, by an almost desperate explosion of military energy. Almost 1,200,000 American troops were thrown into the line before the campaign ended. All this against an enemy weakened by four years of fighting, demoralized by starvation on the home front, and alarmed by a foreshadowing of the defection of its Bulgarian, Turkish, and Austrian allies. Many German divisions were reduced to the size of American regiments, or less, and often the defending forces were outnumbered ten to one, or more; every counterattack was smothered and quickly followed by American units driving in on its flanks and endangering the assault force. The bulk of America's military power was concentrated on a narrow but vital section of the German front; never was a tiny piece of strategic real estate so saturated with men and guns and death, and yet, in the end, the American casualties totaled almost as much as the whole defending force. Had the Meuse-Argonne sector been defended by the German Army of 1915, the cost would have been prohibitive.

In the renewed attack of October 14, the Germans were to be driven back all along the line, with especially violent blows aimed at their center on the heights of Romagne and Cunel. The French XVII Corps, under Pershing's command, was to attack east of the Meuse; west of the Meuse, the American First Army's III and V corps were reinforced with the 5th and 42nd divisions and directed to drive salients into the German lines around the Bois de Romagne and the Bois de Bantheville, while the I Corps held the enemy with its left and advanced with its right in conjunction with the left of the V Corps. The French Fourth Army, operating on the left flank of the American First, was to support these advances by attacking along the west bank of the Aisne and on the eastern edge of the Argonne.

From then until the end of the month there was a steady hammering at the intricate defenses of the Hindenburg Line. Slowly it began to crumble. The 32nd Division, heedless of heavy losses, stormed the Côte Dame Marie and captured the key position of the Kriemhilde Stellung, then went on to take the town of Romagne and the eastern half of the Bois de Romagne. Almost equally important was the assignment of the 42nd Division, which was to advance through the western half of the Bois de Romagne and scale its commanding heights, the Côte de Châtillon.

Summerall, the V Corps commander, planned to take the hill by frontal assault, following artillery preparation. General Douglas MacArthur, now commander of the 84th Brigade of the 42nd, argued in favor of a night bayonet attack. The dispute was settled when MacArthur, examining an aerial map of the position, discovered a gap in the enemy wire. Discarding both plans, they settled on a brilliant compromise: a hundred men rushed through the gap under a brisk covering fire, flanked the German defenses, and held out against a counterattack until the rest of the brigade could move up in force and take the hill at small cost. Pershing did not ordinarily view MacArthur with any great favor, but he praised the shrewd and economical thrust as "an aggressive action against the most obstinate defense." Seizure of the keystone of the Hindenburg Line had resulted in flanking the enemy forces on the Aisne, to the west, and on the heights of the Meuse, to the east.

Something of the cost of these advances was indicated in Pershing's report on how he had to cannibalize divisions fresh from the States to gather up replacements for those engaged at the front. "We now had to use as replacements the personnel of two more arriving divisions, although even these were not enough. In all, we skeletonized four combat divisions and three depot divisions to obtain men for units at the front." The Germans, meanwhile, were drawing in a total of forty-seven divisions, many from the French and British sectors of the western front and others from the Balkan and eastern fronts. Behind them, however, the German will to resist was violently and rapidly disintegrating, with the German Navy mutinying at Kiel on October 29 and igniting a spark of revolt that spread through the nation.

With further local advances, particularly those of the American I Corps and the French Fourth Army around the Bois de Bourgogne flanking the enemy positions on the Aisne, the American armies were ready for the fourth and final phase of the operations in the Meuse-Argonne. Another halt was necessary for regrouping. The attack would be renewed on November 1.

Victory was in their grasp now, but there was no marked easing in the relations of the Allied commanders. Rarely have so many touchy gentlemen been gathered under one banner. Even the exhilarating prospect of success failed to generate much warmth or generosity among them.

Continuing tension in the Allied High Command was indicated by two incidents occurring when Pershing left his headquarters outside Souilly to confer with Foch and Haig late in October, as it was becoming obvious that the German Army could not last out the winter.

Marshal Foch had appointed General Maistre, who commanded the group of armies including the French Fourth, which was moving in unison with the First American Army's left, to "coordinate" the movements of both armies. It was one last stab at establishing control over Pershing's activities. Pershing had already formulated his plans for continuing the advance on November 1 by moving on Boult-aux-Bois and flanking the enemy's forces in the Bourgogne forest and along the Aisne. Foch, through Maistre, submitted his own plan for this operation, changing the direction of the attacks. Pershing refused to consider it on the grounds that "it was quite beyond the Marshal's province to give instructions regarding the tactical conduct of operations."

Marshal Haig, during a conference at Senlis, somehow offended Pershing by remarks which the latter considered disparaging to the American Army. Exactly what Haig said was not recorded, but he wrote Pershing a few days later:

"I have just heard [from Pershing's liaison officer, Major Robert Bacon] that some of the remarks which I made at the conference at Senlis on Saturday were misinterpreted so as to give an idea of 'failure' to the work of the American army since it came to France. . . . I yield to no one in my admiration for the grand fighting qualities of the American soldier and the manner in which you and your staff have overcome the greatest difficulties during the past year. So such an idea had never entered my head."

Pershing rather stiffly replied that he was satisfied with "the official correction that you have made."

In a few days the Allies would be revealing a much wider and more historically important divergence of opinion over how the war was to be concluded.

15. Victory, Peace, and Departure

In the closing days of October, only the wildest of the Pan-German dreamers could have hoped that Kaiser Wilhelm and his spike-helmeted field marshals would find a way of continuing the war. The front was being ruptured in a dozen places, none more seriously than at home, where the red flags were blossoming and revolutionary agitators were becoming bolder and louder every day. The Belgians and the British were heading for the Scheldt on a broad front, the French and the Americans were regrouping for final thrusts toward the Rhine. Defection had broken out among Germany's allies; Bulgaria had quit, Turkey would sign an armistice agreement on October 30, and Austria would resign from the fighting a few days later. Ludendorff departed from the High Command on October 27 rather than witness the scenes of disorder and disintegration that his gamble of that spring had brought about. Europe was ready to let slip the hounds of peace— and vengeance. Only the mechanics of quieting the guns had to be worked out. Meanwhile, thousands would die, would be wounded, would have their lungs seared by poison gas, while their nominal betters searched for a formula.

President Wilson, on whom the Germans were relying for a generous peace, had demanded as preliminaries the acceptance of his Fourteen Points and the evacuation of all occupied territories. The Germans swallowed hard but finally agreed. Then Wilson announced that the terms of the projected armistice would have to be drawn up by the military advisers of the Allied governments, which suggested that the dove of peace might have iron wings and steel claws. Over the bitter protests of his own military leaders, Prince Max of Baden, the new

German Chancellor, who realized better than they that the war could be borne no longer, acceded to Wilson's conditions.

Now it devolved upon the Allied commanders to formulate the terms of an armistice. Foch, Pétain, Haig, and Pershing met in Paris on October 28 to discuss the problem of separating two huge war machines which had been in collision for four years. A paradox soon developed: France and Britain, though they had suffered the most in the war against Germany, favored the more moderate terms, while the American insisted (like his prototype General Grant) on unconditional surrender, that rigid phrase which has hypnotized American commanders ever since.

Haig, who spoke first, pointed out that the German armies were capable of withdrawing to a shorter line and making a strong stand on their own borders. He was also pessimistic about the state of the Allied armies; the French and British were each short about 250,000 men, and the American had sustained 75,000 casualties during its October campaigning. He favored terms which he believed Germany might accept: evacuation of Belgian and French territory, Allied occupation of Alsace, Lorraine, and the fortresses of Metz and Strasbourg, restitution of rolling stock seized by the Germans, and repatriation of the inhabitants of all invaded territory. "If hostilities should be resumed," Sir Douglas told the conference, "I would prefer to find the Germans entrenched behind their old frontier of 1870 than to find them on the right bank of the Rhine."

Marshal Foch was more optimistic about the relative conditions of the Allied and German armies. He pointed out that "we are dealing with an army that has been pounded every day for three months. . . . Certainly the Allied armies are not new, but victorious armies are never fresh. In this matter the question is relative; the German armies are far more exhausted than ours. Certainly the British and French armies are tired; certainly the American Army is a young army, but it is full of idealism and strength and ardor. It has already won victories and is now on the eve of another victory; and nothing gives wings to an army like victory. When one hunts a wild beast and finally comes upon him at bay, one then faces greater danger, but it is not the time to stop, it is time to redouble one's blows without paying any attention to those he, himself, receives."

General Pétain's scheme was to deprive Germany of its matériel to prevent it from continuing the war if the armistice was revoked. He wanted the enemy to be required to withdraw on a schedule which he had worked out and which he believed would force them to abandon much of their heavier equipment. Pétain also favored a German retirement east of the Rhine and the establishment of Allied bridgeheads at Mayence, Coblenz, and Cologne. His terms thus were much severer than Haig's.

Pershing's were harshest of all. "I think that the damage done by the war to the interests of the powers with which the United States is associated against Germany has been so great that there should be no tendency toward leniency.

"The present military situation is very favorable to us. The German forces since the beginning of the counteroffensive on July 18 have been constantly in retreat and have not been able to recover since that time. The condition of the French and British armies can best be judged by the fact that they have been continuously on the offensive since then and that they are now attacking with as much vigor as ever. As to the American Army . . . it is constantly increasing in strength and training . . . there is every reason to suppose that the American Army will be able to take the part expected of it in the event of resumption of hostilities."

In any event, Pershing wanted French and Belgian territory evacuated within thirty days, the Allied occupation of Alsace-Lorraine, the withdrawal of the German armies east of the Rhine, the establishment of bridgeheads to "insure control of that river," the surrender of all U-boats and U-boat bases and "unrestricted transportation of the American Army and its material across the seas."

Haig balked at demanding the surrender of German submarines, saying, "That is none of our affair. It is a matter for the Admiralty to decide."

Pershing with some asperity insisted that "we should have our communications free from danger," and Foch agreed with him.

Wilson's comments on Pershing's proposals included the view that "the terms of the armistice should be rigid enough to secure us against renewal of hostilities by Germany but not humiliating beyond that necessity, as such terms would throw the advantage to the military party in Germany."

Both to the Supreme War Council and the President, Pershing elaborated on his entirely correct estimate that Germany's "internal political conditions" made it absolutely necessary to "ask for an armistice to save the overthrow of her present Government, a consummation which should be sought by the Allies as precedent to permanent peace."

He wanted a "dictated peace" to "insure its permanence."

His appraisal of the military situation was both shrewd and realistic as he pointed out:

"It is the experience of history that victorious armies are prone to overestimate the enemy's strength and too eagerly seek an opportunity for peace. This mistake is likely to be made now on account of the reputation Germany has gained through her victories of the last four years.

"Finally, I believe the complete victory can only be obtained by continuing the war until we force unconditional surrender from Germany, but if the Allied Governments decide to grant an armistice, the terms should be so rigid that under no circumstances could Germany take up arms again."

Pershing wanted the German soldiers to march home "virtually as paroled prisoners of war." The more fearful counsels of the other Allies, particularly the British, prevailed, however, and the vindictiveness was applied instead at the "peace" tables of Versailles, where a measured generosity would have been more seemly both as a human and historic consequence. The result was, as Pershing rather bitterly remarked in his memoirs, that the German troops were permitted to "march back to their homeland with colors flying and bands playing, posing as the victim of political conditions."

General Bullard, commanding the Second American Army, was equally uneasy over the German proposal for an armistice and wrote in his diary that "I had been unable to see that he was hard-pressed by the Allies—well, yes, hard-pressed, but not enough to make him cry out for peace. We have been driving him, but not fast or killingly." Bullard believed that "if peace came now it would be a Boche victory, nothing less. . . ."

On November 1, the American First Army and the French Fourth, with the American Second scheduled to join in several days later, opened their final offensive.

Pershing had been stricken with the grippe during the Allied conference in Paris, but crawled out of his sickbed to return to Souilly and his headquarters the night of October 31. He was determined to be on hand, pale and gaunt though he was, when his armies loosed their hardest punch of the war. In the front line at 5:30 A.M., November

1, from left to right, were the I Corps, with the 78th, the 77th, and 80th divisions; the V Corps, with the 2nd (retrieved from the French) and the 89th; and the III Corps, with the 3rd and 32nd divisions. In corps reserve, immediately behind the line, were the First and 42nd divisions, ready to leapfrog into action. The heaviest blow was to be directed in the center against the Barricourt ridge, followed by a drive to link up the I Corps with the French Fourth Army at Boult-aux-Bois and flank the strong German defenses in the Bourgogne forest.

Summerall had 608 guns, including 155s hauled up to the infantry's positions, on his two-division front.

"What about a counterattack?" correspondents asked him on the evening of October 31.

"Gentlemen," replied the supremely confident Summerall, "there will be no counterattack."

In the gray light of the next morning, the American infantry went forward behind a tremendous barrage that rolled across a zone 1200 yards in depth. Summerall's guns smothered the German lines to the extent that three enemy artillery regiments were captured in the first few hours. Large formations of Allied bombers plastered the German supply and communications lines, ammunition dumps, and moving columns. Three batteries of fourteen-inch naval guns pounded away at the enemy's rail lines far in the rear. Before the day was over, the V Corps took the heights of Barricourt, the III Corps veered over to the Meuse, and the I Corps made lesser gains against the wooded heights on its front. That night the Germans admitted in their communiqué that their line had been broken.

The whole army was moving forward, and that night, when the Germans failed to organize a counterattack, Pershing knew that the enemy was on the run. In the next two days, the III Corps stormed across the Meuse, I Corps took Buzancy, an important road center, and V Corps in the center further exploited its gains beyond Barricourt. Colonel Marshall, the First Army's operations officer, believed that if the Americans had been equipped with their proper quota of tanks they could have taken 100,000 prisoners after Buzancy was captured. Marshall's operations report on November 5 summed up the situation tersely: "Enemy retreating with his infantry in confusion and his artillery actively employed. Situation favorable for pressing the pursuit."

It was tallyho from then on, with Sedan the prize of the chase. The broken and retreating German divisions offered little resistance in the race for the historic city. It would have meant a lot to concede to the French the honor of retaking Sedan, where they had lost the decisive battle of 1870–71; in a later war, when Americans could afford to be more generous, a French armored division would be propelled to the front and lead the march into Paris; but this time the Americans, Pershing above all, were not inclined to consider their ally's sensibilities.

"In view of this historic sentiment," wrote General Harbord, dismayed at the chauvinistic temper of the day, "it does not seem to have been a very happy choice for an American goal, though a very natural one."

The orders resulting in the race for Sedan, which was marked by the sort of recklessness in command and ineptitude in staff work which the French and British had long criticized in the American Army, went out on November 5. It has generally been accepted that this was a spur-of-the-moment decision by the American High Command, but General Pershing's diary shows that two days earlier he had become involved in a row with General Maistre over the movement on Sedan. By that time it was obvious that the French would not be able to push ahead fast enough to reach Sedan ahead of the Americans.

On November 3, Pershing had recorded in his diary that he had a "very plain talk" with Maistre, the French army group commander on his left, "about his overstepping his authority to the extent of giving an order that the First American Army would continue its attack. He meant nothing by it, but the matter could not be overlooked. . . . I remonstrated against his having drawn the line which divides us from the French in such a manner as to oblique the Americans to the right so they strike the Meuse above Sedan. He said it was because the French would have no road unless we did this. *I said I wanted my troops to take Sedan.*"

Two days later Pershing wrote that he had told General Dickman, commander of I Corps, that "I would like to see his Corps have the honor of taking Sedan. . . ." The next day he reported that an agreement had been reached with General Maistre to take Sedan "if we arrive first."

General Maistre, Harbord commented in his history of the A.E.F., "must have felt very much as the American Revolutionary Army would have felt if Rochambeau had asked to be permitted to elbow Washington out of the reviewing stand at Yorktown."

It was an undeniably graceless affair from top to bottom. The result was that Pershing's directive, as framed by his staff and executed by his unit commanders, turned the race for Sedan into a military nightmare which tangled up two of his best divisions and laid the American front open to a disastrous counterattack, had the Germans been strong enough to take advantage of the opportunity.

The first mix-up occurred in the order issued on the evening of November 5, which was directed to the commanding generals of the I and V corps and which read:

"1. General Pershing desires that the honor of entering Sedan should fall to the First American Army. He has every confidence that the troops of the First Corps, assisted on their right by the Fifth Corps, will enable him to realize this desire.

"2. In transmitting the foregoing message, your attention is invited to the favorable opportunity now existing for pressing our advance throughout the night. Boundaries will not be considered binding."

The order was drawn up by Colonel George C. Marshall, but the last sentence was added by General Drum, the chief of staff of the First Army. General Liggett, the commander of the First Army, was away from headquarters and did not even learn of the order until noon of November 7, by which time all the damage had been done.

On receiving this order, General Dickman, I Corps, and General Summerall, V Corps, translated it into action. Next day Summerall ordered the First Division, now under Major General Frank Parker's command, to head for Sedan by the most direct route in five columns. This meant the division would have to cut leftward across the path of the advancing I Corps and elements of the Fourth French Army. Summerall's justification for ordering the movement—if there was any—was the last sentence in the order from First Army Headquarters, which erased the boundaries between I and V corps. In so doing, he disregarded the earlier sentence—expressing Pershing's real intention—stating that his corps was to *assist* I Corps, presumably only if called upon, in the attack toward Sedan.

The result was monumental confusion. In mud and rain the First Division set out on its forced march the night of November 6, proceeding over shell-pitted roads bordered by thick forests, the trucks in the columns traveling without headlights. Thus it blundered into the areas of the I Corps' 42nd and 77th divisions, blocking their advance though they had been closer to Sedan than the First when the race started.

Leading elements of the First Division traded fire with two companies of the 42nd's 168th Iowa Infantry around Haracourt until they realized their mistake. First Division scouts came across Brigadier General Douglas MacArthur of the 42nd's 84th Brigade at his command post near Beaumiel Farm, eyed his informal attire, and decided he was a German officer. MacArthur, whose indignation may be imagined, was taken prisoner and hauled off to a brigade HQ of the First Division, where he was finally given back his freedom. Later in the night the First's 26th Infantry, commanded by Lieutenant Colonel Theodore Roosevelt, Jr., crossed the boundary into the forward area of the Fourth French Army, where their ally's 40th Division intended to lay down a barrage. The French warned Roosevelt that his regiment would be fired upon if it was not withdrawn in an hour. Roosevelt gave ground before the deadline expired.

For several hours during the morning of November 7, a local war threatened to break out between the French and American commands. The 42nd Division, which had also started pushing toward Sedan, similarly ventured into territory the French Army had staked out for itself. Its headquarters was notified by the French at 10 A.M. that their artillery would open up on any troops obstructing the French advance on Sedan.

Late that morning General Liggett finally learned of the scrambled situation of his divisions on the left, flew into an uncharacteristic but well-justified rage, and headed for I Corps Headquarters, where he denounced General Dickman for having caused all the trouble. Dickman, hotly protesting his innocence, showed him that the primary source of the confusion lay elsewhere. Liggett did what he could to restore order by immediately directing his divisions to stay out of the path of the French advance.

Both the First and the 42nd reached the heights south and west of Sedan, but orders were radioed from G.H.Q. holding them there. Marshal Foch had come to the aid of his army by demanding that the boundary between the French Fourth and the American First armies be respected. With this assist, French troops finally claimed the honor of marching into Sedan first, although American patrols had ventured into the city beforehand.

The feckless contest for Sedan set off an eruption of charges and denunciations. An inquiry was ordered with tongue in cheek, but, with so many large reputations endangered, it came to nothing. "Under normal conditions," Pershing wrote in his memoir, "the action of the officer or officers responsible for this movement of the First Division directly across the zones of action of two other divisions could not have been overlooked, but the splendid record of that unit and the approach of the end of hostilities suggested leniency."

A great deal of leniency, as a matter of fact, was spread around in suppressing any inquiry into the clownish advance on Sedan. The ultimate responsibility was Pershing's for having issued the order which initiated the movement and for not seeing to it that it was properly phrased and clearly understood. His statement to General Dickman of November 5 that he wanted V Corps to take Sedan, as quoted in his diary, indicated the operation was clear enough in his own mind.

By the time it reached lower echelons, because of the way it was phrased by Marshall and Drum, the order was regarded as the starting signal for a pell-mell steeplechase which brought out the schoolboy in his generals. Summerall had obviously exceeded his orders in recklessly pushing ahead the First Division rather than supporting a more orderly advance by I Corps on his left. The rashness at corps headquarters naturally infected his unit commanders. Dickman, who "went to his grave embittered and unforgiving," according to Harbord, had obeyed orders to the best of his ability. Liggett was also understandably outraged at the way his army had been maneuvered into a ridiculous impasse without consulting him. One of the many residual mysteries of the whole operation, in fact, is just how he was kept in ignorance of the order until noon of November 7, forty hours after it was issued.

Controversy over the tanglefooted lunge at Sedan was muted, however, by a general rejoicing among the Allies. On November 9, negotiations for an armistice were already in progress; the American First and Second armies were preparing to cross the Meuse on a broad front toward Metz and the Briey iron fields; and the Germans' vital communications in Lorraine had been disrupted. The Americans had fought their way through twenty-five miles of "the strongest fortified position outside of the Verdun-Douaumont area of 1915 and 1916" in the Argonne—a forty-seven-day campaign in which 117,000 men were killed, wounded, or captured. Pershing was able to report to the

War Department that "the strategical goal which was our highest hope" had been attained. "We had cut the enemy's main line of communications and nothing but surrender or an armistice could save his army from complete disaster."

On November 10 the German Emperor fled to Holland, and at 5 A.M. the following day Foch and the German Armistice Commission agreed that a cease fire was to be ordered six hours hence.

In the interval between 5 A.M. and 11 A.M. on November 11, when the fighting on the other fronts died down to an occasional spatter of gunfire, some of the American units were still attacking, possibly because word of the approaching cease fire had not yet reached them.

Herbert Corey, the correspondent of the New York *Globe,* who had a pronounced aversion to war and the brass-hat mentality, wrote of interviewing a general whose troops were still fighting at 8 A.M. that morning. "I have thrown my men against the wire three times," the general exulted. "They were magnificent." The men had suffered heavy losses in that useless operation. Corey also quoted a field surgeon at a dressing station behind that section of the line: "I did not leave the operating table for forty-eight hours after that attack. I did not operate. I just stood there and butchered." The correspondent thought Pershing would be called to account for those last-minute attacks, but the censors "discouraged comment upon them." In his memoirs, Pershing explained those unnecessary sacrifices of the war's last few hours as being due to the fact that "our troops had been advancing rapidly during the preceding two days and although every effort was made to reach them promptly a few could not be overtaken before the prescribed hour."

At 11 A.M. the whole battle line from the North Sea to the Swiss frontier ground to a halt. The last wisps of cordite and poison gas drifted away into the gray sky and an incredible silence enveloped the barbed wire, the shell holes, and the splintered trees which lay between the contending armies. Eastward could be seen the field-gray ranks of the Germans heading back to their ruined country.

There were few celebrations in No Man's Land. Peace had come with stunning impact. Most men tried to grasp it in an unbelieving silence. At the moment they had nothing to say, nothing to cheer; not with millions dead and more millions of lives ruined. During the first numbing hours of the armistice the men of the western front were living in a vacuum, wondering whether the peace was real or the fighting might be resumed, whether the Germans were really through or might use the cease fire to regroup behind another defense line.

Civilians were quicker to grasp the fact of peace. The streets of New York and London erupted immediately with celebrations. In Paris a thousand church bells rang; shops and offices closed, and hundreds of thousands of people poured into the Place de la Concorde to salute their leaders, their soldiers, and each other. All that night the celebrations continued in the Allied capitals.

And what of Pershing during that day of mad rejoicing? A more flamboyant type would have sped to Paris to join other generals on the balconies and respond to the cheers of the multitudes; a more sentimental or publicity-conscious commander would have hastened to his troops and posed for photographs with "our boys at the front," but Pershing, the plain businessman of war, spent the day at his desk in Chaumont. One may wonder whether he even looked up from his work when the eleventh hour struck and the vast establishment he had organized brought its death-dealing activities to a halt. He was busy with plans for following up the German retreat into the Rhineland, as provided in the armistice agreement.

Later in the day General Dawes called him from Paris, thinking that "his mind might be on the victory," but "it was characteristic of the commander-in-chief that he was hard at work, and what he wanted was to talk over the plan for a financial section of the General Staff." To Dawes's congratulations, Pershing replied in his offhand manner that "he would not regard that he had succeeded until the army was safely back in the United States."

Pershing's sense of detachment in moments when everyone else was succumbing to a mass emotion was all but inhuman; it was also the mark of a man who, in pursuing his ambitions, in accepting the loneliness of high places, had schooled himself to retire within himself on great occasions. Who knew better than Pershing what had been accomplished? Only a lesser ego would have to be informed of this by cheering crowds.

He waited until the next day to call on Marshal Foch, hoping the excitement would have subsided by then, but the streets of the capital were still noisy and turbulent with celebration. General Harbord, who was to meet him that evening, wrote that "Paris was still a seething mass of people of all the world but Germany, shouting in all tongues but German." When Billy Mitchell ventured on the streets in his open touring car, twenty-two bibulous strangers clambered aboard, pelted him with flowers, and rode around the city with him.

Pershing managed to slip through the capital unnoticed to suburban Senlis, where Foch was waiting at his headquarters. Here for the first time since the hour of the armistice Pershing's poker-faced features relaxed. Much as they quarreled and as often as they suspected each other's motives, Foch possessed an odd talent for bringing out whatever was emotional in Pershing's nature. The American was particularly touched when Foch told him how much he appreciated Pershing's "straightforward dealing," perhaps because he prided himself most on that. They were so overcome by mutual admiration, Pershing wrote, "that both of us were unable to restrain the tears, and the Marshal in his enthusiasm gave me an old-fashioned French accolade"—that is, a whiskery kiss on each of his comrade's leathery cheeks.

That night, back in the tumultuous heart of Paris, Pershing further relaxed with his old friends, Harbord and Dawes. The latter, according to Harbord, had become "Exhibit A" in Paris society because of his "unconventionality" and his curious habit of demanding that a long cigar and a large cup of coffee be served with dinner. Presumably the fact that Dawes was head of the Military Board of Allied Supply, in charge of purchasing hundreds of millions of dollars' worth of supplies and equipment, did not hinder his social career any more than his much publicized service with the A.E.F. harmed his political aspirations. Harbord believed that his straightening out of the American purchasing system couldn't have been "so well performed by any other living man," and as chief of the S.O.S. he ought to have known.

After dinner the three friends went to the Folies-Bergère to see *Zig-Zag* again. Harbord noticed that Pershing kept "shrinking back unseen behind the high partitions," but he was finally recognized in Dawes's box by the audience and was embarrassed—genuinely, it may be believed—by a wildly enthusiastic demonstration.

The cheering would soon die down as Europe turned back to work, reconstruction, and the long wrangle over peace terms at Versailles. Pershing would have no part in those negotiations, but he foresaw President Wilson's difficulties when the idealism with which America entered the war encountered the pragmatism of a Europe whose feuds went back to the days when barbaric tribes roamed the continent. Having already dealt with Clemenceau and Lloyd George himself, Pershing knew that Wilson's meetings with those savagely political gentlemen were likely to resemble a cutthroat poker game on a Mississippi river boat. The loser also was predictable. "He has been a good President to us, backed the Army well, but he has his hands full now," Pershing said.

The inclination of the Allies to minimize the military importance of American participation was becoming less subtle. Hardly had the guns stopped firing before the fervor with which Americans had been welcomed to Europe was being damped down. Sensing this swift change in attitude, General Bullard, Francophile though he was, wrote in his diary immediately after the armistice that "our work in Europe is finished. I would like to see our army go home on our side of the world. I have recently jokingly proposed to Frenchmen to leave the Allies Mr. Wilson's fourteen articles and go home. The joke amused but the idea worried them." The next day he wrote, "Little things are beginning to happen between American and French authorities which made me feel that it is time for Americans to be going home." An annoying incident had just occurred in Bullard's Second Army area. The President of France had just reclaimed his country estate and found that American troops had cut dead trees on his land. M. Poincaré, who only a few months before had been pleading for American troops to save his country, not only demanded full compensation but complained so incessantly that the American division commander whose troops committed the outrage was relieved of his command to appease him.

On November 21, Pershing attended a liberation ceremony at Longwy, recently evacuated by the Germans and now the III Corps Headquarters, and was wryly amused by the fact that an elderly French lady insisted on referring to her liberators as English. She "read off a most eulogistic document which she had written in honor of the English and the English effort. . . . On termination of her speech she called on the crowd for cheers in honor of England. . . . It added a little touch of humor to the situation which I should have hated to miss."

Whatever claims America had to having "saved the world for democracy" were supported more firmly by the late enemy. The evidence of the German High Command's bitter appreciation of the American effort was gathered, ironically enough, by five U.S. war correspondents who defied A.E.F. regulations to venture into Germany ahead of the Allied armies. Irked by the herding policies and

hidebound censorship of the A.E.F. press section, the five newspapermen commandeered two army Cadillacs, drove through Luxembourg,
and crossed the German frontier on November 21. They headed for
Cassel, Hindenburg's headquarters, passing long columns of retreating German infantry and noting the "splendid discipline of the defeated."

Field Marshal Hindenburg received them only after the local Workers and Soldiers Council leader insisted on it, an indication of how
things were going in the defeated land. The German commander in
chief was naturally disgruntled at taking orders from civilians, but he
finally thawed out and told them what they wanted to hear. According
to a transcript of the interview kept by George Seldes of the Marshall
Syndicate, Hindenburg forthrightly stated: "The American infantry
won the World War in battle in the Argonne." (Later the former German Chancellor, Prince Max of Baden, testified that an armistice became necessary because "the Americans were making progress at the
point—viz., north of Verdun, where they must not be allowed to advance if the Antwerp-Meuse line was to be held any longer.")

The field marshal, according to Seldes, elaborated on how the war
was decided in the Argonne as follows:

"The Argonne battle was slow and difficult. But it was strategic. It
was bitter and used up division after division. We had to hold the
Metz-Longuyon roads and railroads and we had hoped to stop all
American attacks until the entire army was out of northern France.
We were passing through the neck of a vast bottle. But the neck was
narrow. German and American divisions fought each other to a standstill in the Argonne. They met and shattered each other's strength. The
Americans are splendid soldiers. But when I replaced a division it was
weak in numbers and unrested, while each American division came
in fresh and fit and on the offensive. . . .

"Without the American blow in the Argonne, we could have made
a satisfactory peace at the end of a stalemate or at least held our
positions on our frontier indefinitely—undefeated. The American attack decided the war."

Despite the accolade they brought back from Hindenburg, Pershing
was outraged at the fact the correspondents had invaded Germany
ahead of the Army of Occupation and ordered them taken into custody
on their return. They were held for a court-martial and the judge ad-
vocate on Pershing's staff announced that he would see to it that they

spent six months in a military prison. Eventually they were cleared, partly through the intervention of Colonel House, and were allowed to return to their duties, convinced that Pershing was something of an ingrate.

Every day following the armistice the Paris edition of the Chicago *Tribune* published a banner line reading: GET THE BOYS HOME TOOT SWEET, a succinctly phrased echo of the sentiment back home. Americans wanted no further part in the endless European quarrel, were willing to sacrifice in war but not in peace, an unfortunate pattern that was to be repeated after another war. But no matter what the outcry at home, the A.E.F. had not finished its job: there was still the possibility that Germany, its armies defeated but still capable of resistance, would refuse to accept the peace terms and opt for a continuance of the war. The A.E.F. would have to participate in the occupation of the Rhineland, from which it would withdraw in 1923, six years before the British and seven years before the French. In his general order to the A.E.F. immediately after the armistice, Pershing praised its gallantry in action but warned:

"There remains now a harder task which will test your soldierly qualities to the utmost. Succeed in this and little note will be taken and few praises will be sung; fail, and the light of your glorious achievements of the past will sadly be dimmed. . . . Every natural tendency may urge towards relaxation in discipline, in conduct, in appearance, in everything that marks the soldier. Yet you will remember that each officer and each soldier is the representative in Europe of his people. . . . Whether you stand on hostile territory or on the friendly soil of France, you will so bear yourself in discipline, in appearance and respect for all civil rights that you will confirm for all time the pride and love which every American feels for your uniform and for you."

In mid-December, the Allied forces of occupation moved into the Rhineland to keep a watch on the enemy while a peace treaty was being negotiated and to make sure there would be no resurgence of German militarism. The French had every intention of hanging onto their bridgeheads into Germany and making the German people pay for the excesses of their exiled and degraded former leaders. The Americans, and to a lesser degree the British, were naturally less inclined toward a spirit of vengeance.

General Bullard felt that he had to warn his troops, in fact, that the German people "will occupy you if you don't occupy them." The

American soldier was sternly warned against showing any friendly spirit to the conquered, but, as a newspaper correspondent observed, the non-fraternization order "only made John Doughboy keener than ever to fraternize." The German children, close to starvation, then the German women, rather easily broke down the barriers, although their menfolk tended to display a surly disposition at first. Correspondent Wilbur Forrest came across a story early in the occupation which illustrated how fraternization extended quickly upward through the ranks of the American Army. An earnest young lieutenant complained to his two seniors, a colonel and a major, of the young *Fräulein* in the house where he was billeted who made his life miserable by bringing him breakfast in bed and otherwise showering him with her unwelcome attentions. Next day the colonel ordered the regiment's billeting officer to transfer him to the quarters vacated by the priggish young lieutenant. "Sorry, sir," he was told, "but the major engaged that billet early this morning."

It was a matter of serious concern that many Americans soon showed that they not only bore the former enemy no hard feelings but succumbed to an admiration for the cleanliness of the German towns and the orderliness of their people, which encouraged them to forget all too quickly, from the viewpoint of their allies, that clean, orderly German soldiers had only recently been overrunning Europe from the Channel coast to the Ukraine. General Malin Craig, chief of staff of the newly formed Third Army assigned to occupation duty, wrote Pershing's headquarters: "Both the French and British liaison officers have been quite outspoken in their opinions of the necessity of a drastic kind of rules and regulations having for their object what is practically reprisal on boche civilians. . . . It is quite clear to me that both the French and British realize, unless we are forced to deal harshly with the inhabitants of the occupied territory and along the same lines which they expect to use, the German people will shortly favor the Americans and thus raise hell with the political end of the game." It developed that General Mangin, commanding the French Army of Occupation at Mainz, was then trying to bring off a deal through which a Rhineland republic would be established.

Pershing and his generals held themselves aloof from all such political ventures. They regarded themselves as policemen, and their sole concern was to maintain order in their areas of occupation and bring the troops home safely and as soon as possible.

Late in 1919 the French tried to gain a foothold in the American bridgehead at Coblenz, where their agents were busy trying to rally support for the Separatist movement in the Rhineland, having been misled by overly optimistic estimates of the pro-French sympathy of the populace. Pershing reacted to this more or less clandestine activity in his zone by threatening to recommend the withdrawal of the American occupation forces from the Rhine if Foch did not halt this infiltration.

Between Pershing and Foch from then on there was only a frosty politeness. General Allen, commanding at Coblenz, in describing Foch's visit the following spring, remarked on the fact that the marshal, otherwise genial, turned grim and "expressed no desire to see Pershing when I told him he might come this year, nor did he request to be remembered to him."

Much of Pershing's time early in 1919 was spent in reviewing his divisions before they went home. Unlike his brisk trots through the ranks while the Army was preparing for battle, he was now more leisurely and amiable. Perhaps he had decided to take a whirl at playing the father of the regiment—a role in which he was not always conspicuously successful. The troops' reception of his efforts was somewhat colored by reports that their commander was being seriously considered as a candidate for the presidency in 1920, and the suspicion that he might be trying to win their favor.

He reviewed the 165th Infantry, which was largely Irish and prided itself on its former designation as the "Fighting 69th," on St. Patrick's Day in 1919. As he approached the ranks, he was heard to inquire loudly of a staff officer, "What regiment is this?"

"The 165th Infantry, sir," the officer responded.

"What regiment is this?" Pershing demanded again.

"Oh . . . the 69th New York, sir."

"The 69th New York. I understand now."

Down the line Pershing halted in front of an Irishman with three wound stripes on his sleeve and was less successful at repartee.

"Well, my lad, and where did you get these?" Pershing asked, pointing to the stripes.

"From the supply sergeant, sir," the doughboy replied with a straight face.

The late Charles MacArthur, future author of *The Front Page* and other plays, and one of the A.E.F.'s blither spirits, provided a comical

but penetrating account of the impression Pershing made when he reviewed the 149th Field Artillery on the plain near Remagen:

"The General didn't come for two or three hours, and standing at
attention became monotonous. The men began sneaking smokes and
throwing their helmets at jack rabbits and more school kid stuff. . . .
The hours passed. Someone commented on the wondrous authority
that could hold 27,000 men in one place for four hours.

" 'That's all right,' interposed Charlie Jones. 'He's gonna wait longer
than that for my vote for President.' Which restored our perspective
a little.

"The General came at last and cavorted through the ranks on
horseback . . . dismounted and inspected the regiment, stopping here
and there to ask questions. After coaching us up on our right names
and the color of our eyes, some of the officers were horribly surprised
when the General stopped in front of them and asked sensible questions, asking them what percentage of disease existed in their commands and other remarks denoting common sense. All the officers who
had brushed up on expected subjects and were prepared to answer
right off the bat that their name was Julius, got stage fright and were
royally bawled out to our great enjoyment."

General Dickman, now commanding the Third Army, observed that
Pershing was still as concerned with the health of his men as when he
had been a young troop commander. In reviewing a division, he would
question every battalion commander on how many cases of preventable disease they had in their units. If they replied that they had only
one case, he would snap, "One too many." When he found that some
American troops were still encamped on the old Meuse-Argonne battlefields and were prey to influenza and pneumonia, he exploded in
rage and went off to have a personal talk with Foch, who was responsible for the situation, when the Allied commander in chief did not
move them fast enough. He tangled with Foch again when the generalissimo tried to put American troops to work as laborers clearing debris
in the wrecked villages and on the old battlefields. He was almost as
determined to bring the A.E.F. home in good health as he had been
to break the Hindenburg Line.

Aside from overseeing the occupation and the dismantling of the
S.O.S. organization from the ports to the railheads behind the former battle line, Pershing permitted himself to relax for the first time
after almost two years of continuous campaigning from the Mexican

border to the Argonne. Chaumont became the center of festivity instead of crisis, hospitable to visiting bigwigs up to and including President Wilson when he came over for the peace conference. Nor did he shun the company of the beautiful women who motored up from Paris to pay tribute to the victorious soldier. As always, he became a different man in feminine society, a little old-fashioned in his gallantry perhaps, his manner reminiscent of the Old Army posts of the past century, often giving them the dimpled smile that his male associates rarely saw but which transformed his face amazingly.

One of his occasional guests was the wealthy and attractive widow, Daisy Harriman, who had been so vigorous in defending him the previous summer when Parisian gossip had it that he would soon be packed off on the first ship home, and who was to be his friend for many years. Mrs. Harriman wrote in her diary for March 22, 1919, that Pershing had invited her to attend a divisional review and "the General and I came here to Nancy, where I am putting up in the Red Cross Hotel. It is a moonlight night and this beautiful city is a dream."

Pershing also unbent on fairly frequent visits to the uninhibited Razzberry Club, established by the American war correspondents in the Riesen Furtenhof Hotel in Coblenz, whose only rule was "Rank must be left at the doormat." Correspondent Wilbur Forrest observed that Pershing never stood on ceremony and "I have watched the Commander in animated conversation with a high-browed, bespectacled Private who on the other side of our magic threshold would have stood at rigid attention."

The greatest personal satisfaction of Pershing's last months of service in Europe came in April when Secretary of War Baker ordered that his ten-year-old son, Warren, be sent to his father's side. The War Department outfitted Warren in a uniform tailored to his size, decorated with a sergeant's stripes and with the Montenegro Medal and the Philippine War ribbon on his chest. His escort overseas was First Sergeant Joseph Weltz, a combat hero of the 17th Infantry. Once father and son were reunited, however, Warren was turned over to the personal custody of Sergeant Frank Lanckton, Pershing's striker for many years. Warren had been raised by his aunts in Lincoln, Nebraska, and apparently needed a touch of masculine discipline on occasion. Sergeant Lanckton knew how to handle him, as surviving members of Pershing's staff recall. Whenever the boy got out of line, Lanckton would threaten to take away his stripes. In extreme cases, Lanckton

would snap, "Sergeant Pershing, go to your quarters!" and Warren
would obey.

Pershing did his best to bridge the gap of their years of separation
and the even wider gulf between a boy of ten and a father who was
approaching sixty. On all but official occasions they were inseparable,
and Warren remembers that spring of 1919 as the "most wonderful
experience of my early years."

Once at a party at the Prince of Wied's castle at Neuwied in the
occupied territory, Pershing slipped away from the ballroom just before a phone call came from his headquarters. An officer was sent
to find him. The general was finally located in his son's bedroom,
where Warren was sleeping "under a German feather-tick three times
as big as he." Pershing was merely sitting next to the bed and watching
his son sleep.

"I like to be with my boy," Pershing told the officer. "I have seen so
little of him in the last few years that it seems as if we hardly know
each other. I want to see all of him I can. I wouldn't feel right if I
let the evening pass without spending part of it with my son, even if
he is asleep."

Pershing was particularly pleased when Mme. Joffre presented
Warren with a boy-sized uniform of a marshal of France, with seven
stars sewn on its sleeve. Warren, under the influence of the doughty
Sergeant Lanckton, could not be convinced that a French marshal out-
ranked an American three-striper and preferred the American uniform. The boy was watching when Pershing led the American Provisional Regiment, with a blaze of regimental standards representing
the whole A.E.F., under the Arch of Triumph in the Grand Parade
celebrating the Allied victory on Bastille Day, July 14, 1919. Pershing
made a superb picture on horseback, managing his mount like an old
cavalryman, but equally impressive were the two marshals of France,
Joffre and Foch, marching on foot with their batons in hand. Later
that month Pershing and the picked regiment marched in the Victory
Parade in London. The British were unstinting with their honors, and
Pershing was the guest of honor at a royal garden party, had luncheon
at Buckingham Palace, was made an Honorary Freeman of the City,
sat in a box at the theater with the Prince of Wales, and was honored
at a dinner given by Field Marshal Haig, with such luminaries as
Horne, Birdwood, Currie, Monash, and others present. Next day he
was given the Freedom of the City of London and a Sword of Honor.

No other nation does this sort of thing with more graceful ceremony than the British, but General Harbord, who accompanied him, noted that Pershing was not particularly thrilled by all the attention. At a Savoy reception Pershing complained that too much classical music was being played and asked for "some American jazz and ragtime," with the result that the proceedings were enlivened by renditions of *K-K-Katy, The Alcoholic Blues,* and *We Don't Want the Bacon, All We Want Is a Piece of the Rhine.* The general, it appeared, was suffering from a touch of homesickness.

Two more months of pomp and ceremony, and the orders finally came for Pershing to sail for New York, where he would lead the parade of the First Division—"the best damn outfit in the army," he called it—down Fifth Avenue.

On September 8, 1919, he embarked on the *Leviathan* with Warren and an official party including his new aide-de-camp, Colonel George C. Marshall. The peace treaty had been signed, although the United States Senate would balk at its provisions and necessitate a separate agreement between Germany and the United States which was not ratified until two years later. But the war indubitably was over; the Germans would not march for another generation. The world was temporarily safe for democracy, though curious were some of the forms it took. The Russian and German monarchies had fallen, one leaving the vortex of communism, the other a vacuum to be filled by a brutal dictatorship; the Austro-Hungarian and Turkish empires had collapsed; France and Britain were immeasurably weakened. Amid general ruin, the United States emerged as a world power. This would not have happened had Pershing not managed, through a calculated intransigence, to preserve the integrity of the American Expeditionary Force.

One morning while the *Leviathan* was in mid-ocean Warren Pershing was given a message for his father in the ship's wireless room. He ran into his father's stateroom and awakened him by jumping on the bed, then handed him the message. It was a cable from Baker announcing that Congress had voted him the rank of General of the Armies—the first since Washington, when the "armies" amounted to less than a modern division. No officer since Pershing has been given that rank, and perhaps, if the world is luckier than seems possible and a third intercontinental war is averted, no one ever will.

PART THREE

SOLDIER
IN RETIREMENT

16. Chief of Staff

A good soldier is never forgot,
Whether he die by musket or by the pot.

INSCRIPTION ON A TOMBSTONE AT
WINCHESTER COLLEGE IN ENGLAND

Pershing was returning to American shores virtually a stranger. For almost twenty years he had spent most of his time abroad, in Manchuria and the Philippines, below the Mexican border and in France. Before that he had lived outside the mainstream of American life as a soldier on the western frontier. In his mind the United States would always be the expanding, questing nation of his youth, a somewhat rustic America, which it no longer was.

Even since the spring of 1917, when he left with the nucleus of the A.E.F., there had been tremendous changes in American life. Half frontier in his youth, the nation was being industrialized, mechanized, urbanized, and some said feminized at a bounding pace. Automobiles had taken over the roads and were beginning to produce social and economic effects of incalculable force. The labor unions were growing stronger, and men who had been able to afford striped silk shirts on war-time wages would never again be satisfied with the twelve-hour day and bare subsistence pay. Women got the vote and men lost the drink through two new amendments to the Constitution.

Whatever hopes anyone had for an ideal agrarian republic that stayed home and minded its own business had finally been destroyed by the intervention in the European war. There was a temporary retreat into isolationism when the Senate refused to ratify the Treaty of

Versailles or enter the League of Nations, but the United States, through its only partly conscious venture into ancient European feuds, had irrevocably committed itself to the responsibility of a world power.

A new kind of America was being born, in which Pershing and his generation, remembering rail fences, stagecoaches, and Indian uprisings, would never feel entirely at home. Nor would they ever be completely reconciled to the changes that kept cropping up around them— the demand for ease and comfort, the craze for speed, the search for easy money, the yahoo acceptance of slogans, the bare-kneed freedom of the young women—the end, in fact, of what had been a man's world.

Yet this stranger, this returning soldier whose closest connection with politics had been his relationship by marriage to a prominent Republican senator, was being proposed as a candidate for President of the United States. The "Pershing boom" had been under way for some months before he embarked for the United States. There is no evidence that he encouraged it in any way; on the other hand, he was not quite so explicit as General Sherman in rejecting all possibility of accepting the nomination if offered. Less than a month after the armistice, on December 3, 1918, Dawes was writing in his diary that Pershing was "very much annoyed by the newspaper talk about him as a candidate for the Presidency and was contemplating a statement about it, strongly denouncing such gossip. . . . I advised him it was not worthy of notice—at least at present." The Republicans, having no outstanding candidate, claimed him for their own, although Pershing had never indicated any preference, as befitted a professional soldier.

Despite a discouraging silence from the general, Republican politicians and newspapers clamored for his candidacy. They did not reckon with the general aversion to war or anything that smacked of the military. America had become disillusioned; the war had been a fever in the blood only until the casualty lists started clicking out, until Americans were convinced that their "crusade" in Europe was being viewed less idealistically by their allies. *Over There* was no longer a song hit. Few people were really enthusiastic about transferring Pershing, or any other general, from his military headquarters to the White House.

Leslie's Weekly assigned a former *Stars & Stripes* writer, Charles Phelps Cushing, to investigate the potentialities of the Pershing boom. "A good many of us," he wrote, "have a shrewd suspicion that many politicians went to France in the army of joy riders that poured overseas after the signing of the Armistice; and that these politicians carefully sounded out the A.E.F. on the possibilities of Pershing for President. We also have a suspicion that they returned with a report that most of the two million overseas would vote 'NO!' on such a proposition—even on a proposition to put any soldier in the White House. . . .

"Did Pershing lose the opportunity to become a candidate for the highest office in America because he deliberately made himself in France 'something of a machine'? It is possible. Many have a feeling that back of his somewhat forbidding front he was not so cold and colorless a personality as he appeared on inspection tours. Perhaps this was simply his West Pointer's notion of the best way to get a big job done. If so, he is paying the penalty of impersonal efficiency by returning richer in respect than in affection."

Men in the ranks pictured him, Cushing said, as "a businessman with offices in an old barracks, with a town house and a country house like a banker and a garage full of expensive motor cars." He "somehow failed to belong, as some of the other generals did," among whom Cushing cited Liggett, Harbord, and Dickman. "Perhaps he held himself aloof from attempting to catch his men's fancy; perhaps he did not know how."

The movement to make Pershing a candidate for President at the 1920 Republican National Convention never really got off the ground. Nor did he ever give any public indication whether he would accept any bid from the party managers, although some of his friends suspected that he could have been drafted if there had been an overwhelming desire for his candidacy. On June 8, 1920, when the convention was deadlocked, he was quoted as saying "no patriotic American could decline" the presidency. Newspapers reported that he awaited a summons from the party heads in Chicago—but it never came.

When the cigar smoke around the Republican bosses finally cleared, the laurel had been deposited on the deceptively noble brow of Warren G. Harding, the senator from Ohio. Pershing lacked the flexibility and political instinct to have made an outstanding President, but it may be taken for granted that he would never have been manipulated as Harding was, and that while his Administration might have been undistinguished, at least it would not have been disfigured by a Teapot Dome scandal and other criminal follies.

He was given a wholehearted welcome, at any rate, when the *Leviathan* docked at New York on September 9, 1919. All the ships in New York Harbor blew their whistles and sounded their sirens as the liner came up the bay to dock at Pier Four in Hoboken. Secretary of War Baker and Chief of Staff March, along with many members of the A.E.F. staff who had preceded him home, came aboard to greet him. Even General March was cordial. Since the end of the war, Pershing's relations with him had naturally taken a turn for the better, with the removal of wartime tensions and differences. Sixteen days after the armistice, Pershing had taken the conciliatory step of writing March a letter beginning, "I wish I had the time and paper to tell you in a letter all of the details that we have waded through in achieving the organization of our army and fighting it as such. Without this very gratifying outcome, America's part in the war would have been swallowed up in the accomplishment of our allies, and the credit due us would not have come to us. . . . I realize that your own duties are also troublesome and that you have had a pretty hard row to hoe. . . ."

Pershing and his party were showered with ticker tape in a triumphal procession up Broadway from the Battery to City Hall, where Governor Alfred E. Smith and Mayor John F. Hylan waited to receive him on the steps. He went to the Waldorf-Astoria for a reunion with his sisters, Mrs. Bessie Butler and Miss May Pershing, and the following night attended a program in his honor at the Hippodrome, where a display of electric lights spelled out "Happy Days to General Pershing." On September 10 he led the First Division down Fifth Avenue from 110th Street. He was mounted on a charger; the First Division, as usual, made the journey on foot. The cheers rose to a crescendo when he dismounted in front of St. Patrick's Cathedral to shake hands with the heroic Cardinal Mercier of Belgium.

Months of ceremony and public display were to follow, but first Pershing took time out for a month's vacation. The first half of it was spent at the Wood's Hole, Massachusetts, estate of Cameron Forbes, the former governor general of the Philippines under whom he had served. A large house party had gathered there. One of the games they played, on horseback, was Pirates and Cruisers, a sort of hide-and-seek in the saddle. Pershing was a Pirate, and the ladies of the party insisted on vying for the privilege of capturing him. The general was not visibly displeased at losing the game after a chase through the woods. Later he was the guest of the father-in-law of his operations officer, General Fox Conner, at Brandeth Lake, in the Adirondacks, where he spent most of his time hiking and deer hunting.

For the best part of a year, with Colonel Marshall trotting in his wake as aide-de-camp, Pershing fulfilled a ceremonial role, an army commander without an army. It was a year of train rides, public receptions, inspection tours, civic dinners. During that period Pershing at least learned to unbend somewhat, to show the gracious side of his character (hitherto visible only to his friends and closer associates), and even to smile for the newspaper cameras if given sufficient warning. Out of friendship for his aide, Pershing visited Marshall's old school, the Virginia Military Institute, and spent two days there watching the cadets parade in review for the alumni. He even made the statement, astounding for a West Pointer, that he had heard V.M.I. referred to as "the West Point of the South" but after watching its cadets on the parade ground he wondered why West Point was not called "the V.M.I. of the North."

On his coast-to-coast tour shortly after that, he visited Hollywood and incidentally gave one of its future leading lights his first boost up the ladder of the motion-picture industry. Pershing toured the Goldwyn Studios in Culver City, where all former servicemen were drawn up in uniform for his inspection. One of these was William A. Wellman, a former combat aviator with the Lafayette Flying Corps, now a twenty-three-year-old office boy, who had met Pershing on a social occasion in France. The general, recalling that they had met, halted in front of Wellman and whispered, "Is there anything I can do for you?" "Yes, sir," said the quick-witted Wellman. "You'd really make me look good after this thing is over if you'd talk to me a few minutes under that fig tree over there." Pershing nodded and continued his inspection. After the review was over, Pershing cut short his conversation with several studio executives to march over to where Wellman was waiting under the fig tree. They talked together for twenty minutes, to the amazement of Wellman's superiors. Next day they promoted the young man to be an assistant director, and Wellman eventually became one of Hollywood's top directors. Wellman has always credited his rise to fame and fortune to that talk under the fig tree.

In the spring of 1920, after school was out, Pershing picked up his son and took him along on his considerable travels. They journeyed to Panama, where Warren was instructed by his father in the art of tarpon fishing, then on a brief trip to Europe during which Pershing, apparently forgetting that his son was then struggling with long division in school, attempted to explain the fundamentals of physics and mathematics. They were on the move all that summer and drew closer together than they had ever been. Late in the summer they went out west, and on the train ride to Denver, Pershing noted in his diary, he "gave Warren a lesson in spelling and read to him *The Legend of the Moors' Legacy*." After visiting the Warren family's home in Cheyenne, they spent a week in the Rockies, fishing and riding on Senator Phipps's ranch at Wagon Wheel Gap. They wound up the summer in Lincoln, at Pershing's sisters' home, where Warren was left behind to continue his schooling.

On his way back to Washington, Pershing stopped off at Marion, Ohio, to call on Senator Harding and shake a thousand hands at a reception for the man who was shortly to be elected President. He may have been informed on that occasion that he would be appointed chief of staff, succeeding General March. If so, it must have been welcome news. For a man who had worked at top speed all his life, the interval between his arrival in the United States and his assumption of that post must have been irksome and meaningless. He spent much of his time commuting between Washington and New York, where he usually saw his younger brother Jim, a happy-go-lucky fellow who had spent most of his life on the road as a clothing salesman and now operated his own firm. Jim Pershing was living at Forest Hills Gardens and often advised him on stock-market investments. At least Pershing would never have to worry too much about money, Congress having recently voted him a full general's pay for the rest of his life, through the endeavors of Secretary of War Baker.

Social activities filled most of his days in the fall and winter; he was the prize captive of New York and Washington hostesses, and more than one army widow—a type in which Washington abounded, as Pershing observed several times in his diary—conceived hopes of becoming the second Mrs. Pershing. At sixty he was still a fine figure of manhood, and he proposed to stay that way. Almost every day he went to the Frances Fox Institute for scalp treatments, and having his share of vanity about hair, teeth, eyes, and a prepossessing physique he managed to preserve the appearance of a much younger man for many years. For the next decade, rumors of his intended remarriage were to buzz constantly around the upper echelon of Washington society. They were helped along, perhaps, by the fact that Pershing rented the Chevy Chase residence of General Corbin's widow, which was known in capital society as "the Irish legation" and seemed to be roomier than a man set on remaining a widower would require.

Pershing took over as chief of staff, to the intense disappointment of General March, who would have liked to stay in that office. The Army then was undergoing a peacetime crisis. Before Congress and in the War Department a highly vocal war was being waged. The issue at stake was what kind of Army the United States would build for the future—a controversy toward which the public displayed a yawning indifference. Many General Staff officers, March among them, wanted a standing army of thoroughgoing professionals. Pershing and his allies wanted something vastly different, a broadly based "national army" resting on a foundation of universal military training.

By the time Pershing assumed direction of the General Staff, the dispute had been going strong for two years. Just after the armistice he was invited to send a General Staff officer to represent the A.E.F. in the formulation of a permanent military system. Pershing chose General John McAuley Palmer, who had been commanding a brigade in the 29th Division, to participate in the discussions. Eventually Palmer was charged with framing legislation which would define and provide the structure for a modern military establishment.

Pershing and Palmer believed that the citizen army created in the world war should be "perpetuated as a permanent national institution," that it should be a "democratic army" with both Regular Army and civilian components which could be rapidly expanded in the event of war. On his arrival in Washington, however, Palmer found that plans had already been formulated for a standing army of half a million, with "military leadership to be the monopoly of the professional soldier," as Palmer wrote. "At the close of a war against German militarism we were to have a militaristic system in the United States." Such a bill, Palmer rightly believed, was "foredoomed."

The National Defense Act of 1920, when it was finally drafted, represented what Pershing believed would be a workable and efficient compromise. Universal military training, like a large standing army, was "foredoomed" by the prevailing sentiment against anything military. The measure, however, provided for an army of 280,000 enlisted men, enough to organize nine infantry divisions and nine corps areas, under which regular officers and noncoms would train National

Guard, Reserve Officers Training Corps, and Citizens Military Training Camp units.

Despite Pershing's vigorous protests, Congress ordered another army cutback in 1922, this time to 125,000 men. The training centers attached to corps areas had to be abandoned and their personnel returned to Regular Army duties. Disillusioned by the interplay of power politics and national interests at Versailles, already cynical over the war that was to "end war," the United States decided that the best kind of army was the smallest and least visible. War, it was generally held, could be stopped by doing away with armies and navies and their weapons. Laurence Stallings's *What Price Glory?* became the theatrical hit of the decade; college boys whose older brothers had rushed to the colors in 1917 joined pacifist movements or "The Veterans of Future Wars," and soon enough American intellectuals were proclaiming that if all generals could be shelved and all munitions makers could be run out of business there would be no more war.

Meanwhile, Pershing and his staff were pondering the lessons of American participation in the world war and concluding that the A.E.F.'s performance, on the whole, had been brave and enthusiastic, but lacking in skill. In a later war, the American Army might not have time to organize behind a shield held up by its allies or confront a decimated and outnumbered enemy. Pershing assigned Colonel Marshall to compile records on the performances of the various American divisions in France, and undoubtedly Marshall's conclusions, some of which were summarized in an article in the *Infantry Journal,* reflected Pershing's opinions:

"The Americans who fought only at St. Mihiel and in the Meuse-Argonne probably will never realize the vast difference between their enemy then and the German of April or May. Even those who fought in the summer of 1918 will have some difficulty in visualizing the state of mind of troops who are opposed by an enemy far superior in numbers and confident of his ability to defeat them. For this reason it is possible that officers who participated only in the last phase of the war may draw somewhat erroneous conclusions from their battle experiences.

"Many mistakes were made in the Argonne which the Germans at that time were unable to charge to our account. The same mistakes, repeated four months earlier in the war, would have brought an immediate and unfortunate reaction. It is possible that methods successfully employed in the Meuse-Argonne would have invited a successful enemy counter-attack in the spring of 1918.

"It is not intended by this discussion to belittle our efforts in the latter part of the war, for what we actually accomplished was a military miracle, but we must not forget that its conception was based on a knowledge of the approaching deterioration of the German Army, and its lesson must be studied accordingly. *We remain without modern experience in the first phases of a war and must draw our conclusions from history.*"

Next time, if there was a next time, America might not be allowed the time to mobilize men and resources, might not go up against a half-defeated enemy. American luck would not hold forever. In total war, preparations had to be made years in advance. A modern army could not be created in a matter of months.

These thoughts, along with the conviction that the United States had bulled its way to a victory in Lorraine under circumstances that would never repeat themselves, that in a sense the American Army had been almost too lucky and its successes had lulled the people into a foolish belief in American superiority, spurred Pershing's efforts from then until the end of his life toward establishing the Army on an unshakable foundation. Much as he hated public speaking, he was willing to spread the gospel of a democratic army, with so much of the population involved in it—even for a year or two of ROTC or National Guard training—that it would be a part of their life. He wanted Americans to be aware of the kind of world they were living in, as he saw it, a world which technology was making both more comfortable and more dangerous every day. By the end of his term as chief of staff, however, he knew that this effort was also "foredoomed." Only nations with aggressive intentions, bent on vengeance or expansion, are willing to prepare adequately for war in time of peace.

With all his prestige, Pershing could not persuade the gentlemen on Capitol Hill that "economizing" further on the military budget would reduce the Army to a creaking skeleton. The agonies of false economy would have to be suffered by the next generation. Just after he retired in 1924, he wrote Marshall, then serving in China with the 15th Infantry: "I find on my return here that the War Department seems to be up against the real thing. The Budget Officer insists on reducing our estimates so that we shall not be able to have over 110,000 men. Just what this means I cannot understand. I do not know what is going to be done about it, but to my mind it is very discouraging." In 1940, Marshall quoted that letter when, as chief of staff himself, he addressed the Veterans of Foreign Wars convention and cited it as evidence that nothing had changed.

In other matters, particularly the growth of air power, Pershing proved much less farsighted. Astigmatic might be a better word for his vision regarding the future of military aircraft, whose most vociferous apostle was Billy Mitchell. Pershing had an instinctive distrust of the more flamboyant types like Mitchell and MacArthur; perhaps he envied their flair for influencing people, their stage presence, their courting of popularity; but whatever aroused his dislike he definitely wasn't going to put up with officers who wouldn't stay in line. Mitchell's prophecies of the future strategic value of air power struck no sympathetic chord in Pershing. "No airplane," he said more than once, "has ever affected the course of a battle."

Only once had Pershing been willing to go along with one of Mitchell's imaginative schemes for the employment of air power, and that was during the mid-October days when the First Army was bogged down in the depths of the Argonne. In what must have been a moment of weakness, Pershing listened receptively to Mitchell's plans for a paratroop division which could take the German defenses from the rear. Mitchell wrote in his diary for October 17, 1918, that he had just proposed to Pershing that "in the spring of 1919, when I should have a great force of bombardment airplanes, he assign one of the infantry divisions permanently to the Air Service . . . that we arm the men with a great number of machine guns and train them to go over the front in our large airplanes which would carry ten or fifteen of these soldiers. We could equip each man with a parachute, so that when we desired to make a rear attack on the enemy, we could carry these men over the lines and drop them off in parachutes behind the German position. . . . Our low-flying attack aviation would then cover every road in their vicinity, both day and night, so as to prevent the Germans falling on them quickly until they could thoroughly organize the position." Pershing approved of the plan, but the war ended before it could be carried out.

When it came to sharing the War Department's meager budget with the infant Air Corps, however, Pershing was less willing to listen to Mitchell's visionary proposals. If the Army was to be skeletonized, the organization of the ground forces had to be maintained above all, and air power would have to be developed along more modest lines.

Pershing was almost as skeptical as any old-line battleship admiral when the Air Corps, under Mitchell's supervision, began demonstrating the superiority of the plane over the battleship by bombing and sinking old German warships off Old Point Comfort, Virginia, in defiance of the naval mossbacks' dictum that "you can't hit a ship from the air, and if you hit her, you can't sink her." Pershing was one of a large group of high-ranking army and navy officers who watched the Air Corps demonstrations during July 1921. Mitchell and his disciples thought they proved their point when they finally managed to sink the 27,000-ton "unsinkable" German dreadnought *Ostfriesland,* a survivor of the Battle of Jutland. The sinking, said one admiral, "heralded the birth of a new weapon which menaces the old army quite as much as the old navy." This point, too, must have struck Pershing forcibly.

Exhilarated by its obvious successes off the Virginia capes, the Air Corps was stunned by the report of the joint army and navy board, signed by General Pershing, which acknowledged that aircraft could sink or damage "any naval vessel at present constructed" but concluded that "the battleship is still the backbone of the fleet and the bulwark of the nation's sea defense."

Mitchell continued his crusade all the more vigorously after that report was made public. General Menoher, former commander of the 42nd Division, then chief of the Air Service, resigned on September 21, 1921, when the Secretary of War refused to support him in demanding that Mitchell be disciplined—that is, muzzled. Pershing's sympathies, it may be inferred, were all with General Menoher. Certainly they were not inclined toward Mitchell when he faced a general court-martial several years later, after Pershing's retirement as chief of staff.

Much as he hated to attract the attention of Washington's busy gossip mills, Pershing also became unwillingly involved in the private and professional affairs of General Douglas MacArthur during this period. In 1922, MacArthur was in the third year of his service as superintendent of West Point; he was still a bachelor at the age of forty-two, but had fallen in love with the beautiful Mrs. Louise Cromwell Brooks, a twenty-six-year-old divorcee who had decorated New York, Washington, and wartime Paris society since girlhood. She was the daughter of Mrs. Edward Stotesbury, who had long dominated Philadelphia society, and the stepdaughter of a banker whose fortune was said to total $150,000,000. Mrs. Brooks and her brother, Jimmy Cromwell, later the first husband of Doris Duke, met Pershing during the war and were occasional guests of his at the Ogden Mills mansion in Paris.

Despite the buzzing in capital society that Pershing and the wealthy divorcee were "unofficially engaged," Mrs. Brooks announced her engagement to General MacArthur on January 14, 1922. The gossips also had it, as a matter of fact, that Mrs. Brooks was being courted by Colonel Quekemeyer, one of Pershing's aides.

The vivacious Mrs. Brooks, according to two of MacArthur's biographers (Clark Lee and Robert Henschel), told Pershing of her decision to marry MacArthur, whom she had recently met at a West Point ball, at a large dinner party. Pershing's only comment was: "Young lady, you'd better watch out or you'll find yourself in the Philippines."

Three months after the wedding, MacArthur was assigned to a tour of duty in the Philippines and both his and his new wife's friends circulated the charge that he was being "exiled." MacArthur, aside from any possible affront to the chief of staff, stood No. 1 on the list of generals scheduled for foreign service.

Mrs. MacArthur was quoted, according to biographers Lee and Henschel, as saying that "Jack wanted me to marry him. When I wouldn't, he wanted me to marry one of his colonels. I wouldn't do that—so here I am packing my trunks." If her version was correct, it was something new in the history of romance: a rejected suitor who nimbly proposed a replacement.

The gossip grew so rancorous that Pershing finally consented to an interview on the subject.

A member of the New York *Times* Washington bureau reported that Pershing was asked whether there was any truth in the rumor that MacArthur was being "exiled" to the Philippines and that he had been an "unsuccessful suitor for the hand of Mrs. Cromwell Brooks." Pershing's reply was equally forthright and underlined with the contempt he felt for the gossip which had attended almost every phase of his career: "There is no ground for that story. It is all damn poppycock, without the slightest foundation and based on the idlest gossip. If I were married to all the ladies to whom gossips have engaged me, I would be a regular Brigham Young.

"General MacArthur is being ordered to the Philippines because he stands at the top of the list of officers due for foreign service. He has been due for such service, as a matter of fact, for over a year.

"I do not know whether General MacArthur has any intention of resigning from the army. I haven't the slightest intimation to that effect from him. But I can say that I do not believe that General MacArthur would resign from the service merely because he was about to be ordered to a foreign post. I know General MacArthur well. He is one of the most splendid types of soldier I have ever met. All this stuff is idle nonsense."

As it turned out, Mrs. MacArthur found Manila society incredibly provincial and boring after the excitement of wartime Paris. She even served as a part-time policewoman to pass the time. MacArthur, unlike Pershing, refused to dance. Six years later the MacArthurs were divorced, with a parting shot from the lady, "Sir Galahad carried on his courtship as if he were reviewing a division of troops."

If all that the ladies said about Pershing was true, he was leading a rather ardent romantic life for a man in his early sixties. He was not a man to confide such matters to his diary, yet here and there may be found a hint of his extra-military activities. During the early months of his service in France, for instance, there were entries indicating that he was posing frequently, for such a busy man, in the studio of a young portrait painter named Micheline Resco. A charming and highly talented young woman, Mlle. Resco produced a number of sketches and portraits of the general. One served as the frontispiece for his memoirs in both the French and American editions, another hangs in the Museum of the Army in Paris, another in the New York headquarters of the Military Order of the World War. She also executed the official portraits of Marshal Foch, General Fayolle, Admiral Sims, and other Allied leaders.

Mlle. Resco often saw Pershing in the years after the war when she visited New York and Washington.

Several months after the MacArthur affair blew over, on July 27, 1922, Pershing wrote in his diary of receiving a "visit from my sister and Mlle. Resco," indicating his family approved of the young Frenchwoman. Whatever the extent of their relationship, Mlle. Resco never married and was his faithful friend to the end of his life, never more so than during the dreary days of his final hospitalization.

In 1952, four years after his death, the French weekly *Samedi Soir* published a three-column article based on the recollections of an "intimate friend" of Mlle. Resco, who was still living in the studio apartment on the Rue des Renaudes where Pershing had posed for her. "During Thirty Years," the article was headed, "a Frenchwoman Played 'Back Street' for Pershing." According to the "intimate friend," Pershing and the young artist fell in love but hesitated to marry because of the difference in their ages. She kept her friendship with the general out of the limelight, she was quoted as saying, because "I don't want to risk tarnishing his reputation at any price. People would not understand. And then, he has his son. . . ." Pershing himself "considered that her sacrifice was far greater than any he would undergo in affronting public opinion" because of the almost forty-year difference in their ages.

Feminine companionship was always a necessity to him. "He loved the society of women," as General Bullard wrote. "That, too, like other early characteristics, seems to have held with him." Otherwise, austerity governed his later years; he soon gave up the Chevy Chase residence for an apartment at 2029 Connecticut Avenue, where his father-in-law also stayed, later took up even less pretentious quarters at the Metropolitan Club and the Carlton Hotel.

By coincidence he was present during the last tragic scene of President Harding's life. The President had taken a trip to Alaska just as the corruption of various members of his Administration was to be made public, particularly the connection between Secretary of the Interior Albert B. Fall and the Teapot Dome oil leases. Harding died very suddenly and perhaps fortuitously in San Francisco, causing rumors to spread immediately that he had been poisoned, either by himself or someone else. Pershing had been inspecting IX Corps Headquarters at the Presidio on August 2, 1923, and was at dinner that evening when he was notified of the President's death. He hurried over to the Harding suite at the Palace Hotel and found "everyone unstrung." General Sawyer and Dr. Wilbur, the President's physicians, apparently were unable to agree on the cause of death. "The latter [Wilbur] insisted that the cause was plainly arterial schlerosis and that all other symptoms were merely incidental," Pershing wrote in his diary later that night. "General Sawyer did not appear very willing to accept this diagnosis, but Wilbur was most plainspoken in his opinion." At Mrs. Harding's request he accompanied the funeral train to Washington.

On September 13, 1924, Pershing reached his sixty-fourth birthday and "the last day of my active service in the Army." The occasion may have been charged with emotion; certainly it was for other people—members of his staff, old comrades, admirers from civilian life. If Pershing himself was moved by his retirement, and he must have been since the last day of any man's working life has something funereal about it, he managed to conceal it admirably. "Spent the day in my office, where I received a constant stream of callers, who came in to extend greetings and good wishes," was the only comment in his diary. A week earlier he had accompanied his son to New York and had seen him off on the *Leviathan*. The self-possessed Warren Pershing was making his first trip to Europe alone. "He was quite lively during the day until just before the boat sailed," the father noted, "when I think he began to feel a little solemn." The boy cheered up when the liner's captain informed him that he would be seated at a table with Jackie Coogan, the film star.

Within a few weeks after his retirement, time began to hang heavily on his hands and he suddenly decided to join Warren in Europe, where they toured France and Switzerland together.

Shortly after his return to the United States, the government found more work for him to do. Technically he would be on duty to the day of his death, as General of the Armies, and therefore he was available for any assignment the President or the War Department might choose to give him. Until he was too old and ill, he continued to supervise the work of the American Battle Monuments Commission in France, on which both Marshall and Eisenhower served at various times. He also had to be available for appearances at West Point, various army functions, and ceremonies for distinguished visitors. His role in "retirement" was to build and uphold the prestige of the Army—an almost hopeless task in the twenties and thirties.

This time his assignment was more than ornamental. President Coolidge summoned him to the White House to offer him the chairmanship of the commission which was charged with settling the Tacna-Arica dispute in which Peru and Chile, and to a lesser extent Bolivia, had long been embroiled. Pershing eagerly accepted the assignment on March 23, 1925. He would have been less willing, perhaps, had he realized the thorniness of the problem he was called upon to arbitrate and the touchiness of the Latin temperaments he was supposed to reconcile.

The dispute over the province of Tacna-Arica had been going on since 1879, when Chile declared war on Peru and Bolivia after nitrate was found in that forlorn, 500-mile strip of coast. Chile, having defeated the two allies, was ceded the province and its port of Arica in 1883, with the agreement that a plebiscite would be held within ten years to determine whether it would remain under Chilean rule or be returned to Peru. The plebiscite was never held, and ever since then there had been the threat of another war over ownership of the Province. Freshly conscious of its role as big brother to Latin America, the United States was exercising all diplomatic means of arriving at a settlement; the plebiscite must finally be held and enforced, President Coolidge and Secretary of State Frank Kellogg decided, and perhaps a man of the military prestige of General Pershing could persuade the adversaries—particularly Chile—to settle their differences at the voting booth.

On August 2, 1925, Pershing arrived at the port of Arica aboard the U.S.S. *Rochester,* on which he was quartered during most of the six months of negotiation that followed. Among the members of his official party were his aide, Colonel Quekemeyer, and Ralph A. Curtin, his secretary, who had served at A.E.F. Headquarters and returned a lieutenant. Pershing wrote of his arrival, "The band murdered 'The Star-Spangled Banner' horribly and continued to mangle the remains until I dropped my hand from the salute and the Chilean general waved them to stop."

Right from the beginning of his mission, Pershing saw that "it would take a Solomon to render a just judgment" because "both sides see things through a cloud of intense hatred."

In that sweltering port on the nitrate coast, surrounded by desert plateaus and jagged mountains, Pershing spent month after month listening to the recriminations of the Chilean and Peruvian delegates. The Peruvians charged their people were being persecuted by the Chilean carbineers who policed the province. The Chileans claimed that Peru was sending hordes of settlers in, under American protection, to outvote the Chilean colonists at the plebiscite. Under the circumstances, the Chileans announced, they wouldn't participate in the plebiscite or recognize its results.

One of Pershing's first measures was to send to the Panama Canal Zone for twenty Spanish-speaking Americans to "be sent out to the several districts with specific instructions to study conditions" and later to "serve on registration and election boards."

Within two weeks of his arrival at Arica, Pershing was arguing by cable with the State Department over a premature announcement of findings which he had forwarded but didn't want made public. He wrote in his journal of the proceedings on August 15, that he had considered it necessary to warn the Secretary of State to "keep his hands off and not even intimate to the ambassadors of the two countries [Chile and Peru] that I had cabled him the situation." He felt that nothing would be accomplished if the State Department "meddled" through "premature leaks" to the countries involved.

Laborious, exhausting, and exasperating, the negotiations went on for month after month. At night Pershing wrote his reports and whiled away the hours playing blackjack with his associates in the wardroom of the *Rochester*.

Occasionally, in the back country, there were flare-ups of violence between Peruvian settlers and Chilean soldiers. Pershing described a typical incident on November 22, 1925. A Chilean carbineer and two companions broke into a Peruvian's home, tied him up, and raped his wife. Led by the headman of a nearby Peruvian settlement, the victim's compatriots attacked the Chilean military post and killed the rapist. On the Chilean side, Pershing wrote, "The dead carbineer is being heralded as a great hero and charges are flying thick and fast against the Peruvians."

American sympathy was largely pro-Peruvian, particularly since the Chilean press was bitterly critical of "American interference." Occasionally, too, Americans who had come down to Arica out of idle curiosity or looking for excitement caused Pershing embarrassment. One such specimen was an American woman who created an "incident" by loudly charging that she had been fired upon by Chileans while out riding with a couple of Peruvian gentlemen. Pershing couldn't quite believe her story, considered her a sensation seeker in any case, and suggested to the State Department that the "very headstrong" young lady be gently removed from Arica before she started a shooting war between Peru and Chile.

By December 2, Pershing developed what may have been a diplomatic toothache. Little headway was being made in the negotiations, particularly with the Chileans. He found that he needed dental surgery, which could only be performed in the States, he said, suggesting to Secretary of State Kellogg that he "might call me to Washington to a conference as that would seem a plausible thing to do and would not arouse criticism."

Thus Pershing removed himself from the Tacna-Arica dispute, drawing from General March the gleeful comment that his "failure in diplomacy . . . might have been predicted, and the subsequent solution of that matter by our diplomatic representative in Peru, Alexander P. Moore, under direction of the State Department, only showed the truth of the old adage, 'Let the shoemaker stick to his last.'" Actually it took another four years of wrangling to settle the dispute. March, still smarting over his replacement as chief of staff by Pershing and their wartime disagreements, was not entirely just in his observations. After Pershing returned home with his toothache, General William Lassiter took over as Chief United States Commissioner at Arica and also failed to negotiate a settlement. It wasn't until 1929 that Chile and Peru agreed to divide Tacna-Arica between them and finally resolved a half century of bickering.

Pershing was out of the country when General Billy Mitchell was finally called to account for his excessive propagandizing on behalf of an independent and greatly strengthened Air Force. A general court-martial was convened to try Mitchell on charges of having violated the 95th Article of War by publicly accusing the military and naval high commands of "incompetency, criminal negligence, and almost treasonable administration of national defense," thus deliberately choosing martyrdom to continued service in the Air Corps.

While Pershing was still in Arica, he received a cable from his successor as chief of staff, Major General John L. Hines, who had been a corps commander in the A.E.F., asking that Pershing appear at Mitchell's trial. General Hines, Pershing wrote, "stated that counsel for Mitchell had been permitted to develop his defense with great freedom and that the trial was being conducted primarily for the purpose of influencing public opinion."

Pershing decided against appearing as a prosecution witness, though no one was less sympathetic to Mitchell's ideas or methods.

"I do not believe that there need be much worry," he wrote regarding the outcome of the court-martial, "as the War Department stands on too solid a foundation." Brilliant mavericks had been put in their place before, and Mitchell was no exception. Even Mitchell's friend and fellow airman, the late General H. H. Arnold, conceded that "the thing for which Mitchell was really being tried he was guilty of, and except for Billy, everybody knew it, and knew what it meant." Mitchell's career was scrapped, but he achieved the martyrdom he sought and with it the public sympathy which finally resulted in everything he had worked and pleaded for.

Pershing did not gloat, at least not publicly or on the record, over the comeuppance that Mitchell had defied his more conservative brother officers to inflict upon him. Perhaps he realized better than some of his old comrades that the day of the mechanized warrior was coming on just as swiftly as the shades were closing around the cavalrymen who had galloped over the graves of the Sioux.

17. On the Shelf

Twenty-four years, and the blessing (or curse) of an extraordinarily long life, stretched ahead of Pershing after his retirement as chief of staff. They might have been insupportable to a man with his active mind and body without some contact with the working world. He was far luckier than most men in that a sympathetic government found ways of keeping him busy at least part of the time, supplied him with a staff and a suite of offices, kept reminding him that he would always be on "active service" with the government as its senior military adviser, and maintained him on full pay and allowances. Many an old fellow in the soldiers' home could envy his lot.

He divided his time between annual visits to France, winters in Arizona, and living in Washington the rest of the year. On his trips to France he invariably visited General Pétain, whom he admired above all the French soldiers. His principal concern overseas, as head of the Battle Monuments Commission, was to prevent an "unlimited spread of American monuments which gave the impression that Americans had done most of the fighting on the Western Front," as Frederick Palmer said. He had full authority over the number and size of the markers erected by the various units which had fought in France, as well as the vast military cemeteries near the main battlefields. He told a London newspaperman that he visited the battlefields every year in fulfillment of a promise he made in 1919 to "the men who trusted me"—those who had fallen. Nostalgia for the great moments of his career also had a powerful attraction. Invariably he visited the town of Chaumont, where A.E.F. Headquarters had been, seeking out "old friends and familiar scenes." Although offered the hospitality of the château in which he had lived during the war, he insisted on staying at the Hotel de France in town, always in the modestly furnished Room No. 10 which ever since has been known as the "General Pershing Room."

In Washington he led a generally quiet and unsocial life. After a lifetime of rising at dawn, he began operating on a Bohemian schedule, often reading all night in his suite at the Carlton, then going to his office at noon or after lunch. The government assigned him Rooms 256–260 in the old State, War and Navy Building, an impressively dignified, quiet, and high-ceilinged set of offices, with the portraits of his predecessors—Grant, Sherman, and Sheridan—staring down at him. Here he was surrounded by familiar faces: Colonel George E. Adamson, his chief secretary, and Captain Ralph A. Curtin (subsequently a colonel), both of whom had risen from field clerks at A.E.F. Headquarters, and others who helped him with his correspondence, appointments, and writing chores.

The man closest to him in his daily life was his veteran striker, Sergeant Frank Lanckton, a typical Old Army reprobate who knew more ways of getting around the general than any six members of the French High Command. Lanckton attended the general with the maximum of punctilio (in which there was occasionally discernible a touch of satire), flourishing salutes that fairly whipped the air, the indirect form of address, and much heel clicking, all of which may have seemed a little ridiculous to civilians. To Pershing they were a constant and welcome reminder of "cavalry smartness," of the old days on army posts from Manila to El Paso.

Lanckton had started serving as his striker, or body servant, back when Pershing was military governor of Mindanao. Somehow they had become separated during the war and Lanckton had abandoned his employment as "the general's dog-robber" for more active soldiering. Pershing, touring a military hospital outside Paris, found him recuperating from a wound and immediately took him to his residence at 73 Rue de Varenne to convalesce.

His only difficulty with Lanckton was the latter's tendency to tipple occasionally, not extravagantly by most men's standards, but Pershing was a one-drink man himself. Growing suspicious of his striker's behavior, he would demand, "Have you been drinking?"

"No, sir," Lanckton would righteously reply.

"You have been drinking!"

"Yes, sir!" Lanckton would say, unable under protocol to contradict his superior.

When Lanckton was really in bad with Pershing, he would silently remove a photograph from his hip pocket and place it on the general's dresser where he could not help but see it. The photo showed Lanckton posing with all four of the Pershing children outside their home in Zamboanga—mute testimony of his long and faithful service. A glance at that picture quickly allayed the general's annoyance.

His son, Warren, was away at prep school, Phillips Exeter, but he saw to it that they were reunited during the holidays and vacations.

Warren recalls that his father had "only a modicum of success" at supervising his education, though he received a constant stream of encouraging and admonishing letters from his parent, particularly when he was slipping in his studies.

Colonel Curtin remembers that when Warren's marks fell, the general would grumble to his aides that his son was "disgracing the family," but then "he'd get a letter from Warren asking for ten dollars and he'd beam with delight over being needed in some way. He was very proud of Warren, and wanted to be close to him."

The concentrated affection he felt for his only surviving child did not influence him to spoil the boy, however. He had too vivid a memory of his own struggles to acquire an education to permit his son any fancies that he was a member of the idle rich.

Warren, therefore, was required to account for all his expenditures to Colonel Adamson, who handled the general's financial affairs in addition to all his other duties. Occasionally Pershing would cast a stern fatherly eye over those accounts himself.

His son remembers one day when his father seized upon an item in his account—fourteen dollars for a pair of shoes—"a lot of money," he admits, "for shoes in those days."

His father said, "Fourteen dollars is a ridiculous price to pay for a pair of boy's shoes. What do you think, Adamson?"

Colonel Adamson glanced significantly at Pershing's London-made footwear and said, "How much did you pay for the shoes you're wearing, General?"

Pershing hastily dropped the inquiry.

From then on, Warren said, "I always looked on Colonel Adamson as my friend and ally in any dealings with the old gent."

Another member of the family who frequently visited the office was

Pershing's younger brother Jim, who had none of his shyness and was totally unawed by the general's fame and position in the world. Pershing's aides recall that the two brothers, as they grew older and more crotchety, were inclined to argue over almost any point of discussion. Jim, in fact, was one of the few people left on the face of the earth who would give him an argument, in which Pershing apparently took a fierce and secret joy. They remember one exchange as typical of the free-wheeling relationship of the Pershing brothers:

"Jim, you're getting deaf as a post."

"Jackie, you're crazy as hell."

"Damn it all, I say *you're getting deaf!*"—followed by the general's fist slamming on the top of his desk.

"Look here, Jackie," Jim roared back, "you've been an officer all your life and you're used to being kowtowed to, but you can't bulldoze me."

One habit that Pershing clung to, incongruous as it was to his immaculate appearance, was chewing tobacco. He had finally quit smoking some years before, but cavalrymen, like baseball players, were great chewers, and this was one vice that he proposed to afford himself in his old age. He would gnaw off a large section of cigar, Colonel Curtin recalls, with a "sublime expression." He also chewed plug tobacco when a good cigar wasn't handy. His aim at a cuspidor was regarded by his aides as superlative. As he worked over his correspondence or at writing the two-volume account of his services as commander in chief of the A.E.F., his aides in the outer office would hear the frequent *ping* of a well-placed shot.

When a female visitor to his office was announced, the general would invariably inquire, "Is she good-looking?"

If the answer was yes, Pershing would expel his quid and rinse his mouth out in the adjacent bathroom before his caller was admitted.

Being headquartered in Washington, he kept a close eye on military affairs and was particularly diligent about assisting the careers of younger men who had served him well in France. He worked almost as hard at advancing the interests of such men as George C. Marshall as he had years before at promoting his own career. It may be doubted whether Marshall would ever have been appointed chief of staff, to his country's good fortune, without Pershing's constant publicizing of his virtues among highly placed friends.

Pershing's relations with Marshall were close personally as well as professionally. He was Marshall's best man at his marriage to an attractive widow, Mrs. Katherine Tupper Brown, in Baltimore on October 16, 1930. The new Mrs. Marshall wryly observed that a large crowd gathered outside the church, but "my friends were greatly outnumbered, I fear, by those curious to see General Pershing."

Marshall had become assistant commandant of the infantry school at Fort Benning, where a number of brilliant young officers were monkishly striving to work out the tactics of future wars—among them Major Omar N. Bradley, Major Joseph W. Stilwell, and Lieutenant J. Lawton Collins, three of World War II's most competent soldiers. Later such future generals as Walter Bedell Smith, Eisenhower's chief of staff, and John R. Hodge, the postwar commander in South Korea, came under Marshall's pedagogical influence at Fort Benning.

When General Douglas MacArthur succeeded to the post of chief of staff—with absolutely no help from Pershing, one may be certain—the slowly rising curve of Marshall's career suffered an abrupt decline. On MacArthur's orders, Pershing's chief protégé was assigned to take over as senior instructor of the Illinois National Guard, a considerable comedown which Marshall regarded as "a savage blow." Mrs. Marshall said that on receiving the news of his "exile" to Chicago "George had a gray, drawn look which I had never seen before." And when General Charles G. Dawes, former Vice-President and friend of both Pershing and Marshall, heard of the assignment, he exploded, "What! He can't do that. Hell, no! Not George Marshall. He's too big a man for this job. In fact he's the best goddamned officer in the U.S. Army." Pershing's own views on the subject are not a matter of record, but they were equally explosive.

Pershing undertook the unusual gesture of visiting Marshall at his headquarters in Chicago. Marshall had to maneuver carefully so that members of his staff could meet the General of the Armies, who detested being "shown off." As Marshall's biographer has written, "Such introductions involved cunning, for Pershing would send out orders in advance explaining that he had not the least interest in being treated as a visiting fireman. . . . Marshall found pretexts for bringing his staff one by one into the room, and once they had entered Pershing was at their mercy, and the old gnarled General of the Armies [Pershing had begun to suffer from arthritic rheumatism at this time], still upright in spite of great age, shook hands with the stenographers as though he had come deliberately for that purpose."

Pershing soon thereafter wrote President Roosevelt recommending that Marshall be promoted to brigadier general, and the President sent a memorandum to the Secretary of War reading: "General Pershing asks very strongly Col. George S. Marshall (Infantry) be promoted to Brigadier. Can we put in list of next appointments? 54 years old." Secretary of War Dern, however, thought Marshall was "too young." Two years later Marshall was promoted to brigadier and assigned to command the 5th Infantry Brigade at Vancouver Barracks. Pershing, thanks to an earlier Roosevelt, had received his first star when he was ten years younger.

In the summer of 1938, Marshall was transferred to the General Staff in Washington as assistant chief of staff, War Plans Division. Although just recovered from a desperate illness, Pershing again took the trouble to jog the President's elbow on Marshall's behalf, since General Malin Craig, another former A.E.F. staff officer, would soon be retiring. Pershing went to the White House and told Roosevelt, "Mr. President, you have a man over there in the War Plans Division who has just come here—Marshall. Why don't you send for him and look him over? I think he will be a great help."

Fortunately President Roosevelt didn't resent this coaching from the ancient General of the Armies. On the contrary, he emphasized to Pershing that he was to consider himself always as being on active duty. He had reason to be grateful for Pershing's espousal of the Marshall cause: several years hence he would be saying that he couldn't sleep properly when Marshall was out of the country. Twenty years of Pershing sponsorship finally was repaid on September 1, 1939. That day, on which Germany invaded Poland, Marshall was sworn in as chief of staff. In the war years ahead, Pershing considered him the only man with the moral and intellectual capacity to direct the American forces scattered through Asia, Africa, and Europe, an opinion with which most men agreed.

Despite their differences over a wide range of matters, both personal and professional, Pershing and MacArthur eventually were reconciled. Pershing had always respected MacArthur as "a fighter," the only kind of soldier he had any use for, much as he was repelled by the flamboyance of MacArthur's methods. Was it really necessary for a brigade commander to indulge in such theatrical effects as wearing a floppy hat, a knee-length scarf, and a whangee cane while leading his men over the top? Then, too, there was the discomfiting memory of the scandal circulating at the time of MacArthur's first marriage.

While still chief of staff, however, MacArthur had eloquently and successfully opposed the Convery-Taber amendment to the Economy Act, which was designed to cut army retirement pay. Suggestions were made in the subcommittee concerned with the measure that Pershing's $18,000 annual pension be substantially reduced. To these proposals MacArthur indignantly replied that the British Government had been far more generous with Field Marshal Haig, awarding him a $500,-000 trust fund from which his heirs were also to receive the income three generations after his death.

Pershing, who had been wintering in Arizona, wrote from Tucson to thank MacArthur for defending his pension from an economy-minded Congress in that depression year of 1933: "Please allow me to send you my warmest congratulations upon the way you have succeeded in overcoming opposition in Congress to the Army. I think you have much to be thankful for, as we all have. And may I also express my appreciation for the way you have defended the Retired List and especially your reference to me."

Until he was well into his seventies and serious illness overtook him, Pershing kept himself moderately busy. For years he had been laboring over his personal account of commanding the A.E.F. The two-volume work was finally published and widely serialized in 1931, winning the Pulitzer prize for history that year. Considering the bitterness of the Battle of the Memoirs which follows every major war, his account was fairly free from acrimony of the personal kind; it was, in fact, devoid of personality, written in the colorless Olympian style characteristic of most high commanders, relieved only occasionally by the flashes of humor and insight which Pershing could display to his intimates. It is not difficult to believe his aides' insistence that Pershing wrote the book on his own, with only research help and editing from them. Some high-ranking Allied figures—Prime Minister Clemenceau, in particular —did not fare too well in *My Experiences in the World War,* nor was Foch unstintingly praised (as Pétain was), but he did not use his literary work as a platform to even old accounts. General March was mentioned only a half-dozen times, which may have been a comment in itself.

Once that was out of the way, Pershing settled down to write the story of his pre-World War I years, and judging from various drafts and fragments to be found in the Pershing Papers it would have been a far livelier volume. He labored over it for a half-dozen years, with the help of Colonels Curtin and Charles B. Shaw, whose marginal comments and queries sometimes were as sharp, critical, and demanding as those of any editor dealing with an unpublished author. Pershing the writer was far more amenable to criticism than Pershing the soldier had ever been.

His health failed before the story of his early life could be completed for publication. Just before his illness, however, he discussed a motion picture to be based on the work with a Hollywood producer. Gary Cooper was his choice to play the role of John J. Pershing, and considering the restrained style of that actor it was not a bad job of casting. A few years later, as a matter of fact, in *The Real Glory,* a story of the campaigns against the Moros, Cooper played the role of an army major who rather closely resembled Pershing in character and methods.

An extensive correspondence with old friends and comrades, and their widows, also took up much of his time. He was a particularly diligent sender of Christmas cards. Every year, Colonel Curtin recalls, Pershing would pore over the Blue Book listing army officers and their widows living in the Washington area. Occasionally he would pause at the name of a widow and say, "She hates my guts but send her one anyway."

His son Warren realized one summer that he had finally grown up in his father's eyes when he was twenty or twenty-one years old. Warren, then an undergraduate at Yale, was driving his father and his aunt May from Lincoln to Cheyenne. It was a rugged journey in those days, and after nightfall they ran into a driving rainstorm. The general usually sat in the back seat, calling out orders to the driver even though he had never learned to operate an automobile himself. On this rainy night Pershing was riding in the front, next to Warren, and, as his son recalls, "did a lot of back-seat driving from the front seat."

Warren was "getting madder and madder at his suggestions and criticisms. In fact, it's the only time I can recall being angry with the old gent.

"Finally I turned to him and said, 'Why in hell don't you stop telling me what to do? After all, I'm driving the car.'

"My father said, 'Yes, but it happens to be *my* car.'

"I said, 'But I happen to be the only one who can drive *your* car.' "

The journey continued in silence as the General of the Armies pondered this matter of insubordination. Pershing and his sister checked into a hotel in North Platte, Nebraska, while Warren brought in their luggage, including an old Gladstone bag which his father always carried on his travels and which contained many bottles of medicine and a flask of brandy.

"Up in our adjoining rooms, my father leaned out of the bathroom and waved the flask at me, and said, 'I think it's about time you and I had our first drink together.' I'd had a few drinks before which he didn't know about and which I saw no reason for mentioning. The invitation was my father's way of indirectly apologizing for his backseat driving and at the same time recognizing that I had reached manhood."

Warren grew up in his father's physical mold, with the same blond hair and gray-blue eyes, tall erect figure and soldierly bearing that distinguished the elder Pershing from his cadet days. But he had absolutely no desire to follow his father into the military profession. Pershing never pressed the point, though he was somewhat disappointed, when Warren showed no interest in entering West Point. He thoroughly respected his son's determination to make his own career. There is none of the "iron commander" manner which Pershing imposed on himself in the personality and outlook of his son. Apparently having inherited much of his uncle Jim's geniality and his maternal grandfather's talent for persuasion, Warren was elected the most popular man in his class at Yale. On graduation he headed straight for Wall Street and a growing prominence in the financial world. He now heads the large brokerage bearing his name.

In retirement, as during his A.E.F. command, Pershing's closest friends were General Harbord, who became president and later board chairman of the Radio Corporation of America on leaving the Army, and Charles G. Dawes, who was Vice-President under Coolidge. They frequently visited him in Washington and at the El Conquistador Hotel in Tucson during the winter. Harbord still addressed him with the deference of A.E.F. days as "General" and always remembered to send him telegrams on anniversaries and holidays; Dawes was the only man aside from his brother and sisters who called him "Jack." In their letters, Harbord and Pershing spent more time discussing their mutual literary efforts, the sales and reviews of their books, than military affairs. Harbord had authored two exceedingly valuable books on the A.E.F.—*Leaves from a War Diary* and *The American Army in France*. On September 22, 1936, Pershing wrote Harbord consolingly after Cameron Forbes, their mutual friend in Boston and former governor general of the Philippines, had been critical of the latter work in a newspaper review. "You must remember," Pershing wrote, "that neither of us is from Harvard and of course we are unable to give the Harvard touch to anything we do."

Pershing was in Paris when Harbord's first wife, the former Emma Ovenshine, the daughter of a general, died in the Harbord home at Rye, New York. "The little lady had your wonderful red roses on her last day on earth," Harbord wrote Pershing, addressing him as "my dear longtime friend." "You lost a good friend when Emma went away. She loved you not only for all you have been to me, but on her own accord. As the years went by, she had a constantly growing pride that you kissed the bride at our wedding."

Death and illness were taking so many of the friends he had known since service on the frontier. Pershing himself was resisting old age with all the vigor at his command, but he admitted in a letter to Harbord, "I am riding almost every day but the reporter who wrote in such glowing terms of my health stretched it considerably." Mr. and Mrs. Dawes were living in a cottage on the grounds of his hotel in Tucson and "we have done little but talk over old times."

Rather than settling down in one place, Pershing continued his migrations from hotel to hotel, in Tucson, Washington, New York, Paris, Chaumont. Death at least would have a hard time pinning him down. In London during the spring of 1937 he suffered a "slight" heart attack, and arthritis was making its inroads. Soon he was no longer able to take his morning rides. He substituted walks instead, even when a cane became necessary. He had to keep moving somehow.

Early in 1938 he fell seriously ill and was removed to the Desert Sanitarium outside Tucson. His heart and arteries were deteriorating and his kidneys had failed to function—and he was seventy-eight years old. His physician, Dr. Roland Davison, ordered him placed under an oxygen tent; his relatives were summoned, and newspapers were preparing his obituary, noting that Haig, Foch, Clemenceau, and most of the leading figures of the world war had already preceded him in death.

Through the month of February, Pershing, in a coma much of the time, struggled for his life, his face sunken and gray under the tent which kept him breathing. Specialists who examined him doubted that he could live more than a few weeks.

The Army prepared to undertake the last solemn rites in Arlington. His uniform was flown out. The IX Corps area dispatched a special train to take his body back to Washington, and Major General H. J. Brees was ordered from Fort Sam Houston to take charge of the arrangements.

All premature. The doctors had not reckoned sufficiently with his powerful constitution and his grip on life. The General of the Armies began to take disgusted notice of the grave, head-shaking atmosphere of his sickroom. He was highly annoyed when he became aware of the elaborate preparations being made to convey him to Arlington and the magnificence of his last rites. There might be a faltering beat in his arteries, but he wasn't ready for the beat of muffled drums and the last ride on the black-draped caisson. Anger seemed to act as a tonic. On March 1, the New York *Times* was able to announce that he had "improved considerably," furthermore that he was demanding solid nourishment.

His son, who was living with his aunt May in a wing of the sanitarium, told how the general rallied at the point of death. "One night the doctors said he couldn't live for more than a few days. You could almost see him sinking into death. Then, a few nights later, he made an almost visible effort to gather up his last resources of strength and vitality; it was as though he had made a firm decision not to die. Next morning he raised himself up and swung his legs over the side of the bed. His first words in days were, 'I want you to go ahead with your marriage.' I had planned to be married in April but thought it would have to be postponed. 'I'll be at your wedding,' he said."

Dr. Davison himself was convinced that Pershing was recovering a few mornings later when he started to leave the sickroom while Pershing was being served his breakfast. "Don't you go away," Pershing snapped. "You said you'd be right back and you'd better be."

Against his doctors' advice, Pershing not only attended Warren's wedding in New York the following month but made his annual pilgrimage to France. In August he was waiting in Paris when Warren and his bride stopped off there on their round-the-world honeymoon. His father was in their suite when a waiter brought up a large tray of wines and liquors with the compliments of the hotel. Pershing eyed the array of bottles and half seriously cautioned his son, "It doesn't mean you have to drink all of them, you know."

Once again war flamed on the horizon in Europe. Two decades earlier, Pershing had urged that the lesson of military defeat be impressed upon the whole German nation. By failing to advance farther than the Rhineland, the Allies, against his advice, allowed the German nationalists to proclaim before a new generation that their armies had never been defeated, that collapse and treachery at home had forced their withdrawal and the shameful submission to the Treaty of Versailles. Hitler and his Nazis, winning one reckless gamble after another, had cleared the French out of the Rhineland, engulfed Austria, bluffed the British and the French at Munich, seized part, then all of Czechoslovakia, and now were preparing to reach out for Danzig, the Corridor, Poland.

President Roosevelt was assuring American parents their sons would never fight another war. But he was a politician, aware of American opposition to entanglement in another European war. Pershing, less inhibited, began speaking out against the prevailing lassitude. In the spring of 1939 he urged that an army of 400,000 men be trained and organized immediately. Many of his fellow citizens considered him a senile old warmonger and approved of World Peaceways advertisements in the newspapers showing a crippled war veteran in a wheel chair and headed, "Hello, Sucker!"

Then France and England went to war with Germany and her allies, and it looked like 1918 all over again when the Germans, having blitzed Poland out of existence as a sovereign nation, turned a steamroller offensive loose and once again Sedan fell, the Meuse was crossed, the French and British armies were split apart . . . only this time the German war plan worked. Part of France was occupied; the rest became a Nazi vassal under Marshal Pétain, older than Pershing himself, a tragic and confused relic of more glorious days. With England standing alone against a Nazi-occupied continent, World War II appeared to be lost less than a year after it began.

On a warm May afternoon during the battle for France, President Roosevelt summoned the General of the Armies to the White House, partly for counsel, perhaps, but mostly to remind the American people of their historic relationship with France and England. Newspaper photographers gathered on the White House porch as Pershing, leaning heavily on his cane, approached the door. He wrathfully raised his cane; at eighty he still didn't want his picture taken until he looked his best. The photographers lowered their cameras until he could put his cane aside, draw himself up at attention, and glower at posterity like the younger Black Jack, his gray Homburg settled squarely on his white head, black suit sharply pressed, mustache clipped to a firm line of bristles, chin thrust out. Then he waved his cane almost jauntily and marched inside to see the President.

Shortly thereafter he made a nationwide radio address designed to counter, with all his prestige, the prevailing sentiment against involvement in the European crisis.

"It is not hysterical to insist that democracy and liberty are threatened," he told the nation. "By sending help to the British, we can still hope to keep this war on the other side of the Atlantic where the enemies of liberty, if possible, should be defeated. . . .

"And I am telling you tonight, because it is my duty to warn you before it is too late, that the British Navy needs destroyers and small craft to convoy merchant ships, to escort its warships and hunt submarines, and to repel invasions.

"We have an immense reserve of destroyers left over from the other war, and in a few months the British will be completing a large number of destroyers of their own. The most critical time, therefore, is the next few weeks or months. If there is anything we can do to save the British fleet during that time, we shall be failing in our duty to America if we do not do it.

"Tomorrow may be forever too late to keep war from the Americas."

Shortly afterward the United States, under a Lend-Lease arrangement, sent her overage destroyers to Britain.

Pershing made his last appearance at the annual dinner of the Baltic Society, which was composed of men who accompanied him to Europe as the advance element of the A.E.F. Harbord, as usual, sat on his right. On his left was his former aide, Major General George S. Patton, Jr., now commanding an armored division.

Long before the reunion dinner came to a close, he quietly rose from his place and left, on orders from his physician. His appearance shocked his old comrades that night, and most of them doubted they would ever see him alive again. "It seemed as though suddenly he had become a very old man," Frederick Palmer wrote. "His stoop, his feeble steps as he withdrew, suggested that whatever the course of events in the warring world he might not be alive on the next anniversary of the day of his departure in 1917 for Europe on the steamer *Baltic*."

Pershing soon entered Walter Reed Hospital to spend the rest of his days there, except for brief excursions outside. From that time on he would be wrapped in a cocoon of attention and solicitude, all but isolated from the world, all but forgotten as new armies were raised and new leaders were acclaimed. In the hospital he would be secure, he would be looked after properly, he would not have to face the numbing terror of a paralytic stroke alone in a hotel room, as must be expected by a man with his brittle arteries—so the doctors told him—but he went along unwillingly, cantankerously. He still hated to be fussed over, told what to eat and when to go to bed and whom he could see. He knew that this was a kind of surrender—conditional, perhaps, but no less humiliating to a man of his pride.

Never again did he go to the office in the State, War and Navy Building, now abandoned by the armed services in favor of the new Pentagon, but it was still his official headquarters, with "General of the Armies" on the door and Colonel Adamson sitting at his desk just inside. But his own office stayed empty from then on, its ornate fireplace cold, the long mirror over it reflecting no living presence.

Almost every day Colonel Adamson or Colonel Curtin went out to Walter Reed Hospital to discuss the general's correspondence. Often Colonel Curtin joined him on an afternoon ride through Rock Creek Park, whose bridle paths he had traveled every morning during his more vigorous years. A sergeant drove them—not Lanckton, he was gone like so many other friends.

General Marshall, now chief of staff, went out to the hospital every other Sunday afternoon to keep him posted on the growing United States Army and developments in Europe, where the Germans were invading Russia on a broad front and the British were fighting to maintain themselves in the Mediterranean. Recalling those visits, Mrs. Marshall wrote in *Together*: "Often I would go with him [General Marshall] and some Sundays we would lunch together in the General's sitting room. George would go over the whole situation with him and bring him up to date. General Pershing was very feeble at this time but still dapper and immaculate in his dress."

The news of Pearl Harbor, penetrating the walls of insulation his doctors designed to separate the old man from the wartime excitement, came as a distant thunderclap. He was told of the Japanese attack after his nap that December afternoon. His first thought, naturally dismaying to his doctors, was that somehow he could be of service to the government, if only as an adviser. The man who had disdained strategy as the empty theorizing of military intellectuals like Foch now spent hours studying maps of the world, communiqués from the fighting fronts, and newspaper dispatches, trying to relate this new kind of war, leaping from continent to continent on the wings of the long-range bombers which he had scorned in Mitchell's proselytizing days, to his own narrower experiences as a commander of expeditionary forces. Those columns he led against the Moros and against Villa, even the A.E.F. itself, must have seemed incredibly antiquated. Yet he felt that he had something to offer. He immediately wrote President Roosevelt a letter tendering his services to the "last ounce of my strength." The President replied, "You are magnificent. You always have been and you always will be"—but he made no mention of accepting the offer. Instead he regularly sent bouquets of red roses to Pershing's hospital suite.

The old general fretted in his unwelcome isolation, felt he was being ignored and neglected. Couldn't they find something for the General of the Armies to do? He was hurt, too, that General Marshall no longer had the time to come out to see him every other Sunday.

His only consolation was that his son, Warren, was keeping the Pershing name alive—though very quietly and inobtrusively—in the records of the Army of the United States. Warren had called him one day to announce, with some trepidation, that he had entered the Army as an enlisted man; he also wanted it made clear that he wanted no help from the Pershing legend, no influence brought to bear on his behalf by his father's friends. Subsequently, Warren was admitted to an officer candidate school and won his lieutenant's bars at Fort Belvoir in the Corps of Engineers. One gesture from his father's friends he could not forestall: General Marshall came over to Fort Belvoir to pin the insignia on him at the commissioning ceremony. A short time later General Patton wanted to make Warren his aide, as Patton had been Pershing's, but the latter advised against it and told Patton that Warren was determined to "make it on his own." By the war's end, Warren had risen to the rank of major, had served with the 75th Division and later on the staff of the First Army in its operations from Normandy to the Elbe.

Feeling ignored and forgotten as he did, Pershing sometimes tended to view events with a jaundiced eye. "There seems to be a lack of confidence in the management of affairs. . . ." he wrote Harbord in the spring of 1942, and he still suspected the British of being inclined to treat the Americans as a colonial army. "There is one phase of this that I am rather uneasy about and that is the tendency of the British to grab the command wherever the troops are thrown together."

Pershing was offended when generals departing for commands abroad failed to take their leave of him. He believed they owed that much to the General of the Armies, busy and preoccupied though they might be. Eisenhower had never been one of "Pershing's boys," but the old man was highly irritated when the leader of the second A.E.F. hurried off to Europe without seeing him. "I don't even know the man," Pershing growled when someone brought up Eisenhower's name a short time later.

Patton, now, whatever anyone said about his tendency to bellow and his pistol-packing showmanship, had a proper cavalryman's respect for the amenities. When Patton left Pershing's headquarters in 1917 to take up tank training instead of remaining as his aide, Pershing had written Mrs. Patton, "This is the second time Patton has left my staff. I am writing to tell you he has not been fired." Pershing, however, managed to forgive him for quitting the horse cavalry in favor of the "clanking iron monsters."

Before leaving the States to command the armored forces in the North African campaign, General Patton called on his old commander and wrote in his diary that day (October 11, 1942):

". . . He did not recognize me until I spoke. Then his mind seemed quite clear. He looks very old. It is probably the last time I shall see him but he may outlive me. [He did.] I said that when he took me to Mexico in 1916 he gave me my start. He replied, 'I can always pick a fighting man and God knows there are few of them. I am happy they are sending you to the front at once. I like Generals so bold that they are dangerous. I hope they give you a free hand.' He recalled my killing the Mexicans and when I told him I was taking the same pistol he said, 'I hope you kill some Germans with it.' "

Pershing told him that "at the start of the war he was hurt because no one consulted him, but he was now resigned to sit on the sidelines with his feet hanging over."

Patton said that Pershing "almost cried" as he told of being ignored. "It is pathetic how little he knows of the war.

"When I left I kissed his hand and asked for his blessing. He squeezed my hand and said, 'Good-by George, God bless you and keep you, and give you victory.'

"I put my hat on and saluted when I left, and he returned it like he used to, and twenty-five years seemed to drop from him. He said that when he started World War I he was just my age. A truly great soldier."

The following year, when the late Henry Wales of the Chicago *Tribune* visited him, having maintained an acquaintance with the general since covering A.E.F. Headquarters in the other war, Pershing complained "on several occasions" that no one came to see him any more. "I haven't seen Marshall for a long, long time. Those maps you see"—he gestured toward the wall, which was covered with maps clipped from newspapers—"are all I have seen." The calumny heaped on Marshal Pétain as chief of state of the Vichy regime also bewildered Pershing. "The general," Wales wrote, "cannot believe that the Marshal is a traitor and cannot understand the reasons why Pétain, after those years of service, is in disgrace."

Pétain's fate, as a matter of fact, preyed on the old man's mind almost to the day of his death.

When General Harbord sent him a copy of Philip Guedalla's just published *The Two Marshals,* a corrosive study of the lives of Bazaine (who surrendered Metz in 1871) and Pétain, Pershing wrote a letter of thanks and added that "I shall be particularly interested in reading this indictment of Marshal Pétain."

Undoubtedly Harbord was reflecting Pershing's opinion, too, when he wrote the general, "This man Guedalla is one of the most brutal writers in a keen, smooth way that I have read. . . . I think the book is unjust to Pétain. . . . I think he is the victim of the most unfortunate lot of circumstances that ever faced a Commander in his old age. I do not think it was a defeatist tendency of Pétain that lost the war in France. It was the character of the French themselves—the tendency to Communism, with the Blum Front Populaire, and all those things. . . . It is a calamity that these things struck Marshal Pétain in his old age, but I think the old boy has done as well as anybody could with the same setup."

In this mutual loyalty to their old friend, the two elderly gentlemen stood almost alone, refusing to blame Pétain for the excesses of the Vichy regime or the brutal oppressions of its Nazi-directed police.

The memories they shared, and the understanding, the inobtrusive sympathy Harbord gave him in those war years when everyone else seemed to have forgotten him, were a constant prop to Pershing's morale as he sat day after day in his wheel chair, placed at the window of his suite, watching the play of a fountain in the courtyard outside.

Harbord always remembered to write or telegraph on the anniversary of the Battle of Saint-Mihiel. On September 11, 1943, Harbord wrote that "I am thinking about how your mind must be turning this afternoon to the eve of St. Mihiel twenty-five years ago—to the rush of great events transpiring around you as a center and inspiration that night. . . . We both have a lot of precious memories . . . a lot that no one else has. . . . What a life you have lived, what a record you made, what miracles you wrought. . . . You will loom larger and larger in history as the years go by. . . ."

A year later Harbord wrote him, "It is very cheering to read of the achievements of Patton, Patch and others, and I think your training and your example live on in the achievements of the American Armies during the last few months. It must have made you a little homesick to read of the place names, as it did me."

Just once Pershing was permitted to step toward the center of the wartime stage. That was during the fall of 1943 when the British and American joint chiefs of staff decided at their Quebec meeting that General Marshall would be named to command OVERLORD, the invasion of Normandy, and Eisenhower would be recalled to take over as chief of staff. President Roosevelt, Secretary of War Stimson, and Marshall himself, above all, wanted the latter to lead the invasion of the Nazi-held French coast. Many high-ranking officers in Washington were alarmed at the prospect, believed that only Marshall had the capacity to oversee the campaigns in all the theaters of war. They prevailed on General Malin Craig, former chief of staff and presently head of the War Department's Personnel Board, to persuade General Pershing to write President Roosevelt protesting the Marshall-Eisenhower transfer. Pershing agreed at once and on September 16, 1943, wrote the President:

"I am so greatly disturbed by the repeated newspaper reports that General Marshall is to be transferred to the tactical command in England, that I am writing to express my fervent hope that these reports are unfounded.

"We are engaged in a global war of which the end is still far distant, and for the wise strategical guidance of which we need our most accomplished officer as Chief of Staff. I voice the consensus of informed military opinion in saying that officer is General Marshall. To transfer him to a tactical command in a limited area, no matter how seemingly important, is to deprive ourselves of the benefit of his outstanding strategical ability and experience. I know of no one at all comparable to replace him as Chief of Staff.

"I have written this, Mr. President, because of my deep conviction that the suggested transfer of General Marshall would be a fundamental and very grave error in our military policy."

A very flatteringly phrased "no" was President Roosevelt's reply four days later. His letter to Pershing read:

"You are absolutely right about George Marshall—and yet, I think you are wrong, too. He is, as you say, far and away the most valuable man as Chief of Staff. But, as you know, the operations for which we are considering him are the biggest that we will conduct in this war. . . . The best way I can express it is to tell you that I want George to be the Pershing of the second World War—and he cannot be if we keep him here. I know you will understand."

Several months later, however, Roosevelt decided against naming Marshall as Supreme Commander in Europe and told him, "I feel now that I will not be able to sleep at night with you out of the country." Pershing's letter must have played some part in persuading the President to change his mind, with the result that Eisenhower stayed on to lead his "crusade in Europe" and with that enormous prestige as his springboard to serve two terms in the presidency.

Pershing and Harbord frequently discussed the various American commanders in their letters and decided that MacArthur was the ablest of the generals in the field, that Patton was the best combat leader in the European theater. "Am glad to see MacArthur doing so well," Pershing wrote Harbord late in 1944, at the height of MacArthur's steppingstone campaign across the western Pacific. "I am sure that you, like all the other oldtimers who have served in the Islands, have been particularly thrilled by his recent successes." Neither was particularly enthusiastic about Eisenhower, Harbord writing on February 20, 1945, "Confidentially, I do not see much to General Eisenhower except as a great coordinator of a lot of different agencies. Perhaps I do him an injustice though." Pershing thought the command in Europe should have gone to General Lesley McNair, who was kept at home to supervise the ground-force training but who was killed while observing operations in Normandy when American bombers attacked their own troops' positions by mistake. The highest praise Pershing could give an officer was to say that "he's a fighter, a *fighter*." Eisenhower had to subordinate the "fighter's" role to his wider responsibilities; he was the Foch, not the Pershing, of World War II.

As for the way the American operations in Europe were conducted, according to Frederick Palmer, Pershing was opposed to the costly and laborious campaign up the Italian peninsula and favored striking directly across the Channel at the French coast rather than assaulting the Norman beaches.

He was determined to live long enough to see another Allied victory, and this wish was granted him in full measure. He took great comfort in Harbord's letter on V-E Day, May 8, 1945: "I still think ours was a properly fought war and that you are the greatest soldier of our time and, if your views had been adopted at the end of the last war, the present one would not have occurred." Very few veterans of World War I would not have agreed with him; the end of that war left more than its share of untidy and complex problems, but the Russo-American confrontation on the Elbe, the fatal hesitation to take Berlin, the Russian seizures in eastern Europe, pointed to an even untidier future.

Close to the end of the war in the Pacific, from one of its remotest corners, came word of an incident peculiarly satisfying to the eighty-five-year-old general in Walter Reed Hospital. Shortly after the victory over the Japanese forces on Mindanao, General Robert Eichelberger, the army commander under MacArthur, General George Kenney, the Air Force commander in that area, and Major General Jens Doe, commanding the 24th Division, landed on the island of Jolo. The first man who came to greet them was the wizened old Sultan of Jolo, who recalled that he had submitted to Captain Pershing as a young warrior in 1905. Ever since then, he said, he had been loyal to the Americans. Japanese soldiers who ventured any distance from their posts were invariably killed by the Moros. The Japanese occupation forces in the southern Philippines, in fact, feared the Moros far more than the returning American Army. In that far corner of the Pacific, at least, the work of Black Jack Pershing was not forgotten.

18. Muffled Drums—and Taps

In his last years Pershing was the unwilling and occasionally rebellious captive of his doctors, his nurses, and his severely watchful sister May. His world had shrunken to the confines of the two-room penthouse on the third floor of the Walter Reed Hospital, quarters which he often urged the doctors to turn over to the war wounded. He was caged in the antiseptic hush of hospital routine, of cajoling doctors, and of dietitians proclaiming the virtues of poached eggs and creamed spinach, and worst of all in the growingly helpless husk of his once powerful body. May Pershing moved into the penthouse suite to keep him company, see to it that he obeyed the doctors, and bar the door to all but a few visitors—Harbord, Dawes, Warren and his wife (who had provided Pershing with two grandsons, John and Richard).

The general was bored, restless, resentful in his necessary confinement. He protested when his office was finally moved to the Pentagon. When the War Department asked him to pose for a photograph, he told them to go to hell. He didn't want to be remembered this way. All he wanted now was to be left alone.

There was the De Gaulle Incident to prove his point. When the leader of the Free French came to Washington, someone thought it would be a nice gesture to present him to Pershing, apparently unaware of his stubborn sympathy for Marshal Pétain, who was to spend his last years in an island prison.

"And how is Marshal Pétain?" Pershing demanded, amid general consternation, immediately after being introduced to the Free French leader.

Most of those present, regarding the question as tactless, if not insulting, looked as though the roof had fallen on them.

General de Gaulle, who once served under Pétain, understood the soldierly spirit in which the question was asked. He handled himself "admirably," according to one person present at the meeting, and didn't even blink at the blunt question. So far as he knew, he gravely and politely replied, the marshal was in good health.

Aside from those infrequent recognitions of his past fame, an occasional hearty lunch was one of the few consolations permitted the old man. Every noon the staff dietitian would appear and read off the menu, which was seldom inspiring to a man of Pershing's educated palate.

"Jackie," Miss Pershing would say to her brother, using the name by which she had called him since childhood and which never failed to startle any new member of the hospital staff present, "why don't you have some of this nice clear soup."

Pershing would glower at her over the rim of his glasses. "May, you do as you please about eating and let me alone!"

Fairly often he would be permitted to send over to the Carlton for a dozen oysters or some other dish he fancied—invariably over the protests of his sister.

Once he threatened to move out of his "prison" and back to the Carlton, but Major General Shelly Marietta, the head of Walter Reed Hospital, talked him out of it.

Just once Pershing managed to have a brief fling outside the hospital walls, when he went A.W.O.L. for the first time in his life. How that happened has been related by Colonel John M. Virden, one of whose duties on reassignment to the Pentagon was to take charge of a bulky folder titled "Procedures to be followed in the event of the death of General John J. Pershing." The first order of procedure read:

"You, as the responsible officer, will be the first person notified in the event of the passing of General Pershing. At whatever hour this message reaches you, whether day or night, you will immediately notify the President of the United States, in person."

All the documents in that folder hardly prepared Colonel Virden for what happened a short time later.

One day he received an excited call from Walter Reed: "General Pershing has disappeared!"

This was one eventuality the Pentagon hadn't counted on. Virden began calling everyone who had known Pershing and finally came up with a lead. Pershing had always been very fond of the sedate old Carlton, where he had lived off and on for many years. The colonel checked with the hotel and found that Pershing had indeed moved in.

A doctor was dispatched immediately from Walter Reed. He found the general in his old suite, brooding over the remains of a feast. Pershing had checked into the hotel that morning, demanded a large drink of bourbon to whet his appetite, and then ordered up a roast-duck dinner with all the trimmings. He was just sipping a pony of brandy when the doctor arrived.

"Ah, sir," he growled at the doctor, "you've found me, have you? Well, you can remove yourself from my sight now while I finish my brandy."

The doctor withdrew as ordered, and a few minutes later his patient consented to return to the hospital and his diet of cottage cheese and baby food.

The visits of his friends, Harbord and Dawes, were fewer and fewer with each passing year. Dawes could barely walk with the help of a cane, but he was still talkative and jovial. Harbord had been stricken with nephritis and barely survived. He wrote Pershing on April 11, 1946, explaining why he hadn't visited the capital for almost a year: "I have more friends in Arlington than I have in Washington." The next year he resigned as chairman of the board of RCA, and five weeks later, on August 20, 1947, Major General James G. Harbord, one of the three or four ablest officers who served with the A.E.F., died quietly in his home outside New York. By then the world outside, even the deaths of his closest friends, had become very dim and far away to the General of the Armies. He had suffered a stroke which paralyzed one side of his body, and he had to be lifted in and out of bed. He spent his days in a rather odd costume: a pair of pajamas from Sulka with a high Russian collar, around which he fastened a tie, and four dressing gowns and bathrobes to keep any stray draft from chilling an old man's bones. Frail and sunken-eyed, he passed hours in his wheel chair, staring out at the fountain in the courtyard and perhaps, through the veil of water, recaptured other and happier, livelier scenes. Few men, certainly, were able to look back on a fuller life, with heaping measures of personal tragedy and public triumph.

No one except members of his immediate family and the hospital staff came to the door any more. Mlle. Resco had spent the wartime years in Washington and frequently visited him, but she had returned to Paris and was living in the apartment in the Rue des Renaudes, its walls covered with mementos, a bronze bust and a portrait of Pershing in the salon, krises and other weapons seized during his Philippine campaigns, several swords presented to him by Allied governments, one of the red, white, and blue pennants that flew from his automobile on his tours of the front in 1917 and 1918.

Henry Wales of the Chicago *Tribune,* one of the few newspapermen Pershing ever took into his confidence, called at the hospital in September of 1947 to find the door guarded against all visitors by May Pershing. He caught only a glimpse of Pershing:

"Propped up by four pillows, the General lay on a narrow cot near the window, his eyes wide open and fixed on me in the doorway. They flickered as he recognized me and he moved as though to speak, but Miss Pershing tugged at my arm. 'I'm sorry I can't let you talk to him,' she whispered, 'but they have given me specific instructions he cannot receive visitors.'"

During the summer of the following year, Pershing sank lower and lower, his pulse only a faint flutter, his eyes clouded with the recognition of death. Washington was full of excitement that summer; the Russians had denied their former allies access to Berlin and the tremendous effort required to supply the former German capital by air was under way; and there were rumors that World War III could break out at any moment.

Preoccupied as it was, however, the capital took pause at the final bulletin to be issued from the Pershing suite at Walter Reed Hospital.

The General of the Armies was dead.

At 3:50 A.M. on the morning of July 15, 1948, in his eighty-eighth year, John J. Pershing simply stopped living. The cause of death was given as arteriosclerosis and auricular fibrillation.

Outside of the family, President Truman was the first to be informed of his death, receiving the news as he stepped off a train from Philadelphia shortly before dawn at the Union Station. The President had served in the A.E.F. as a captain in the field artillery. "Embodied in General Pershing's character," he said, "were all those soldierly qualities that are essential to a great captain: brilliant leadership, steadfast courage, tireless energy, unswerving loyalty and constant devotion to duty."

All over Washington the mimeograph machines ground out the official tributes. General Marshall, then Secretary of State, said that Pershing had "perfection in soldierly qualities, dynamic leadership, and American patriotism. A great soldier, devoid of personal and political ambitions . . . his influence went far toward shaping the destinies of our armies in two great wars."

To Secretary of Defense Forrestal he "symbolized the best in the military traditions of our nation."

Secretary of War Kenneth C. Royall emphasized that he should be remembered for his service as chief of staff, the development of a citizens' army, the modernization of the General Staff, and the expansion of the system of military education as well as his victories in the field, and that he should be credited with "the development of techniques which led to the victories of World War II."

Old grudges long forgotten, General MacArthur, commanding the occupation forces in Tokyo, said that "Pershing represented the legendary ideal of a past era" and that his qualities would be "stamped on the United States Army for all time."

Three days later Pershing's body lay in state, resting on the catafalque fashioned for Abraham Lincoln, in the rotunda of the Capitol.

The next day, July 19, Pershing was given one of the most impressive funerals in Washington's history. The procession moved in a driving rain from the Capitol to Arlington, where he was to be buried on a slope which had once been part of Robert E. Lee's estate. Three thousand five hundred soldiers, sailors, and marines, including the 456th Airborne Field Artillery Battalion from Fort Bragg, the 3rd Infantry Regiment from Fort Myer, and 500 West Point upperclassmen marched along the four-mile route to the slow beat of muffled drums. Three hundred thousand persons watched the procession.

The casket was borne on a caisson, followed by a caparisoned black horse with reversed boots in the stirrups.

Generals Eisenhower and Bradley led the General Staff and a large group of general officers, in a rain-spattered phalanx, down the broad avenues to Arlington.

There was a brief Episcopal service at the graveside, with General Marshall and members of the Pershing family standing nearby.

Nineteen guns boomed a last salute to the General of the Armies.

Taps sounded sweet and clear through the heavy summer air.

Then soldiers and civilians alike turned slowly back to Washington to deal with a kind of non-shooting war which could hardly have been imagined by the general who was being lowered into the earth with all the dead memories of Indian wars and colonial campaigns.

He should have died content; all the honor that the nation owed him was paid in full. In the muster roll of American generalship he is enshrined for all time as one of a very small and select company: George Washington, Winfield Scott, Ulysses S. Grant, Robert E. Lee, possibly one or two of the World War II generals. The Army has never let his name be forgotten; a tank and a missile presently are named for him, and more importantly he is held up as the best recent example of the prescribed military career. No one in American military history deviated less from what was expected of an officer. He was strictly Government Issue.

His achievements owed more to character than intellect, to strength and simplicity and clearheadedness rather than to originality, native genius, or even talent. "If he was not a great man," wrote Frank H. Simonds, "there have been few stronger."

Despite what were uttered as verbal wreaths on his death, he was not a great captain, certainly not in the sense of a Caesar, a Napoleon, a Belisarius, or a Lee. He was the kind of practical, sensible, straight-thinking soldier, in direct lineage to Wellington and Grant, who was victorious when he was supplied with the means of victory. Innately he was aware of this; "furnish me with the men, the equipment and the supplies," he said at the start of World War I, and he would do the job. How well he would have done with inferior resources or fighting against insuperable odds can never be known. He was never confronted by an enemy who could outnumber or outgun him.

And there were two serious deficiencies in his nature which barred him from military greatness. One was his lack of ability to inspire the men under him; he could make them do their duty but rarely more, and never with a soaring enthusiasm; the cheers he heard were always a trifle sullen. Shyness enclosed in a brusque and peremptory manner gave the impression of a cold-blooded driver. To the A.E.F. as a whole, he was the granite-faced man in the rear of a Cadillac that splashed mud on them as they marched to the front. He not only lacked the common touch but despised it. It rarely occurred to him that citizen-soldiers, unlike the tough professionals he led in the Philippines, might expect a fatherly smile now and then.

Another defect was his strong conservatism, his attitude toward unorthodox men, new weapons and methods. He allowed the employment of tank and plane, but they never aroused much enthusiasm in him. Neither he nor any of his high-ranking contemporaries seemed to grasp how war was being transformed by technology. To him a soldier was a man with a rifle, not an operator of weird mechanisms.

The most amazing thing about the Pershing legend was his absolute rightness for every important situation in which he was cast in a leading role, a rightness that owed more to his ability than to the famous "Pershing luck." His achievements as a soldier and administrator in the southern Philippines were one of the most attractive parts of his career. In dealing with the Moros on a human level, he was an innovator, ahead of his time, progressive in colonial administration as he was conservative in large-scale warfare. There he showed elements of greatness, in a far corner of the world where his name is still honored above all other white men. In the futile pursuit of Villa he behaved with dignity, discretion, and forbearance—exactly what was required of him. His career bridged the Old Army of the last century and the modern army which fought two world wars; "not the last of the Old," as the faithful Harbord wrote, "he is one of the first of the New."

All that he was trained to be, all the remarkable opportunities handed to him were more than balanced by his performance as the commander in chief in France. There have been many justifiable criticisms of his ability as a diplomat, administrator, and tactician. He was an abrasive influence on Allied councils, made many mistakes in organizing and equipping his army, and lacked deceptiveness, subtlety, and originality in fighting his campaigns (all qualities which tended to be submerged, in any case, in the slugging matches of the western front). He was no military statesman. A military statesman would have knuckled under to the Allies, with incalculable results. Instead, Pershing clung to one idea: the American Army would fight as an integrated force under his command.

No other available man could have matched his accomplishments in France. There his single-mindedness was invaluable. A less determined man, even if he had managed to keep his army intact from the encroachments of the Allies, might well have hesitated at the fearful day-by-day cost of the fighting in the Meuse-Argonne. It took more than genius, or inspiration, or what Lawrence of Arabia called the "irrational tenth" of intuition and insight, to break the Hindenburg

Line, to keep hammering when it was a question of whether his own men or the enemy would crack first. When he found staff officers considering the possibilities of retreat, as was their duty, he told them, "Never mind planning how to conduct a retreat. You find out how to get guns and wagons over bad roads and enemy trenches—damn quick." That was his style and his method—limited, undoubtedly, but effective enough in that set of circumstances. The best summation of his achievements in France was written by Captain Liddell Hart, one of the severest critics of World War I generalship. "There was perhaps no other man who would, or could, have built the American Army on the scale he planned. And without that army the war could hardly have been saved and could not have been won." No American historian could have paid him a more resounding tribute.

What he was and what he stood for, both as a man and a general, will always be a part of the American military tradition. If he did not achieve the romantic designation of great captain, he was one of a larger but no less worthy company. He was a good soldier in every hour of his life.

NOTES ON SOURCES AND BIBLIOGRAPHY

The author is especially indebted to Mr. F. Warren Pershing, of New York, for reminiscing at length about his father, and on the same score to Colonels Ralph A. Curtin and Charles B. Shaw, both of whom went overseas on the *Baltic* as field clerks and later served for many years on the general's staff. Colonel Curtin, a wise and witty Irishman, now secretary of the United States District Court for the District of Columbia's Committee on Admissions and Grievances, served with Pershing for thirty years, until his death. Colonel Shaw, now attached to the American Battle Monuments Commission, was a member of Pershing's office staff for twenty years. Both of these gentlemen, along with Mr. Pershing, deserve much gratitude for having preserved and having placed in such excellent order the vast collection of Pershing Papers, now in custody of the Library of Congress's Manuscript Division. The author also appreciates the various kinds of assistance provided by David C. Mearns, Daniel J. Reed, John de Porry, and their colleagues in that library's Manuscript Division; two fellow workers in the same field, Mr. A. A. Hoehling and Donald Smythe, S.J., Georgetown University, both of Washington; Mr. Will Fowler, of Encino, California, and Mr. L. F. Moore, chairman of the Pershing Park Memorial Association, Laclede, Missouri.

The task of any Pershing biographer, of course, has been immensely aided by the recent availability of his papers. Their range is enormous: journals and notebooks kept in his early years as an officer, almost 200 large boxes of correspondence, twenty-eight huge scrapbooks, his war diary (continued for several years afterward), the various drafts for an unpublished memoir of his pre–World War I career, and practically every Christmas card and invitation he received. The general attached a great deal of sentimental significance to Christmas cards. In the millions of words contained in this collection, most of the days of his life are accounted for —but only in physical detail and occasionally in his opinion on public matters. He rarely revealed the man underlying the officer, apparently considering this of little significance or historic interest. To reveal himself would have violated his sense of proportion. He always insisted that he must be judged on the record. The record, with a few curious lapses, is there for everyone to see.

The author is neither a "scholar" nor a military historian, in any formal sense, but the following notes account for the bulk of the sources used in this work.

CHAPTER 1

The descriptions of Laclede and Pershing's early years were drawn from Pershing's notes for his unpublished memoir, Box Nos. 373, 374, and 380, Pershing Papers, and data supplied by the Pershing Park Memorial Association of Laclede. Information on the Pershing ancestry came principally from *Family Tree*, by the Reverend J. H. Pershing, an undated pamphlet privately published in Greensburg, Pennsylvania, which may be found in the Pershing Papers, and from *The Pershing Family in America*, by E. J. Pershing. Other details of Pershing's boyhood years may be found in Tomlinson's and Palmer's earlier Pershing biographies, as well as Avery D. Andrews's memoir, *My Friend and Classmate, John J. Pershing*.

An account of Pershing's fist fighting was given in the *Missouri Historical Record* for April–July 1917; Clay Biggers's recollections on the same subject, in the Kansas City *Star*, July 9, 1916. Perry Floyd's characterization of Pershing as a boy was included in George MacAdam's series on Pershing for *The World's Work*, November 1918. MacAdam's series was invaluable on Pershing's life up to World War I, since MacAdam, an able and diligent reporter, interviewed many of the persons (now dead) who knew him in his youth.

Information on his college education from the records of the Northeast Missouri State Teachers College at Kirksville, Missouri. His sister May's recollection of his concern over his appearance from McCracken's *Pershing*. West Point reminiscences are drawn from Andrews's *My Friend and Classmate* and Lieutenant General Robert Lee Bullard's candid and clear-eyed *Personalities and Reminiscences*.

Pershing's own memories of his first days at West Point were contained in a letter to the Class of 1886, written March 15, 1911, from Zamboanga, Mindanao. His communications to his classmates invariably conveyed a depth of affection and nostalgia rarely found in any of his other writings.

Pershing's painful recitation was described by his classmate Walcott in Andrews's memoir. Same source for Pershing's description of the trip west to his first post, a letter dated March 9, 1887, and addressed to his class.

Sources for his participation in the Apache campaign of 1886 include his unpublished memoir, Box 380, Pershing Papers; Lieutenant General Nelson A. Miles's *Serving the Republic;* Fairfax Downey's *Indian-Fighting Army;* Paul I. Wellman's *The Indian Wars of the West;* Andrews's *My Friend and Classmate,* and MacAdam's series in *The World's Work,* November 1918.

Pershing as one of the "Three Green Peas" was described by Sophie A. Poe in her *Buckboard Days.* She was the wife of John Poe, the peace officer who accompanied Sheriff Pat Garrett the night Billy the Kid was shot and killed. Fort Stanton had been the center of strife and scandal during the Lincoln County cattle war several years before Pershing served there. Its commanding officer, Lieutenant Colonel Nathan A. M. Dudley, was removed for openly taking sides in the long and bloody dispute between the cattle barons headed by John Chisum and the smaller ranchers of the Murphy-Dolan-Riley faction. Lucrative government beef contracts were at the bottom of the Army's involvement. In addition to Pat Garrett and John Poe, Pershing also made the acquaintance of Buffalo Bill Cody during this period, and in later years was inordinately proud of his meetings with these frontier celebrities.

Pershing's capture of the three horse thieves on the Zuñi reservation was described by 6th Cavalry officers to MacAdam, *The World's Work,* November 1918. Same source for Sergeant Stephenson's praise of his qualities as an officer. Description of Pershing's activities during the Wounded Knee campaign from his notes in Box 380, Pershing Papers.

CHAPTER 2

Pershing's career as a faculty member of the University of Nebraska was described in MacAdam's series, *The World's Work,* March 1919; Andrews's *My Friend and Classmate,* and notes and drafts for his unpublished memoir in Box 380, Pershing Papers. His friendship with Charles G. Dawes was told in Dawes's *A Journal of the Great War.* Dawes's early political career is outlined in Margaret Leech's *In the Days of McKinley.* Colonel William Hayward's statement was given MacAdam for his *The World's Work* series, March 1919.

Meeting of Pershing and Theodore Roosevelt was described in Andrews's *My Friend and Classmate.* MacAdam dug out the West Point source of Pershing's "Nigger Jack" and "Black Jack" nicknames, *The World's Work,* March 1919.

Official descriptions of Pershing's role in the Santiago campaign were contained in the reports to the Adjutant General's Office of the 10th Cavalry's officers, Colonel Baldwin, Major Wint, commanding the 2nd Squadron, and Lieutenant John Bigelow, Jr., commanding Troop D, whose place Pershing took after Bigelow was wounded. Pershing's account of the Cuban fighting was delivered before the Hyde Park Methodist Episcopal Church in Chicago the evening of November 27, 1898. His brother Jim was a lay official of the church. All the quotations attributed to Pershing are from this account. Regarding the Cuban campaign, Pershing was particularly proud of the fact that one of the first volunteer regiments to offer its services was the 1st Nebraska from the University of Nebraska. A firsthand account of the 71st New York Volunteers' panicked retreat at San Juan Hill was quoted in William A. Ganoe's *The History of the United States Army*.

Pershing was recommended for staff duty by Colonel Leonard Wood, who praised him for "marked gallantry and efficiency" in the advance on Santiago in a letter dated July 30, 1898, and addressed to the Adjutant General's Office. At least twice, Wood boosted Pershing's career, then and later in the Philippines. Pershing, however, rejected Wood for a divisional command in the A.E.F.

Root's work with the Bureau of Insular Affairs is concisely told in Margaret Leech's *In the Days of McKinley*.

Pershing's story of his tour of the Woolwich Arsenal is from a draft for his unpublished memoir, Box 374, Pershing Papers.

CHAPTER 3

Pershing's estimate of the Moro character was included in a field-message notebook which he used briefly as a diary early in his Philippine tour, Box 1, Pershing Papers.

A report on General Smith's "kill and burn" orders and his concentration camps appeared in the Manila *Times* of November 4, 1901. The general was subsequently court-martialed, but his sentence was light. He was "to be admonished."

The religious and political background of the southern Philippines is concisely analyzed in Volume II of Cameron Forbes's *The Philippine Islands*. As governor general of the islands, Forbes was an unusually keen and sympathetic observer.

The Moro laws are quoted from the Mangindanao Code in *Studies in Moro History, Law and Religion*, Department of the Interior Ethnological Survey Publications, Volume IV, Manila, 1905.

The account of the Cagayan River campaign was drawn from Captain

Mays's and Pershing's reports to departmental headquarters, Box 1, Pershing Papers. Also the general in chief's report for 1901.

Pershing's comment on Colonel Baldwin's intentions was made in notes for his unpublished memoir, Box 373, Pershing Papers. Bullard's observations on Pershing's receiving the Camp Vicars command from *Personalities and Reminiscences*. Pershing's playing chess with the Moros and entertaining them at the Fourth of July celebration were described to MacAdam (*The World's Work,* May 1919) by officers who had served at Camp Vicars.

The Manila *Times* account of the storming of the Sultan of Maciu's fort was published October 22, 1902; its editorial praising his "attitude toward the customs of the people," April 10, 1903.

Incident of Pershing and the "talking machine" and his persuasion of the Moro chiefs from the *Army Register*, September 20, 1958. Description of Pershing's visit to the Sultan of Bayan's stronghold from the Manila *Times* issues of November 1903; MacAdam's series in *The World's Work*, May 1919, and notes for his memoir, Box 374, Pershing Papers. Pershing's boast of his influence with the Moros and his adoption of four Moro children are contained in a field-message notebook he kept briefly as a diary, Box 1, Pershing Papers.

A copy of Pershing's report on the capture of Fort Bacolod may be found in his field notebook, Box 1, Pershing Papers. Regarding the Moro losses at Bacolod, the Manila *Times* correspondent estimated them at 120 to 150 killed.

Pershing's description of the action at Taraca was contained in telegrams to General Sumner at the Malabang base, copies of which may be found in a field-message notebook, Box 3, Pershing Papers. The interview with Henry Savage Landor appeared in the Hong Kong *China Mail* July 11, 1903. Clippings describing Pershing's return to the United States and visits with his family may be found in Box 381, Pershing Papers. Secretary of War Root's remark concerning Pershing's promotion to brigadier was quoted in Andrews's *My Friend and Classmate*.

CHAPTER 4

A concise account of the formation of the General Staff, and arguments for and against it, may be found in Ganoe's *History of the United States Army*.

Senator Warren's background and early career were described in a *Saturday Evening Post* article, December 2, 1911. Descriptions of his daughter from the Washington *Post* and *Star*, January 10, 1905; also from

MacAdam's series (*The World's Work*, May 1919), which contained details of her romance with and marriage to Pershing. A detailed account of the wedding was carried by the *Army and Navy Journal* in its January 28, 1905, issue.

The historic significance of the Russo-Japanese War is brilliantly analyzed in Major General J. F. C. Fuller's *A Military History of the Western World*, Volume III.

Pershing's recollections of the other military attachés in Manchuria were included partly in his published memoir, *My Experiences in the World War*, also in notebooks to be found in Box 3, Pershing Papers. Activities at the observers' camp were described in Frederick Palmer's *With My Own Eyes*, General Max Von Hoffmann's *The War of Lost Opportunities*, and Palmer's *With Kuroki in Manchuria*.

Pershing's report as the United States military observer was included in Box 371, Pershing Papers.

Bullard's comment on Pershing's promotion, *Personalities and Reminiscences*. Pershing himself clipped a wide selection of the editorial comment on his promotion (Box 381, Pershing Papers). Pershing's demand for the arrest of a hotel doorman is mentioned in Colonel R. Ernest Dupuy's *Compact History of the United States Army*. Report of Pershing's tentative assignment to command the Department of the Visayas from the Washington *Star*, October 21, 1906. Senator Warren's denial of the charges made against Pershing was published by the Washington *Star* and *Post*, December 21, 1906. Clippings from the Manila newspapers on Pershing's engaging an attorney to refute the charges against him may be found, undated, in a scrapbook in Box 382, Pershing Papers.

Pershing's tactfulness in assuming command of Fort McKinley was related to MacAdam (*The World's Work*, May 1919) by Colonel Kingsbury. Shortly after Pershing took over this command, his brother Ward retired from the Army because of ill health. Ward Pershing died several years later, his health ruined by tropical diseases which infected him during his Cuban and Philippine service.

Governor General Forbes's comment on Pershing's administration was included in his *The Philippine Islands*, Volume II; also the account of Pershing's establishment of the *Sulu News*. A description of his plan for harnessing the Tumaga River was published by the *Voz de Mindanao* on May 18, 1910. Letters and reports concerning the marriage of Lieutenant F. to a Filipino are contained in Box 371, Pershing Papers. The letter of an officer's wife describing the dangerous conditions of life in Zamboanga was published by the New York *World*, September 21, 1913. Pershing's description of a *juramentado* attack was contained in a letter to General Bell from Jolo, April 22, 1911, Box 371, Pershing Papers; same source for the letter from General Bliss.

The mass meeting of the Moros and the Christian Filipinos was described in Forbes's *The Philippine Islands,* Volume II; likewise the description of the baseball game in which he and Pershing participated. Pershing's recommendations for a realignment of military forces and the description of the Subano uprising from his report to the War Department, June 30, 1910; his proposals for army reforms in his report of the succeeding year. The Moro Constabulary was organized by Captain James G. Harbord, who was Pershing's chief of staff during the early stages of the A.E.F. Pershing's letters to his wife regarding the 1911 campaign may be found in Box 3, Pershing Papers. His letter of February 28, 1913, on the Jolo situation was quoted by Forbes in *The Philippine Islands,* Volume II. His report to the commanding general on the Bagsak action is in Box 382, Pershing Papers. The account of the Bagsak fighting given by John McLeod was published July 31, 1913, in the Washington *Herald,* as well as other American newspapers.

CHAPTER 5

Departure of Pershing and his regiments for the Mexican border from the San Francisco *Examiner* and *Chronicle,* April 20–28, 1914. Pancho Villa's personality is captured in *Bullets, Bottles, and Gardenias* by Timothy Turner, then an El Paso newspaperman who covered Mexican revolutionary activities; also Louis Stevens's and Edgcumb Pinchon's works on Villa. Pershing's description of Villa and Obregón from a draft of his unpublished memoir, Box 373, Pershing Papers.

How Pershing received the news of his wife's and daughters' deaths was described in MacAdam's series (*The World's Work,* June 1919), based on interviews with Pershing's staff. Details of the fire at the Presidio from the San Francisco *Chronicle* and *Examiner,* August 28–30, 1915. The editorial quoted appeared in the *Chronicle,* August 30.

Much of the pre-American phases of World War I was drawn from the following general histories: Cyril Falls's *The Great War, 1914–1918;* General Fuller's *A Military History of the Western World,* Volume III; Winston Churchill's *The World Crisis;* and *A History of the World War, 1914–1918,* by B. H. Liddell Hart.

General Scott's denunciation of the recognition of Carranza from his *Some Memories of a Soldier.* The story of the Columbus raid is told in some detail by Colonel Frank Tompkins's *Chasing Villa* and Colonel H. A. Toulmin's *With Pershing in Mexico.* Tompkins commanded the squadron which chased Villa back across the border after the raid. Lieutenant Lucas's account of the fighting in Columbus was quoted from his book.

Pershing's selection to command the punitive expedition is recounted in Frederick Palmer's *Bliss, Peacemaker*. Bullard's comment from his *Personalities and Reminiscences*. General Funston's remark on the job facing Pershing was quoted in *World Alive*, the autobiography of Robert Dunn, a correspondent for the New York *Tribune*, who accompanied the punitive expedition.

CHAPTER 6

General Scott's account of the intrigue in Washington against Pershing from *Some Memories of a Soldier*.

Colonel Toulmin's quotation from *With Pershing in Mexico*. Pershing's comment on the First Aero Squadron from *My Experiences*, Volume I. Account of the initial efforts of the squadron from the report of Captain Benjamin Foulois, its commanding officer, to the War Department, March 15–August 15, 1916. The military aviation was then part of the Signal Corps, since it was designed more for observation than combat.

Pershing's statements to the press and his relations with the correspondents were recalled in Dunn's *World Alive*.

Tompkins's talk with Pershing at Bachíniva the night of April 1 was related in his *Chasing Villa;* Dunn's observation on Pershing's "taking it on the chin" from his *World Alive*. Damon Runyon's dispatch was published in the New York *American* April 2, 1916.

Pershing's organization of the district commands was detailed in General Order No. 28, issued from his field headquarters at Namiquipa. Account of the Ojos Azules fight from Major Howze's report to Pershing; also an article in the *Cavalry Journal* (January 1917) by First Lieutenant M. S. Williams, who commanded a troop in Howze's squadron.

The one-armed General Obregón later became President of Mexico and eventually was assassinated—ironically enough—at Parral, where American troops were lured into the ambush that didn't come off. Villa also was assassinated several years after the end of World War I.

The caustic comment on the rumors concerning Villa's fate was published in the Kansas City *Journal* of July 1, 1916. Lieutenant Patton's exploits were recounted in Harry H. Semmes's *Portrait of Patton*, which quotes Patton's letter to his wife from Pershing's headquarters.

Threatening maneuvers of the Carranzistas in early June were detailed in Tompkins's *Chasing Villa*. The exchange of telegrams between Pershing and Trevino took place on June 16.

Junius B. Wood's interview with Pershing at Colonia Dublán appeared in the New York *Globe*, July 20, 1916. The New York *Sun's* comment on his promotion was published on September 28, 1916. General Scott's approval was conveyed in his memoir, *Some Memories of a Soldier*. The editorial urging the evacuation of the expeditionary force appeared in the New York *Herald* of November 24, 1916.

Pershing's reports on the renewal of Villa activity were contained in telegrams to General Funston, his immediate superior, November 2 and December 16, 1916. General Scott's reflections on the failure of the volunteer system were included in his annual report as chief of staff, September 30, 1916.

CHAPTER 7

All quotations from General Pershing's war diary are to be found in Box 4–5, Pershing Papers.

Marshal Foch's statement from his *Memoirs*. General Bliss's memos to Scott and Baker are quoted in Palmer's *Bliss, Peacemaker*. General Harbord's comments on the departure of Pershing and his staff for France are to be found in his readable and enlightening *Leaves from a War Diary*. Frederick Palmer's recollection of Colonel George M. Harvey loudly announcing the ship on which Pershing was sailing was included in his *Newton D. Baker*, Volume I. Harvey was also violently anti-Baker, characterizing the Secretary of War as "a chattering ex-pacifist." In his subsequently established, war-hawking *Harvey's Weekly* he generally referred to Baker as "Newtie Cootie."

Pershing's account of his departure on the *Baltic* from his war diary. His conversation with Frederick Palmer on "bloodshed and destruction" was recorded in Palmer's *John J. Pershing, General of the Armies*. Harbord's comments on their reception in England from his *Leaves from a War Diary*.

Description of the landing at Boulogne from Wilbur Forrest's *Behind the Front Page*. Forrest covered that event as a correspondent for the United Press.

CHAPTER 8

Pershing's comments on Pétain were made in *My Experiences*, Volume I. A terse and unfriendly summation of Pétain's career may be found in Philip Guedalla's *The Two Marshals*. Pershing read this book, published during World War II, and didn't like it a bit. Pershing's observations on civilian morale in France also from *My Experiences,* Volume I. Harbord's report on the talk of corruption in high places was included in the June 19 and July 12, 1917, entries in his *War Diary.* Forrest's description of temporary A.E.F. Headquarters from *Behind the Front Page.*

Breakdown of communications with the War Department and the pile-up of orders, dispatches, and reports there: Pershing's *My Experiences* and his war diary, Box 4–5, Pershing Papers; Harbord's *War Diary* and *The American Army in France;* Colonel T. Bentley Mott's *Twenty Years as a Military Attaché.* Bliss's habit of slipping papers under his blotter was related in Palmer's *Bliss, Peacemaker.*

A rundown on the success of the Anglo-American naval effort in the Atlantic may be found in Frederic L. Paxson's *America at War, 1917– 1918.*

Haig's comment on Pershing from his diary, November 4, 1917, quoted in Alfred Duff Cooper's *Haig.* Account of Pershing's visit from *My Experiences,* Volume I, his war diary, and Harbord's *War Diary.*

Palmer reported his conversation with Pershing in the garden of the house on Rue de Varenne in *With My Own Eyes,* his autobiography.

Pershing's explanation of his reasons for taking over the Lorraine front was extracted from his *Final Report,* published in 1919.

Enrollment of the "three musketeers" was recorded in Palmer's *With My Own Eyes.*

CHAPTER 9

Pershing's continuing sorrow over his family tragedy was related by Charles G. Dawes in *A Journal of the Great War,* Volume I. Palmer's comments on Pershing's "fading" human quality from *With My Own Eyes;* Bullard's from *Personalities and Reminiscences.* Baker's report to Pershing on Stateside feeling against the Sam Browne belt was quoted in Palmer's *Newton D. Baker,* Volume II, from a letter written on August 19, 1918.

Pershing's recollection of the joke he played on General Pétain from *My Experiences,* Volume I; likewise his account of observing the French attacks on the Meuse. Pershing noted with obvious concern that the four days of artillery preparation for the French attacks cost a total of $75,- 000,000 in ammunition expended.

Pershing's program for employing his army in open warfare was outlined in *My Experiences,* Volume I, and his war diary, Box 4–5, Pershing Papers.

Clemenceau's remarks on Pershing from his farewell fusillade, *Grandeur and Misery of Victory.* A striking profile of the Clemenceau personality may be found in *Dusk of Empire,* by Wythe Williams, an American correspondent stationed in Paris who knew Clemenceau well before and after he became Premier. Pershing's account of Clemenceau's visit to the First Division while a senator from *My Experiences,* Volume I.

Colonel Mott's comparison of Foch and Pétain from his *Twenty Years as a Military Attaché;* also for his description of Pershing and Foch groping toward an understanding.

How the A.E.F. ordered and canceled on gantry cranes was told in Palmer's *Newton D. Baker,* Volume I. Stateside purchasing mistakes were detailed in Forrest's *Behind the Front Page.*

Pershing's plea for younger officers was contained in a confidential letter to the Secretary of War, October 4, 1917.

Appointment of Charles G. Dawes as general purchasing agent for the A.E.F. from Dawes's *A Journal of the Great War* and Harbord's *War Diary.* Incident of Dawes saluting Pershing with a cigar in his mouth from Forrest's *Behind the Front Page.*

Colonel Repington's observations on the Chaumont scene from his *The First World War, 1914–1918,* Volume II.

Pershing's gifts of food to the children living in a section house between Chaumont and Paris from MacAdam's series (*The World's Work,* September 1919).

Mrs. Theodore Roosevelt, Jr.'s embarrassing run-in with Pershing in Paris was recalled in her lively autobiography, *Day Before Yesterday.*

CHAPTER 10

The Westbrook Pegler incident was related in Emmet Crozier's *American Reporters on the Western Front.* Pershing quoted on press interviews and propaganda in Palmer's *With My Own Eyes.* Quote from Herbert Corey's letter may be found in Crozier's *American Reporters.* Heywood Broun's articles on Pershing and the A.E.F. were published in the New York *Tribune* in January 1918 and were collected in book form in *The A.E.F.* Palmer's account of Pershing's handling of the Broun situation from *With My Own Eyes.*

Harbord's description of life at G.H.Q. from *War Diary* and *The American Army in France.*

Bullard's description of a trench raid from *Personalities and Reminiscences.*

Episode of Pershing's missing hat and belt from the October 27, 1917 entry in Harbord's *War Diary*. The account of his travels around Saint-Nazaire from the same source and from Pershing's war diary, Box 4–5, Pershing Papers.

Statistics on the results of the "war of attrition" were given by General March in his *The Nation at War*.

Pershing's view of the Supreme War Council was quoted by MacAdam (*The World's Work*, June 1919). His report on the views of his fellow commanders in chief on the same subject was contained in *My Experiences*, Volume I. Harbord's report of Colonel House's preconference remarks to the United States delegation was given in the November 30, 1917 entry of his *War Diary*.

Dawes's description of Pershing exercising in the snow from his diary, December 22, 1917, quoted in Volume I of *A Journal of the Great War*.

Bullard's criticism of French morale and Pershing's "pacifism" was extracted from November and December entries in his diary, quoted in his *Personalities and Reminiscences*. Same source for his word portrait of General Liggett. General Bell's "heartbreak" was related in Palmer's *Baker*, Volume II. Bliss's letter to Baker on General Wood, dated January 22, 1918, was quoted in Palmer's *Bliss, Peacemaker*. Baker's dealings with Wood, including his letter concerning a reflection on Pershing's personal reputation, were detailed in Palmer's *Baker*. March's comment from his *The Nation at War*.

March's portrait is drawn in part from his own *The Nation at War*, Palmer's *Baker*, Pershing's *My Experiences*. Baker's recital of March's ruthlessness was part of a lecture given by the Secretary of War at the Army War College on May 11, 1929. Harbord's comments on the Pershing-March situation from *The American Army in France*.

Pershing's description of his reception by the King and Queen of Belgium from *My Experiences*, Volume I.

CHAPTER 11

Field Marshal Haig's eagerness to acquire American replacements was recounted in Colonel Repington's *The First World War*, Volume II. Bliss's memorandum of December 18, 1917, was quoted in Palmer's *Baker*. Harbord's remarks on the pressure exerted by the Allies were made in *The American Army in France;* his account of the dispute between Pershing and Pétain from the January 28, 1918 entry in his *War Diary*. Pershing's conversation with Joffre was related in *My Experiences*, Volume I.

General Henry T. Allen's comment on Compiègne from his diary, which may be found in the Allen Papers in the Manuscript Division of the Library of Congress.

Both sides of the differences between Pershing and Bliss on the issue of sending 150 battalions to the British are stated in Pershing's *My Experiences,* Volume I, and Palmer's *Bliss, Peacemaker.* Bliss told of his support of Pershing's position before the Supreme War Council in a letter to Baker dated August 29, 1931. Haig's predictions are from his diary, January 30, 1918, quoted in Duff Cooper's *Haig.* Quotation from Dawes in his *Journal* under date of January 28, 1918. Colonel Rageneau's secret report was quoted by Major General J. T. Dickman in his *The Great Crusade.*

Harbord's criticism of the swarm of propaganda makers and orators from his *War Diary* under date of March 15, 1918.

Baker's request of Pershing that he name a possible successor was told by the Secretary of War to his biographer, Palmer (*Newton D. Baker,* Volume II).

A concise account of the planning behind Ludendorff's 1918 offensives may be found in Ludwig Reiner's *The Lamps Went Out in Europe.*

Haig's recital of the byplay at the Doullens conference is quoted from his diary (Duff Cooper's *Haig*).

Pershing's account of his offer of U.S. divisions from his diary; same source for the Beauvais conference.

Dawes's story of the overcoat button from his *Journal,* entry of April 21.

Events leading up to and through the Pershing-Milner agreement in London were told in Pershing's war diary, Harbord's *Leaves from a War Diary,* and Lloyd George's *War Memoirs,* Volume V.

CHAPTER 12

Lloyd George's comment on Pershing from his *War Memoirs,* Volume V; Clemenceau's on Pétain, quoted in Guedalla's *The Two Marshals.*

The story of the Abbeville conference is drawn from Lloyd George's *War Memoirs,* Volume V; Pershing's war diary and *My Experiences,* Volume II, and Clemenceau's *Grandeur and Misery of Victory.* Haig's remarks about the French were quoted in Pershing's diary, May 30, 1918 entry.

Pershing's address to the officers of the First Division was quoted in Bullard's *Personalities and Reminiscences.*

Telephone conversation between the German G.H.Q. and the chief of staff of the corps covering Cantigny was found in the German *Reichsarchiv* at Potsdam after the war and was among the bales of military documents translated by members of the United States Army's historical section.

Mimeographed and bound copies of the documents relating to the operations of German units opposed to American divisions on the western front have been deposited with the New York Public Library.

Pershing's comments on American regimental commanders were confided to his war diary, June 21, 1918; his denunciation of General Bridges's suggestions, same source, date of August 25.

Harbord mentioned his feelings on leaving as Pershing's chief of staff in his *War Diary*, May 14; his comments on the demoralization of the French, June 17 entry. Pétain's defeatist remarks, quoted by Marshal Foch, from Guedalla's *The Two Marshals*.

Pershing's chewing out of Douglas MacArthur was described in Frazier Hunt's *The Untold Story of Douglas MacArthur.*

Pershing's aviation difficulties were told in *My Experiences,* Volume II; General March's *The Nation at War;* Isaac Don Levine's *Mitchell: Pioneer of Air Power;* Quentin Reynolds's *They Fought for the Sky.*

Various aspects of the proposal for General Goethals to take over the S.O.S. were taken up in Pershing's *My Experiences,* Volume II; Palmer's *Baker;* March's *The Nation at War;* Harbord's *War Diary.*

Allied attitudes at the Bombon conference were admirably summed up in Colonel McEntee's *Military History of the World War.* A footnote to that conference: the Allies agreed to send forces to Russia, ostensibly to rescue Czech prisoners of war fighting their way toward Vladivostok. Pershing, in principle, was opposed to helping the "so-called White Army of Russia" because "it would simply mean scattering our resources." Like all western-front commanders, Pershing resented any operation which might divert men and supplies from his forces. A Siberian Expeditionary Force was dispatched by the United States and soon became embroiled in disputes with Red and White Russians, the Japanese, and the other Allies. Other expeditionary forces to North Russia also foundered in the turmoil of the revolution and counterrevolution.

CHAPTER 13

Account of their tour of S.O.S. facilities from Harbord's and Pershing's war diaries, also Harbord's *The American Army in France.*

A first-rate character sketch of General Summerall may be found in the late Fletcher Pratt's lively study of the art of command, *Eleven Generals.*

Pershing's renewed struggle with the French and British may be traced in his war diary and *My Experiences,* Volume II, and Harbord's *The American Army in France.* Sir Henry Wilson's statement from the *Life and Diaries of Sir Henry Wilson,* Volume II. The dialogue between Pershing and Pétain was quoted by the former in *My Experiences,* Volume II.

The topography of the Saint-Mihiel salient is described in Colonel Mc-Entee's *Military History of the World War.* Observation on German military cemeteries in the Saint-Mihiel salient from Elmer W. Sherwood's *Diary of a Rainbow Veteran.* A brief biographical sketch of General von Gallwitz was included in the United States Army translations of the military documents found in the *Reichsarchiv* at Potsdam. Same source for the information that the Germans were in the midst of preparations for withdrawal from the salient when the Americans attacked. Pershing's Belfort deception plan was thoroughly described in Crozier's *American Reporters on the Western Front.*

An account of the 2nd Cavalry's charge near Vigneulles is given in war correspondent Thomas M. Johnson's *Without Censor.* Incident of German officers being compelled to work along with enlisted men from Sherwood's *Diary of a Rainbow Veteran.* Bullard's comment from *Personalities and Reminiscences.*

CHAPTER 14

Marshall's background from Robert Payne's *The Marshall Story* and William Frye's *Marshall: Citizen Soldier.* Quotation from Pershing in *My Experiences,* Volume II, and Marshall's from *The United States Army in the World War, 1917–1919.*

Pershing's "Combat Instructions" were included in *My Experiences,* Volume II. His diary comments on Foch's attitude were made under the entries of October 1, 7, and 13.

Pershing's "crisis of the will" was described briefly in Simonds's *They Won the War;* General Allen's account of what Pershing told him was contained in his diary, October 17, 1918, which may be found with the Allen Papers in the Manuscript Division of the Library of Congress.

On Clemenceau's effort to have Pershing removed: Dawes's *Journal of the Great War;* Mrs. Harriman's observations from her memoir, *From Pinafores to Politics;* Bliss to March on Anglo-French maneuvers from the Bliss Papers, Library of Congress Manuscript Division. Foch's exchanges with Clemenceau on the proposed removal of Pershing from the former's *Memoirs.* Clemenceau's arguments with Foch over the extent of his authority from the former's *Grandeur and Misery of Victory.*

Haig's letter to Pershing was quoted in Duff Cooper's *Haig.* Pershing did not mention the incident in any of his own writings.

CHAPTER 15

The account of the armistice conference October 28 is drawn largely from Pershing's, Haig's, and Foch's memoirs and diaries.

Marshall's opinion that with the proper number of tanks the Americans could have cut off and captured 100,000 Germans after the capture of Buzancy was expressed in a letter to General Harbord which was included in the latter's *The American Army in France.*

The complicated story of the American strike for Sedan and the tangle in which the First and 42nd divisions found themselves may be traced through the orders and operational reports of the First American Army; Pershing's *My Experiences,* Volume II; General Dickman's *The Great Crusade;* and Pershing's war diary, entries from November 3 to 6.

How Pershing spent November 11 was indicated in his war diary and Dawes's *Journal of the Great War.* Same sources for his activities the following day; also Harbord's *War Diary.*

Field Marshal Hindenburg's comments on the military impact of the Americans from George Seldes's *You Can't Print That!* The journey of the five correspondents is described in Crozier's *American Reporters on the Western Front.*

Charles MacArthur's account of Pershing's review of the Rainbow Division from *A Bug's Eye View of the War;* the 165th Infantry incident was related in the Reverend Francis P. Duffy's *Father Duffy's Story.*

Quotation from Mrs. Harriman's diary was included in her *From Pinafores to Politics.*

Pershing's visits to the Razzberry Club in Coblenz were recounted in Forrest's *Behind the Front Page.*

CHAPTER 16

Pershing's November 27, 1918, letter to General March may be found in Box 373, Pershing Papers.

The account of his reception in New York is drawn from the New York *Globe, Times, Mail,* and *Tribune.*

Pershing's vacation at Wood's Hole and in the Adirondacks from his diary, September 15 to October 30 entries, Box 4–5, Pershing Papers. Pershing continued his diary for several years after the war.

William A. Wellman's fortunate encounter with Pershing in Hollywood was told the author by Mr. Wellman.

For General Palmer's role in organizing the postwar army, his *America in Arms* is the best authority. Palmer said that when Pershing sent him to Washington he gave him no directive, being too deeply involved in organizing the American phase of the Rhineland occupation, but told him, in effect, to use his own best judgment. Palmer already was known as one of the Army's "intellectuals."

Pershing letter to Marshall on the 1924 army cutbacks was quoted in Payne's *The Marshall Story*.

Billy Mitchell's activities and the sinking of the German warships off Virginia from the New York *Times*, June 30–July 24, 1921; also Isaac Don Levine's *Mitchell*.

The Pershing-MacArthur rivalry over Mrs. Brooks was related in Hunt's *The Untold Story of Douglas MacArthur* and Clark Lee's *Douglas MacArthur*. Pershing made no mention of the lady in any of his diaries.

A translation of the *Samedi Soir* article on Pershing's relationship with Mlle. Resco appeared in the Chicago *Tribune*, November 30, 1952.

Pershing at Arica from his diary, August 2, 1925–January 19, 1926–a two-volume journal which covered every exhausting detail of the Tacna-Arica proceedings (Box 334, Pershing Papers); also the recollections of Colonel Curtin, one of his staff, which were given to the author, and March's *The Nation at War*.

Pershing's remarks on the Mitchell court-martial from his Tacna-Arica journal, date of November 22, 1925, Box 334, Pershing Papers.

CHAPTER 17

Pershing gave the reason for his battlefield visits to the London *Daily Express*, June 8, 1939.

Details of Pershing's daily life after retirement from the recollections of his son, F. Warren Pershing, and Colonels Curtin and Charles B. Shaw.

Mrs. Marshall's description of her husband's disappointment on being assigned to the Illinois National Guard from her memoir, *Together*. Pershing's introduction to members of Marshall's staff in Chicago is quoted from Payne's *The Marshall Story*.

Pershing's February 23, 1933, letter to MacArthur is quoted in Hunt's *The Untold Story of Douglas MacArthur*.

The Pershing and Harbord letters exchanged in 1936 and 1937 may be found in Box 88, Pershing Papers.

Details of Pershing's near-fatal illness from Mr. Warren Pershing and the New York *Times*, February 15–March 31, 1938.

Frederick Palmer's comment on Pershing's appearance at the 1941 meeting of the Baltic Society from his *John J. Pershing*.

Pershing's letter to Harbord on the "lack of confidence," May 20, 1942, Box 89, Pershing Papers.

Pershing's annoyance at Eisenhower's failure to see him before leaving for North Africa was reported in *Time* magazine, November 15, 1943.

General Patton's account of his visit to Pershing is from his diary, quoted in Semmes's *Portrait of Patton*.

Harbord letter to Pershing on Guedalla's *The Two Marshals* from Box 89, Pershing Papers.

Palmer (*John J. Pershing*) is the authority for the statement that Pershing preferred General McNair as commander in Europe. Harbord on Eisenhower, letter of February 20, 1945, Box 89, Pershing Papers.

CHAPTER 18

Colonel Virden's account of Pershing's "escape" from Walter Reed Hospital was given Harold H. Martin of the Atlanta *Constitution*, reprinted in *Reader's Digest*, October 1955.

Harbord letter to Pershing of April 11, 1946, Box 89, Pershing Papers.

Henry Wales's stories on Pershing were published in the Chicago *Tribune*, September 28, 1947, and November 30, 1952.

Accounts of Pershing's death and the tributes paid him from the New York *Times*, Washington *Post*, *Star*, and *Times-Herald*, July 16–20, 1948.

Frank H. Simonds's quotation is from his *They Won the War*.

SELECTED BIBLIOGRAPHY

Andrews, Avery D., *My Friend and Classmate John J. Pershing*, Harrisburg, Pa., 1939.

Broun, Heywood, *The A.E.F.*, New York, 1918.

Broun, Heywood Hale, (editor) *Collected Edition of Heywood Broun*, New York, 1941.

Bullard, Robert Lee, *Personalities and Reminiscences*, New York, 1925.

Captured German Documents, *Reichsarchiv*, Potsdam, translated by the United States Army, mimeographed copy deposited with the New York Public Library.

Clemenceau, Georges, *Grandeur and Misery of Victory*, New York, 1930.

Cooper, Alfred Duff, *Haig*, New York, 1936.

Crozier, Emmet, *American Reporters on the Western Front*, New York, 1959.

Dawes, Charles G., *A Journal of the Great War*, Boston, 1921.

DeWeerd, H. A., *Great Soldiers of the Two World Wars*, New York, 1941.

Dickman, Joseph T., *The Great Crusade*, New York, 1927.

Downey, Fairfax, *Indian-Fighting Army*, New York, 1941.

Duffy, the Rev. Francis P., *Father Duffy's Story*, New York, 1919.

Dunn, Robert, *World Alive*, New York, 1956.

Dupuy, R. Ernest, *The Compact History of the United States Army*, New York, 1956.

Falls, Cyril, *The Great War*, New York, 1959.

Foch, Ferdinand, *Memoirs of Marshal Foch*, New York, 1931.

Forbes, W. Cameron, *The Philippine Islands*, Boston, 1928.

Forrest, Wilbur, *Behind the Front Page*, New York, 1934.

Frye, William, *Marshall: Citizen Soldier*, Indianapolis, 1947.

Fuller, J. F. C., *A Military History of the Western World*, New York, 1936.

Ganoe, William A., *The History of the United States Army*, New York, 1942.

Grasty, Charles H., *Flashes from the Front*, New York, 1918.

Guedalla, Philip, *The Two Marshals*, London, 1943.

Harbord, James G., *Leaves from a War Diary*, New York, 1925.

——, *The American Army in France*, Boston, 1936.

Harriman, Mrs. J. Borden, *From Pinafores to Politics*, New York, 1923.

Hunt, Frazier, *The Untold Story of Douglas MacArthur*, New York, 1954.

Johnson, Thomas M., *Without Censor*, Indianapolis, 1928.

——, and Pratt, Fletcher, *The Lost Battalion*, Indianapolis, 1938.

Lee, Clark, and Henschel, Robert, *Douglas MacArthur*, New York, 1952.

Leech, Margaret, *In the Days of McKinley*, New York, 1959.

Levine, Isaac Don, *Mitchell: Pioneer of Air Power*, New York, 1943.

Liddell Hart, B. H., *A History of the World War*, Boston, 1935.

——, *Strategy*, New York, 1954.

Liggett, Hunter, *Commanding an American Army*, Boston, 1925.

Lloyd George, David, *War Memoirs*, London, 1936.

MacArthur, Charles, *A Bug's Eye View of the War*, Chicago, 1919.

McCracken, Harold, *Pershing*, New York, 1931.

McEntee, Girard L., *Military History of the World War*, New York, 1937.

March, Peyton C., *The Nation at War*, New York, 1932.

Marshall, Katherine Tupper, *Together*, New York, 1946.

Miles, Nelson A., *Serving the Republic*, New York, 1911.

Millis, Walter, *Arms and Men*, New York, 1956.

Mott, T. Bentley, *Twenty Years as a Military Attaché*, New York, 1937.

Palmer, Frederick, *Bliss, Peacemaker*, New York, 1934.

——, *Newton D. Baker*, New York, 1931.

——, *John J. Pershing*, Harrisburg, 1948.

——, *With Kuroki in Manchuria*, New York, 1904.

——, *With My Own Eyes*, Indianapolis, 1934.

Palmer, John M., *America in Arms*, New Haven, 1941.

Paxson, Frederic L., *America at War, 1917–1918*, Boston, 1939.

Payne, Robert, *The Marshall Story*, New York, 1951.

Pershing, E. J., *The Pershing Family in America*, Philadelphia, 1924.

Pershing, the Rev. J. H., *Family Tree*, Greensburg, Pa. (undated).

Pershing, John J., *Final Report*, Washington, 1919.

——, *My Experiences in the World War*, New York, 1931.

Poe, Sophie A. (edited by Eugene Cunningham), *Buckboard Days*, Caldwell, Idaho, 1936.

Pratt, Fletcher, *Eleven Generals*, New York, 1949.

Reiner, Ludwig, *The Lamps Went Out in Europe*, New York, 1957.

Repington, C. A., *The First World War, 1914–1918*, Boston, 1920.

Reynolds, Quentin, *They Fought for the Sky,* New York, 1957.

Roosevelt, Mrs. Theodore, *Day Before Yesterday,* New York, 1959.

Scott, Hugh L., *Some Memories of a Soldier,* New York, 1928.

Seldes, George, *You Can't Print That!,* New York, 1929.

Semmes, Harry H., *Portrait of Patton,* New York, 1955.

Sherwood, Elmer, *Diary of a Rainbow Veteran,* Terre Haute, Indiana, 1929.

Storey, Moorfield, and Lichauco, Marcial P., *The Conquest of the Philippines by the United States, 1898–1925,* New York, 1926.

Tomlinson, Everett T., *The Story of General Pershing,* New York, 1937.

Tompkins, Frank, *Chasing Villa,* Harrisburg, Pa., 1934.

Toulmin, H. A., *With Pershing in Mexico,* Harrisburg, 1935.

Turner, Timothy, *Bullets, Bottles, and Gardenias,* Dallas, 1935.

Von Hoffmann, Max, *The War of Lost Opportunities,* New York, 1925.

Wellman, Paul I., *The Indian Wars of the West,* New York, 1954.

Williams, Wythe, *Dusk of Empire,* New York, 1937.

Wolff, Leon, *In Flanders Fields,* New York, 1958.

NEWSPAPERS

Kansas City *Star*
Kansas City *Journal*
St. Louis *Post-Dispatch*
St. Louis *Globe-Democrat*
Chicago *Tribune*
Chicago *Inter-Ocean*
Chicago *Daily News*
Manila *Times*
Manila *Sun*
Manila *American*
Atlanta *Constitution*
New York *Times*
New York *World*
New York *Globe*
New York *Evening Mail*
New York *Herald*
New York *Tribune*
New York *Journal*
New York *American*
New York *Sun*
San Francisco *Chronicle*
San Francisco *Examiner*

MAGAZINES

Saturday Evening Post
Time
The World's Work
Review of Reviews
Literary Digest
Reader's Digest
Leslie's Weekly
Collier's
Army Register
Army and Navy Journal
Infantry Journal
Cavalry Journal
Samedi Soir (Paris)
The Missouri Historical Record

INDEX

Pershing, John J. (*cont'd*)

Bayard, 27–30; early army reputation, 30–31; transferred to Fort Stanton, 32–33; action against Sitting Bull, 33–34; teaches at University of Nebraska, 37–41; meets Charles G. Dawes, 40; admitted to Nebraska bar, 41; at Fort Assiniboine, 42; teaches at West Point, 42–44; meets Theodore Roosevelt, 43; on active service, 45; action in Cuba, 45–51; War Department, Washington, 51–52; goes to Philippines, 52–54; Moro campaign, 57–59; in command at Camp Vicars, 60–73; becomes honorary datu, 68–69; at Army War College, 77; meets Frances Warren, 77–78; marries, 79; children, 79; American observer in Manchuria, 80–84; promoted from captain to brigadier general, 85–86; to Fort McKinley, Philippines, 87; charged with illegitimate children, 87–89; second tour in Philippines, 90–104; at Presidio, San Francisco, 105; action against Villa, 105–10, 112–19, 121–40; death of wife and daughters, 111–12; goes to Washington, May, 1917, 146; named Commanding General, A.E.F., 146–47; gathers staff in Washington, 149–51; opposes fragmentation of American troops, 150, 152; embarks for France, 152–54; interview with Pres. Wilson, 153; opinions on World War I, 155–56; in England, 156–58; goes to France, 158–60; friendship with Pétain, 161–62, 164; early A.E.F. problems, 166–72; meets Field Marshal Haig, 173–74; organizes lines of communication, 175–77; general staff at Headquarters, 177–78; Harbord's appraisal, 183–84, 188; "Every private a Pershing," 185; training of A.E.F., 188–89; hostility of Clemenceau, 190–93; problem of supply, 193–95; problem of officers, 195–97; makes Dawes purchasing agent, A.E.F., 196–98; Headquarters moves to Chaumont, 198–200; French "nursemaid" missions, 200; and American correspondents, 203–7; and propaganda, 207; "Valley Forge winter," 208–28; First Division at Nancy, 210–11; tours French battlefields, 211; painted by Mlle. Resco, 212; formation of Supreme War Council, 214–15; Inter-Allied Conference, 215–16; maintains army discipline, 217–20; and Gen. March, 222–27; and King Albert, 229; British and French designs on A.E.F., 230–37; German push toward Paris, 238–41; Foch's refusal of American troops, 243–45; in England for conference on troops, 248–50; Cantigny, Belleau Wood, Soissons, 251 ff., 2nd Battle of Marne, 258; and Rainbow Division discipline, 265–66; and Air Service, 266–69; and Billy Mitchell, 267–69; and S.O.S., 270–79; made Grand Commander of Bath, 275; moves to Ligny-en-Barrois, 282; refuses to give up U.S. troops, 285–87; Saint-Mihiel offensive, 287 ff.; and George C. Marshall, 299–301; Argonne-Meuse salient, 299 ff.; and French interference, 309–17; insists on unconditional surrender, 324–26; contest for Sedan, 327–32; armistice, 332–34; conflict with Foch over Rhineland, 339–40; joined by Warren, 341–42; returns to America, 343; mentioned for presidency, 348–49; New York victory parade, 350–51; chief of staff, 353–56; skeptical of Air Corps, 357; and Col. MacArthur, 357–59; and Mlle. Resco, 359–60; death of Pres. Harding, 360; retires, 361–62; Tacna-Arica settlement, 361–64; Mitchell court-martial, 364–65; and Gen. Marshall, 370–72; writing war memoirs, 374; 1937 heart attack, 376; believed dying, 376–77; recovers, 377–78; World War II, 378; enters Walter Reed Hospital, 380; De Gaulle incident, 387–88; goes A.W.O.L. to Carlton Hotel, 388–89; death, 390; burial in Arlington, 391–92

Pershing, Mary Margaret, 79, 101, 110–11